Brahms Patriotic and Political

Eastman Studies in Music

Ralph P. Locke, Senior Editor
Eastman School of Music

Additional Titles of Interest

Analyzing Wagner's Operas: Alfred Lorenz and German Nationalist Ideology
Stephen McClatchie

*Anton Bruckner and the Reception of His Music:
A History of Dichotomies and Controversies*
Miguel J. Ramirez

Anneliese Landau's Life in Music: Nazi Germany to Émigré California
Lily E. Hirsch

Bach to Brahms: Essays on Musical Design and Structure
Edited by David Beach and Yosef Goldenberg

Brahms and the Shaping of Time
Scott Murphy

*Brahms's "A German Requiem": Reconsidering Its
Biblical, Historical, and Musical Contexts*
R. Allen Lott

*Good Music for a Free People: The Germania Musical Society
in Nineteenth-Century America*
Nancy Newman

Karl Straube (1873–1950): Germany's Master Organist in Turbulent Times
Christopher Anderson

Minna Wagner: A Life, with Wagner
Eva Rieger
Translated by Chris Walton

*Music and Desire among the Austro-German Romantics:
Beethoven, Schubert, Wagner, Brahms, and the Schumanns*
Chris Walton

A complete list of titles in the Eastman Studies in Music Series
may be found on our website, www.urpress.com

Brahms Patriotic and Political

David Brodbeck

UNIVERSITY OF ROCHESTER PRESS

Copyright © 2025 David Brodbeck

All rights reserved. Except as permitted under current legislation, no part of this work may be photocopied, stored in a retrieval system, published, performed in public, adapted, broadcast, transmitted, recorded, or reproduced in any form or by any means, without the prior permission of the copyright owner.

First published 2025

University of Rochester Press
668 Mt. Hope Avenue, Rochester, NY 14620, USA
www.urpress.com
and Boydell & Brewer Limited
PO Box 9, Woodbridge, Suffolk IP12 3DF, UK
www.boydellandbrewer.com

Our Authorised Representative for product safety in the EU is Easy Access System Europe - Mustamäe tee 50, 10621 Tallinn, Estonia, gpsr.requests@easproject.com

ISBN-13: 978-1-64825-107-8
ISSN: 1071-9989

Portions of chapters 2 and 3 have appeared previously in print in "Settling for Second Best: Brahms's *Männerchor-Lieder* in Historical Context," *Rethinking Brahms,* ed. Nicole Grimes and Reuben Phillips (New York: Oxford University Press, 2022).

Library of Congress Cataloging-in-Publication Data
Names: Brodbeck, David Lee, author.
Title: Brahms patriotic and political / David Brodbeck.
Other titles: Eastman studies in music ; 203.
Description: Rochester : University of Rochester Press, 2025. | Series: Eastman
 studies in music, 10719989 ; 203 | Includes bibliographical references and index.
Identifiers: LCCN 2024056891 (print) | LCCN 2024056892 (ebook) |
 ISBN 9781648251078 (hardback) | ISBN 9781805436379 (pdf) | ISBN
 9781805436386 (epub)
Subjects: LCSH: Brahms, Johannes, 1833–1897.—Criticism and interpretation. |
 Brahms, Johannes, 1833–1897. Lieder, men's voices, op. 41. | Brahms,
 Johannes, 1833–1897. Triumphlied. | Brahms, Johannes, 1833–1897. Fest- und
 Gedenksprüche. | Music—Political aspects—Germany—History—19th century. |
 Patriotic music—Germany—19th century—History and criticism. | Choral music—
 Germany—19th century. | Nationalism in music. | Germany—History—1789–1900.
Classification: LCC ML410.B8 B734 2025 (print) | LCC ML410.B8 (ebook) |
 DDC 780.92--dc23/eng/20241126
LC record available at https://lccn.loc.gov/2024056891
LC ebook record available at https://lccn.loc.gov/2024056892

A catalogue record for this title is available from the British Library.

In memory of my parents

All hail, praise, and thanksgiving for the hour when you were born to the nation!

—Hermann Levi, 1871

Contents

List of Illustrations	ix
Acknowledgments	xi
Note on Nomenclature, Place Names, and Orthography	xiii
Introduction	1
Prologue: A Young Man's Political Formation	8

Part I. *Fünf Lieder für Männerchor*, op. 41

1	Liedertafel and Liberal Nationalism	25
2	Soldiers' Songs and the German Question	48
	Excursus 1: From the German War to *A German Requiem*	76

Part II *Triumphlied*, op. 55

3	"A Song to Paris"	89
4	Sounding the Nation	113
	Excursus 2: National Holidays, Monuments, and Celebrations	151

Part III *Fest- und Gedenksprüche*, op. 109

5	"Words quite lovely and for us Germans uplifting"	167
6	The Stuff of Tragedy?	183
7	Revanche and Response	201
	Epilogue: An Old Man's Political Disillusionment	225

Appendix	247
Bibliography	253
Index	285

List of Illustrations

Tables

1	Brahms's biblical notebook, fols. 15v–16v.	192
2	Brahms's biblical notebook, fols. 15v–19r.	198

Figures

1   Caricature of Napoleon as the Son of the Devil, ca. 1813–14. Public domain.   10

2   Concert program, *Singakademie*, Bremen, April 7, 1871, p. 1. Reproduced with permission from the Brahms-Institut an der Musikhochschule, Lübeck.   101

3   Concert program, *Singakademie*, Bremen, April 7, 1871, p. 4. Reproduced with permission from the Brahms-Institut an der Musikhochschule, Lübeck.   102

4   Johannes Schilling's model for *Das National-Denkmal auf dem Niederwald*, reproduced in *Die Gartenlaube* 33 (1874): 534–35. Public domain.   157

5   Concert program, *Hamburgische Gewerbe- und Industrie-Ausstellung 1889*, Hamburg, September 9, 1889 (*Erstes Fest-Konzert*). Reproduced with permission from the British Library Collection: Abonnement Concerte, Hamburg (1886–96) 1609/3137, Volume 2, n.p. (1889–90).   176

6   Heinrich von Treitschke, *Zwei Kaiser, 15. Juni 1888*, pp. 16–17. Reproduced with permission from the Archive of the Gesellschaft der Musikfreunde, Vienna.   189

7   Title page, "Boulanger Maître d'Ecole en Alsace." Public domain.   203

8   Certificate of Brahms's Honorary Presidency of the Vienna branch of the Association for the Unhitching of the Horses. Reproduced with permission from the Archive of the Gesellschaft der Musikfreunde, Vienna.   241

Musical Examples

1   Brahms, *Fünf Lieder für Männerchor*, op. 41, no. 3 ("Geleit"), mm. 37–42.   41

2   Mendelssohn, *6 Gesänge*, op. 47, no. 4 ("Es ist bestimmt in Gottes Rath"), mm. 20–26.   42

3a   Brahms, *Fünf Lieder für Männerchor*, op. 41, no. 2 ("Freiwillige her!"), mm. 1–15.   57

3b   Brahms, *Fünf Lieder für Männerchor*, op. 41, no. 2 ("Freiwillige her!"), mm. 31–48.   58

4   Brahms, *Fünf Lieder für Männerchor*, op. 41, no. 5 ("Gebt Acht") (stanza 1 only).   62

5   Brahms, *Fünf Lieder für Männerchor*, op. 41, no. 1 ("Ich schwing' mein Horn ins Jammerthal") (stanza 1 only).   69

6   Comparison of "Heil and Preis" (Brahms, op. 55, first movement) and "Heil Dir im Siegerkranz" (unofficial Prussian national anthem).   104

7   Brahms, *Triumphlied*, op. 55, first movement, mm. 66–74 (reduction).   108

8   Brahms, *Triumphlied*, op. 55, second movement, mm. 110–19 (voices only, *f sempre*).   125

9a   Brahms, *Triumphlied*, op. 55, second movement (reduction), mm. 143–49.   128

9b   Brahms, *Triumphlied*, op. 55, second movement (reduction), mm. 172–end.   129

10   Brahms, *Fest- und Gedenksprüche*, op. 109, first movement, mm. 1–15.   210

11   Brahms, *Fest- und Gedenksprüche*, op. 109, second movement, mm. 1–7.   214

12   Brahms, *Fest- und Gedenksprüche*, op. 109, second movement, mm. 41–50.   215

13   Brahms, *Fest- und Gedenksprüche*, op. 109, third movement, mm. 43–67.   221

Acknowledgments

The publication of this book would not have been possible without the support of a number of friends, colleagues, and librarians. For providing me with copies of essential primary sources, I am deeply grateful to Thomas Aigner and Marcel Atze (Wienbibliothek im Rathaus), Mirijam Beier (Staats- und Universitätsbibliothek Hamburg Carl von Ossietzky), Katrin Eich (Musikwissenschaftliches Institut der Universität Kiel), Bill Emery (British Library), Silvia Kargl (Historisches Archiv der Wiener Philharmoniker), Jürgen Neubacher (Staats- und Universitätsbibliothek Hamburg Carl von Ossietzky), Johannes Prominczil (Archiv der Gesellschaft der Musikfreunde in Wien), and Wolfgang Sandberger and Stefan Weymar (Brahms-Institut an der Musikhochschule Lübeck). Ivana Rentsch (Institut für Musikwissenschaft, Universität Hamburg) kindly put me in touch with a number of fellow scholars who could assist me in various facets of my research. Others to whom I owe thanks for research assistance along the way include Maike Arnemann, Johannes Behr, Britta Berg, George S. Bozarth, Eva-Maria Breuer, Scott Ellwood, Virginia Hancock, Claude Keisch, Sandra McColl, Reuben Phillips, Carsten Schmidt, John H. Smith, Birgitte Straubel, and Maximilian Zauner.

Over the years I have presented versions of material that eventually made its way into this book at the North American Conference on Nineteenth-Century Music (Vanderbilt University, 2017, and the University of North Carolina, Chapel Hill, 2019), the Cambridge Brahms Requiem Conference (Cambridge, UK, 2018), and the annual conference of the Royal Musical Association (Manchester, 2019). Portions of Chapters 2 and 3 have appeared previously in print in "Settling for Second Best: Brahms's *Männerchor-Lieder* in Historical Context," *Rethinking Brahms*, ed. Nicole Grimes and Reuben Phillips (New York: Oxford University Press, 2022).

Unless otherwise noted, all translations from the German are my own. I would be remiss, however, not to thank Anke Biendarra, Josef Eisinger, Kai Evers, Peter Krapp, and Philipp Lehmann for helping me to polish a few of those translations. To Frank Lehmann I express my deepest gratitude for his expert transcription of a number of primary sources written in *Kurrentschrift*.

Sincere thanks go to my colleague Amy Bauer, for producing the musical examples for this book with speed and good spirits, and to Melissa Torres of

xii ❧ ACKNOWLEDGMENTS

the Interlibrary Loan staff of the Langson Library, University of California, Irvine, for managing my seemingly endless requests so graciously and professionally. Generous financial support was provided by a faculty research grant from UC Irvine's Claire Trevor School of the Arts and publication subventions from the American Brahms Society and the John Daverio Fund of the American Musicological Society, supported in part by the National Endowment for the Humanities and the Andrew W. Mellon Foundation.

Finally, I am most grateful for the interest taken in my work by a pair of noted historians of nineteenth-century Germany, Celia Applegate (Vanderbilt University) and Neil Gregor (University of Southampton). Each provided helpful comments and advice after reading an early version of what eventually found its way into Chapters 4 and 5. My thanks go, too, to Ralph Locke, the Senior Editor of the Eastman Studies in Music series, for his enthusiastic embrace of my project, and to Sonia Kane, Editorial Director, and her entire team at the University of Rochester Press, for seeing it into print.

My wife, Leonora Saavedra, has been a bulwark of support in more ways than she might imagine during the years it took to bring this project to fruition. She is, as ever, my intellectual inspiration and the love of my life.

This book is dedicated to the memory of my parents, Richard Miller Brodbeck and Virginia Anne Niebel Brodbeck.

Note on Nomenclature, Place Names, and Orthography

In this book I follow the historian Helmut Walser Smith in trying to avoid making the German word *Volk* more peculiar than it is. In most instances, I do not hesitate to translate it, usually as "people" but sometimes as "nation." By contrast, the adjective *völkisch*, which began to come into vogue in populist circles in Austria in the 1870s as a Germanization of *national*, I leave untranslated. The word was soon understood to connote a form of ethnic nationalism that was highly charged with the ideologies of racism and Social Darwinism.[1] Like *völkisch*, the word *Heimat*, a particularly German concept, has no direct semantic equivalent in other languages, and I do not attempt to offer one. The word can refer to one's native country or region or, for that matter, to any place where one has planted deep roots or feels at home. At all events it has much more to do with the warm feelings evoked by the landscape, customs, and traditions of a place than with national identity. As for the name of the German state founded in 1871: *Deutsches Reich* is usually translated into English as German Empire, even though *Reich* literally means "realm," not "empire" (which is *Kaisertum*), does not necessarily have monarchical implications (the Weimar Republic retained *Deutsches Reich* as its official name), and is close in meaning to the English term *commonwealth*. Hereafter I will generally use the partially translated name "German Reich."

I also generally use the German names for places with no English name in which more than one language was spoken during the nineteenth century, although at the first mention I cite the names in both languages in use there (e.g., Breslau/Wrocław). The German writers quoted in this book frequently used German orthography when giving the names of Czechs. I retain these spellings in my quotations but otherwise use the proper Czech orthography. When quoting passages in German and when citing German publication titles, I invariably use the original orthography. Finally, I use the unhyphenated spelling of the word antisemitism. This is not only in

---

1   Günter Hartung, "Völkische Ideologie," in *Handbuch zur "Völkische Bewegung" 1871–1918*, ed. Uwe Puschner, Walter Schmitz, and Justus H. Ulbricht (Munich: K. G. Saur, 1996), 22–41.

keeping with the German origins of this neologism—*Antisemitismus* was coined only in 1879—but also avoids the unfortunate implication given by the still commonly encountered hyphenated spelling ("anti-Semitism") that there once existed a threatening racial ideology of "Semitism" that needed to be combatted.

Introduction

On January 11, 1896, Johannes Brahms spent several memorable hours in the company of Adolph Menzel, the dean of German artists in the second half of the nineteenth century. Menzel had recently marked his eightieth birthday, and Brahms, who enjoyed a warm friendship with the artist in his autumn years, had come to join him in a belated private celebration at his Berlin atelier. After ascending four flights of stairs, the composer was greeted by his host in the corridor and escorted into the studio. Upon entering he would have immediately caught sight of the large unfinished oil painting "Frederick the Great Addressing His Generals before the Battle of Leuthen" (1859–61), which was prominently displayed on one of the studio walls. The two men soon sat down to a deluxe meal of oysters served with fine wine. The drinking was heavy, the examination of the artist's work so engrossing, that Brahms lost all track of time and barely made it to a dinner that had been arranged in his honor by the Prussian Academy of Arts.

Max Kalbeck, the author of the first substantial biography of the composer, described the visit in characteristically flowery prose:

> The tiny hoary [Menzel], in whom a sorcerous necromancer was hiding, had held [Brahms] spellbound. One glass after another was emptied as libation for the spirits that emerged from the books and folders all around and took on flesh and blood when the conjurer, to the boundless astonishment of his guest, called them all by name. He knew all those whom he had once conquered with his imagination and captured with his eyes, had told them who they would be and given them eternal life. A true "seer" who read the past and future from the present, he thought through what he saw and saw through what he thought [*durchdachte er, was er sah, und durchschaute er, was er dachte*]. [1]

---

1   My account here is based on that given in Max Kalbeck, *Johannes Brahms*, rev. ed., 4 vols. in 8 (Berlin: Deutsche Brahms-Gesellschaft, 1915–21; repr., Tutzing: Hans Schneider, 1976), 4: 421–23. Kalbeck's principal source of information concerning this encounter was likely Clara Simrock, the widow of Brahms's principal publisher, Fritz Simrock, whose Berlin home the composer frequented during his visits to the German capital. Cf. Alfred Bock, "Erinnerungen an Clara Simrock und Johannes Brahms," *Zeitschrift für Musik* 97 (1931): 477–78. It appears that Kalbeck, exercising considerable poetic license, also drew some of the details of his highly embroidered anecdote from

2 &❧ INTRODUCTION

We might surmise that among the books Brahms was shown that day—at least in Kalbeck's imagination—was a rare first edition of *Die Armee Friedrichs des Grossen in ihrer Uniformung* (Frederick the Great's army in uniform), published in three volumes between 1851 and 1857 in a limited run of only thirty copies.[2] As he continues his account, Kalbeck seems to draw a great contrast between these exquisite drawings of the uniformed officers and soldiers, more than 400 in number, and the period ball in eighteenth-century dress that the German Emperor William II, costumed as Robert Scipio von Lentulus, Frederick's devoted adjutant general, had hosted in honor of the artist's birthday jubilee seven months earlier at the Potsdam Palace. Notably, this event included a *tableau vivant* of Menzel's "Frederick the Great Playing the Flute in Sanssouci" (1852) performed in the very music room in which this famous painting is set:

> Half of the old Prussian army, with Frederick the Great at its head, marched past [in the mind's eye] in parade, livelier and more genuine than the costumed honor guard that Emperor William II presented to the Court and Military Painter of the House of Hohenzollern at the festival of the Frederician period in Sanssouci, whereupon Menzel addressed the monarch with a serious jest [*ernsthaft scherzend anredete*]: "I have the honor of seeing the Adjutant General Lentulus before me?"[3]

To conclude his roundabout anecdote, Kalbeck sets this "imperious stage show" at Sanssouci against the entirely more intimate get-together of Menzel and Brahms in the quiet and secluded setting of the artist's studio:

> The history painter could scarcely have paid a nobler compliment to the emperor, who was the sole creator, organizer, and performer of this clever homage; the spoken epigram thanking His Majesty could not have been more flattering. And no greater joy could the one friend give to the other,

---

    an account of a visit to Menzel's studio that had nothing to do with Brahms; see Ottomar Beta, "Gespräche mit Adolph Menzel," *Deutsche Revue über das gesamte nationale Leben der Gegenwart* 23/2 (April–June 1898): 45–58.

2   *Die Armee Friedrichs des Grossen in ihrer Uniformirung, gezeichnet und erläutert von Adolph Menzel*, 3 vols. (Berlin: L. Sachse, 1851–57). Most of the copies were intended for royal and princely houses; a few were reserved for Prussian officials and only five were earmarked for the art trade.

3   A. v. W [Anton von Werner], "Flötenkonzert in Sanssouci," *Vossische Zeitung, Abend-Ausgabe* (June 14, 1895): 3. The emperor's welcome address is given in E. Schröder, *Ein Tagebuch Kaiser Wilhelms II., 1888–1902 nach Hof- und anderem Berichte* (Breslau: S. Schottlaender, 1902), 206–7. Kalbeck is alluding here to Goethe's famous letter to Wilhelm von Humboldt from 1832 in which he apostrophized his *Faust II* as "these very serious jests" (*diese sehr ernste Scherze*).

the patriot to the compatriot, the painter of Prussia's and Germany's power and glory to the composer of the *Triumphlied*, the F Major Symphony, the *Fest- und Gedenksprüche*, than with this quiet and moving celebration in his studio. Before the colossal painting of "Frederick the Great before the Battle of Leuthen" [*sic*], the like-minded brothers emptied their glasses to the future of Germany, in which they, together with Frederick II's biographer Carlyle, saw "the future of the world."[4]

Menzel was a remarkably versatile artist, and the works of his Frederician period, as significant as they are, cannot have been all that Brahms asked to see.[5] Still, by bringing Frederick the Great to the fore in his account, Kalbeck furthered his principal aim of underscoring Brahms's true-blue German patriotism.[6] The biographer may well have taken certain liberties in the interest of telling a good story, and he does not get all his facts straight.[7] Yet, the central point of his anecdote is confirmed, as we shall discover, by numerous other sources. Moreover, Brahms's interest in Frederick the Great, intimately tied up with his interest in Menzel's art, was at its height in the composer's later years. In 1892, for example, he was very happy to receive a copy of *Adolph Menzel's Illustrationen zu den Werken Friedrich des Großen, Jubiläums-Ausgabe* (Adolph Menzel's illustrations to the works of Frederick the Great, 1886). Writing to thank his publisher Fritz Simrock for this present, he added that he had recently read Franz Kugler's *Geschichte*

---

4   I borrow my characterization of this "imperious stage show" from Eva Giloi, *Monarchy, Myth, and Material Culture in Germany 1750–1950* (Cambridge: Cambridge University Press, 2011), 267–74.

5   On Brahms's deep affinity for the artist's work, see Reinhold Brinkmann, "Zeitgenossen: Feuerbach, Böcklin, Klinger und Menzel," in *Johannes Brahms: Quellen—Text—Rezeption—Interpretation: Internationaler Brahms Kongress Hamburg 1997*, ed. Friedhelm Krummacher and Peter Petersen (Munich: G. Henle, 1999), 71–94 (esp. 84–88). On the Frederick works, see Werner Busch, *Adolph Menzel: The Quest for Reality*, trans. Carola Kleinstück-Schulman (Los Angeles: Getty Research Institute, 2017), 61–86, 129–70. See also Françoise Forster-Hahn, "Adolph Menzel's 'Daguerrotypical' Image of Frederick the Great: A Liberal Bourgeois Interpretation of German History," *Art Bulletin* 59 (1977): 242–61; and Françoise Forster-Hahn, "Adolph Menzel: Readings between Nationalism and Modernity," in *Adolph Menzel, 1815–1905: Between Romanticism and Impressionism*, ed. Claude Keisch and Marie Ursula Riemann-Reyher (New Haven and London: Yale University Press, in association with the National Gallery of Art, Washington, 1996), 103–12.

6   On this point, see also Sandra McColl, "A Model German," *Musical Times* 138 (1997): 7–12.

7   For example, Menzel's studio was located at Sigismundstraße 3, not, as Kalbeck has it, in the Margaretenstraße.

4　❧　INTRODUCTION

des Friedrichs des Grossen, mit 400 Illustrationen von Adolph Menzel (History of Frederick the Great, with 400 illustrations by Adolph Menzel, 1867). Although this popular edition was thought to be outdated, Brahms nevertheless believed it could yet bring "pleasure and contentment."[8]

In the popular imagination of the later nineteenth century, Frederick was no longer primarily the stern Prussian general-king who had waged war on fellow German-speaking peoples, as at Leuthen in 1757, when his army defeated the numerically superior forces of Maria Theresa's Austria in the decisive battle of the Third Silesian War. Nor was he any longer the Francophile, flute-playing philosopher-king who preferred to be left to his cultural pursuits at Sanssouci.[9] Both images had largely been eclipsed by that of Old Fritz, a figure "wise and approachable, feared yet benevolent, just, and, most important, prototypically German."[10] German, not solely Prussian; that is the important thing here. At the same time, the proclamation of the German Reich in January 1871 marked the culminating step in what many, reflecting the influence of the Prussian School of historians, had come to understand as Prussia's historical mission to unify the German states in a "Smaller German" solution that excluded Austria. Seen in this light, it was only to be expected that Old Fritz, who in the previous century had used his military prowess to become the first Hohenzollern to threaten traditional Habsburg hegemony in Germany, would now be celebrated as the figure who had set this historical mission into motion.

8　Letter to Simrock of November 21, 1892, in *Johannes Brahms Briefwechsel* (hereafter *Briefwechsel*), 19 vols. to date (consisting of 16 orig. vols., rev. eds., Berlin, 1912–22; repr. Tutzing: Hans Schneider, 1974; and a *Neue Folge* consisting of 3 vols. to date, Tutzing: Hans Schneider, 1991–), vol. 12: *Briefe an Fritz Simrock*, ed. Max Kalbeck (1919): 86–87. The books in question are L[udwig] Pietsch, *Adolph Menzel's Illustrationen zu den Werken Friedrich des Großen, Jubiläums-Ausgabe*, 2 vols. (Berlin: R. Wagner, 1886), which is preserved in Brahms's library; and Franz Kugler, *Geschichte des Friedrichs des Grossen, mit 400 Illustrationen von Adolph Menzel* (Leipzig: Mendelssohn, 1867), which is not. Unless otherwise noted, for information regarding the contents of Brahms's library I rely on Kurt Hofmann, *Die Bibliothek von Johannes Brahms: Bücher- und Musikalienverzeichnis* (Hamburg: Karl Dieter Wagner, 1974).

9　On the role Menzel had played in shaping the latter image, see, in addition to Forster-Hahn, "Adolph Menzel's 'Daguerrotypical' Image of Frederick the Great," Christopher B. With, "Adolph von Menzel and the German Revolution of 1848," *Zeitschrift für Kunstgeschichte* 42 (1979): 195–214.

10　Brent O. Peterson, *History, Fiction, and Germany: Writing the Nineteenth-Century Nation* (Detroit: Wayne State University Press, 2005), 97–145 (at 98).

INTRODUCTION ❧ 5

Kalbeck, born in 1850 in Menzel's home town of Breslau/Wrocław, the largest city in Prussian Silesia, had always taken the Hohenzollerns' historical mission for granted. By the time he came of age, around 1870, Prussian dominance in, and Austria's exclusion from, Germany were *faits accomplis*. Brahms's experience was different. He was born in 1833, a proud son of the Free and Hanseatic City of Hamburg. He was old enough to have vivid adolescent memories of the failed Revolutions of 1848–49, and he entered early manhood shortly thereafter during a period of conservative retrenchment. Although at one time he probably considered himself a democrat, Brahms seems to have adopted the political profile of a moderate liberal fairly early on, and once he did that never really changed. What did change was his attitude toward the prospect of Prussian leadership in German affairs and the corollary it would necessarily entail, Austria's banishment from Germany.

Concerns about Prussian expansionist intentions had always run deep in Hamburg, and never more so than when the conservative Otto von Bismarck rose to the pinnacle of political power in Berlin in September 1862, a position he would hold for most of the next three decades. Bismarck was a figure of even greater loathing at this point in Vienna, a city to which the composer was increasingly drawn. When liberal-nationalist aspirations stirred openly once more in the early 1860s, Brahms lined up with the "Greater Germans" in hoping that Austria would play a leading role in national unification. But after Prussia's decisive military victory over its Habsburg rival in the summer of 1866 was followed by Austria's removal from German political affairs, the composer came straight to terms with the new reality, as we shall discover. And from the founding of the German Reich four-and-a half years later until his death in 1897, Brahms would remain an ardent *Reichsdeutscher*—he never naturalized as an Austrian—and an admirer of both Bismarck and the first German Emperor, William I, even while choosing to make his home outside the Reich in Vienna.

Although Brahms observed national politics closely throughout his adult life, he rarely composed music that directly engaged the pressing national-political issues of the day. Lying at the heart of this book are studies of the three works that do—the *Fünf Lieder für Männerchor*, op. 41; the *Triumphlied* for eight-part chorus and orchestra, op. 55; and the *Fest- und Gedenksprüche* for eight-part chorus *a cappella*, op. 109. This roster of works is similar to but not identical with the list mentioned at the end of Kalbeck's description of the visit Brahms paid to Menzel in his studio. The Third Symphony, op. 90, certainly can be read as a commentary on contemporary *musical* politics, but no convincing argument can be made—Kalbeck offers no argument at all—that Brahms intended for anyone to hear it as a

6　❧　INTRODUCTION

homage to "the power and glory" of Germany, much less of Prussia alone.[11] And though Kalbeck discusses the *Fünf Lieder für Männerchor* in passing, he is not much interested in this opus since, as he asserts, it embodies what he called Brahms's "myopic" (*kurzsichtig*)—which is to say, his Greater German—understanding of the national question at the time when the songs were written.[12] But getting to the heart of Brahms's understanding of that crucial question at that early stage in his political development, myopic or not, is precisely why these songs are of interest to me.

The national-political aspects of the *Triumphlied* and the *Fest- und Gedenksprüche* are considered in English-language monographs by Ryan Minor and Daniel Beller-McKenna, as well as in a number of studies in German that will be cited in due course.[13] Minor's is an extended consideration of the use of choral singing in the nineteenth century, by Brahms and several other composers, to give voice to the German nation. Beller-McKenna takes a different tack. His interest lies primarily in connecting Brahms's undoubted identity as a patriotic German to his identity as a Protestant Christian, albeit one of a heterodox kind. *A German Requiem*, op. 45, therefore, is for Beller-McKenna a key work for understanding Brahms's patriotic or German-national sensibilities—what it is not for Minor or for me. As will become clear throughout large portions of this book, I have profited from the work of both authors, whom I have long counted among my scholarly friends, even when, as is not infrequently the case, my take on things differs from that of one or the other or both.

Unlike Beller-McKenna and Minor, whose critical analyses of the works they explore are often insightful, I have aimed to keep my music-technical discussion to a minimum, although with a composer whose music is as complex as that of Brahms, it cannot, of course, be dispensed with entirely. In doing so, I seek to situate this book in what Celia Applegate, a historian of modern Germany who has made it her business to study musical culture,

---

11　David Brodbeck, "Brahms, the Third Symphony, and the New German School," *Brahms and His World*, rev. ed., ed. Walter Frisch and Kevin C. Karnes (Princeton: Princeton University Press, 2009), 95–116.

12　Kalbeck, *Johannes Brahms*, 2: 14n, 219.

13　Ryan Minor, *Choral Fantasies: Music, Festivity, and Nationhood in Nineteenth-Century Germany* (Cambridge: Cambridge University Press, 2012); Daniel Beller-McKenna, *Brahms and the German Spirit* (Cambridge, MA, and London: Harvard University Press, 2004). For a comprehensive earlier study that studiously pushes national questions aside, see Siegfried Kross, *Die Chorwerke von Johannes Brahms*, 2nd ed. (Berlin: Max Hesses Verlag, 1963). The national question lies even further outside the scope of Hans Michael Beuerle, *Untersuchungen zu den A-cappella-Kompositionen: Ein Beitrag zur Geschichte der Chormusik* (Hamburg: K. D. Wagner, 1987).

INTRODUCTION & 7

has called "a kind of Schengen zone of scholarship ... among historians and musicologists."[14] This is a tricky zone to navigate. Because I hope to provide a more nuanced understanding of the intersections of Brahms's music and questions of German patriotism, liberalism, and nationalism than has been customary in the field of historical musicology, I endeavor to provide a fairly thick historical context in which to read the music in question, with generous quotation of letters, journalistic writings, and other primary sources.[15] This is in keeping with my desire to approach Brahms's political works, "not [with] the clarity of hindsight [but with] the confusion of the moment," to borrow an expression from Marianne Wheeldon.[16] I beg the indulgence of historians of Central Europe (for whom I hope the book will have some appeal) for the lengths I go to provide the reader with basic historical background and context. But experience has taught me that what may go without saying to specialists in German history may well need to be provided to a broader community of readers, including those who are well versed in the history of music and musical style but not in political history.

The book opens with a prologue that takes stock of Brahms's political formation during the years extending from the Revolutions of 1848–49 up to the time of his decisive first stay in Vienna in 1862–63. That is then followed by fairly extensive accounts of three works from the 1860s, 1870s, and 1880s, respectively: the five early *Männerchöre* (covered in Chapters 1 and 2), the *Triumphlied* (Chapters 3 and 4), and the *Fest- und Gedenksprüche* (Chapters 5, 6, and 7). The concluding epilogue offers a rumination on Brahms during his twilight years with an emphasis on his unwavering devotion to Bismarck right up until his death in 1897. Two excursuses, interspersed along the way, provide additional historical context to aid in understanding.

---

14   Celia Applegate, *The Necessity of Music: Variations on a German Theme* (Toronto, Buffalo, and London: University of Toronto Press, 2017), 4.

15   For an exception to my generalization here, see Barbara Eichner, *History in Mighty Sounds: Musical Constructions of German National Identity 1848–1914* (Woodbridge, UK, and Rochester, NY: Boydell Press, 2012), especially 1–40.

16   Marianne Wheeldon, "Anti-Debussyism and the Formation of French Neoclassicism," *Journal of the American Musicological Society* 70 (2017): 433–74 (at 433).

Prologue

A Young Man's Political Formation

Liberalism—German unification, two concepts that are inseparably linked. It was the national idea that gave liberalism the inner strength to seize the hearts of the German people in the nineteenth century.[1]

—Karl Heinz Holst

On September 21, 1848, the fifteen-year-old Johannes Brahms gave a concert of his own for the first time in his hometown of Hamburg. It made hardly a ripple. "The world had other things to do," as Max Kalbeck would later wryly explain, "than to be concerned with a new pianist."[2] Indeed, Brahms's debut came in the midst of a tumultuous period in the city's history, as Hamburg was swept up in the revolutionary wave that had begun in Paris in February, and in March had moved eastward into the German lands and well beyond.[3] Common to all the revolutions of 1848 were liberal demands for constitutional government and the rule of law, suffrage rights, effective parliaments, freedom of the press, and freedom of association. But in Germany liberalism was only part of the story; the delegates who gathered in the Frankfurt National Assembly (May 18, 1848–May 31, 1849) also pushed for the creation of a unified constitutional German state.[4]

This was a dream that had animated liberals since the Napoleonic era. Napoleon's dramatic defeat of combined Prussian and Saxon forces in the twin battles of Jena and Auerstedt in October 1806 had hit hard. Large-scale

---

1   Karl Heinz Holst, *Die Stellung Hamburgs zum inneren Konflikt in Preussen, 1862–1866* (Wismar: Albert Sander, 1932), 1.

2   Kalbeck, *Johannes Brahms*, 1: 45.

3   Christopher Clark, *Revolutionary Spring: Europe Aflame and the Fight for a New World, 1848–49* (New York: Crown, 2023).

4   Dieter Langewiesche, "Revolution in Germany: Constitutional State–Nation State–Social Reform," in *Europe in 1848: Revolution and Reform*, ed. Dieter Dowe et al., trans. David Higgins (New York and Oxford: Berghahn Books, 2001), 120–43.

PROLOGUE ❧ 9

French occupation ensued, the states of the German Rhineland were made to function as French military satellites, and eventually some parts of Germany, including Hamburg, were formally annexed into the French Empire.[5] Fiercely anti-French sentiment thus animated the work of such early nationalists as Johann Gottlieb Fichte, author of *Reden an die deutsche Nation* (Addresses to the German nation, 1808); Friedrich Ludwig Jahn, founder of the *Turnverein* (gymnastics society) movement (1811); and Ernst Moritz Arndt, author of numerous patriotic anthems, including the iconic "Was ist des Deutschen Vaterland?" (What is the German's fatherland?, 1813). Anti-Napoleonic resistance soon spawned a veritable industry of patriotic pamphlets, poetry, songs, and engravings. In one widely circulated engraving, Napoleon is depicted as the son of the devil; the caption—"Das ist mein lieber Sohn an dem ich Wohlgefallen habe"—parodies the voice of God quoted in the first chapter of the Gospel of Mark: "You are my beloved son; with you, I am well pleased" (Figure 1). In Arndt's "Lied der Rache" (Song of revenge) of 1812, Napoleon is identified, not as the son of Satan, but as Satan himself: "Denn der Satan ist gekommen / Er hat sich Fleisch und Bein genommen / Und will der Herr der Erde sein" (For Satan has come. He has taken on flesh and bone and wants to be lord of the earth).[6]

For all that, German nationalist sentiment was not broadly felt during the early years of the nineteenth century. As John Breuilly has argued, anti-French sentiment among the "common people" at the time was more likely to be based on the material hardship imposed by the French than on German nationalist fervor.[7] Such was most likely the case, for example, with Brahms's mother, who was toiling as an unmarried, twenty-two-year-old seamstress in Hamburg when the French took control of the city. Arndt's "Was ist des Deutschen Vaterland?" was designed precisely to convince (in truth, not all that successfully) the far-flung and nationally indifferent German-speaking peoples to think of themselves as *ein deutsches Volk*.[8] Later

---

5   Karen Hagemann, "Francophobia and Patriotism: Anti-French Images and Sentiments in Prussia and Northern Germany during the Anti-Napoleonic Wars," *French History* 18 (2004): 404–25; and Karen Hagemann, "Occupation, Mobilization, and Politics: The Anti-Napoleonic Wars in Prussian Experience, Memory, and Historiography," *Central European History* 39 (2006): 580–620.

6   E. M. Arndt, *Lieder der Teutsche* (n.p., Im Jahr der Freiheit 1813), 38–39. This song is quoted and briefly discussed in Philip Dwyer, *Citizen Emperor: Napoleon in Power* (New Haven and London: Yale University Press, 2013), 442.

7   John Breuilly, *Austria, Prussia, and the Making of Germany, 1806–1871*, 2nd ed. (Harlow, UK: Pearson, 2011), 12–22.

8   As Breuilly notes (ibid., 15), in the early nineteenth century, the word *Volk* generally connoted the subjects of a particular ruler (of Prussia, of Saxony, and so forth) rather more than it implied the people of a German nation.

Figure 1. Anonymous, "Das ist mein lieber Sohn an dem ich Wohlgefallen habe," satirical print showing a seated devil cradling his "son," Napoleon, 1813–14. ©The Trustees of the British Museum. Shared under a Creative Commons Attribution-Non-Commercial-ShareAlike 4.0 International (CC BY-NC-SA 4.0) license.

nationalist myth-makers had this same goal in mind when they took to formulating the anti-Napoleonic Wars of 1813–15 in terms of national liberation. To be sure, two competing narratives soon emerged. Were the conflicts wars for freedom (*Freiheitskriege*), concerned with the bourgeois struggle for political participation as well as for the establishment of a constitutional nation-state? Or were they wars of liberation (*Befreiungskriege*) fought for

PROLOGUE 11

King and Fatherland?[9] By either nomenclature, the anti-Napoleonic wars could be construed by the liberal nationalists of the early nineteenth century as a fight against French hegemony in Central Europe waged, not by the various German dynastic states that, for reasons of their own, had sent troops into battle with Napoleon's forces, but by *Germany*, a state of mind if not yet a nation-state.[10]

Visions of realizing just this sort of Germany helped to call the *Burschenschaft* movement to life in the immediate post-war era. At the University of Jena on June 12, 1815, the various traditional regional student fraternities (the *Landsmannschaften*) voluntarily disbanded and joined together in a single undivided new fraternity, the *Urburschenschaft*, the first German student corporation formed with a political purpose in mind. The recently concluded Congress of Vienna, chaired by the reactionary Austrian Minister of State Klemens von Metternich, had dashed hopes for a post-Napoleonic, constitutional pan-German state by restoring conservative monarchical rule in a loosely bound German Confederation (*Deutsches Bund*), a kind of streamlined version of the old Holy Roman Empire of the German Nation. Frustrated and disappointed by this turn of events, the *Urburschenschaft* was determined to agitate for the creation of a unified, constitutional state that embodied notions of liberty.[11]

Many of the founders were veterans of the Wars of Liberation—hereafter I shall generally use the name that eventually became dominant—and

---

9   Christopher Clark, "The Wars of Liberation in Prussian Memory: Reflections on the Memorialization of War in Early Nineteenth-Century Germany," *Journal of Modern History* 68 (September 1996): 550–76 (here at 558–59); Dirk Göttsche, "Nationalism, Regionalism, and Liberalism in the Literary Representation of the Anti-Napoleonic 'Wars of Liberation,'" in *Nationalism before the Nation State: Literary Constructions of Inclusion, Exclusion, and Self-Definition (1756–1871)*, ed. Dagmar Paulus and Ellen Pilsworth (Leiden and Boston: Brill, 2020), 147–70; Peterson, *History, Fiction, and Germany*, 202–8; Kirstin Anne Schäfer, "Die Völkerschlacht," in *Deutsche Erinnerungsorte*, 3 vols., ed. Etienne François and Hagen Schulze (Munich: C. H. Beck, 2001), 2: 187–201.

10   Brian E. Vick, *The Congress of Vienna: Power and Politics after Napoleon* (Cambridge, MA, and London: Harvard University Press, 2014), 4–5, and the references cited there. Notably, the place of publication of Arndt's *Lieder der Teutsche* is given as "Im Jahr der Freiheit 1813" (In the year of freedom 1813); see above, footnote 6.

11   Karen Hagemann, "Celebration, Contestation and Commemoration: The Battle of Leipzig in German Memories of the Anti-Napoleonic Wars," in *War, Demobilization and Memory: The Legacy of War in the Era of Atlantic Revolutions*, ed. Alan Forrest, Karen Hagemann, and Michael Rowe (New York: Palgrave Macmillan, 2016), 335–52.

12 ❧ PROLOGUE

they adopted as their colors the black, red, and gold of the famous Lützow Free Corps, the only unit among the anti-Napoleonic troops made up of volunteers from all the German lands. The first large-scale meeting of the organization was held on October 18, 1817, at the Wartburg Castle near Eisenach. The timing and venue were chosen carefully. This marked both the tercentenary of the beginning of the Lutheran Reformation, the historical turn that Fichte had recently called "the last great and, in a certain sense, completed world deed [*Welt-That*] of the German people," and the fourth anniversary of the decisive Battle of Leipzig (known as the *Völkerschlacht*, or Battle of Nations), which had ended years of French domination of the German lands.[12] The Wartburg Castle was where Martin Luther had produced his translation of the New Testament of the Bible into German, a key document in the emergence of the modern German language and of German national consciousness. Here were several signs of how the student activists, by "mixing past with present in a bit of political theater," sought to connect their revolutionary national political project to old German traditions, including Protestant Christianity, which they understood, in contrast to cosmopolitan and oppressive Roman Catholicism, to represent religious, moral, and intellectual freedom.[13] As Arndt put it, "Germany is the land of Protestantism [because] Protestantism seems to be purely Germanic [and] effortlessly attracts to it all things Germanic."[14]

None of this went down well with Metternich, the architect of the repressive measures that characterized political life during the period before the March Revolution of 1848 (the so-called *Vormärz*).[15] Taking advantage of the widespread concern aroused by the assassination, on March 23, 1819, of the conservative dramatist August von Kotzebue by the *Burschenschaftler* Karl Ludwig Sand, Metternich convened a conference in August in the Bohemian resort of Carlsbad at which he convinced the leaders of the several German states in attendance of the necessity of rooting out and eliminating every trace of liberal and national agitation. The resulting Carlsbad Decrees,

---

12   Johann Gottlieb Fichte, *Fichte: Addresses to the German Nation*, ed. Gregory Moore (Cambridge: Cambridge University Press, 2008), 73.

13   Steven Michael Press, "False Fire: The Wartburg Book-Burning of 1817," *Central European History* 42 (2009): 621–46 (quoted at 622).

14   Ernst Moritz Arndt, *Ansichten und Aussichten der Teutschen Geschichte* (Leipzig, 1814); quoted in Wolfgang Altgeld, "Religion, Denomination and Nationalism in Nineteenth-Century Germany," in *Protestants, Catholics and Jews in Germany, 1800–1914*, ed. Helmut Walser Smith (Oxford: Oxford University Press, 2001), 49–65 (at 52).

15   A concise overview is provided in David Blackbourn, *History of Germany 1780–1918: The Long Nineteenth Century*, 2nd ed. (Malden, MA: Blackwell, 2003), 90–103.

issued on September 20, 1819, disbanded the *Burschenschaften*, called for the firing of politically suspect professors, and expanded press censorship. Later that year August Daniel von Binzer, another *Burschenschaftler*, penned the text of "Wir hatten gebauet ein stattliches Haus" (We had built a stately house) to mourn the loss. The next-to-last stanza alludes plaintively to the flag of the now-banned fraternity ("The ribbon is cut into pieces / It was black, red, and gold / And God did not prevent it / Who knows his ways"). And in the final stanza Binzer makes explicit the nationalists' appropriation of the Reformation as a German revolutionary movement, by way of recalling Luther's iconic chorale "Ein feste Burg ist unser Gott," what Heinrich Heine would later call the "Marseillaise of the Reformation" ("The house may collapse / Would it matter? / The spirit lives within us all / And our fortress is God").[16]

Eventually the black, red, and gold tricolor of the banned fraternity came to symbolize the liberal-nationalist movement at large, first at the Hambach Festival in May 1832 and then, in 1848–49, at the Frankfurt National Assembly, which adopted the colors in connection with its attempt to create a unified constitutional state.[17] Yet in Frankfurt the national dream foundered once more, in part on account of differences between moderate liberal and more radical democratic activists, in part on the question of how or even whether to include the multinational Austrian Empire. Although the liberals and democrats were united in their demands for national unity and constitutionalism, the latter went further than the former with their demands for universal male suffrage and an elective, not hereditary, executive. The so-called German Question also marked a fault line. Was there to be a Greater German solution that would include all the German states and be dominated by Habsburg Austria, or a Lesser German solution that would exclude Austria and be dominated by Hohenzollern Prussia? This defining question, in which Brahms took great interest, would remain unresolved for years to come.

Early on, the liberals at Frankfurt prevailed over their democratic brethren in determining that the new state would be a constitutional monarchy, not a republic, and in June 1848 the Habsburg Archduke Johann accepted appointment as the Imperial Regent of the short-lived German Reich. In November, Austria rejected the Assembly's proposal of a modified Greater German solution in which only Austria's predominantly German-speaking

---

16 Heine's essay "Zur Geschichte der Religion und Philosophie in Deutschland" (1835) is quoted in Heinz Schilling, *Martin Luther: Rebel in an Age of Upheaval* (Oxford: Oxford University Press, 2017), 102.

17 On the Hambach Festival, see James J. Sheehan, *German History 1770–1866* (Oxford: Clarendon Press, 1989), 610–12.

14 &❧ PROLOGUE

lands would be incorporated, leaving the Lesser German solution as the only viable option. That, too, came to nothing. In April 1849, King Frederick William IV of Prussia refused the imperial crown he was offered, and the delegates to the Assembly went home empty-handed.[18]

The liberal nationalists may not have achieved German unity, but their efforts were not entirely ineffectual. For one thing, most German states retained their recently gained parliaments and constitutions in whatever weakened form.[19] Austria became an exception when its short-lived constitution of 1849 was revoked two years later, ushering in a period of neo-Absolutism. Prussia, too, lived under a form of neo-Absolutism for most of the 1850s, but because its constitution and parliament survived, liberals tended to hold it in higher esteem than its rival Austria.[20] "The apparent political slumber of the 1850s was deceptive," writes David Blackbourn, even if "the exuberant mass mobilization and popular politics" of the revolutionary era had now come and gone. The lesson the liberals had learned from their sobering experience was to seek to bring about progressive reform, not through revolutionary action, but in incremental steps.[21]

The revolution in young Brahms's home town followed a course different in certain respects from those, say, in the larger capital cities of Berlin and Vienna and elsewhere in Germany.[22] As a thriving commercial seaport, the Free and Hanseatic City of Hamburg had always looked outward into the world more than it had looked inward toward the rest of Germany. (Hamburg was one of four republican city-states in the German Confederation; the other thirty-five members were monarchies of various kinds.) The Hamburg Senate, dominated by the city's mercantile oligarchs, was highly protective of the city's autonomy, and its representatives to the Frankfurt National Assembly were concerned primarily with the city's

---

18 On the deliberations in Frankfurt, see Brian E. Vick, *Defining Germany: The 1848 Frankfurt Parliamentarians and National Identity* (Cambridge, MA, and London: Harvard University Press, 2002); and James J. Sheehan, *German History 1770–1866* (Oxford: Clarendon Press, 1989), 656–729. For a more succinct account, see Mary Fulbrook, *A Concise History of Germany*, 3rd ed. (Cambridge: Cambridge University Press, 2019), 116–22.

19 Clark, *Revolutionary Spring*, 408–9.

20 Christopher Clark, *Iron Kingdom: The Rise and Fall of Prussia, 1600–1947* (Cambridge, MA: Belknap Press of Harvard University Press, 2006), 468–509.

21 Blackbourn, *History of Germany*, 130–31.

22 John Breuilly and Iorwerth Prothero, "The Revolution as Urban Event: Hamburg and Lyon during the Revolutions of 1848–49," in *Europe in 1848: Revolution and Reform*, ed. Dieter Dowe et al., trans. David Higgins (New York and Oxford: Berghahn Books, 2001), 371–98.

PROLOGUE 🙣 15

political and economic interests.[23] There was no monarchy in Hamburg to seek to reform (much less to overthrow), although this is not to suggest that no efforts were made to liberalize and even democratize the institutions of the city-state's governance. If street skirmishes in Hamburg were fewer in number and less bloody than in the Prussian and Austrian capitals, they did occasionally occur, such as on the night of June 9, 1848, when one of the city's toll gates was burned down, and with greater frequency in August and September. In proudly independent Hamburg the national question became more present now, primarily as a result of its proximity to the Elbe duchies of Schleswig and Holstein, the status of which was a subject, as we shall see, of fierce dispute between Denmark and the German Confederation that soon became the cause of war. Even still, heightened concern in Hamburg about the fate of the duchies had as much to do with market and other economic considerations as it did with the national question *per se*.[24]

Brahms was only fifteen as these revolutionary events unfolded. He was too young to be an active participant and, besides, he had a musical career to go about beginning. Nevertheless, already in his youth he seems to have been a devoted reader of the ephemeral works of Adolf Glassbrenner, a humorist, democrat, and champion of the lower classes in the Prussian state during the *Vormärz*.[25] A budding bibliophile who used the earnings from his musical activities to buy books, the young Brahms soon made himself acquainted with political writings of a higher *niveau*.[26] From *Des Jungen Kreislers Schatzkästlein* (*The Young Kreisler's Little Treasure Chest*), a handwritten anthology of favorite passages encountered in Brahms's wide range of reading, we can determine that by the early 1850s he knew the work of many notable liberals and democrats.[27] Among the collections of political poetry

---

23 Katherine Aaslestad, *Place and Politics: Local Identity, Civic Culture, and German Nationalism in North Germany during the Revolutionary Era* (Leiden and Boston: Brill, 2005), 327–28.

24 Richard J. Evans, *Death in Hamburg: Society and Politics in the Cholera Years, 1830–1910* (New York: Penguin, 2005), 4–5.

25 David Brodbeck, "Settling for Second Best: Brahms's *Männerchor-Lieder* in Context," in *Rethinking Brahms*, ed. Nicole Grimes and Reuben Phillips (Oxford: Oxford University Press, 2022), 56–69 (at 56).

26 On Brahms's passion for books and reading, see Kurt Hofmann, "Brahms the Hamburg Musician, 1833–1862," in *The Cambridge Companion to Brahms*, ed. Michael Musgrave (Cambridge: Cambridge University Press, 1999), 3–30 (at 16); and especially Reuben Phillips, "Between Hoffmann and Goethe: The Young Brahms as Reader," *Journal of the Royal Musical Association* 146 (2021): 455–89.

27 Johannes Brahms, *Des jungen Kreislers Schatzkästlein: Aussprüche von Dichtern, Philosophen und Künstlern*, ed. Carl Krebs (Berlin, 1909); Eng. trans. as *The*

16 &♥ PROLOGUE

acquired by Brahms at this time was Ferdinand Freiligrath's *Neuere politische und soziale Gedichte* (Recent political and social poems, 1849–51).[28] In the first volume of the *Schatzkästlein*, Brahms quotes Freiligrath's wildly popular poem of July 1848, "Die Todten an die Lebenden" (The dead to the living), in which those who had fallen on the barricades in Berlin in March 1848 exhort those who had survived the debacle to be undaunted by the defeat they had endured and to continue the revolution until they had successfully overthrown the repressive Prussian monarchy and replaced it with republican government.

The stanza that Brahms thought to enter into his notebook is particularly salient on this point:

O Volk, und immer Friede nur in deines Schurzfells Falten?
Sag' an, birgt es nicht auch den Krieg? Den Krieg herausgeschüttelt!
Den Zweiten Krieg, den letzten Krieg mit Allem was dich büttelt!
Laß deinen Ruf: "die Republik!" die Glocken überdröhnen,
Die diesen allerneuersten Johannesschwindel tönen!

[Oh People, always only peace within the folds of your Masonic apron? Say, does it not also harbor war? The war unloosed! The second war, the final war with everyone who agitates you. Let your cry, "The Republic!" drown out the bells that ring in this latest swindle by Johannes.]

The Johannes here was not Brahms, of course, but the newly proclaimed Imperial Regent, the Austrian Archduke Johann. For the Prussian authorities, the very passage that Brahms quoted, with its incitement of an armed overthrow of the government, was justification for arresting Freiligrath for sedition in August 1848. For Brahms's biographer Kalbeck this notation and others like it provide evidence of the young musician's partiality for writing down passages from poems that embody the revolutionary sentiments of the time.[29] Even many years later, after the founding of the German nation-state in 1870–71, Brahms made a point of acquiring Georg Herwegh's *Gedichte*

Brahms Notebooks: The Little Treasure Chest of the Young Kreisler, trans. Agnes Eisenberger, annotations by Siegmund Levarie (Hillsdale, NY: Pendragon Press, 2003). On this important source, see Reuben Phillips, "Brahms as Reader" (PhD diss., Princeton University, 2019), 1128; and Reuben Phillips, "Between Hoffmann and Goethe."

28   Ferdinand Freiligrath, *Neuere politische und soziale Gedichte*, vol. 1 (Cologne: Selbstverlag der Verfassers; Düsseldorf: W. H. Scheller, 1849), and Ferdinand Freiligrath, *Neuere politische und soziale Gedichte*, vol. 2 (Düsseldorf: Selbstverlag der Verfassers, 1851).

29   Kalbeck, *Johannes Brahms*, 1: 183.

eines Lebendigen (Poems of a living man, 1841–43), which had been banned on political grounds in *Vormärz* Prussia.[30]

No less anathema to the Prussian authorities than Freiligrath and Herwegh was August Heinrich Hoffmann von Fallersleben, author of the iconic "Lied der Deutschen" (Song of the Germans, 1841), with its call to repudiate traditional German particularism (*Kleinstaaterei*) in favor of German unity ("Deutschland über Alles").[31] On July 17, 1853, Brahms met the poet in the home of the Göttingen music director, Arnold Wehner, and he immediately set four of his lyric poems to music (op. 3, nos. 2–3, and op. 6, nos. 5–6). Later that summer, with those new songs in his knapsack, Brahms called on Hoffmann von Fallersleben at his home in Neuwied while on a walking tour of the Rhineland that would take him to Düsseldorf at the end of September for his introduction to Robert and Clara Schumann.[32]

Brahms would spend a good deal of time over the next few years in the company of the many friends he made that fateful summer, not only the Schumanns in Düsseldorf, but also Joseph Joachim in Hannover, Julius Otto Grimm in Göttingen, and Albert Dietrich in Bonn and later Oldenburg. His goal, however, was to base his career at home in Hamburg, where he was forging relationships with the city's leading musicians, including Theodor Avé-Lallement, Carl Georg Peter Grädener, and Georg Dietrich Otten.[33] By the late 1850s and early 1860s Brahms had put the emotional turmoil created by Robert Schumann's tragic end and his complicated early relationship with Clara Schumann behind him. And following something of a fallow period during those troubled years, he was composing actively again and beginning to publish the works of his first maturity. What is most relevant

---

30   Georg Herwegh, *Gedichte eines Lebendigen*, 9th printing (Stuttgart: G. J. Göschen, 1871).

31   Jost Hermand, "On the History of the "Deutschlandlied,'" in *Music and German National Identity*, ed. Celia Applegate and Pamela Potter (Chicago and London: University of Chicago Press, 2002), 251–68. Brahms's library includes a copy of August Heinrich Hoffmann von Fallersleben, ed., *Politische Gedichte aus der deutschen Vorzeit* (Leipzig: Wilhelm Engelmann, 1843).

32   [August Heinrich] Hoffmann von Fallersleben, *Mein Leben*, 6 vols. (Hannover: Carl Rümpler, 1868), 5: 215, 224. Both visits are discussed briefly in Peter Clive, *Brahms and His World: A Biographical Dictionary* (Latham, MD: Scarecrow Press, 2006), 227.

33   Styra Avins and Josef Eisinger, "Six Unpublished Letters from Johannes Brahms," in *For the Love of Music: Festschrift in Honor of Theodore Front on his 90th Birthday*, ed. Darwin F. Scott (Lucca: Antigua, 2002), 105–36 (at 115–19). On Hamburg's middle-class musical milieu, see Celia Applegate, "The Musical Worlds of Brahms's Hamburg," in her *The Necessity of Music* (Toronto, Buffalo, and London: University of Toronto Press, 2017), 167–80.

18 ❧ PROLOGUE

to this discussion, however, is the composer's immersion in liberal culture in Hamburg during a crucial period in the city-state's history.

In 1858, Hamburg's liberals renewed their demand for constitutional reform. In doing so, they took inspiration from the liberalizing New Era initiated in Prussia that year when the Hohenzollern Prince William assumed the duties of the throne after his brother Frederick William IV was incapacitated by a series of strokes.[34] Two years later, they achieved their goal at last with the adoption of a liberal constitution. The political system they envisioned consisted of a male-dominated discursive space comprising voluntary associations, newspapers, pamphlets, and public speech, what Jürgen Habermas famously called the "bourgeois public sphere."[35] Rational consensus was to be achieved through a process of ongoing public discussion conducted by self-reliant, mature, and autonomous males able to adjudicate matters of civic importance in accordance with disinterested logic. "The new, liberal government," writes Madeleine Hurd, "would be accountable, transparent, and neutral." With the notable exception of state-financed public education, it would also be strictly libertarian.[36]

This exception for education was critical, in that education was the foundation on which everything else rested. As Hurd explains:

> Rational debate required a general understanding of the "natural laws" of science, economy, and society, while shared knowledge of the nation's high culture would further the abolition of particularist interest. Secular primary schools—and their sisters, the educational voluntary associations—freed men politically. They taught their pupils to penetrate the lies of the tyrant, the obfuscating superstitions of the church, and the simplistic teachings of communism. The individual was freed from state and corporation in his economic life; education gave him mental autonomy.[37]

---

34 Abigail Green, "Political and Diplomatic Movements, 1850–1870: National Movement, Liberal Movement, Great-Power Struggles, and the Creation of the German Empire," in *Germany 1800–1870*, ed. Jonathan Sperber (Oxford and New York: Oxford University Press, 2004), 69–90 (at 76–84).

35 Jürgen Habermas, *The Structural Transformation of the Public Sphere: An Inquiry into a Category of Bourgeois Society*, trans. Thomas Burger (Cambridge, MA: MIT Press, 1989).

36 Madeleine Hurd, "Oligarchs, Liberals, and *Mittelstand*: Defining Civil Society in Hamburg, 1858–1862," in *Paradoxes of Civil Society: New Perspectives on Modern Germany and British History*, ed. Frank Trentmann (New York: Berghahn Books, 1999), 283–305 (quoted at 284). See also Madeleine Hurd, *Public Spheres, Public Mores, and Democracy: Hamburg and Stockholm, 1870–1914* (Ann Arbor, MI: University of Michigan Press, 2000), 1–92.

37 Hurd, "Oligarchs, Liberals, and *Mittelstand*," 284–85.

PROLOGUE &» 19

It is an easy matter to see traces of Brahms in this account, beginning with
the value placed on liberal education as an indispensable means of attain-
ing political maturity. To be sure, Brahms's formal schooling had ended at
age fourteen, but he worked hard thereafter to acquire the liberal hallmark
of *Bildung* (self-cultivation). In the summer of 1853, for example, he and
Joachim became informal students in history of Ludwig Aegidi, an erst-
while student revolutionary who was then working as a private lecturer in
Göttingen.[38] Studies of this kind continued in Hamburg in 1860–61, when,
as Brahms reported to Clara Schumann, he was starting "all kinds of new
lessons now" in the homes of new acquaintances.[39]

One of these acquaintances was the merchant Johann Gottfried Hallier.
Two of Hallier's daughters were members of Brahms's Hamburg Women's
Choir; one of his sons, Emil, was a professor at the city's Academic
Gymnasium. Brahms attended Emil Hallier's lectures in art history and also
received tuition from him in Latin. At the same time, he attended classes
in history once more with Aegidi, who was now lecturing on the subject
as Hallier's colleague at the Academic Gymnasium. The composer regularly
joined in readings of Shakespeare in the home of Avé-Lallement, and he frequented the weekly gatherings in the Halliers' home of artists and artistically
inclined persons, where he not only provided entertainment at the piano
but was an avid participant in discussions ranging across social, cultural, and
political issues. An inveterate reader of newspapers—the daily political press
was, of course, a critical component of the bourgeois public sphere—he was
given to expressing strong opinions on all such matters of the day, a practice
he retained for the rest of his life.[40] Nor did he make any secret of his religious unorthodoxy, another liberal hallmark. Brahms was, in short, a young
man of mental autonomy.[41]

---

38 Ludwig Aegidi, "Erinnerung an und von Emanuel Geibel," *Deutsche Revue
    über das gesamte nationale Leben der Gegenwart* 23/1 (January–March 1898):
    6–24 (at 13n).

39 See Brahms's letter to Clara Schumann of January 30, 1861, in Berthold
    Litzmann, ed., *Clara Schumann–Johannes Brahms: Briefe aus den Jahren 1853–
    1896*, 2 vols. (Leipzig: Breitkopf & Härtel, 1927, repr. Hildesheim and New
    York: Georg Olms, 1970), 1: 348–49 (at 348).

40 Benedict Anderson, *Imagined Communities: Reflections on the Origin and
    Spread of Nationalism*, rev. ed. (London and New York: Verso, 2006). Useful,
    too, are James Retallack, "From Pariah to Professional? The Journalist in
    German Society and Politics, from the Late Enlightenment to the Rise of
    Hitler," *German Studies Review* 16 (1993): 175–223; and Eleanor Turk, "The
    Press in Imperial Germany," *Central European History* 10 (1977): 329–37.

41 Walter Hübbe, *Brahms in Hamburg* (Hamburg: Lütcke & Wulff, 1902),
    35; Florence May, *The Life of Brahms*, 2 vols. (London: Edward Arnold,

20 ❧ PROLOGUE

Meanwhile in Prussia, the prince regent William's initiatives to reform the military and to increase appropriations for it were stymied by the liberal majority in the Diet. The military leadership wanted to increase the size of the army, to fix a three-year term of conscription, and to reduce the role and size of the *Landwehr* (voluntary people's militia). The liberals were opposed, not to a strengthening of the state's military power, but out of ideological reasons, fearful that the reforms were designed in part to inculcate in the military a personal loyalty to the crown that could be used against them.[42] By the summer of 1862, this stalemate had brought William I—the regent had acceded to the throne upon his brother's death on January 2, 1861— to the brink of abdication in favor of the liberal Crown Prince Frederick William. At the last minute, however, the king thought the better of things and, on September 23, 1862, he put the final nail in the coffin of the New Era by making the conservative Otto von Bismarck his new minister-president. A week later, in one of his most famous speeches—what the liberals could only view as an attack on constitutional parliamentary democracy— Bismarck famously proclaimed: "The position of Prussia in Germany will not be determined by its liberalism but by its power.... The great questions of the time will not be settled by speeches and majority decisions—that was the great mistake of 1848 and 1849—but by iron and blood," that is, by building Prussia's military-industrial base and being willing to resort to a strategic use of war if necessary to achieve one's goals.[43]

In the end, Bismarck would have his way. Through a series of three military conflicts won over a period of six years—with Denmark, in 1864; with Austria, in 1866; and with France, in 1870—a Smaller German nation-state was delivered by means of a stunning revolution from above.[44] Brahms would eventually come to venerate Bismarck and would celebrate his great achievement in the splendiferous *Triumphlied* (1872). But like his fellow liberals, he initially disdained the Iron Chancellor, not least for resorting

---

    1905), 1: 259. Reuben Phillips makes the insightful point that Brahms's reading might well be understood as an attempt "to gain admittance to a social world removed from his own more modest background and potentially also as a means compensating for his lack of a university education." See Phillips, "Between Hoffmann and Goethe," 470.

42   Clark, *Iron Kingdom*, 510–17; Frank Lorenz Müller, "The Spectre of a People in Arms: The Prussian Government and the Militarisation of German Nationalism, 1859–1864," *English Historical Review* 122 (2007): 82–104 (at 87–88).

43   Otto von Bismarck, speech to the Prussian Landtag, September 30, 1862 ("Blood and Iron"), quoted in English translation in germanhistorydocs.ghi-dc.org/sub_document.cfm?document_id=250.

44   For an excellent concise account, see Blackbourn, *History of Germany*, 184–95.

PROLOGUE ❧ 21

to extraconstitutional means to bring about the modernized military that would prosecute the Wars of Unification. In this early period of German liberal discontent with Bismarck, Brahms composed a work even more explicitly political, if more modestly scaled, than the *Triumphlied*. This is the music with which we begin.

Part I

Fünf Lieder für Männerchor, op. 41

Chapter One

Liedertafel and Liberal Nationalism

> The rubric of "German nationalism" encompasses more than antisemitism, xenophobia, chauvinism, and racialism…. Scholars not working in German studies … tend to treat an absurdly homogenized "German" nationalism as the paradigmatic example of "ethnic nationalism," whether formulated as Hans Kohn's "Eastern nationalism" or some other variant of the "bad" half of a theory of "Good and Bad Nationalism."[1]
>
> —Alexander Maxwell

The *Fünf Lieder für Männerchor* (Five songs for men's chorus), op. 41, is the only essay Brahms saw fit to publish in a genre that had been a prime medium for the expression of patriotic and liberal-nationalist sentiment dating back to the years of Napoleonic domination of the German lands. Writing in the first edition of George Grove's *Dictionary of Music and Musicians* (1880), Franz Gehring provided a concise description of the social milieu in which the genre had originally flourished:

> LIEDERTAFEL, originally a society of men, who met together on fixed evenings for the practice of vocal music in four parts, drinking forming part of the entertainment. They arose during the political depression caused by Napoleon's rule in Germany; and the first, consisting of 24 members only, was founded by Zelter in Berlin, Dec[ember] 28, 1808. Others soon followed at Frankfort [*sic*] and Leipzig, gradually relaxing the rules as to numbers. Bernhard Klein founded the "Jüngeren Berliner Liedertafel," which aimed at a higher standard of art. These societies gave an immense impetus to men's part-singing throughout Germany. Since the establishment of the

---

1   Alexander Maxwell, "Hungaro-German Dual Nationality: Germans, Slavs, and Magyars during the 1848 Revolution," *German Studies Review* 39 (2016): 17–39 (at 33).

26 ❧ CHAPTER ONE

Männergesangvereine proper (male singing societies), the word Liedertafel has come to mean a social gathering of the "Verein," *i.e.* a gathering of invited ladies and gentlemen, at which the members perform pieces previously learned. They are in fact informal concerts, where the guests move about, eat, drink, and talk as they please, provided they keep silence during the singing. The Liedertafeln of the large male singing societies of Vienna, Munich, and Cologne, are pleasant and refined entertainments, not without a musical significance of their own.[2]

In contrast to Carl Friedrich Zelter, founder of the first society, the Swiss liberal democrat Hans Georg Nägeli envisioned male choral singing as a means of educating the masses. From this tradition came the *Sängerfeste* (singing festivals). From fairly modest roots in the 1820s, these gatherings eventually grew into multi-day regional and even national affairs involving dozens of male choral societies with singers numbering in the thousands. During the repressive *Vormärz* and then in the neo-Absolutist decade of the 1850s, they provided a reasonably safe space, in some locales more than in others, for the expression of longing for national unification, civil rights, and freedom. Only later, as a result of liberalization in Prussia, Austria, and elsewhere, could such political speech be made more openly and boldly.[3]

Various hypotheses have been advanced to explain Brahms's relative lack of interest in this genre. It may in some degree have been an absence of opportunity and demand. By far the largest number of his many female part-songs date from the years 1859–62, when he served as the director of

---

2   F. G. [Franz Gehring], s.v. "Liedertafel," *A Dictionary of Music and Musicians,* ed. George Grove, 4 vols. (London: Macmillan, 1879–89), vol. 2 (1880): 136.

3   The literature from the past quarter century is considerable. Fundamental is the work of two German scholars in particular. See Friedhelm Brusniak and Dietmar Klenke, "Sängerfeste und die Musikpolitik der deutschen Nationalbewegung," *Die Musikforschung* 52 (1999): 29–54; Dietmar Klenke, *Der singende 'deutsche Mann': Gesangvereine und deutsches Nationalbewußtsein von Napoleon bis Hitler* (Münster: Waxmann, 1998); and Friedhelm Brusniak and Dietmar Klenke, eds., *"Heil deutschem Wort und Sang!": Nationalidentität und Gesangskultur in der deutschen Geschichte* (Augsburg: Wißner, 1995). The classic study is Otto Elben, *Der volksthümliche deutsche Männergesang: Geschichte und Stellung im Leben der Nation, der deutsche Sängerbund und seine Glieder,* 2nd ed. (1887); repr. ed., ed. Friedhelm Brusniak and Franz Krautwurst (Wolfenbüttel: Möseler, 1991). For a brief but insightful discussion in English, see Celia Applegate, "The Building of Community through Choral Singing," in *Nineteenth-Century Choral Music,* ed. Donna DaGrazia (New York and London: Routledge, 2013), 1–20 (esp. 8–10). See also Eichner, *History in Mighty Sounds,* 181–97; and James Garratt, *Music, Culture, and Social Reform in the Age of Wagner* (Cambridge: Cambridge University Press, 2010), 84–127.

LIEDERTAFEL AND LIBERAL NATIONALISM ❧ 27

the Hamburg Women's Chorus.[4] He had no similar involvement with any ensemble that might have prompted a similar production for male voices. At the same time, the paucity of Brahms's output in this genre may indicate a lack of affinity for a style in which simple textures and homorhythm predominated or a lack of compatibility with a genre whose once culturally significant character had shaded into mere *Liedertafelei* (singsong joviality). As we shall discover, Brahms's *Männerchöre* are not exactly fun and games, not all of them at any rate.

Opus 41 is not only singular in Brahms's oeuvre with respect to its genre. The disparate provenance of its texts is striking as well. The composer found the verse of the first song, "Ich schwing' mein Horn in's Jammerthal" (I blow my horn into the vale of tears), in an anthology he owned of Old High and Low German *Volkslieder*, where it is attributed to Ulrich, Duke of Württemberg (1487–1550).[5] Brahms's musical setting may have originated in 1847 in Winsen an der Luhe, a hamlet located along the Elbe River about fifteen miles southeast of Hamburg, where—as a fourteen-year-old boy engaged for the summer as the piano tutor to the daughter of one of his father's friends—he composed at least four short pieces for a local male chorus to sing.[6] In any case, the song must have been composed by ca. 1859–60, when he arranged it for his Hamburg Women's Chorus.[7]

---

4   Sophie Drinker, *Brahms and His Women's Choruses* (Merion, PA: Sophie Drinker, under the auspices of Musurgia Publishers, A. G. Hess, 1952).

5   Ludwig Uhland, *Alte hoch- und niederdeutsche Volkslieder mit Abhandlung und Anmerkungen herausgegeben.* 2 vols. (Stuttgart and Tübingen: J. G. Cotta'schen Buchhandlung, 1844–45), 1: 481.

6   May, *Life of Brahms*, 1: 70–82. Brahms later sought to destroy most of, if not all, these juvenilia, but a copy containing one of the pieces, a setting of Wilhelm Müller's "Postillions Morgenlied," as well as a setting of Emanuel Geibel's "Goldne Brücke seien alle Lieder mir" that might be another, eluded him and turned up several years ago in Celle, where they had been performed in a concert by Brahms and the violinist Eduard Reményi on 2 May 1853. Helmut Lauterwasser, "'Von seinen Jugendstreichen bewahrt man nicht gern die sichtbaren Zeichen': Johannes Brahms' älteste erhaltene Kompositionen im Stadtarchiv Celle entdeckt," *Brahms-Studien* 16 (2011): 101–12; and Johannes Brahms, *Zwei Lieder für Männerstimmen a cappella*, ed. Helmut Lauterwasser (Wiesbaden: Breitkopf & Härtel, 2010).

7   In the part-book of Friedchen Wagner, one of the leading members of the Hamburg chorus, the first soprano part is inscribed "originally written for four men's voices" (*Ursprünglich für 4 Männerst. geschr.*) See Drinker, *Brahms and His Women's Choruses*, 95. Drinker assumed that this reference was to one of the male choral part-songs composed in Winsen. The only extant autograph of "Ich schwing' mein Horn in's Jammerthal," op. 41, no. 1, is undated. It was discovered in the archive of the Altonaer Singakademie and acquired at

28 &♦ CHAPTER ONE

The texts of the other four songs were drawn from a large omnibus collection of *Lieder und Gedichte* published in 1861 by Carl Lemcke (1831–1913). "Geleit" (Procession), op. 41, no. 3, was selected from a miscellany of twenty-five songs (*Vermischte Lieder*). "Freiwillige her!" (Volunteers, come forth!), "Marschiren" (Marching), and "Gebt Acht" (Take heed), op. 41, nos. 2, 4, and 5, respectively, were drawn from a subgroup of seven *Soldatenlieder* found in a chapter headed "Im Volkston" (In the popular style).[8] Kalbeck assigned the date of Brahms's composition of "Geleit" to the summer of 1862 and held that the three soldiers' songs were probably written "around the same time (1861–62) in Hamburg."[9] Yet, since the composer's exemplar of the *Lieder und Gedichte* is inscribed "Johs. Brahms 1862," it is difficult to imagine that any of his settings from this volume would have been written during the year before. Moreover, as we shall see, it is unlikely that any was composed before 1863 or after 1864.[10]

Taken in the order in which they were eventually published, the four Lemcke songs unfold a thematically unified and tonally compatible set in C. "Freiwillige her!," in C minor, exhorts the able-bodied men of all the German lands to come together to defend the fatherland from foreign aggression. "Geleit" is not one of Lemcke's specially designated soldiers' songs, but it fits in easily with those that are, inasmuch as it depicts a battlefield burial of a fallen comrade-in-arms. Brahms composed it in E♭ major, the closely related

---

auction in 1980 by the Staats- und Universitätsbibliothek Carl von Ossietzky, Hamburg.

8   Carl Lemcke, *Lieder und Gedichte* (Hamburg: Hoffmann und Campe, 1861). On Brahms and Lemcke, see Natasha Loges, *Brahms and His Poets: A Handbook* (Woodbridge, UK: Boydell Press, 2017), 265–75.

9   Kalbeck, *Johannes Brahms*, 2: 13. Siegfried Kross is more circumspect than Kalbeck in acknowledging that the time of origin of the songs is "absolutely unsettled" (*völlig ungeklärt*) but then does not really disagree with Kalbeck's supposition. See Kross, *Die Chorwerke von Johannes Brahms*, 148–50.

10   Hofmann, *Die Bibliothek von Johannes Brahms*, 69. The only extant autographs of the three soldiers' songs were discovered, along with that of "Ich schwing mein Horn in's Jammerthal," in the archive of the Altonaer Singakademie and were acquired at auction by the Österreichische Nationalbibliothek, Vienna, in 1980. Of these only "Freiwillige her!," op. 41, no. 2, carries a signature with date: "Januar 1864 / Joh. Brahms." For unexplained reasons, Margit McCorkle expressed doubt about the relevance of this inscription to the date of composition, placing greater credence on Kalbeck's claim that the songs were written in ca. 1861–62; see Margit L. McCorkle, *Johannes Brahms: Thematisch-bibliographisches Werkverzeichnis*, published following joint preliminary work with Donald McCorkle (Munich: Henle, 1984), 148. No autograph of "Geleit" is extant, but other primary evidence, which I will explore, points to 1863 as the date of composition.

major mediant key of the prevailing tonic, C. "Marschiren" tells a timeless, light-hearted generic tale of a bored garrison soldier who is eager to see some action after spending two years confined to barracks (or, as Lemcke put it, using the salty and perhaps drunken language of a soldier, "*in der ver-dammten Ki, Ko, Ka, in der Kasern[e]*" [in the damned bi-bo-ba, in the bar-racks]). All five stanzas begin in C minor and end with a refrain in C major. And like the opening "Freiwillige her!," the concluding "Gebt Acht" is in C minor and concerned with guarding the nation's borders against affronts from abroad.

Lemcke, an aesthetician and art historian as well as a poet and novelist, and later the rector at the University of Stuttgart, studied at Göttingen in the early 1850s, where he was a member of the Burschenschaft Hannovera Göttingen, founded in the early months of the 1848 Revolution. His sol-diers' songs must therefore be read in a mid-century German liberal-nation-alist context, not with glances ahead to military aggression, to say nothing of the world wars of the twentieth century.[11] Yet many modern commentators, more apt to think of Hitler's Germany than of the unified constitutional state about which the liberal nationalists had traditionally dreamt, have struggled to find the right tone in which to discuss Brahms's voicing of the belligerent sentiments expressed in some of the soldiers' songs. (The text of the set's opening number, "Ich schwing' mein Horn in's Jammerthal," has caused no such consternation.) That tension is evident in Siegfried Kross's pioneer-ing survey of the composer's choral music, a product of the early years of Germany's struggle to account for its Nazi past (*Vergangenheitsbewältigung*). Kross recognized that to the audiences of the 1950s and beyond, Brahms's male part-songs could only come off as "unconscionably nationalistic, almost a little chauvinistic," even if, as Kross allowed, such attitudes would have seemed far-off to the composer. Still, Kross was relieved that audiences had grown "deaf to the [songs'] national and patriotic emotionalism," and so had rendered the work, in effect, "completely dead." As if it that were indeed its fate, Hans Michael Beuerle gave Opus 41 not so much as a pass-ing mention in his own extensive survey from twenty-five years later.[12]

Even those post-war scholars who have offered commentary on this music have done so only fleetingly, almost sheepishly. Most focus on what Burkhard Meischein calls the "aggressive-chauvinistic tenor" of the "ideologically

---

11   It is not inconceivable that Brahms crossed paths with Lemcke in Göttingen during his weeks spent there with Joachim in the summer of 1853.

12   Kross, *Die Chorwerke von Johannes Brahms*, 153, 160–61; Hans Michael Beuerle, *Untersuchungen zu den A-cappella-Kompositionen: Ein Beitrag zur Geschichte der Chormusik* (Hamburg: K. D. Wagner, 1987). Kross's account originated in his dissertation, completed in 1957 and first published the fol-lowing year.

30 &♥ CHAPTER ONE

suspect … verse." Like Kross, Daniel Beller-McKenna acknowledges that the music was written in the context of traditional German liberal nationalism, but he never really dismisses his charge of chauvinism.[13] An indictment of chauvinism is not to be made lightly, in my view, and we should be wary of allowing the shadow of jingoistic Wilhelmine militarism, not to speak of the horrors of the Third Reich, to eclipse from thoughtful consideration music from an earlier era solely on account of its open display of German patriotism, even German nationalism. Locutions that may offend today carried very different meaning in the years before German unification and even for a period beyond. Indeed, during the time in which Opus 41 originated they were part and parcel not only of the men's choral societies, but also of the gymnastics clubs and sharpshooters' clubs (*Schützenvereine*), both of which had long been associated with traditional German liberal nationalism.[14] Indeed, Karl Geiringer thought it "a pity" that Brahms's only set of male part-songs had fallen into oblivion.[15] As Geiringer knew, and as Friedhelm Brusniak instructs us, it was once possible to be "unmistakably national but not nationalistic" and to retain a "remarkably tolerant and open-minded attitude in ideological and political views."[16] It is high time, therefore, to

---

13   Burkhard Meischein, "Weltliche Chorwerke A Cappella," in *Brahms Handbuch*, ed. Wolfgang Sandberger (Stuttgart and Weimer: J. B. Metzler, 2009), 314–29 (at 319). Daniel Beller-McKenna, *Brahms and the German Spirit*, 149–51 (at 150); Daniel Beller-McKenna, "The Scope and Significance of the Choral Music," in *The Cambridge Companion to Brahms*, ed. Michael Musgrave (Cambridge: Cambridge University Press, 1999), 171–94 (at 178), and Daniel Beller-McKenna, "5 Lieder, for Four-Part Men's Chorus, Opus 41," in *The Compleat Brahms*, ed. Leon Botstein (New York: Norton, 1997), 342–44.

14   Berit Elisabeth Dencker, "Popular Gymnastics and the Military Spirit in Germany, 1848–1871," *Central European History* 34 (2001): 503–30; Daniel A. McMillan, "Energy, Willpower, and Harmony: On the Problematic Relationship between State and Civil Society in Nineteenth-Century Germany," in *Paradoxes of Civil Society: New Perspectives on Modern German and British History*, ed. Frank Trentmann (New York: Berghahn, 1999), 176–95; and Dieter Düdling, *Organisierter gesellschaftlicher Nationalismus in Deutschland (1808–1847): Bewegung und Funktion der Turner- und Sängervereine für die deutsche Nationalbewegung* (Munich: Oldenbourg, 1984).

15   Karl Geiringer, *Brahms: His Life and Work*, 3rd ed. (New York: Da Capo, 1982), 299.

16   Friedhelm Brusniak, "Der Deutsche Sängerbund und das 'deutsche Lied,'" in *Nationale Musik im 20. Jahrhundert: kompositorische und soziokulturelle Aspekte der Musikgeschichte zwischen Ost- und Westeuropa: Konferenzbericht Leipzig 2002*, ed. Helmut Loos and Stefan Keym (Leipzig: Gudrun Schröder, 2004),

rethink accounts that use historical hindsight to render Opus 41 irredeemable, and instead to offer a reading of the work in the context of the period in which it was written. Kerstin Schüssler-Bach made a brief initial foray in this direction some years ago, but much remains to be considered.[17]

Meeting Liberal Vienna

Austria was in the early stages of profound political transformation when Brahms traveled to Vienna for the first time in the middle of September 1862 to begin what turned out to be an extended stay lasting nearly eight months. Three years earlier, Emperor Francis Joseph had blundered into a war he could ill afford with the Second French Empire of Napoleon III and the Savoyard Kingdom of Sardinia and ended up not only losing face but also most of his monarchy's Italian territories. (The lessons Prussia learned while standing outside the fray about the centrality of force to the resolution of entrenched power-political conflicts led the prince regent William to begin pushing for the dramatic reform of his military that ultimately led to Bismarck's installation as minister-president a few years later.)[18] Weakened at home by the debacle in Italy, and now under increasing pressure both from his bankers to put the monarchy's shaky finances in order and from restive liberals in Hungary looking for greater autonomy, Francis Joseph recognized that he would have to loosen the strictures of neo-Absolutism and allow movement toward some form of constitutional governance in order to shore up public support for his regime.[19] This happened in fits and starts, but by 1867 the Austrian Empire would be no more, replaced by a new Austro-Hungarian Monarchy, both halves of which Francis Joseph would rule as a constitutional monarch.

With the relaxed police oversight that had accompanied the beginnings of this liberal thaw in the early 1860s came a rapid growth in Austria in voluntary associations, what Gary B. Cohen succinctly characterized as "free,

---

409–21 (at 410). See also the discussion in Blackbourn, *History of Germany 1780–1918*, 321–22.

17 Kerstin Schüssler-Bach, "'Einigermaßen zeitgemäß': Brahms' Männerchöre im politischen Kontext der 1860-er Jahre," *Brahms-Studien*, vol. 16, ed. Beatrix Borchard and Kerstin Schüssler-Bach (Tutzing: Hans Schneider, 2011), 113–26. See also the brief discussion in Verena Naegele, "Brahms und die Politik," in *"Hoch aufm Berg, tief im Thal ...": Die Schweizer Inspirationen von Johannes Brahms*, ed. Sibylle Ehrismann (Zurich: Musik Hug, 1997), 49–77 (at 53–55).

18 Clark, *Iron Kingdom*, 510–17.

19 Steven Beller, *The Habsburg Monarchy 1815–1918* (Cambridge: Cambridge University Press, 2018), 107–27.

32 ❧ CHAPTER ONE

formal organization[s] of individuals established independently of the state for joint purposes other than earning a livelihood."[20] Ranging from reading clubs to gymnastics clubs to clubs organized around any number of other commonly held interests, these groups of like-minded men constituted a middle-class public sphere in which liberal *Bürger* could agitate for the self-governance that had eluded them in 1848.

Of great general importance, and of particular interest here, are the male choral societies. "Voluntary associations are now springing up like mushrooms in our country, especially associations of men in four parts, and the display of flags, slogans, and German patriotic sentiments is in full bloom." Thus began a report on the musical goings-on in Vienna published in August 1862 in the *Signale für die musikalische Welt*. The report continues:

> This stuff is necessary for the many festivities that take place in Vienna, and it is truly fortunate that the gymnasts are mute when it comes to music, as otherwise it would be unbearable to hear them singing "What is the German's Fatherland?" The Viennese man, to whom the clubs and societies were for so long forbidden by the police, now literally revels in them, and it will in all probability be a long time until he ... can look upon singers in black tails, gymnasts in twill jackets, and large banners and maintain his cool.[21]

The *Wiener Männergesangverein* (Vienna Men's Choral Society), founded in 1843 under the wary eye of Metternich's police, was the oldest and most prestigious association of this kind in the Habsburg capital. For fifteen years it was the only such group permitted there, but between 1858 and 1863, sixteen other Viennese male choral societies came into existence.[22] Interest was now such as to warrant the founding, in January 1861, of *Die Liedgenossen* (Comrades in song), a newsletter of sorts that covered the groups' activities and other matters of common interest.

At the time of Brahms's arrival, Vienna was not only a city in the midst of this boom in the number of male choral societies; it was also beginning to experience—what is not entirely unrelated—a significant Schubert boom. One example of this interrelationship took place on August 9, 1862, when

---

20 Gary B. Cohen, *The Politics of Ethnic Survival: Germans in Prague, 1861–1914*, 2nd ed., rev. (West Lafayette, IN: Purdue University Press, 2006), 42, and the references cited there.

21 "Wiener musikalische Skizzen," *Signale für die musikalische Welt* 20 (September 4, 1862): 441–42 (at 441).

22 Rudolf Hofmann, *Der Wiener Männergesangverein: Chronik der Jahre 1843 bis 1893* (Vienna: Verlag des Wiener Männergesangvereines, 1893); Eduard Kral, *Taschenbuch für Deutsche Sänger* (Vienna: Hoffmann & Ludwig, 1864), 249–54.

the newly established male choral society *Biedersinn* (Upright Mentality) hosted a singers' festival in the Vienna suburb of Hietzing on the occasion of the dedication of its banner. On the fairgrounds stood a large bust of Schubert surrounded by the banners of all thirty-four participating male choral societies, from Vienna and throughout Lower Austria. Moreover, the proceeds of the festival were earmarked for the Schubert Monument that would eventually be dedicated ten years later in the *Wiener Stadtpark*.[23] It was not for nothing, then, that a portrait of the Viennese composer was used as the frontispiece for Eduard Kral's comprehensive *Taschenbuch für Deutsche Sänger* (Handbook for German singers, 1864), or that this volume included an essay by Schubert's early biographer, Heinrich Kreissle von Hellborn, that describes his importance for the male singing movement in general.[24] All this is evidence of the important role played by groups of this kind in the elevation of Schubert's stature to that of a German *Großmeister*.[25]

From the pages of *Die Liedgenossen* we can gain a good sense of the atmosphere of male bonhomie mixed with Greater-German liberal nationalist sentiment that surrounded Brahms during this first Viennese sojourn. Consider this report from October 1862:

> Some time ago the Viennese choral society "Zion" under its choirmaster Mr. [Carl] Goldmark, welcomed the Vienna Gymnastics Club [*Wiener Turnverein*] on a gymnastics tour with an impromptu singing of its motto and a chorus. The joyfully surprised gymnasts responded with a hearty "*Gut Heil,*" and also performed some songs under the direction of their choral master, [Franz] Mair, whereupon [Gottfried] Bergamenter, the society's *Sangwart* [singing coach] gave a longer speech to the "Zion" singers, thanking his comrades for their kindness. He emphasized that Art knows no one side or the other and everywhere sings to the same god, whose heavens shine down with equal serenity upon all peoples, upon Germany's green bushes and meadows, as it did long ago upon the sublime glory of Mt. Zion. At the end, he invited [the members of Zion] to join the gym-

---

23 Among other reports, see Ed. H. [Eduard Hanslick], "Sängerfest in der 'Neuen Welt,'" *Die Presse* (August 11, 1862): 1; "Niederösterreichisches Gesangsfest," *Ost-Deutsche Post* (August 11, 1862): 1; "Das niederösterreichisches Sängerfest," *Fremden-Blatt* (August 10, 1862): 5; Dr. F, "Die Fahnenweihe des Wiener Gesangvereines: 'Biedersinn,'" *Die Liedgenossen* 2/4 (October 1862): 26–27.

24 Kreissle's essay, entitled "Franz Schubert in seinem Verhältniss zu mehrstimmigen, insbesondere Männergesang," is found in Kral, *Taschenbuch für Deutsche Sänger*, 323–30.

25 Helmut Loos, "Franz Schubert im Repertoire der deutschen Männergesangvereine: Ein Beitrag zur Rezeptionsgeschichte," *Archiv für Musikwissenschaft* 57 (2000): 113–29.

nasts in singing "Das deutsche Lied," a proposal that was cheerfully accepted. "Das deutsche Vaterland" [i.e., "Was ist des Deutschen Vaterland?"], performed with equal enthusiasm by Jews and Christians, followed, and the two honest and upright [*wacker*] societies parted with shouts of "*Gut Heil!*" and "*Die Sänger hoch!*"[26]

It bears noting that the Germanized Jews who formed the membership of Zion—they sometimes provided the music on the High Holy Days and on other occasions in Vienna's Leopoldstadt Synagogue—sang Gustav Reichardt's setting of [Arndt's] "Das deutsche Vaterland" (1826) and Johann Wenzel Kalliwoda's setting of "Das deutsche Lied" (1838), both standard *Männerchor* fare at the time, as a matter of course, and that the members of the *Turner-Sängerchor*, as the Vienna Gymnastic Club's own choral society was called, felt bound in brotherhood to the members of the *Gesangverein Zion*.[27] Among the several friendships Brahms made in these circles at this time was one he struck up with Carl Goldmark, the director of the Zion and an ascendent composer of Germanized Jewish-Hungarian origin to whom he remained close thereafter.[28] Another bond was made with the Moravian-born conductor, composer, teacher, and publisher J. P. Gotthard (born Bohumil Pazdirék), who had recently founded another male choral society of his own. It was through Gotthard that Brahms came to compose the first of his Lemcke settings for male chorus, "Geleit."

Kalbeck was misled into thinking that this song was composed in the summer of 1862 by his uncritical reading of Gotthard's important,

---

26   *Die Liedgenossen* 2/4 (October 1862): 30. *Gut Heil!* (To your health!) was the official greeting of the gymnastics movement, *Die Sänger hoch!* (Hail to the singers!) the official greeting of the singers' movement. *Sangwart* was a prestigious title that dates back to the founding of the *Burschenschaften*.

27   On the importance of singing in the gymnastics clubs, see McMillan, "Energy, Willpower, and Harmony," 179–80, and the references cited there. It is perhaps symbolic that in 1865 *Sion*, as the Zion Choral Society was known in Hebrew, changed its name to *Eintracht* (a German word meaning "concord"). On the strong desire by upward-striving Jews in Vienna during this period to acculturate as German liberals, see Jonathan Kwan, "Politics, Liberal Idealism and Jewish Life in Nineteenth-Century Vienna: The Formative Years of Heinrich Jacques (1831–1894)," *Leo Baeck Institute Yearbook* 64 (2019): 197–218; and Lisa Silverman and Deborah Holmes, "Jewish Difference in the Austrian Context," *Austrian Studies* 24 (2016): 1–12. On Goldmark and Zion, see David Brodbeck, *Defining Deutschtum: Liberal Ideology, German Identity, and Music-Critical Discourse in Liberal Vienna* (New York: Oxford University Press, 2014), 68–69, and the references there.

28   David Brodbeck, "Notes from the Lives of Two Viennese Composers," *The American Brahms Society Newsletter* 32/1 (2014): 1–5.

turn-of-the-century recollection of Brahms. Gotthard's memoir has the advantage of having been written by one of the composer's first Viennese friends, but it contains a number of inaccuracies all the same. The first of these, which Kalbeck surely recognized, occurs in the very title of the manuscript: "My Personal Relationships with Viennese Artists and in particular with the Master Johannes Brahms during his Intermittent Viennese Sojourns from 1861 to 1872" (1901).[29] As we have seen, Brahms's first stay in the Austrian capital did not begin until September 1862; by December 1871 he had settled into an apartment in the Karlsgasse, in Vienna's Fourth District, in which he would spend the rest of his years. Such errors are easily rectified, however, and, once that has been taken care of, the recollection is in fact quite informative.

Gotthard was instrumental not only to Brahms's turn to the genre of the male choral part-song, but also to his deepening knowledge of the music of Schubert, a composer whom he had long admired.[30] His "most beautiful hours" there, as he explained to the Swiss publisher J. Melchior Rieter-Biedermann, were spent in examination of Schubert's unpublished manuscripts. Many of these were in the hands of Gotthard's employer, C. A. Spina, the Viennese music dealer who had acquired them when he took over the firm of Diabelli & Co. some years before.[31] Among them—some borrowed and taken home for study—were several male choral part-songs. Perhaps most notable among that group is the beautiful "Der Entfernten"

---

29 "Meine persönlichen Beziehungen zu Wiener Künstlern und insbesonders zum Meister Johannes Brahms während seines zeitweisen Wiener Aufenthaltes von 1861 bis 1872, Biographischer Beitrag von J. P. Gotthard, Vöslau 15./9/1901," Staats- und Universitätsbibliothek Hamburg, Carl von Ossietzky. On Gotthard, see also Alexander Weinmann, *J. P. Gotthard als später Originalverleger Franz Schuberts* (Vienna: Ludwig Krenn, 1979).

30 For overviews, see James Webster, "Schubert's Sonata Form and Brahms's First Maturity (II)," *19th-Century Music* 3 (1979/80): 52–71 (at 55); and Robert Pascall, "Brahms and Schubert," *Musical Times* 124 (1983): 286–90. For a more detailed account, see David Brodbeck, "Brahms as Editor and Composer: His Two Editions of Ländler by Schubert and His First Two Cycles of Waltzes, opp. 39 and 52" (PhD diss., University of Pennsylvania, 1984), 13–38.

31 Letter of February 18, 1863, in *Briefwechsel*, vol. 14: *Johannes Brahms im Briefwechsel mit Breitkopf & Härtel, Bartolf Senff, J. Rieter-Biedermann, C. F. Peters, E. W. Fritzsch und Robert Lienau*, ed. Wilhlem Altmann (1920), 77–78 (at 77). Gotthard was Spina's stock manager (*Sortimentschef*). That same month Gotthard helped to arrange for the firm's publication of Brahms's setting for women's chorus of Psalm 13, op. 27, and his four Duets for Alto and Baritone, op. 28. See Gotthard, "Meine persönlichen Beziehungen zu Wiener Künstlern und insbesonders zum Meister Johannes Brahms," 4, 8.

36 ❧ CHAPTER ONE

(To the distant beloved), D. 331, which the Schubert enthusiast Johann Herbeck conducted in a concert given in the Imperial-Royal Large Ballroom by his Vienna Men's Choral Society on March 15, 1863. Twelve days later, Herbeck led the first performance of the unfinished oratorio *Lazarus* in the concerts of Vienna's Gesellschaft der Musikfreunde (known locally as the Musikverein). Brahms, who thought enough of the *Lazarus* fragment to make a copy of it for himself, was present for the latter concert and, given his present preoccupation with Schubert, very likely attended the former as well.[32]

Herbeck's Vienna Men's Choral Society was the oldest but by no means the only such group in Vienna by the time Brahms first visited the city. Toward the end of August 1862 Gotthard began weekly rehearsals of a new choral society of his own made up of young men from Vienna's business community. Upon receiving the necessary approval from the Viennese authorities, the *Wiener kaufmännische Gesangverein* (Vienna Mercantile Choral Society) was formally established on November 10, 1862. Several weeks later, on December 16, came the ensemble's *Gründungs-Liedertafel* (Inception Liedertafel), at which its motto was introduced. Its words— "German song, free and noble / ring out across the land. / Trade by land and sea / forges ties between peoples!"—are indicative of the liberal-bourgeois orientation these associations shared.[33] The evening continued with choruses by Schubert, Mendelssohn, and Gade, among other composers, and concluded with the ubiquitous "Was ist des Deutschen Vaterland?" and "Das deutsche Lied."[34] "The following months," writes Gotthard, "were

---

32 Letter of March 26, 1863, from Brahms to Adolf Schubring, in *Briefwechsel,* vol. 8: Johannes Brahms, *Briefe an Joseph Viktor Widmann, Ellen und Ferdinand Vetter, Adolf Schubring,* ed. Max Kalbeck (1915), 196–98.

33 As Gotthard writes: "Die Constituierung erfolgte unter enthusiastischen Kundgebungen der Versammlung und schon acht Tage später war ich in der angenehmen Lage, den von mir rasch improvisierten und vertonten Wahlspruch: "Deutsches Lied, frei und hehr / Tön' durch alle Lande / Handel über Land und Meer / Schließe Völkerbande!" der jungen Sängerschar einüben zu können." On the founding of the organization, see "Neuer Gesangverein," *Der Zwischen-Akt* (August 29, 1862): 4; "Kaufmännischer Gesangverein," *Das Vaterland* (November 4, 1862): 3. Gotthard's musical setting of the motto is provided in *Festschrift zur Feier des 50jährigen Gestandes des Wiener Kaufmännischen Gesangvereines am 5. und 6. Januar 1912* (Vienna: Verlag des Wiener Kaufmännischen Gesangvereines, 1912), second frontispiece. Another version is provided in Weinmann, *J. P. Gotthard als später Originalverleger Franz Schuberts,* fig. 1, where the noun "Handel" is replaced with the first-person singular verb "ziehe."

34 The program, which also included some songs and instrumental pieces, is given in *Festschrift zur Feier des 50jährigen Gestandes des Wiener*

spent in diligent choral studies and already at the beginning of 1862 [*recte*: May 20, 1863] the chorus was able to appear before the public to put its raison d'être to the test," namely, forging ties between peoples through music.[35] This concert, like that given by the Vienna Men's Choral Society two months earlier, included a hitherto unperformed four-part men's chorus by Schubert, "Der Wintertag" (The winter day), D. 984, on a text by an unidentified poet, and with a piano accompaniment provided by Gotthard in lieu of Schubert's lost original.[36]

As he continues, Gotthard confuses this successful Liedertafel with another that did not take place until the end of year. In doing so, he obscures a matter that is critical for our understanding of the genesis of Opus 41:

> What is more, a gala Fest-Liedertafel in the Sperlsaale (Leopoldstadt) [on December 17, 1863] for the benefit of the Schubert Monument Fund, with solo performances by the famous flute brothers [Franz and Karl] Doppler and the phenomenally gifted Frau Marie Wilt, who was still unfamiliar at that time, turned out well beyond all expectations, and I came to the decision under such circumstances to organize as soon as possible a performance of brand new and never before heard choral pieces.[37]

Kaufmännischen Gesangvereines, 17. For a review, see "Theater und Kunst (Kaufmännischer Gesangverein)," *Fremden-Blatt* (December 18, 1863): 5. This correspondent reported that the Liedertafel lasted until nearly midnight and was one of the "jolliest" (*gemüthlichst*) he could remember.

35   In its notice of the choir's *Gründungs-Liedertafel, Die Liedgenosse* reported a somewhat different version of this raison d'être: "[The choral society's] mission 'of using the income generated by concerts etc. for humane purposes' is so praiseworthy that from this point of view we wished it every success." *Die Liedgenossen* 3/1 (January 1863): 3.

36   "Die nächsten Monate gingen im fleißigen Chorstudium dahin und bereits Anfang des Jahres 1862 konnte der Verein vor die Öffentlichkeit treten, um Proben seiner Daseinsberechtigung abzulegen." For brief reports, see "Theater und Kunst (Liedertafel)," *Fremden-Blatt* (May 23, 1863): 5; and *Die Liedgenossen* 3 (June 1863): 24. Kreissle identifies the name of the person who made the new accompaniment as "Herr Gottdank," but he surely meant Gotthard. See Heinrich Kreissle von Hellborn, *Franz Schubert* (Vienna: G. Gerold's Sohn, 1865; repr. ed., Hildesheim: Georg Olms, 1978): 608. Spina published this work with Gotthard's accompaniment as Op. 169.

37   "Auch eine zum Besten des Schubert-Monumentfonds im Sportsaale (Leopoldstadt) veranstaltete, mit Solovorträgen der berühmten Flöten-Brüder Doppler und der damals noch unberühmten, mit phänomenaler Singstimme begnadeten Frau Marie Wilt, reich ausgestattete Fest-Liedertafel fiel über alle Erwartung gut aus und reifte in mir den Entschluß, bei solchenUmständen sobald als möglich eine Aufführung von ganz neuen, noch nirgends bekannt gewordenen Chorstücken zu veranstalten." The Schubert Monument Fund

38 &♣ CHAPTER ONE

Gotthard goes on to imply that this planned performance of novelties was to take place in a festival to be held the following August. But that cannot be the case since by March 1864 Gotthard had resigned his position with the chorus he had founded a year and a half earlier.[38] The pieces of the puzzle fit together perfectly, however, if we assume that it was not the Schubert benefit Liedertafel of December 1863, but rather the Liedertafel given in May of that year, with its successful performance of a previously unheard Schubert chorus, that gave Gotthard the idea of seeking out new works for performance that summer.

This chronology needs to be borne in mind as we read the continuation of Gotthard's recollection, which mentions Brahms's setting of "Geleit" by name:

> With the agreement of the society's leadership, I contacted the most out-standing masters of German song for contributions to a music festival of the Vienna Mercantile Choral Society planned for the month of August and asked Johannes Brahms in particular to send me a choral work of his choice. Almost immediately I received a letter from Hamburg, followed by a male chorus "Geleit" written in quarto and sent as printed material. In response to my inquiry as to whether the chorus could be published by the performance date, I received the following lines:
>
>> Dear Sir, allow me to report in all haste and brevity that the cho-ral song in question, "Geleit," will probably not be published by August. At least, I have not yet given any thought to gathering up songs for men's chorus for that purpose. Perhaps if you put off the performance a bit? I could look forward to hearing it all the more. Forgive me for saying Addio on the first page. Kindly remember me to Herr Doppler, and I think we will soon chat about a few things. Best regards, Joh. Brahms.[39]

---

had been founded by the *Wiener Männergesangverein* in June 1862; see Heinrich v[on] Billing, *Neunter Jahresbericht des Wiener Männer-Gesang-Verein für das Vereinsjahr von 1. Oktober 1862 bis 1. Oktober 1863* (Vienna: Friedr[ich] und Moritz Förster, 1863), 6. On the benefit concert given by the Vienna Mercantile Choral society, see "Concerte," *Blätter für Musik, Theater u[nd] Kunst* (December 22, 1863): 1–2 (at 2).

38   *Fremden-Blatt* (March 12, 1864): 5.

39   "Im Einvernehmen mit der Vereinsleitung wendete ich mich an die hervor-ragendsten Meister des deutschen Liedes um Beiträge zu einem im Monat August geplanten Musikfeste des Wiener Kaufmännischen Gesangvereins und bat vor Allem Johannes Brahms um Zusendung eines ihm beliebigen Chores. Ich erhielt fast umgehend aus Hamburg einen Brief, dem unter Kreuzband alsbald ein auf Großquart geschriebener Männerchor 'Geleit' nachfolgte und auf meine Anfrage, ob der Chor bis zum Aufführungstermine gedruckt

Before taking up the musical festival in question here, let us consider what other things Brahms may have wanted to chat about with Gotthard. These surely must have included the edition he hoped to publish with Rieter of a beautiful gathering of twelve German dances by Schubert. Brahms had seen the autograph of this set during his recent stay in Vienna, not at Spina's but in the possession of the family of the late Austrian court counselor Karl von Enderes. After returning to Hamburg in May, and with the help of another new Viennese friend, Josef Gänsbacher, he arranged to purchase it. But this did not, as he knew, confer on him the right to publish the music as he pleased. Citing the contract Diabelli had signed many years earlier with Ferdinand Schubert, the brother of the late composer, Spina claimed the publication rights not only to the music in the manuscripts he owned but also to that in any that might turn up elsewhere. Brahms must have hoped that Gotthard, and perhaps also Franz Doppler, the flutist who was also the general manager of Spina's firm, would be able to arrange something with their employer to allow the proposed edition to go forward with Rieter. Nothing came of it, however, and in the following year Brahms saw the music into print with Spina himself as Schubert's *Twelve Ländler*, op. 171.[40]

It was therefore in the midst of an intense enthusiasm on Brahms's part for the music of Schubert that he responded to Gotthard's request by composing "Geleit," probably as a one-off and with no larger "gathering up" of other male choral part-songs in mind. Its *mise en scène* is a battlefield burial; its persona, a soldier who lays to rest an honorable comrade-in-arms

---

sein könnte, erhielt ich nachstehende Zeilen: Geehrter Herr, Erlauben Sie, daß ich in aller Eile u. Kürze melde, daß besagtes Chorlied 'Geleit' bis zum August vermutlich nicht gedruckt sein wird. Wenigstens habe ich noch nicht daran gedacht Lieder für Männerchor zu dem Behuf zusam[m]en zu suchen. Vielleicht, wenn Sie die Aufführung etwas hinaus schöben? Desto sicherer könnte ich auch darauf rechnen es mit zu hören. Verzeihen Sie daß ich jetzt auf der ersten Seite Addio sage. Empfehlen Sie mich Hrn. Doppler freundlich u. ich denke bald plaudern wir ein Mehreres. Mit besten Grüßen ergeben Joh. Brahms." The original of Brahms's undated letter is housed in the Archiv der Wiener Philharmoniker, B/29, Nr. 8. The erroneous date found at the head of the letter (1862) is not in Brahms's hand.

40   David Brodbeck, "Dance Music as High Art: Schubert's Twelve Ländler, Op. 171 (D. 790)," in *Schubert: Critical and Analytical Studies*, ed. Walter Frisch (Lincoln, NE: University of Nebraska Press, 1986): 30–47. See also Brahms's letters to Rieter-Biedermann of May 15, 1863, and December 15, 1863, in *Briefwechsel*, 14: 79–80, 81–83; and his letter of May 30, 1863, to Gänsbacher, quoted in Kalbeck, *Johannes Brahms*, 2: 75–77.

40 & CHAPTER ONE

with promises to join him someday soon. German militarism or chauvinism is nowhere in sight:

> Was freut einen alten Soldaten?
> Drei Salven über sein Grab.
> Die geben die Kameraden;
> Die Musketen werden geladen
> Senkt man den Sarg hinab.
>
> Du Bruderherz, den wir tragen,
> Du freust dich wohl zur Stund';
> Daß tapfer du einst geschlagen,
> Die lauten Musketen es sagen
> Mit ihrem Eisenmund.
>
> Du Bruderherz, den wir tragen,
> Bestell' mir nun Quartier;
> Wir haben zusammen geschlagen,
> Bald werden sie mich auch tragen,
> Kamerad' bald folg' ich dir.

> [1. What comforts an old soldier? / Three salvos over his grave / given by his comrades. / The muskets are loaded. / The coffin is lowered. // 2. Dear brother, whom we carry, / you are well pleased now. / That you once fought bravely / the loud muskets tell / with their iron barrels. // 3. Dear brother, whom we carry, / order my quarters now; / We have fought together. / Soon they will carry me too. / Comrade, I will follow you soon.]

Brahms's setting shows an understanding of what, in the succinct description of James M. Brinkman, the members of a mid-century amateur men's chorus valued: "the singing of a meaningful text in good harmony."[41] Lemcke's poem is moving—it concerns a pair of war buddies separated, albeit only temporarily, by the battlefield death of one of them—and Brahms provides it with a strophic setting in E♭ major in a moderate march tempo (Example 1).[42] The mixing of a prevailingly diatonic homophonic texture with the occasional shift to unison singing, as well as the uncomplicated rhythmic flow, are entirely typical of the prevailing mid-century style. The sudden and dramatic shift to flat-side harmony in measures 5–8, however, is not. Nor is the counterpoint that begins in measure 9 and carries the last line

---

41 James M. Brinkman, "The German Male Chorus at the Beginning of the Nineteenth Century," *Journal of Research in Music Education* 18 (1970): 18–24 (at 22).

42 For brief discussions, see Beller-McKenna, *Brahms and the German Spirit*, 150; and Kross, *Die Chorwerke von Johannes Brahms*, 156–58.

Example 1. Brahms, *Fünf Lieder für Männerchor*, op. 41, no. 3 ("Geleit"), mm. 37–42.

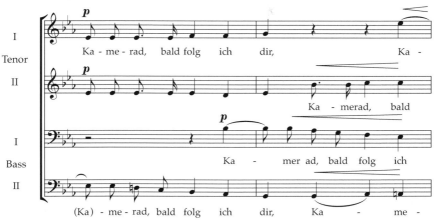

Example 2. Mendelssohn, 6 *Gesänge*, op. 47, no. 4 ("Es ist bestimmt in Gottes Rath"), mm. 20–26.

of the stanza ("the coffin is lowered") through to its quiet and peaceful close five measures later. On the words "I will follow you soon," set to the melodic turn 5–3–4–3, Brahms alludes to the final cadence of Mendelssohn's "Es ist bestimmt in Gottes Rath," op. 47, no. 4, with its closing "Auf Wiedersehen" sung using the same melodic turn (Example 2). Here, as Schubert had done in "Der Entfernten," to cite one example with which Brahms had recently become familiar, the composer goes beyond, but not too far beyond, the norms of the Liedertafel tradition.[43]

---

[43] Brahms's allusion to Mendelssohn's song is noted in Hermann Kretzschmar, "Johannes Brahms," in his *Gesammelte Aufsätze über Musik und Anderes*, ed. Alfred Heuss (Leipzig: Breitkopf & Härtel, 1910), 196; and Walter Niemann, *Brahms* (Berlin: Schuster und Loeffler, 1920), 352. Written in the remarkable key of C♯ major, "Der Entfernten" ends with a codetta that includes a delicate flat-side excursion based on the note A (first as the dominant of the Neapolitan, D, and then as the bass of the German-sixth of the tonic, C♯ major) before the final close.

Two Festivals, Two Farces, and Anti-Prussian Sentiment in Two German Cities

During Brahms's time back home from Vienna in the summer of 1863, Hamburg played host to the first International Agricultural Exhibition in the Heiligenstadtfeld, located in the suburb of St. Pauli.[44] This large exhibition attracted some 163,000 attendees during its seven-day run, beginning on July 14. Some of these patrons undoubtedly also found their way into the nearby summer theater of the actor and impresario Carl Schultze, where they could take in a performance of a timely new hit play by Heinrich Volgemann and Heinrich Wilken entitled *Wilhelm Keenich und Fritze Fischmarkt aus Berlin auf der Reise zur Ausstellung in Hamburg* (Wilhelm Keenich and Fritze Fischmarkt from Berlin on the journey to the exhibition in Hamburg).[45] This farce, partially delivered in *Plattdeutsch*, featured local themes and topical allusions expressed in spoken word and song. (The genre was known as the *Lokalposse*.) It also contained numerous political allusions, and few who saw it could have failed to perceive that the two title characters—the one a gentleman of means from the Prussian capital, the other his man Friday—were caricatures of König Wilhelm and Otto Bismarck, respectively. The script is peppered with biting commentary by the house servant Hannes Buttje, played by Schultze, who makes light of Bismarck's barbed parliamentary speeches, his budget disputes with the liberals in the Prussian parliament over military funding, and other such matters.[46] Hamburg's police were not much bothered by this, but the production raised the hackles of the Prussian ambassador to the city-state, who finally succeeded in pressuring the local authorities to pull it off the boards, albeit not before it had been performed upwards of forty times to full houses.[47] Brahms very likely would have taken in at least one of those performances—Kalbeck

---

44   Anne Steinmeister, *Im Weltgarten zu Hamburg: Die internationalen Hamburger Gartenbauausstellungen des 19. Jahrhunderts* (Munich: Akademische Verlagsgemeinschaft, 2014), 143–48.

45   The discussion that follows is based primarily on Hermann Geering, "Tagesereignisse im Spiegel des Hamburger Volks- und Garten-Theater: Ein Beitrag zur Geschichte des Hamburger Volkstheaters im Mittel des 19. Jahrhundert," *Beiträge zur deutschen Volks- und Altertumskunde* 15 (1971): 69–96; and Karl Theodor Gaedertz, *Die plattdeutsche Komödie im neunzehnte Jahrhundert* (Berlin: A. Hofmann, 1884), 129–34.

46   Local ire toward Prussia was stimulated in part by Prussia's half-hearted participation in the exhibition. See "Die internationale landswirthschaftliche Ausstellung in Hamburg," *Klagenfurter Zeitung* (July 29, 1863): 1–2 (at 1).

47   Although the farce was originally billed as *Wilhelm König und Fritze Fischmarkt aus Berlin auf der Reise zur Ausstellung in Hamburg*, its title

44 ❧ CHAPTER ONE

implies that he may have done so—but he would have been familiar with the production in any case from the considerable public notice it generated.[48]

This *Lokalposse*, and others like it that would feature in Schultze's theater over the next few years, gives evidence of the high degree to which Bismarck was a hated figure in Hamburg before 1866.[49] Brahms undoubtedly shared this sentiment. As a proud son of his home town, he must have kept a wary eye on Prussia, fearful of the threat to Hamburg's sovereignty posed by Bismarck's expansionist ambitions in the north and west of Germany. As a liberal, he must have been disappointed that the hopes raised by the New Era in Prussia had been dashed so quickly. And now, having experienced Vienna at first hand, he cannot have been pleased by the growing signs that Bismarck was intent on ensuring that Austria would be left out of whatever German nation-state might finally arise. (Such was the essential message that the "iron and blood" speech was meant to convey: Prussian military superiority within the German sphere would bring unity where parliamentary debates in Frankfurt had not.) That the city of Haydn, Mozart, Beethoven, and Schubert might not remain a city at the symbolic center of Germany—might not remain in Germany at all—cannot have been something the composer was pleased to contemplate.

Meanwhile, in Vienna Francis Joseph was working to avoid just such a fate for his realm. The emperor's strong desire to reestablish hegemony in Germany may have been motivated primarily by a desire to obtain compensation for his losses in Italy, but it also suited the national wishes of the Austrian liberals and the Greater Germans more generally. After meeting privately with the Prussian king at the beginning of August to inform him of his intention to seek a dramatic reform of the German Confederation, the Austrian emperor proceeded to call for a meeting of all the German princes later that month in Frankfurt. From this *Fürstentag* (Princes' Diet) he hoped to achieve something like a genuine parliamentary German federal government, with Austria, crucially, chairing a newly created executive organ, a critical element that the German Confederation had always lacked. Francis Joseph's proposal had widespread support among those who planned to attend; the problem was that the Prussian king, under prodding by Bismarck,

---

   was quickly changed for reasons that are uncertain but probably also reflect Prussian pressure.

48   Kalbeck, *Johannes Brahms*, 2: 14, where Wilhelm Keenich (the parody of the Prussian king) is misidentified as Anjust Lehmann. For excerpts from a number of local newspaper reviews, see Geering, "Tagesereignisse im Spiegel des Hamburger Volks- und Garten-Theater," 79–81.

49   On anti-Prussian sentiment in Hamburg during these years, see Holst, *Die Stellung Hamburgs zum inneren Konflikt in Preussen.*

was threatening to boycott the proceedings, a development that would have left the Austrian proposal with nowhere to go.[50]

It is in this context that we should consider the occasion for which Gotthard commissioned what became Brahms's "Geleit," namely, a *Volksfest* (popular festival) held in the Vienna Prater under the sponsorship of the city's municipal government on August 23, 1863.[51] (Originally scheduled for August 18, Francis Joseph's birthday, it had to be postponed for five days because of inclement weather.) The schedule ran from 3 o'clock in the afternoon until midnight and included musical performances by all the city's many male choral societies, the orchestras of Johann Strauss Jr. and Franz Morelly, eleven military bands, and the Vienna *Dienstmannscapelle* (Vienna Porters' Band), as well as demonstrations by the Vienna Gymnastics Club. The male choral societies went on at 5:30 p.m. on three separate stages. On one stage, erected in the circus meadow, were positioned some five hundred singers from six *Männerchöre*, including Gotthard's Vienna Mercantile Choral Society, who joined forces in a well-attended *Monstre-Concert*.[52]

It is hard not to think that Brahms, newly returned from Hamburg to take up his duties as director of the Vienna Singakademie, would have been among the large crowd of as many as 300,000 persons (if press reports are to be believed) who swarmed that day into the Prater, and not only because Vienna's iconic park was already one of his most beloved locales in the city.[53] The monster concert was, after all, the program on which his "Geleit" would have been performed if only it had been published and thereby been made

---

50 Jonathan Steinberg, *Bismarck: A Life* (Oxford: Oxford University Press, 2011), 196–98; Edgar Feuchtwanger, *Bismarck: A Political History*, 2nd ed. (London and New York: Routledge, 2014), 96–98.

51 For a contemporaneous discussion of popular festivals of various types at this time, see s.v. "Volksfest," in *Pierer's Universal-Lexikon*, 4th ed., 19 vols. (Altenburg: H. A. Pierer, 1859–65), 18 (1864): 658–59 (www.zeno.org/Pierer-1857/A/Volksfeste).

52 *Die Liedgenossen* 3 (September 1863): 35; *Wiener Zeitung* (August 5, 1863): 5; and "Fest-Anzeige," *Fremden-Blatt* (August 6, 1863): 4–5; Billing, *Neunter Jahresbericht des Wiener Männer-Gesang-Verein für das Vereinsjahr von 1. Oktober 1862 bis 1. Oktober 1863*, 39.

53 We can estimate the date of Brahms's arrival as August 18 or thereabouts based on what we know about his three-day stopover along the way in Baden-Baden to visit Clara Schumann. See Renate Hofmann and Kurt Hofmann, *Johannes Brahms in Baden-Baden* (Baden-Baden: Brahmsgesellschaft Baden-Baden; Karben: CODA, 1996), 30; and Berthold Litzmann, *Clara Schumann: Ein Künstlerleben, nach Tagebücher und Briefen*, 3 vols. (Leipzig: Breitkopf & Härtel, 1923–25); repr. ed. (Hildesheim and New York: G. Olms, 1971), 3: 142n.

46 &❧ CHAPTER ONE

practical for the occasion through the availability of a sufficient number of parts. Although this *Volkfest* was no *Sängerfest*, its monster concert would not have been out of place at one. The impressive combined forces of six choral societies and five hundred singers gave vivid testimony to "the unifying power immanent to German song," a power that Otto Elben, one of the founders of the *Deutsche Sängerbund* (German Federation of Singers), was certain could "strengthen the sense of national cohesion among the German peoples and [contribute] towards the unity of power of the fatherland."[54] Everywhere it was evident that the united fatherland envisioned in Vienna was a Greater Germany governed under the imperial dignity of the Habsburg monarch. As the Vienna *Fremden-Blatt* reported:

> The Monstre Concert ... held several thousand listeners in enthusiasm. The patriotic songs especially were greeted with true jubilation; during the "German Fatherland" ["Was ist des Deutschen Vaterland?"] and the "German Song" ["Das deutsche Lied"] countless cheers rang out for Austria, for His Majesty the Emperor and the Empress, and when at the end the *Volkshymne* [the Habsburg national anthem] was intoned, the enthusiastic crowd joined in with enthusiastic *Vivats*.[55]

Throughout the day, the question of whether King William I of Prussia would join the other German princes in Frankfurt to negotiate a reformed German Confederation was very much on the popular mind.[56] According to one report, when a group of Prussians attending the fair shared with an Austrian their assumption that the Viennese must now be speaking ill of the Prussian government because of its recalcitrance with respect to the matters under discussion at the Princes' Diet, the Austrian cut them off with obvious sarcasm: "On the contrary, we are quite enchanted by your king and your Bismarck.... If the emperor's efforts for Germany should succeed, Austria

---

54   Elben, *Der volksthümliche deutsche Männergesang*, 172–73, quoted in translation in Eichner, *History in Mighty Songs*, 188.

55   "Das Volks-Fest," *Fremden-Blatt* (August 24, 1863): 5–6 (at 6). On the *Volkshymne*, see Andrew Barker, "Setting the Tone: Austria's National Anthems from Haydn to Haider," in *Austrian Studies* 17 (2009): 12–28. The name "Volkshymne" was first used when Haydn's famous *Kaiserhymne* (1797), set originally to a text beginning "Gott erhalte Franz den Kaiser, unsern guten Kaiser Franz" (God preserve Francis the emperor, our good emperor Francis), was given new words in 1854 by Johann Gabriel Seidl: "Gott erhalte, Gott beschütze, Unser Kaiser, unser Land" (God preserve, God protect, Our emperor, our country).

56   "What will Prussia do?" read the opening sentence of the lead article in Vienna's flagship liberal newspaper on the day of the festival. "Wien, 20. August," *Die Presse* (August 21, 1863): 1.

would owe this entirely to the conduct of your king and his Bismarck."[57] One tavern keeper in the nearby Novaragasse posted this witty inscription above his door: "Noch besser und billiger gebe ich Bier und Wein / Dringt Franz Joseph durch in Frankfurt am Main" (The beer and wine will flow freely if Francis Joseph is successful in Frankfurt am Main.)[58] In the event, the beer and wine would not flow freely: the Prussian king followed through on his threatened boycott, and the Austrian emperor would return to Vienna empty-handed.

This fiasco gave stimulus in Hamburg to a new farce by Louis Schöbel, one Brahms may have heard about but could not have witnessed, entitled *Wilhelmine Keenich; oder, Die Frau setzt das Geschäft fort* (Wilhelmine Keenich; or, The wife carries on with business), which opened on August 31, 1863. Here pointed allusion is made to the unsuccessful Princes' Diet not only through Keenich's absence from the story, emblematic of William's decision not to go to Frankfurt, but also by the name of the gimpy, gout-afflicted horse—*Bundestag*—on which Hannes Buttjes enters the stage, a symbol of the federal diet itself, which would now be left to carry on with its business as ineffectually as before.[59]

The failure of the Princes' Diet marked a turning point. Liberals had once held Prussia in higher regard than Austria on account of its institutions of parliamentary-constitutional governance, as weak as they were after 1848. But as a result of Bismarck's roughshod treatment of those institutions and the contempt shown for Francis Joseph's relatively modest proposal for national reform, Austria, hitherto the more reactionary of the two German major powers, began to look better to some liberals by comparison.[60] This was all the more reason for Brahms to be happy about signing on for another season in Vienna.

---

57   *f. s.*, "Das Volksfest im Prater," *Sonntags-Blatt* (August 30, 1863): 136–38 (at 137).

58   A. L., "Das Volksfest," *Die Presse* (August 25, 1863): 1–3 (at 2).

59   This farce is briefly discussed in Geering, "Tagesereignisse im Spiegel des Hamburger Volks- und Garten-Theater," 81–82, but without mention of the happenings in Frankfurt.

60   Beller, *The Habsburg Monarchy, 1815–1918*, 113.

Chapter Two

Soldiers' Songs and the German Question

Later national chauvinism and the Germanomania of beer-drunken brothers in song [*bierselige sangesbrüderliche Deutschtümelei*] made people forget that this "unity" [of the Germans' fatherland] was about the unanimity of a political will to bring about constitutional states of law and with them justice and freedom.[1]

—Ulrich Hermann

Brahms's return to Vienna coincided with the first Viennese visit of Robert von Hornstein (1833–1890), a Swabian-born composer whose one-act operetta *Die Pagen von Versailles* (The pages of Versailles) was given its première at the city's Carltheater on October 13, 1863. In his memoirs, Hornstein discusses at length the many pleasant interactions he had during this visit with Vienna's leading musical figures.[2] He spent a good deal of time in particular in the company of the music critic Eduard Hanslick and his friends. It is probable, therefore, that Brahms, who was already on Du-terms with Hanslick, was among those who made Hornstein's acquaintance.[3]

What is beyond doubt is that Brahms would have been familiar with Hanslick's high regard for the visitor's music. In his review of the first performance of *Die Pagen von Versailles*, the critic wrote:

---

1 Ulrich Hermann, "Was ist des Deutschen Vaterland?," *Die Zeit Online* (December 4, 1987); https://www.zeit.de/1987/50/was-ist-des-deutschen-vaterland/seite-3 (accessed July 6, 2020).

2 Robert von Hornstein, *Memoiren* (Munich: Süddeutsche Monatsheft, 1908), 249–64.

3 Brahms used the familiar form of address for Hanslick in his correspondence with the critic from the summer of 1863; see Christiane Wiesefeldt, "Johannes Brahms im Briefwechsel mit Eduard Hanslick," in *Musik und Musikforschung: Johannes Brahms im Dialog mit der Geschichte*, ed. Wolfgang Sandberger and Christiane Wiesenfeldt (Kassel: Bärenreiter, 2007), 275–348 (at 282).

SOLDIERS' SONGS AND THE GERMAN QUESTION ❧ 49

We were interested in this new work because not long ago we were convinced by this composer's songbooks that a pleasing, popular talent has appeared here, which is as if it were made for the badly neglected field of the light-hearted Singspiel. The first three of Hornstein's [four] *Soldatenlieder*, op. 28—"Hans Ziethen" [no. 2], "Seidlitz" [no. 1] and "Grenadierlied" [no. 3]— astounded us with their simple popular power, which is so seldom encountered in our days of refined and over-refined composition.[4]

If Hornstein is to be believed, Brahms was already admiring of his early piano music. And in view of Hanslick's praise of Hornstein's songs—in the following year he called them "exquisite"—it seems probable that Brahms made a point of getting to know them as well.[5]

The texts of these songs were taken from the same gathering of *Soldatenlieder* in Lemcke's *Lieder und Gedichte* that Brahms would mine as well for "Freiwillige her!," "Marschiren," and "Gebt Acht."[6] All were "to some degree topical" (*einigermaßen zeitgemäß*), as Brahms would later put it to Simrock, in that they embody the new rhetoric of militarization that began to seep into the German national movement in the early 1860s.[7] Hornstein's songs highlight figures drawn from the annals of Prussian military history. Hans Joachim von Ziethen and Friedrich Wilhelm von Seydlitz were much-decorated cavalry officers in service to Frederick the Great during the War of Austrian Succession (1740–42) and the Seven Years' War

---

4   Ed. H. [Eduard Hanslick], "Musik," *Die Presse* (October 15, 1863): 1–2 (at 2). The *Soldatenlieder* had appeared in September. See *Hoffmeister Monatsberichte* (September 1863): 171.

5   Hornstein, *Memoiren*, 335; Ed. H. [Eduard Hanslick], "Oesterreichische Componisten und Musikverleger," *Oesterreichische Wochenschrift* 2 (1864): 1031–41 (at 1036); repr. in *Eduard Hanslick Sämtliche Schriften. Historisch-kritische Ausgabe*, vol. 1, no. 7: *Aufsätze und Rezensionen 1864–1865*, ed. Dietmar Strauß, with Bonnie Lomnäs (Vienna, Cologne, and Weimer: Böhlau Verlag, 2011): 235–48 (at 242).

6   In addition to the three songs mentioned by Hanslick, Hornstein's set includes a fourth entitled "Kasernenlied" (Barracks' song), op. 28, no. 4. Hornstein's "Kasernenlied" and Brahms's "Marschiren" are settings of the same text. Brahms's song retains Lemcke's given title.

7   Frank Lorenz Müller, "The Spectre of a People in Arms: The Prussian Government and the Militarisation of German Nationalism, 1859–1864," *English Historical Review* 122 (2007): 82–104; Dietmar Klenke, "Nationalkriegerisches Gemeinschaftsideal als politische Religion: Zum Vereinsnationalismus der Sänger, Schützen und Turner am Vorabend der Einigungskriege," *Historische Zeitschrift* 260 (1995): 395–448. Here I quote from the same correspondence between Brahms and Simrock that Schüssler-Bach quotes in the title of her article cited in Chapter 1, footnote 17. We will consider these letters in due course.

50   & CHAPTER TWO

(1756–63), respectively; the "Grenadierlied" is written from the point of view of a Pomeranian soldier in service against the French in 1813 under the command of Field Marshal Gebhard Leberecht von Blücher in the Battle of Katzbach. For Schüssler-Bach, Brahms's decision not to compose these three texts suggests a reluctance to glorify past Borussian military victories, something that would have run counter to what were his anti-Prussian attitudes at this point.[8] There may be something to this surmise. But it by no means tells the whole story.

The Italian War of 1859 provided liberal nationalists with a proximate example of how armed conflict could further national unification efforts, not German in that case, of course, but Italian. And with Napoleon III making no secret of his desire to incorporate all the German lands west of the Rhine into his Second French Empire, war was now seen as "imminent and inevitable." More than that, after the Italian example, it was rationalized "as a catalyst of change and progress, as a 'tool for the creation of a national future.'"[9]

If German liberal nationalists in the early 1860s were beginning to countenance military action as a means to their desired end, the prospect of such a war was at the same time sobering owing to obvious inadequacies in the defense system of the German Confederation.[10] The solution would be found, they thought, not in the institution of Germany's various standing armies, dominated by aristocratic leadership in unconditional service to the crown (as in the historical cases of the armies successfully led by Ziethen, Seydlitz, and Blücher), but in the bourgeois institution of the *Landwehr* (militia). Indeed, traditional liberal-nationalist hostility toward a military that was the tool of a monarch and not of the people was a key factor in the objection by Prussia's liberal parliamentary majority to the proposed military reform and funding bill. By the nationalists' lights, only an army of the people could save Germany in its time of need. Brahms's soldiers' songs can be fruitfully understood in precisely the context of such an idealized world of the bourgeois militia.

This is demonstrated most clearly by the case of "Freiwillige her!" The autograph of this song is inscribed "Januar 1864 / Joh. Brahms." [11] Margit

---

8   Schüssler-Bach, "'Einigermaßen zeitgemäß,'" 116–17.

9   Müller, "The Spectre of a People in Arms," 85, quoting in translation Nikolaus Buschmann, *Einkreisung und Waffenbruderschaft: Die öffentliche Deutung von Krieg und Nation in Deutschland 1850–1871* (Göttingen: Vandenhoeck & Ruprecht, 2003), 310.

10   The discussion that follows relies on Müller, "The Spectre of a People in Arms," 85–91.

11   This manuscript, together with the undated autographs of "Marschiren" and "Gebt Acht," was discovered in the archive of the Altonaer Singakademie and acquired at auction in 1980 by the Österreichische Nationalbibliothek, Vienna.

McCorkle expressed doubt about the relevance of Brahms's handwritten date to the date of composition, placing greater credence on Kalbeck's claim that the songs were written in ca. 1861–62, a claim we have already undermined in our discussion of "Geleit."[12] But Brahms ought to be taken at his word here, as the song can be convincingly related to a watershed historical event that began precisely in January 1864. Lemcke's summons to German patriots everywhere reads:

Freiwillige her! Freiwillige her!
Von der Memel bis zum Rhein,
Von den Alpen bis zum Meer,
  Freiwillige her!
Schwarz Roth Gold ist das Panier,
Für dich, Deutschland, kämpfen wir!

Freiwillige her! Freiwillige her!
Nehmt die Büchsen, zielet gut!
Auf zu Roß mit Schwert und Speer!
  Freiwillige her!
Schwarz Roth Gold ist bedroht —
Vaterland! Sieg oder Tod!

Freiwillige her! Freiwillige her!
Duldet ihr der Feinde Spott?
Ist der Fluch noch nicht zu schwer?
  Freiwillige her!
Dänen, Welsche, wer es sei —
Nieder fremde Tyrannei!

Freiwillige her! Freiwillige her!
Durch das Volk da braust der Sturm:
Einig! Keine Trennung mehr!
  Freiwillige her!
Einig! ruft's im Schlachtenroth!
Deutsches Volk, Sieg oder Tod!

[1. Volunteers, come forth! Volunteers, come forth! / From the Memel to the Rhine, / from the Alps to the sea, / Volunteers, come forth! / Black, red, gold is our banner, / for you, Germany, we fight! // 2. Volunteers, come forth! Volunteers, come forth! / Take your rifles and aim well! / Mount your horses with sword and lance. / Volunteers, come forth! /

At the same auction, the autograph of "Ich schwing' mein Horn," op. 41, no. 1, also discovered in the archive of the Altonaer Singakademie, was acquired by the Staats- und Universitätsbibliothek Carl von Ossietzky, Hamburg.

12 See above, Chapter 2, footnote 10.

52 &❧ CHAPTER TWO

Black, red and gold is at risk. / Fatherland! Victory or death! // 3. Volunteers, come forth! / Do you tolerate the enemy's mockery? / Is the curse not yet strong enough? / Volunteers, come forth! / Danes, Frenchies, whoever it may be— / Down with foreign tyranny! // 4. Volunteers join the ranks! / A storm is brewing among the people: / United! No more division! /Volunteers join the ranks! / United! It's calling in the blood of battle! / German nation, victory or death!]¹³

Although Lemcke cites no national heroes by name in this song, the text is nonetheless full of national allusions.¹⁴ Like the members of the Lützow Free Corps in 1813, and under the same liberal colors of black, red, and gold, Lemcke's volunteers are summoned from the farthest reaches of Germany to unite as one in defense of the fatherland. The delineation of the geographical borders of the historic German nation recalls Hoffmann von Fallersleben's "Lied der Deutschen": what in Hoffmann's famous song was the Maas River in the west, Memel River in the east, Etsch River in the south, and Baltic straits in the north now becomes the Memel River in the east, Rhine River in the west, Alpine region in the south, and Baltic Sea in the north. Moreover, by its images of a storm of national sentiment let loose among the people and of the bloodshed of battle called for by the great moment of national awakening (*Schlachtenroth*), Lemcke recalls Theodor Körner's "Männer und Buben" (Men and boys, 1813), one of a large number of songs from a posthumous collection of patriotic poetry by this legendary Lützower that quickly became staples of the *Burschenschaften*.

These poems remind us that attachment to the *Vaterland*—as opposed to *Heimat*, with its associations with everyday experiences in a specific locale for which one has the warm feelings of home—was something that had to be inculcated in the popular mind. As Anna Wierzbicka has observed, its "point of reference was not experiential but political, with a particular emphasis on the unity of a large abstract entity, seen against the background of a number of smaller, local entities." Poems such as "Freiwillige her!"—and by extension musical settings of them—were designed to do important nation-building work.¹⁵

At the same time, Lemcke's refrain alludes to Hoffmann's "Die Freiwilligen" (The volunteers). That poem, together with Nikolaus Becker's

---

13 On "Welsche" as a prejorative for the French, see Ute Schneider, "Die Erfindung des Bösen: Der Welsche," in *"Gott mit uns": Nation, Religion und Gewalt im 19. und frühen 20. Jahrhundert*, ed. Gerd Krumeich and Hartmut Lehmann (Göttingen: Vandenhoeck & Ruprecht, 2000), 35–51.

14 A few of these are noted in Schüssler-Bach, "'Einigermaßen zeitgemäß,'" 119. I add several more here.

15 Anna Wierzbicka, *Understanding Culture through Their Key Words: English, Russian, Polish, German, and Japanese* (New York and Oxford: Oxford University Press, 1997), 156–70 (quoted here at 163).

"Rheinlied" (Rhine song), Max Schneckenburger's "Die Wacht am Rhein" (The watch on the Rhine), and countless other similar topical poems (*Zeit-Gedichte*), was born of the Rhine Crisis precipitated in 1840 when France, frustrated by the failure of its attempt to expand its influence in the Levant, sought compensation closer to home by reasserting the claim that its natural eastern border ran to the Rhine River. This French provocation engendered, to the consternation of the various conservative governments of the German Confederation, widespread and fervent bourgeois nationalist response at home, including in poetry and song.[16]

Something of that fierce response can be seen in "Die Freiwilligen." In the first of its two stanzas, Hoffmann von Fallersleben proudly recalls the decisive German defeat of Napoleon in the Battle of Nations in 1813; in the second he calls for the Germans to act once more with similar selflessness and determination to thwart the renewed French threat in 1840:

> Frei und willig gingt ihr in die Schlacht,
> Frei und willig littet ihr den Tod,
> Und die Rettungs Deutschland ward vollbracht,
> Hell ging auf der Freiheit Morgenroth.
>
> Stelltet ihr euch heute wieder ein
> Für das Vaterland in seiner Noth —
> Heute dürftet ihr nur willig sein,
> Weil man frei zu sein der Welt verbot.

[1. Freely and willingly you went into battle, / freely and willingly you suffered death, / and Germany's salvation was accomplished. / The morning star rose on freedom. // 2. Did you stand up again today / for the fatherland in its misery, / Today you must be willing / because the world was forbidden to be free.]

The Wars of Liberation of 1813 and the Rhine Crisis of 1840 were not the only patriotic topics to come within the purview of Lemcke's "Freiwillige her." By the time the *Lieder und Gedichte* were published, the Rhineland had once again come under threat from France, this time by Napoleon III, who had his eye on the rich mining region of the Saar.[17] Moreover, in the third stanza, the poet makes an unmistakable reference to the so-called Schleswig-Holstein Question. This complex matter—one "so complicated," as Lord Palmerston famously quipped, that "only three men in Europe ever understood

---

16 James M. Brophy, "The Rhine Crisis of 1840 and German Nationalism: Chauvinism, Skepticism, and Regional Reception," *Journal of Modern History* 85 (March 2013): 1– 35. See also Cecilia Hopkins Porter, "The *Rheinlieder* Critics: A Case of Musical Nationalism," *Musical Quarterly* 63 (1977): 74–98.

17 Paul Bernstein, "The Economic Aspect of Napoleon III's Rhine Policy," *French Historical Studies* 1 (1960): 335–47.

54 ❧ CHAPTER TWO

it"—concerned the relations of the Elbe duchies of Schleswig (a Danish fief) and Holstein (a German fief) to the Danish crown, on the one hand, and to the German Confederation, on the other. At the heart of the dispute was the question of whether linguistically and culturally mixed Schleswig was indissolubly united to Holstein and therefore a rightful part of Germany.[18]

James J. Sheehan explains how things stood at the beginning of 1848, when the childless Frederick VII succeeded to the Danish throne:

> The duchies were ruled [in personal union] by the King of Denmark; they were legally inseparable [as set out by charter when the Danish king Christian I was accepted as duke in 1460], but only Holstein belonged to the German Confederation. Moreover, they were governed under Salic Law, which stipulated that their sovereign must be a male. Since the male line of the Danish royal house was about to die out, the duchies' future was in doubt. Although they were linguistically mixed—Germans in the south, heavily Danish in the north—German nationalists hoped to use the impending constitutional crisis to unhitch the duchies from Denmark and turn them into a German state.... However, the new Danish government, which had no intention of abandoning the duchies, annexed Schleswig on 21 March. The Germans in the south rebelled and established their own provisional government [under Prince Christian August II of Augustenburg]. When the Danes sent troops to back up their claims, the Germans [i.e., Schleswig-Holsteiners] sought support from Prussia and a few smaller [German] states.[19]

Shaken by the revolt that had engulfed Berlin earlier that month, King Frederick William IV of Prussia reckoned that he could win the support of the liberal and democratic revolutionaries by sending his military to aid the Schleswig-Holsteiners. This intervention did not last long. Prussian troops quickly occupied Schleswig, but by the summer, under international pressure, they had been withdrawn. Fighting continued sporadically thereafter in what was a civil war but led to no conclusive settlement of the underlying issues. The terms of the ensuing London Protocol (1852) simply

---

18 For a concise but lucid discussion, see Randall Lesaffer, "1864," in *Oxford Public Law International* (https://opil.ouplaw.com/page/545/1864). For a thoughtful extended treatment, see Mark Hewitson, *Nationalism in Germany, 1848–1866: Revolutionary Nation* (New York: Palgrave Macmillan, 2010), 291–344.

19 James J. Sheehan, *German History 1770–1866* (Oxford: Clarendon Press, 1989), 682. On the state of the Schleswig-Holstein question from the German liberal point of view in 1848, see Brian E. Vick, *Defining Germany: The 1848 Frankfurt Parliamentarians and National Identity* (Cambridge, MA, and London: Harvard University Press, 2002), 142–49. Also useful is Steen Bo Frandsen, "Denmark 1848: The Victory of Democracy and the Shattering of the Conglomerate State," in *Europe in 1848: Revolution and Reform*, ed. Dieter Dowe et al., trans. David Higgins (New York and Oxford: Berghahn Books, 2001), 289–311.

re-established the *status quo ante bellum*. The Danish king would continue to rule the Elbe duchies in personal union but make no further attempt to annex them. At the same time, the Augustenburg prince renounced his claim to the duchies in exchange for payment, and the right to succession was transferred by the female heirs to Prince Christian of Glücksburg.

Things stood thus for eleven years until matters erupted anew.[20] On November 13, 1863, in violation of the London Protocol, the Danish parliament passed a new constitution that annexed Schleswig once more. Two days later Christian IX succeeded to the Danish throne upon the death of his father, Frederick VII. Mindful of the legal perils of abrogating the same treaty that had established his right to succession in the duchies, but also of the need not to antagonize his Danish subjects, Christian signed the constitution on November 18. This set off a clamorous German liberal response, and, under the unusual combined lead of both the pro-Greater Germany *Reformverein* (Reform Association) and the pro-Lesser Germany *Nationalverein* (National Association), some 900 Schleswig-Holstein associations were quickly established throughout Germany. In late November, over the objections of conservative Prussia and Austria, the Confederal Diet voted to recognize Prince Friedrich of Augustenburg, the eldest son of Christian August II, as Duke of Schleswig-Holstein, envisioning that the united duchies would then join the German Confederation. In December, after Denmark failed to change course in response to this pressure, confederal troops from Hannover and Saxony were dispatched to Holstein.

Ignoring the national question and still offering no support of the liberal-backed Augustenburg candidate, Prussia and Austria now took things into their own hands. (In the words of Abigail Green, neither appeared to "g[iv] e a damn about German public opinion or the liberal nationalist agenda."[21]) On January 16, 1864, the two major German powers issued an ultimatum to Denmark that gave it forty-eight hours to rescind the November constitution and pledged in exchange to support the Danish king's claims to the duchies. In effect, Prussia and Austria were insisting that all parties continue to honor the terms of the London Protocol. Denmark once again held firm, and on January 21 Austrian and Prussian troops entered Holstein. On February 1, they crossed the Eider into Schleswig and fighting began. The Danes' defeat in the Battle of Dybbøl/Düppel in April was the decisive

---

20 Here I rely on Hewitson, *Nationalism in Germany*, 291–344; Green, "Political and Diplomatic Movements," 82–85; Sheehan, *German History 1770–1866*, 890–92; and John Breuilly, "Revolution to Unification," in *Nineteenth-Century Germany: Politics, Culture and Society, 1780–1918*, 2nd ed., ed. John Breuilly (London: Bloomsbury Academic, 2020), 123–42 (at 129–31).

21 Green, "Political and Diplomatic Movements, 1850–1870," 82. On Brahms and the succession question, see Kalbeck, *Johannes Brahms*, 2: 14n.

56 ❧ CHAPTER TWO

engagement in the short war that followed. There were a few remaining skirmishes, but on August 1 Denmark sued for peace. By the terms of the Treaty of Vienna (October 30, 1864) Denmark gave up all its claims to the duchies, the ultimate fate of which was left to be decided later.[22]

Most Hamburgers sided with the Duke of Schleswig-Holstein and supported membership of the united duchies in the German Confederation, a far cry from Bismarck's hope of annexing them into the Prussian kingdom.[23] In Brahms's case, family ties also played a role in his support for the Schleswig-Holsteiners. His father had been born in Holstein, where he remained until moving to Hamburg when he was nineteen. Brahms visited his father's hometown of Heide as a boy and met his relatives there; later he encouraged his father to maintain that family connection.[24] Although Brahms's mother was a native of Hamburg, her father had come from Tondern (now Tønder), in the German-speaking south of Schleswig, and her mother from the town of Itzehoe in Holstein.

It is not surprising, then, that after the Schleswig-Holstein question flared up again in 1863, Brahms gave clear voice to his sympathies in music. He could not, of course, have foreseen the outcome of war with Denmark or its long-term ramifications when, in January 1864, he composed "Freiwillige her!" But he could certainly rally the troops, so to speak, for the great national cause. Suddenly the reference in Lemcke's poem to the Germans' defense against Danish actions around mid-century acquired new, more proximate meaning.[25] More than he had done in "Geleit," written with Gotthard's nascent choral society in mind, here Brahms pushed well past the limits of typical Liedertafel fare (Example 3a). Marked *Allegro*

---

22   For a good account, see Clark, *Iron Kingdom*, 523–31.

23   Aaslestad, *Place and Politics*, 328, and the references cited there. Notably, *Christian oder Friedrich? oder Hannes Buttje im Lager der Alliierten* (Christian or Frederick?; or, Hannes Buttje in the Allied Camp), a timely new *Lokalposse* by Louis Schöbel, was a great success following its opening in Schultze's theater on June 19, 1864. Gaedertz, *Die plattdeutsche Komödie im neunzehnten Jahrhundert*, 134; Johann Heinemann, *Johann Meyer, ein schleswig-holsteinischer Dichter: Festschrift zum 70. Geburtstag*, 3 vols. (Hamburg: Boysen, 1899–1900), vol. 3: *Johann Meyer als dramatischer Dichter* (1900): 45.

24   Peter Russell, *Johannes Brahms and Klaus Groth: The Biography of a Friendship* (Aldershot, UK, and Burlington, VT: Ashgate, 2006), 17–21.

25   On the boom in "patriotic war songs and heroic celebratory rhetoric" occasioned by this historical moment, see Friedhelm Brusniak and Dietmar Klenke, "Sängerfeste und die Musikpolitik der deutschen Nationalbewegung," *Die Musikforschung* 52 (1999): 29–54 (at 40). The authors do not make mention of Brahms's Opus 41. Schüssler-Bach and Kross both seem to sense that Op. 41 is related in some way to events in the Elbe duchies, but because, like McCorkle, they follow Kalbeck in dating the songs to 1861–62, they are unable to make the case for it. Schüssler-Bach, "'Einigermaßen zeitgemäß,'" 122; and Kross, *Die Chorwerke von Johannes Brahms*, 150–51.

Example 3a. Brahms, *Fünf Lieder für Männerchor*, op. 41, no. 2 ("Freiwillige her!"), mm. 1–15.

Example 3b. Brahms, *Fünf Lieder für Männerchor*, op. 41, no. 2 ("Freiwillige her!"), mm. 31–48.

con fuoco, "Freiwillige her!" unfolds a modified strophic form in C minor. Stanzas 1 and 2 share the same music and, with their tonicizations of the key of the mediant, are suggestive of the opening half of a binary form. In Brahms's setting of the first four lines, insistent calls for volunteers to step forward, sounded in urgent, unison triplets, are sandwiched around a homophonic passage written in forceful dotted block chords. In measure 9, as he returns to the chordal texture, Brahms underscores Lemcke's invocation of the liberal-nationalist tricolor with horn calls in triplets and the beginning of the tonal shift to the heroic key of E♭ major. Then in measure 10, he introduces yet another textural change, this time to imitative polyphony, for both stanzas' salient final line ("For you, Germany, we fight!" and "Fatherland! Victory or death!"). Things close, still in E♭ major, with several final outbursts of the cry for volunteers, not in unison but rhythmically augmented in the first tenor, superimposed on repeated iterations in the usual rhythm in the second tenor and first bass, and over a strong cadential line in the second bass.

The third stanza follows the same general course, except that now the homophonic passage in dotted rhythm is replaced by one marked legato in two-part voice leading that is seemingly intended to cajole the uncertain into fighting ("Do you tolerate the enemy's mockery? / Is the curse not yet strong enough?"). The final stanza presents a louder, faster version of the third (*ff, animato*) until taking its own course at measure 38 with the accented climactic final two lines of text (Example 3b): "United! This calls for bloody battle! German nation, victory or death!" To make the point, Brahms then sets the last line once more, now with the added urgency of a four-fold imitative triadic arpeggiation on the words "German nation" (*Deutsches Volk*). All this is done now, not in E♭, but in C, the tonic major. In that key, this dramatic passage initiates the final cadence that is completed by one final iteration of the call for volunteers.

If "Freiwillige her" bids men from throughout Germany to come together under the liberal-nationalist tricolor, and "Marchiren" concerns a soldier eager to go into battle for the nation, in "Gebt Acht" the ranks are implored to stand guard in the fatherland's defense:

> Gebt acht! Gebt acht!
> Es harrt der Feind,
> Der schlimm es meint,
> Ihr Brüder wacht!
> Im Westen, Süden, im Osten, Nord
> Sind wir uns selbst der einz'ge Hort —
>   Gebt acht!

Gebt Acht! Und baut
Auf Gott und euch
Und Schwertesstreich,
Sonst Niemand traut![26]
Man triebe gern ein schnödes Spiel,
Nur uns're Schwäche ist ihr Ziel —
 Gebt acht!

Gebt acht! Seid fest
In aller Noth
Bis in den Tod!
Gott nicht verläßt,
Wer treu für Recht und Wahrheit ficht,
In Ehr' und Vaterlandes Pflicht —
 Gebt acht!

Gebt acht! Es tagt —
Zum Kampf bereit
Mit Schwert und Kleid!
Seid unverzagt!
Und ob der Feind wie Meeressand,
Wir retten doch das Vaterland—
 Gebt acht!

[1. Take heed! Take heed! / The enemy is waiting / who means us harm, / Brothers, keep watch! / In the west and south, in the east and north / we are our only stronghold, / Take heed! // 2. Take heed! And trust in God / and in yourselves and in the sweep of your sword. / Trust no one else! / They would like to do a vile deed / and aim at our weak spot / Take heed! // 3. Take heed! Be steadfast / in all danger / even unto death! / God does not forsake / those who fight faithfully for justice and truth / in honor and duty to the fatherland / Take heed! // 4. Day is breaking, / ready for battle / with sword and cloak / be not afraid! / And whether the enemy is like the sand of the sea, / we shall save the fatherland! / Take heed!]

Hard evidence of the dates of composition of "Marchiren" and "Gebt Acht" is lacking. But it seems plausible that the latter at least can be traced back to the period following the Battle of Dybbøl/Düppel of April

---

26 In the first edition of this song—and in all subsequent editions to date—the first four lines of the second stanza are given erroneously as "Gebt acht! Und baut / auf Gott und auf / des Schwertes Streich / sonst Niemand traut!" Brahms's autograph score (Beinecke Rare Book and Manuscript Library, Yale University) gives the correct text.

1864, when it became clear that the Elbe duchies would be wrested from Danish control.[27] If so, this song, too, imparts to its text a meaning somewhat different from that which Lemcke could have intended when he wrote it some years earlier. Although it was evident that the separation of Schleswig-Holstein from Denmark could only strengthen the position of the hated Bismarck, this victory in the first of the so-called Wars of German Unification was an occasion of great rejoicing among the liberal nationalists throughout the German Confederation: here national sentiment briefly trumped anti-Bismarck attitudes.[28] What Kross criticized as the "somewhat monotonous uniformity" of Brahms's strophic setting, with its frequently recurring open fifths and fourths that impart to the music an Old German sound, might better be heard then as a sign of its solemn, steadfast, resolute character: what Germany seemed posed to gain—a satisfactory national solution to the Schleswig-Holstein question—must not now be lost (Example 4).[29]

At all events, Brahms's *Soldatenlieder*, despite the militant rhetoric that reflected the tenor of the times, ought not to be written off too quickly as a disreputable manifestation of hyper-Germanness and *Deutschtümelei*. This is sober liberal-nationalist stuff, composed at a moment when liberals might still hope that a unified German state was coming into sight. What Brahms could not yet have anticipated, however, was that Vienna, the historic city in which he was rapidly building a network of close personal and professional relationships, was about to be cut loose from the Germany of which it had for centuries stood as the titular head.

---

27 Among Brahms's personal effects when he died were photographs of some of the Prussian military commanders and of the decisive Battle of Dybbøl. See Renate Hofmann and Kurt Hofmann, *Johannes Brahms: Zeittafel zu Leben und Werk* (Tutzing: Hans Schneider, 1983), 64.

28 On this point with respect to Brahms's hometown, see Holst, *Die Stellung Hamburgs zum inneren Konflikt in Preussen*, 60.

29 Kross, *Die Chorwerke von Johannes Brahms*, 160.

Example 4. Brahms, *Fünf Lieder für Männerchor*, op. 41, no. 5 ("Gebt Acht") (stanza 1 only).

The German Question Settled

Tensions between Prussia and Austria quickly came to a boil over the future of the newly acquired Elbe duchies. Bismarck was set on absorbing them into the Prussian kingdom; Austria preferred that they remain autonomous duchies ruled jointly from Berlin and Vienna. The compromise terms of the ensuing Gastein Convention (August 14, 1865), which gave Austria control of Holstein and Prussia control of Schleswig (with free passage through Holstein to Prussian territory to the south), satisfied no one and only served to create further tensions that Bismarck would soon exploit to advance his long-term goal of excluding Austria from the German Confederation altogether.

As the two German major powers played this game of chess, the Third Germany could only watch and wonder what would happen. Brahms passed this summer of 1865 in the Grand Duchy of Baden, a liberal stronghold in the southwest of Germany. The composer's rented rooms were in Lichenthal bei Baden, within easy walking distance of the home of Clara Schumann, whom he saw often. Deepening friendships with the conductor Hermann Levi and the copper engraver and photographer Julius Allgeyer, a veteran of the 1848 Revolution, also led to extended visits to nearby Karlsruhe. Bismarck was no more popular in these parts, and among these friends, than he was in Hamburg or Vienna.[30] And when, in September 1865, Brahms was given the opportunity to meet Bismarck in the home of the Prussian ambassador to the Badenese court, Count Albert von Fleming, he turned it down for what he later remembered, with some regret, as "democratic reasons."[31]

---

30   Ekkehard Schulz, "Brahms' Karlsruher Freundes- und Bekanntenkreis," in *Johannes Brahms in Baden-Baden und Karlsruhe: Eine Ausstellung der Badischen Landesbibliothek Karlsruhe und der Brahmsgesellschaft Baden-Baden e. V.*, ed. Badische Landesbibliothek Karlsruhe unter Mitarbeit von Joachim Draheim et al. (Karlsruhe: Selbstverlag der Badischen Landesbibliothek Karlsruhe, 1983), 35–57 (here 43). See also Alfred Orel, *Johannes Brahms und Julius Allgeyer: Eine Künstlerfreundschaft in Briefen* (Tutzing: Hans Schneider, 1964), 35–53. On the attitudes of Prussia and Baden toward one another at this time, see Hewitson, *Nationalism in Germany, 1848–1866*, 321–24; and Abigail Green, *Fatherlands: State-Building and Nationhood in Nineteenth-Century Germany* (Cambridge: Cambridge University Press, 2001), 16–17.

31   Entry from May 1883 in the diary of Laura von Beckerath, in Kurt Stephenson, *Johannes Brahms und die Familie von Beckerath* (Hamburg: Christians Verlag, 1979), 28: "Erzählung der Möglichkeit, mit Bismarck bei Graf Fleming in Baden zusammengetroffen zu sein, aber aus demokratischen Gründen zu seinem jetzigen Ärger gemieden." This opportunity seems to have arisen in the first week of September 1865. On Bismarck's presence in Baden-Baden at that time, see Otto Graf zu Stolberg-Wernigerode, "Ein unbekanntes Bismarckgespräch aus dem Jahre 1865," *Historische Zeitschrift* 194/2 (April 1962): 357–62 (at 358).

64   ❧   CHAPTER TWO

Brahms was living in Allgeyer's home when, in the spring of 1866, it became evident to everyone that Bismarck's intended showdown with Austria was fast approaching.[32] In an essay published in April, Gustav Freytag, one of the editors of the liberal quarterly *Die Grenzboten*, tried to strike a hopeful tone, albeit not entirely convincingly:

> Every day brings new reports about the hostilities between the two great powers of the German Confederation; ... the people listen in anxious fear to official statements from Berlin and Vienna.... It is not impossible that in both [capitals] it might still be thought more useful to come to a mutual understanding.... And the consolation remains that in our time it is difficult to start a great war against the will of the people. That it cannot be reliably waged against the will of the people is, of course, a poor consolation, for this truth does not protect against fateful steps.[33]

Writing to Gänsbacher just before departing Karlsruhe in the middle of April for an extended stay in Switzerland, Brahms conveyed the news that the young soprano Marie Wilt, one of Gänsbacher's former students, had recently turned down Levi's invitation to perform at the Grand Ducal Theater in Baden in order to accept an engagement in the Prussian capital: "Berlin and Bismarck! Here, like you [in Vienna], we have to lie low [*stillhalten*]!"[34] Political questions held front of mind throughout the Swiss sojourn that followed.[35] Levi's letter of May 5 would have brought Brahms up to date on the situation in Baden: "The hubbub about war has been let loose here. We poor *Mittelstaatler* don't even know whom we'll fight against tomorrow.... Herren von Goeler and Gemmingen [members of the upper house of the Badenese parliament] are shouting at table, 'Better French than Prussian!' and the privy counselor wants to die before the war. He is right. The thought of a civil war [*Bürgerkrieg*] puffs up even my modicum of patriotism."[36]

---

32   For an insightful account, see Feuchtwanger, *Bismarck: A Political History*, 120–47.

33   G[ustav] F[reytag], "Krieg oder Frieden?," *Die Grenzboten* 25/2 (April 1866): 64–69 (at 64, 69).

34   Quoted in Kalbeck, *Johannes Brahms*, 2: 219–20. Brahms may have been thinking here of Ludwig Pfau's "Badenisches Wiegenlied" (Baden Lullaby), written after Prussian troops had put down the liberal revolution in Baden in 1849. Its refrain reads: "Sleep, my child, sleep quietly. / The Prussian is outside." See John Eckhard and David Robb, *Songs for a Revolution: The 1848 Protest Song Tradition in Germany* (Rochester, NY: Camden House, 2020), 218–34.

35   Naegele, "Brahms und die Politik," 55–59.

36   *Briefwechsel*, vol. 7: *Johannes Brahms im Briefwechsel mit Hermann Levi, Friedrich Gernsheim sowie den Familien Hecht und Fellinger*, ed. Leopold Schmidt (1910): 26–27. H. A. Winkler has argued that the concepts of civil

Three days later, on May 8, the Berlin *Kreuzzeitung*, the flagship organ of Prussian conservatism, published a remarkable leading article entitled "Krieg und Bundesreform" (War and reform of the Confederation). Written by Ernst Ludwig von Gerlach, this impactful piece showed that it was not only the liberals, with their liberal principles, who were outraged by Bismarck's *Realpolitik*, but now also his former friends among the conservatives.[37] Gerlach made a public break here with Bismarck, a former protégé who never forgave him, warning, on the grounds of political morality, "against 'a fundamentally destructive war' between Prussia and Austria, one that could only 'injure Germany, and especially Prussia and Austria, in their vital organs, with perhaps fatal consequences, no matter who emerges the victor.'"[38] Shortly thereafter, Brahms shared with Allgeyer his pessimism regarding precisely this prospect: "One does forget everything over a political lead article. And unfortunately, whether they fight now for 30 or for 7 years, the fight is as little on behalf of mankind as in those days when they fought for 30 and 7 years."[39] The composer's allusion to the bloody Thirty Years War of the seventeenth century and the Seven Years War of the eighteenth, both of which saw Austria and Prussia on opposing sides, is self-evident, and its meaning is clear: like the arch-conservative Gerlach, the liberal nationalist Brahms believed that "Germany [would] no longer [be] Germany if Prussia is missing or Austria is missing."[40]

The war that everyone had been fearing came at last on June 14; what surprised everyone was how quickly it concluded, in only six weeks' time. The

---

war and fraternal war are both misplaced in this context, in that the soldiers who went into battle against one another in 1866 fought for king and country in regular armies, not as guerilla or irregular forces, and against enemies, not brothers. H. A. Winkler, *Germany: The Long Road West*, vol. 1: *1789–1933*, trans. A. J. Sager (Oxford and New York: Oxford University Press, 2000), 160. Still, as Winkler notes, in the popular imagination of the Third Germany, the war did feel like one between brothers in a way that it did not in multinational Prussia or Austria, where state patriotism and German patriotism were felt more readily as things apart from one another. Of relevance here, with an emphasis on the Kingdom of Hannover, is Jasper Heinzen, *Making Prussians, Raising Germans: A Cultural History of Prussian State-Building after Civil War, 1866–1935* (Cambridge: Cambridge University Press, 2017).

37 Feuchtwanger, *Bismarck: A Political History*, 137.

38 Ludwig von Gerlach, "Krieg und Bundesreform," *Neue preussische Zeitung (Kreuzzeitung)* (8 May 1866): 1; quoted in translation in Winkler, *Germany: The Long Road West*, 1:164.

39 This undated letter can be placed around May 10 on the basis of its content. Orel, *Johannes Brahms und Julius Allgeyer*, 39; trans. in *Johannes Brahms: Life and Letters*, ed. Styra Avins, trans. by Josef Eisinger and Styra Avins (Oxford and New York: Oxford University Press, 1997), 341.

40 Gerlach, "Krieg und Bundesreform," 1.

66 &❧ CHAPTER TWO

decisive battle took place on July 3, when Prussia routed the numerically superior forces of Austria and the South German *Mittelstaaten* near the Bohemian towns of Königgrätz/Hradec Králové and Sadowa/Sadová. By the terms of the ensuing Peace of Prague, signed on August 23, Bismarck achieved nearly all his goals: the German Confederation was dissolved, Austria was forced to give up all its authority in German affairs, and Prussia annexed the German states north of the Main River into the new North German Confederation.[41]

Finding a Publisher

Throughout this period of profound geopolitical transition, Brahms sought to bring his patriotic male part-songs to light. This proved to be more difficult than he may have expected, perhaps in part because of that geopolitical change. In a letter of September 6, 1865, written around the time when he declined the opportunity to meet Bismarck, Brahms offered the Bonn publisher P. J. Simrock a batch of new works, comprising the String Sextet in G major, op. 36, and the Cello Sonata in E minor, op. 38, together with several choral songs of varying description, including one set that he characterized as "a small volume of songs for male chorus that might even be called topical [*zeitgemäß*]." After some back and forth between the publisher and the composer over the next several weeks, Simrock finally agreed to take the two instrumental chamber works, but he seems to have had no interest at all in the *Männerchöre* or in any of the other vocal works.[42] Meanwhile, after learning of Simrock's initial rejection of the works on or before September 16, Brahms offered largely the same set of compositions to Breitkopf & Härtel in Leipzig. The Leipzig publisher initially accepted sight unseen both the sextet and duo sonata, but showed no more interest than Simrock had in the vocal pieces. Worse still, the firm soon sought to renege on the commitment it had made for reasons that Brahms found deeply insulting. Although by then Simrock had reconsidered his own initial judgment and informed the composer that he would publish the chamber works after all, Brahms was still left with no publisher for the Lemcke-Lieder.[43]

---

41 Sheehan, *German History, 1770–1866*, 899–911.

42 See Brahms's letters to Simrock of September 6, October 2, October 10, and October 21, 1865, in *Briefwechsel*, vol. 9: *Johannes Brahms: Briefe an P. J. Simrock and Fritz Simrock*, ed. Max Kalbeck (1917): 45–49. Simrock's side of the exchange has not been preserved.

43 Brahms's correspondence with Breitkopf & Härtel is recorded in part in *Briefwechsel*, 14: 116–19 (Brahms to Breitkopf & Härtel on September 16; Breitfopf & Härtel to Brahms on September 18), and in George S. Bozarth, "Brahms and the Breitkopf & Härtel Affair," *Music Review* 60 (1994): 202–13

SOLDIERS' SONGS AND THE GERMAN QUESTION ❦ 67

Nine months later, and with war between Prussia and Austria on the horizon, Brahms reached out to Simrock once more: "Should our terrible times not prevent you from thinking of us … composers, then I could tell you how I would first keep the engravers, and finally even the publishers, gainfully employed." Simrock quickly replied: "Do satisfy my curiosity right away and give us news about this latest brainchild of yours to which you attach such importance. In the hopeless conditions of our time, it really is necessary that people awake again to poetry and art." To that invitation, Brahms responded on June 18, four days after the outbreak of hostilities. In addition to his new Trio for Piano, Waldhorn, and Cello, op. 40, he once again proposed publication of several short vocal pieces, including some of those offered the year before. Among the latter was what he now described as "a small volume of 5 male choral songs. Quite easy to sing, needless to say rather topical." Although Simrock accepted the trio, once again he passed over the male part-songs without mention. What did not go unmentioned, however, was the latest military conflict: "The events of the war, which I would not have believed could happen, have surprised and depressed us ever since."[44] It was evidently not a set of topical songs but a trio featuring the pastoral sound of the natural horn that seemed best suited, in Simrock's view, to serve as the balm to the nation called for by the troubled times.[45]

It cannot escape notice that what Brahms had previously described to Simrock as a volume of male choral songs of unspecified number was now said to consist of five. Obviously, the composer's letter to Simrock of June

---

(Breitkopf & Härtel to Brahms on September 29; Brahms to Breitkopf & Härtel, October 5; and Breitkopf & Härtel to Brahms on October 7). The last three letters first appeared in print in Alfred von Ehrmann, *Brahms: Weg, Werk und Welt* (Leipzig: Breitkopf & Härtel, 1933), 186. For a thorough recent study, see Peter Schmitz, *Johannes Brahms und der Leipziger Musikverlag Breitkopf & Härtel* (Göttingen: V & R unipress, 2009), 131–47.

44   Letters from Brahms to P. J. Simrock of May 26 and June 18, 1866, in *Briefwechel*, 9: 51–52; and from P. J. Simrock to Brahms of May 29 and June 20, 1866, in *Johannes Brahms und Fritz Simrock: Weg einer Freundschaft*, ed. Kurt Stephenson (Hamburg: J. J. Augustin, 1961), 42–43.

45   Simrock's reaction to the outbreak of war brings into question Naegele's suggestion that he decided not to accept the *Männerchöre* for publication out of "sympathy with Prussia." Naegele, "Brahms und die Politik," 54. It is evident from her account that she is confusing Peter Joseph Simrock with his son Fritz Simrock, who for a time served as a Prussian light cavalry officer (*Husarenoffizier*). In 1870, two years after inheriting the family firm, the Prussophile Fritz moved its editorial offices from Bonn to Berlin; he became a close friend of Brahms and his principal publisher. Naegele's suggestion that Breitkopf & Härtel also turned down the male choir songs on account of its own Prussian sympathies is unsupported. It is worth nothing that the Leipzig firm was based in the Kingdom of Saxony, which had allied with Austria in the war against Prussia.

68 &❧ CHAPTER TWO

18, 1866, establishes the *terminus ante quem* of the definitive five-song gathering that would eventually see print. Does it also help us to ascertain its *terminus post quem*? Do we have reason to think, in other words, that it was only at this later time that Brahms decided to preface the four Lemcke songs with "Ich schwing' mein Horn in's Jammerthal"?

As noted in the previous chapter, Brahms's setting of Duke Ulrich's poem must have been composed by 1860 at the latest and perhaps considerably earlier than that (Example 5). The Old German text reads:

> Ich schwing' mein Horn ins Jammerthal,
> Mein Freud ist mir verschwunden,
> Ich hab gejagt, muss abelahn,
> Das Wild lauft vor den Hunden,
> Ein edel Thier in diesem Feld
> Hatt' ich mir auserkoren,
> Das schied von mir, als ich wohl spür,
> Mein Jagen ist verloren.
>
> Fahr' hin, Gewild, in Waldes Lust,
> Ich will dir nimmer schrecken,
> Mit Jagen dein schneeweisse Brust,
> Ein Ander muss dich wecken,
> Mit Jagdgeschrei, und Hundebiss,
> Daß du nit magst entrinnen:
> Halt dich in Hut, mein Thierle gut!
> Mit Leid scheid ich von hinnen.
>
> Kein Hochgewild ich fahen kann,
> Das muss ich oft entgelten;
> Noch halt ich stät auf Jägers Bahn,
> Wie wohl mir Glück kommt selten.
> Mag mir nit g'bührn ein Hochwild schön,
> So lass ich mich begnügen,
> An Hasenfleisch, nit mehr ich heisch,
> Das mag mich nit betrügen.

[1. I blow my horn into the valley of sorrow, / my joy has escaped me. / I have been hunting but must now abandon the chase. / The game eludes my hounds. / I had chosen a noble beast in this field; / it fled from me, / and I well see / all my hunting is in vain. // 2. So run away, my prey, into the delight of the forest. / I shall never frighten / your snow-white breast with my hunting. / Another will have to rouse you / with hunting cries and biting dogs / so that you cannot escape. / Be on your guard, good little doe, / with a heavy heart I take my leave. // 3. I cannot catch any noble beast, / I must often suffer for that, / yet I shall constantly follow the hunter's track, / although good fortune seldom comes my way. / If no lovely doe will ever fall to my lot, / I must learn to relish / hare's flesh; I ask no more, / that won't deceive me.]

Example 5. Brahms, *Fünf Lieder für Männerchor*, op. 41, no. 1 ("Ich schwing' mein Horn ins Jammerthal") (stanza 1 only).

* Durchaus nicht zu langsam und ziemlich frei vorzutragen.

70 &♦ CHAPTER TWO

It is difficult to imagine what Brahms might have considered topical about Ulrich's poem when the Schleswig-Holstein crisis filled *Bürger* throughout the German Confederation with a patriotic fervor that is reflected in his four Lemcke settings. Matters were different during the lead up to war between the two German major powers in 1866. Suddenly the concerns of Ulrich's heartfelt allegory of love and resignation and duty seemed not only time- less but timely. Brahms's song can be understood as a salve to what Gerlach rightly predicted would be fatal wounds inflicted on Greater Germany. Ulrich loved Elisabeth, Countess of Brandenburg, but was obliged to enter into a marriage with Sabina, Duchess of Bavaria, that had been arranged for political reasons by Emperor Maximilian I. Elisabeth was the lovely doe; Sabina, the less comely hare. The hunter would prefer to eat venison but must resign himself to having rabbit instead. Like Ulrich, Brahms could not have what he really wanted. In the end, he would have to settle for a Lesser Germany, for a Germany without Austria, for Sabina instead of Elisabeth.

And so too, of course, would his many friends in Vienna. Somewhat tact- lessly, the composer said as much in his next letter to Gänsbacher, written in August, as this new reality began to sink in:

> Since I am personally untouched by the war and by the present state of af- fairs, there is much, a great deal, that draws me to Vienna, and I am only held up by some practical and essential matters. You will have experienced how deeply one's entire self is affected by what has occurred. The mood where you are must be so distressing, that one might almost hope for a most joyous experience coming along soon. But the world makes progress slowly and meanwhile we can, I suppose, be grateful to the Prussians for the brouhaha they have caused, for nothing moves forward without that.[46]

Here Brahms, in his own ham-handed way, expressed empathy with the Viennese in their plight while expressing no grievance with Prussia for hav- ing caused their trauma.

This is significant. It has often been noted that in 1866 many North German liberals went from hating Bismarck to worshipping him as a national hero almost overnight. To be sure, the left wing of the Prussian Progressives remained implacably opposed, but a larger, more moderate faction, taking the name National Liberals, began to rationalize Bismarck's illiberal actions as the price of obtaining national unity. Besides they were heartened by his restoration of the constitutional rule he had suspended four years ear- lier in his dispute with the liberals over the military budget and the reform

---

46   Undated letter of August 1866 from Brahms to Gänsbacher, in Orel, *Johannes Brahms und Julius Allgeyer*, 40.

SOLDIERS' SONGS AND THE GERMAN QUESTION ❧ 71

of the Prussian army.[47] In the new political landscape, Brahms eventually fell into ideological lockstep with this moderate camp and began what became a lifetime interest in the work of the cultural and political historians of the Prussian School. These influential scholars and state servants held that the Hohenzollern monarchy had historically pursued policies that were in Germany's best interests, and that Prussian leadership in Germany was therefore inevitable.[48] Notably, among the books found in Brahms's library is the fifth edition of the first volume of Freytag's *Bilder aus der deutschen Vergangenheit* (Pictures of the German past) (1867), whose dedicatory preface, dated October 18, 1866, ends: "Since the [Hohenstaufen] Frederick I, nineteen generations of our ancestors have done without a great and powerful German Reich; in the twentieth generation, the Germans have won back through Prussia and the triumph of the Hohenzollern what to many has seemed as alien as the barbarian migration and crusades [*Völkerwanderung und Kreuzzüge*]: their state."[49]

As a new order of things began to take hold in Central Europe, Brahms persisted in his efforts to see his male choral pieces into print. "Opuses 41–49 [*recte*: 43] are not out yet because of the war," he reported to Rieter in a letter of September 16, 1866. "There are three six-voice choral pieces [op. 42], one small volume of men's choral pieces [op. 41], and songs [op. 43] which I offered to Simrock along with the Horn Trio. Since the Treaty [of Prague]

---

47   For an early articulation of this turn, see Hermann Baumgarten, *Der deutsche Liberalismus: Eine Selbstkritik* (Berlin, 1866; ed. and enlarged Adolf M. Birke, Frankfurt and Vienna, 1974).

48   Historians who held university positions were expected, as state officials, to show public loyalty to the monarchy. But, as Alastair Thompson notes, "for most [such] historians support for a Prussian-led Germany was less a matter of careerism and conformity than of inner conviction." Alistair Thompson, "'Prussians in a Good Sense': German Historians as Critics of Prussian Conservatism, 1890–1920," in *Writing National Histories: Western Europe since 1800*, ed. Stefan Berger, Mark Donovan, and Kevin Passmore (London and New York: Routledge, 1999), 97–110 (at 97).

49   Gustav Freytag, *Aus dem Mittelalter*, vol. 1 of *Bilder aus der deutschen Vergangenheit*, 5th ed. (Leipzig: S. Hirzel, 1867), [v–vi]. Freytag's reference is to Schiller's "Völkerwanderung, Kreuzzüge, und Mittelalter" (1792). On Freytag's popular cultural history, see Larry L. Ping, "Gustav Freytag's *Bilder aus der deutschen Vergangenheit* and the Meaning of Germany History," *German Studies Review* 32 (2009): 549–68. For a thoughtful account within the literature on Brahms, see Mark Burford, "Brahms's Sybel: The Politics and Practice of German Nationalist Historiography," *Nineteenth-Century Music Review* 16 (2019): 417–39. Helpful, too, in this context is Herbert Flaig, "The Historian as Pedagogue of the Nation," *History: The Journal of the Historical Association* 59 (1974): 18–32.

72 ❧ CHAPTER TWO

I haven't needed any money."[50] Rieter failed to take the hint, and so four months later, in a letter of January 17, 1867, Brahms brought the matter of publishing his *Männerchöre* up again, this time in connection with a possible performance by the Vienna Men's Choral Society: "You know about my small volume of male choral pieces and do not seem interested in it. One of the songs happens to appear in a volume of Lieder with piano. For this reason, and because I wouldn't want to make the work Prussian or Austrian by dint of the title page, I am prompted to turn to you once again."[51]

Despite Brahms's allusion to the recent war between the German states, it was not political but rather practical considerations that led him to offer these part-songs to the Swiss publisher. He needed a publisher sooner rather than later, and neither Simrock nor Breitkopf & Härtel had shown any interest. The composer explained:

> Three of the five songs may be sung in the next concert of the local male choral society. The decision will come tomorrow, and I wouldn't want to have the parts in manuscript, but would rather provide the publisher with the sales right away. In the event that the Committee says "Yes," would you like to take over the small work, and could you quickly get us the necessary parts?[52] By mid-February at the latest? The concert is on March 17.... However, don't be embarrassed [to decline], and if the Committee says "No" because of the text or the music, it's nothing anyway.

Evidently the Committee did say "No," and Brahms was represented on the program, not by his male choral pieces, but by five of his recent Waltzes for Four-Hand Piano, op. 39, newly arranged for the piano duo of the sisters Stephanie Vrabély and Seraphine Vrabély-Tausig. Writing to Rieter on February 7, the composer put the best face on things: "My men's choral pieces could not stand

---

50 *Briefwechsel,* 14: 132–33 (at 133). Rieter had already by this time put the composer's Twelve Songs and Romances for Women's Chorus into production with the opus number 44; see Brahms's letter of August 1866 to Rieter's wife, in *Briefwechsel,* 14: 129–30 (at 130).

51 Letters to Rieter of September 16, 1866, and January 17, 1867, in *Briefwechsel,* 14: 132–33 (at 133); ibid., 137–39 (at 138–39), from which the following quotation also is taken. An arrangement of "Ich schwing mein Horn in's Jammerthal," op. 41, no. 1, was included in the Four Songs, op. 43, which Rieter would publish in 1868.

52 The large size of the Vienna Men's Choral Society—in 1863 it had 262 members—made the availability of printed parts, as in the case of the Monster Concert in the Prater, the only practical way to perform the music. See Kral, *Taschenbuch für Deutsche Sänger,* 249.

the rush in the Carnival amusement, so I let it go."[53] But we cannot rule out the possibility that the Committee had demurred, as Brahms had already acknowledged might be possible, because of the songs' texts. This would hold especially true if, as seems probable, the three pieces in question included the overtly nationalist "Freiwillige her!," "Gebt Acht," or both. Nerves were still raw following Austria's ignominious and devastating defeat by Prussia and enforced removal from the German fatherland, and who among the Viennese at the time would wish to have all that thrown in their faces on a Sunday afternoon?

Following a last push by Brahms, the *Fünf Lieder für Männerchor* finally appeared under Rieter's imprint in November 1867.[54] Both "Marschiren" and "Ich schwing mein Horn in's Jammerthal" were performed for the first time before the year was out—on November 27, by the *Wiener Akademische Gesangverein* (Vienna Academic Choral Society), and December 30 on a subscription concert by the Baden Court Orchestra in Karlsruhe, respectively. "Gebt Acht" was given its première in a concert by the Vienna Academic Choral Society on December 8, 1871. Three months later, on March 4, 1872, "Freiwillige her!" was performed for the first time in Prague by the *Liedertafel der deutschen Studenten* (German students' Liedertafel). "Geleit," the first of the Lemcke songs to be composed, was the last to be heard in public: its belated première came in a concert by the Vienna Academic Choral Society on March 4, 1891, nearly thirty years after the *Volksfest* in Vienna for which Gotthard had requested it.

Changed Circumstances

If Brahms took pride in the establishment of the North German Confederation, he was also a man who was well on his way to putting down roots in Austria. The balancing act this required in the immediate aftermath of the German War can be observed in an incident that took place in August 1867, when he and his father were on holiday together in the Austrian Alps. While hiking one day on the famous Schafberg, the two men encountered Julius Magg and his wife en route to the summit. Magg, a young Viennese lawyer who would become a prominent progressive-liberal politician, later recounted the events of the day to Max Kalbeck:

> An hour later we were up in the *Gaststube* with many young men, North and South Germans. One group sang the famous Burschenschaft song

---

53   *Briefwechsel*, 14: 139–41 (at 140); Rudolf Hofmann, *Der Wiener Männergesangverein: Chronik der Jahre 1843 bis 1893* (Vienna: Verlag des Wiener Männergesangvereines, 1893), 156–57.

54   Letter to Rieter of March 8, 1867, in *Briefwechsel*, 14: 143–44 (at 143).

"Wir hatten gebauet ein stattliches Haus." After the plaintive conclusion, some of the Prussians objected angrily to treating the great achievements of the previous year in this way. I said, "But gentlemen, you are here in Austria! We Austrians may have to cope with our feelings, but don't tear open our wounds with your bickering." Since Brahms was in wholehearted agreement with me, he tried to placate the others, and soon peace was made. Perhaps this was the only time Brahms intervened in a semi-political debate.[55]

The Austrians' singing of "Wir hatten gebauet ein stattliches Haus," composed in 1819, as we have seen, to mark Metternich's dissolution of the liberal-nationalist *Urburschenschaft*, carried unmistakable overtones of a cry of lament for the injustice Bismarck had done nearly half a century later by shattering the dream of a unified Greater Germany, and it was surely this insinuation that offended the young Prussians that day. For the most radical student activists in Austria, exile from their German fatherland left a bitter taste that would linger for decades to come and eventually lead to baleful consequences.[56] Yet the mainstream German liberals who formed the social circle in which Brahms felt most at home in Vienna, including the likes of men such as Magg, soon got over their sense of loss (or at least thought they could live with the loss until it could be reversed at some point in the future). They grasped that by framing Austria's defeat as a failure of Habsburg conservatism—of the aristocracy, church, and military—they could exploit it to advance their goal of liberal constitutional rule. In fact, this point was made forcefully by the *Neue Freie Presse*, Vienna's newest and most important liberal newspaper, already on August 19, 1866:

> We in Austria ... can only look on the triumph celebrated in the world of Prussian politics with regretful resignation. A test of self-conquest of almost unimaginably great difficulty has been imposed on our state and its peoples, especially on the German-Austrians. Yet it must be overcome. May favorable fortune at least attune statesmen to the sufferings and grievances of these peoples, who, after so great a sacrifice of treasure and blood, deserve a strong state of public law that gives new scope to their bourgeois activity to recover, by labor and thrift, from the defeats suffered, and to straighten themselves up anew by freedom, in whose sun alone paralyzed Austria can find healing.[57]

---

55 Kalbeck, *Johannes Brahms*, 2: 230–31.

56 Steven Beller, "Hitler's Hero: Georg von Schönerer and the Origins of Nazism," in *In the Shadow of Hitler: Personalities of the Right in Central and Eastern Europe*, ed. Rebecca Haynes and Martyn Rady (London: Taurus, 2011), 38–54 (esp. 43–44).

57 "Wien, 18 August," *Neue Freie Presse* (August 19, 1866).

Brahms must have had something like this in mind at that moment when he suggested to Gänsbacher that Prussia had done Austria, not an injustice, but a favor. In any event, movement in a liberal direction came swiftly in the Austrian Empire. With all the traditional pillars of his strength weakened following the humiliating expulsion from Germany, Emperor Francis Joseph was now forced to make certain concessions in order to build support among the middle and upper middle classes.[58] In June 1867, working to appease the Hungarian liberals, he accepted the crown of the Kingdom of Hungary, thereby formalizing the recently negotiated Compromise of 1867 that dissolved the Austrian Empire in favor of a new Dual Monarchy (officially known as the Austro-Hungarian Monarchy but often called Austria-Hungary) composed of two largely independent, multinational states in Austria and Hungary. (The full and proper name of the former was The Kingdoms and Lands Represented in the Imperial Council; of the latter, The Lands of the Holy Hungarian Crown of St. Stephen. Since the two halves of the monarchy were roughly divided by the Leitha River, they were commonly called, as viewed from Vienna, Cisleithania and Transleithania, respectively.) Then at the end of the year he ratified a broadly liberal constitution in the new Austrian half of the monarchy and appointed its first parliamentary cabinet. Known as the *Bürgerministerium* (Bürger Ministry), this government represented a clear triumph of liberalism, since the majority of its members were "solidly middle class" (*gut bürgerlich*) and had risen to their new positions, as Vienna's *Die Presse* put it, by dint of nothing other than their talent, energy, and industry.[59] The ambitious Brahms was increasingly making Vienna the base of operations for his career, and this new government of liberal "self-made men" was one in which he could feel at home.

---

58   Pieter M. Judson, *Exclusive Revolutionaries: Liberal Politics, Social Experience, and National Identity in the Austrian Empire, 1848–1914* (Ann Arbor, MI: University of Michigan Press, 1996), 105–15.

59   "Biographisches über das neue Ministerium," *Die Presse* (December 31, 1867): 18. The term *Bürger* here is to be understood in the sense of both *citoyen* and bourgeois. Hereafter I shall refer to the Bürger Ministry. Five of the nine members (including one who had been ennobled some years earlier) were commoners; four were members of the nobility by birth.

Excursus I

From the German War to
A German Requiem

As far as the text is concerned, I will confess that I would very gladly
omit the "German" and simply put "Human."[1]

—Johannes Brahms

During the same period that saw the resolution of the German Question,
Brahms was completing a major work in which "German" was written into
its very name. *Ein deutsches Requiem nach Worten der heiligen Schrift*, op.
45, for solo voices, chorus, and orchestra, is the longest and in many respects
the most ambitious work of Brahms's career, and the one that first brought
him widespread international fame. What it is not, in my view, is a German
nationalist work, at least not in the political sense that is seen so clearly in the
Fünf Lieder für Männerchor. (The national significance that would attach
to the work after 1870, however, is another matter altogether, as we shall
see.) Although the slow funeral march heard in the second movement evidently derives from an aborted duo sonata that was conceived under the
pall cast by Robert Schumann's tragic collapse in 1854, most of the composition dates from the mid-1860s. Whatever the connection to Schumann
may be, it is reasonable to assume that the death of the composer's beloved
mother, on February 2, 1865, was the work's primary motivation. Writing
to Clara Schumann in April of that year, Brahms made mention of the
first two movements and included a piano score of the fourth, which he
described as a "choral piece ... from a kind of German Requiem." Brahms
followed up with more information about the "aforementioned [*besagtem*]

---

1   Letter of October 9, 1867, to Karl Reintahaler, in *Briefwechsel*, vol. 3: *Johannes
     Brahms im Briefwechsel mit Karl Reinthaler, Max Bruch, Hermann Deiters,
     Friedr. Heimsoeth, Karl Reinecke, Ernst Rudorff, Bernhard und Luise Scholz,*
     ed. Wilhelm Altmann (1908): 9–10.

German Requiem" in a letter to Clara of April 24.[2] Work continued in 1866 in Karlsruhe, Winterthur, Zurich, and Lichtenthal. (Finishing the *Requiem* was surely the most important of the "practical and essential matters" that, as he explained to Gänsbacher, kept Brahms away from Vienna longer at this time than he may have wished.) Originally completed in six movements, the *Requiem* was heard in that form for the first time on Good Friday 1868 (April 10) at Bremen's Cathedral of St. Peter under the composer's direction.[3] Shortly after the Bremen première Brahms rehearsed an additional number, a beautiful soprano solo that was inserted after the fourth movement to form a new seven-movement whole. This definitive version was heard for the first time, in Leipzig, on February 18, 1869. Publication that year quickly brought numerous performances throughout the German-speaking world, in Britain, and beyond.

By this stage of his career, Brahms had considerable experience in setting biblical and other religious texts.[4] These were mostly small-scale works, ranging from exercises in Renaissance and Baroque counterpoint (some of which later surfaced in published compositions) to evocations of J. S. Bach's motet style (in *Es ist das Heil uns kommen her*, op. 29, no. 1), to more modern-sounding, lyrical expressions such as the *Marienlieder*, op. 22, *Ave Maria*, op. 13, and *Geistliches Wiegenlied*, op. 91, no. 2. Paul Berry has perceptively

---

2 Berthold Litzmann, ed., *Clara Schumann–Johannes Brahms: Briefe aus den Jahren 1853–1896*, 2 vols. (Leipzig: Breitkopf & Härtel, 1927, repr. Hildesheim and New York: Georg Olms, 1989), 1: 504–6. For an English translation of the letter of April 24, 1865, see Avins, *Johannes Brahms*, 321–22. Daniel Beller-McKenna's translation of "besagt" as "so-called" leads him to argue that Brahms had misgivings about the title and was concerned about how the cultural meaning ascribed to it might be understood in light of the "political circumstances in Germany during 1866." The letter in question, however, dates from 1865, not 1866, and would seem to have nothing to do with the tensions between Prussia and Austria. See Daniel Beller-McKenna, *Brahms and the German Spirit* (Cambridge, MA, and London: Harvard University Press, 2004), 76.

3 The first three movements had been tried out previously in Vienna with mixed success on December 1, 1867, occasioning Brahms's new friend Theodor Billroth, a Prussian-born surgeon recently appointed to the medical faculty of University of Vienna, to wonder whether the music was too "Protestant-Bach-like" to go down well there. Billroth's observation is quoted in translation in Michael Musgrave, *Brahms: A German Requiem* (Cambridge: Cambridge University Press, 1996), 61.

4 On Brahms's interest in the Bible, see Jan Brachmann, *Kunst–Religion–Krise: Der Fall Brahms* (Kassel, Basel, London, New York, Prague: Bärenreiter, 2003); and Beller-McKenna, *Brahms and the German Spirit*, 31–64.

78 &❧ EXCURSUS 1

described this labor as an effort to achieve "compositional discipline."[5] If this discipline was lacking in much of the earlier instrumental music, Brahms surely thought it would be necessary to achieve if he were ever to justify the claim made in Robert Schumann's famous encomium "Neue Bahnen" (New paths) of 1853 that he was destined to play a truly decisive role in the history of German music, indeed was called to serve as the messiah of contemporary Art-Religion.[6]

Opus 45 can be understood in precisely those terms. This was no outgrowth of a compositional study, but a major seventy-minute work comprising sixteen separate texts culled by the composer from the Luther Bible and set to music that integrates an array of genres drawn from three centuries of sacred choral music into a thoroughly modern musical idiom. Clara Schumann, in attendance at the Bremen première, experienced this performance as the moment when the composer fully realized the expectations her late husband had placed on him fifteen years earlier in "Neue Bahnen": "As I saw Johannes standing there, baton in hand, I could not help thinking of my dear Robert's prophesy, 'Let him but once grasp the magic wand and work with orchestra and chorus,' which is fulfilled today. The baton was really a magic wand and its spell was upon all present, even upon his bitterest enemies."[7]

For August Wilhelm Ambros, the *Requiem* was a "modern palingenesis," a "reshaping" and "revitalization … in a new spirit" of the church cantatas of J. S. Bach.[8] Ambros draws particular attention to Bach's *Gottes Zeit ist die allerbeste Zeit*, BWV 106, suggesting that the two works share "a very similar basic idea." To be sure, the texts of each are taken from disparate parts of the Bible (although the cantata also includes some chorale texts by Luther). But whereas Bach is intent on preparing the faithful for death, Brahms, as we shall see, seems concerned primarily to comfort the bereaved. Herein lies, in fact, a critical difference between the basic ideas of the two compositions, not to speak of the basic sensibilities of the two composers.

---

5   Paul Berry, "Brahms, Johannes," in *The Oxford Encyclopedia of the Bible and the Arts*, ed. Timothy Beal, 2 vols. (Oxford: Oxford University Press, 2015), 1: 115–19 (here 116–17).

6   Robert Schumann, "Neue Bahnen," *Neue Zeitschrift für Musik* 39 (October 28, 1853): 185–86.

7   Berthold Litzmann, *Clara Schumann: Ein Künstlerleben nach Tagebüchern und Briefen*, 3 vols. (Leipzig: Breitkopf & Härtel, 1920), 2: 258 (quoting Schumann, "Neue Bahnen," 186). The early previews and reviews of this performance similarly tie this achievement to the claims made in "Neue Bahnen"; see Musgrave, *Brahms: A German Requiem*, 60–64.

8   A[ugust] W[ilhlem] Ambros, "Das 'Triumphlied' von Johannes Brahms," *Wiener Zeitung* (December 11, 1872).

EXCURSUS 1 &❧ 79

Unlike Bach, and despite his traditional Lutheran upbringing, Brahms held with no orthodox Christian belief.[9] This explains the composer's decision to avoid setting in the *Requiem* any verse in which Jesus Christ is mentioned by name, something that Bach does in several key moments of *Gottes Zeit ist die allerbeste Zeit*. Carl Reinthaler, the music director in Bremen who was beginning to prepare the chorus for the première, found Brahms's reluctance to present a more forthcoming Christian message puzzling, and in a letter from early October 1867 this former student of theology urged the composer to set some additional lines of text near the end that would make clear to the listener "the point on which everything turns," the redemptive power of the death of Jesus. Reinthaler offered two suggestions concerning where such an addition might occur, but then concluded, perhaps anticipating that Brahms would not follow either, by writing: "Anyhow, you say in the last movement: 'Blessed are the dead that die in the Lord from henceforth,' that can only mean, after Christ has brought his salvation work to completion."[10]

In his elliptical response (fleshed out here to make the meaning clearer), Brahms took pains to distance himself from any such profession of the Christian faith: "As far as [my omission in] the text [of any direct reference to Jesus] is concerned, I will confess that I would very gladly omit the 'German' [from the title as well] and simply put 'Human' [in its place], [and] also quite deliberately and consciously do without passages such as John 3:16." As for the texts he did set, Brahms implies that his decisions were motivated by his needs as a composer, not by those of a believing Christian, and that those needs had caused him to admit into his work

---

9   Brahms had never made a secret of his unorthodox religious views; see Florence May, *Life of Brahms*, 1: 258. For concise recent discussions, see Jan Brachmann, "Brahms zwischen Religion und Kunst," in *Brahms Handbuch*, ed. Wolfgang Sandberger (Stuttgart and Weimer: J. B. Metzler, 2009), 128–33; Paul Berry, *Brahms among Friends: Listening, Performance, and the Rhetoric of Allusion* (Oxford and New York: Oxford University Press, 2014), 81–88; and David Brodbeck, "Politics and Religion," in *Brahms in Context*, ed. Natasha Loges and Katy Hamilton (Cambridge: Cambridge University Press, 2019), 259–68. For longer studies, see Hanns Christian Stekel, *Sehnsucht und Distanz: Theologische Aspekte in den wortgebundenen religiösen Kompositionen von Johannes Brahms* (Frankfurt am Main: Peter Lang, 1997); and Brachmann, *Kunst, Religion, Krise.*

10 *Briefwechsel*, 3: 7–8, translated in Beller-McKenna, *Brahms and the German Spirit*, 42. On the close personal relationship that developed between Brahms and Reinthaler, see Sabine Giesbrecht-Schutte, "Gründerzeitliche Festkultur: Die 'Bismarckhymne' von Carl Reinthaler und ihre Beziehung zum 'Triumphlied' von Johannes Brahms," *Die Musikforschung* 52 (1999): 70–88.

80 & EXCURSUS 1

biblical passages in which he had no personal belief: "On the other hand, I did accept many a thing because I am a musician, because I was making use of it, because I cannot challenge or strike out the text of my revered bards, not even a 'from henceforth.'" And if that pointed last remark were not enough to convince Reinthaler that Brahms did not accept Christian dogma regarding the immortality of the soul, the composer goes on to add: "But—I'll stop without having said all I have to say," in other words, presumably "before I say something that you, as a believer, may well not want to hear from me."[11]

It is notable that Brahms did want Reinthaler to know that he had willfully done without John 3:16, the very verse that Luther had famously called "the Gospel in a nutshell": "For God so loved the world, he gave his only begotten Son that whosoever believeth in him should not perish, but have everlasting life." Brahms's concern in the *Requiem* is not with God's promise to the living faithful upon their deaths, much less with the fate of the soul of the deceased, as in the Catholic ritual; he seems to have believed in none of that. Rather, as suggested, he sought simply (and nobly) to bring comfort and consolation to the grieving in the here and now. The solacing message of this "Human Requiem," he wanted Reinthaler to understand, was intended to be universal in nature, not limited to the believer, German or otherwise.

None of what I am recounting here is new: this assumption of Brahms's "universal" intentions in the work has long been generally accepted.[12] But some years ago, Daniel Beller-McKenna challenged the received view, arguing that it developed in the second half of the twentieth century as a strategy for disassociating Brahms from the tainted German nationalism of the period of National Socialism and even earlier, and led to an unfortunate obscuring in post-war writings of Brahms's strong sense of German identity.[13] At all events, if we are to come to grips with Brahms's *Deutschtum* as he understood it, it is critical not to lose focus on the cultural context in which he

---

11   *Briefwechsel*, 3: 9–10. Beller-McKenna takes a different approach to explaining this passage in *Brahms and the German Spirit*, 42–44.

12   For a recent, thoroughly researched but in my view ultimately unconvincing study that takes a revisionist point of view on this question, see R. Allen Lott, *Brahms's A German Requiem: Reconsidering Its Biblical, Historical, and Musical Contexts* (Rochester, NY: University of Rochester Press, 2020). See also Ronald Knox, "Brahms and His Religion," *Il Saggiatore musicale* 22 (2015): 215–49.

13   Daniel Beller-McKenna, "How 'deutsch' a Requiem? Absolute Music, Universality, and the Reception of Brahms's 'Ein deutsches Requiem,' op. 45," *19th-Century Music* 22 (1998): 3–19; adapted as chap. 3 of Beller-McKenna, *Brahms and the German Spirit*.

EXCURSUS 1 &❧ 81

lived it. In Brahms's day, to be a German patriot, even a German nationalist, was not necessarily also to be a German chauvinist. We do well to remember, as historian David B. Dennis has put it in his discussion of the *Requiem*, "It was once possible to be a German (even a patriotic one) *and* a humanist."[14]

There is nothing new in that idea either, of course. Kalbeck, in fact, made this point long ago in a *feuilleton* published in 1888 and later reworked for his monumental biography of the composer:

> [The] *Requiem* is German not in the sense of being a translation or adaptation of the old Latin text ...; it is German according to its character, which is expressed in the thoughtful, conscientious selection of its text[s]. One might also call it Protestant, if the concept of Protestantism is conceived more broadly than the Orthodox conceive it, and if open-minded research into the Holy Scriptures is regarded as one of its principal features. The German has with his blood won the right to biblical license and with that has deprived the priestly power of its most powerful weapon. The German artist [Brahms], therefore, merely exercised his Protestant right when he allowed himself to interpret and combine parts from the Old and New Testaments that seemed to him to be fit for his ideal purpose.[15]

Brahms knew the Bible inside and out but valued it, not as the revealed word of God, but as "an article of his Germanness and personal story."[16] His views on religion can thus be aligned with Culture Protestantism (*Kulturprotestantismus*). This ideology, the roots of which lay in Schleiermacher and Hegel and which grew prominent within the North German educated bourgeoisie during the years in which the *Requiem* was first making the rounds, regarded Protestantism, with its legacy of "freedom from ecclesiastical tutelage, this-worldliness, and national self-determination," as the source of modern German cultural development and saw it, in a suitably modernized and secularized form, as "the basis for a free

---

14   See, for example, Beller-McKenna, *Brahms and the German Spirit*, 151. David
      B. Dennis, "Johannes Brahms's *Requiem* eines Unpolitischen," in *Searching
      for Common Ground: Diskurse zur deutschen Identität 1750–1871*, ed.
      Nicholas Vazsonyi (Cologne: Böhlau, 2000), 283–98 (here at 287). See also
      Blackbourn, *History of Germany 1780–1918*, 321.

15   Max Kalbeck, "Ein deutsches Requiem von Joh. Brahms," *Die Presse*
      (December 21, 1888): 1–3 (here 1); Kalbeck, *Johannes Brahms*, 2: 234.

16   Hanns Christian Stekel, "Brahms und die Bibel—historisch-theologische
      Aspekte," *Brahms-Studien* 11 (1997): 49–54 (here 52). For a detailed account
      of Brahms's annotations in his copy of the Luther Bible, see Beller-McKenna,
      Brahms and the German Spirit, 37–64.

82 &• EXCURSUS 1

and progressive political life."[17] As David Blackbourn has argued, Culture Protestantism ran like a powerful current through German middle-class consciousness. German culture was understood to be Protestant, and Culture Protestantism was understood to represent progress.[18]

Yet as Kalbeck continues, he shifts into his characteristic poetic mode and makes evident his view that the message inherent in the *Requiem* was not intended for the cultured German Protestant alone:

> What [Brahms] had in mind was the simple and humane idea, worthy of a man wise in the ways of the world, that it was not the dead but rather the living who were in need of peace and consolation. This idea is secular but not irreligious; it is philosophical but devout and beautiful, and it is thoroughly anti-dogmatic. For it embraces in its simple grandeur and boundless love every confession and throws open the unknown gates of a new Hypaethral temple, whose roof is the blue heavens above and whose hall, bedecked in the cypresses of sadness and the roses of love, stands ready to include the bereaved of every nation and sect in a single community of brothers and sisters connected through sacred pangs.[19]

We are not yet done with Brahms's correspondence with Reinthaler in October 1867. Beller-McKenna argues that the composer's "misgivings" about the title of his new work—should he replace "German" with "Human"?—may suggest a reluctance to be seen as siding with "northern Protestantism as opposed to Austrian Catholicism" as well as his anxiety that the *Requiem* would be "construed in political terms that had been associated with the Austro-Prussian War," and in particular that he would be seen as in agreement with the Prussian cause.[20] This seems unlikely. To be sure, in his correspondence with Rieter from earlier that year, Brahms had indicated that he did not want to make Op. 41 either "Prussian" or

---

17 George S. Williamson, "Protestants, Catholics, and Jews, 1760–1871: Enlightenment, Emancipation, New Forms of Piety," in *The Oxford Handbook of Modern German History*, ed. Helmut Walser Smith (Oxford: Oxford University Press, 2011), 211–33 (at 224–25). I have quoted here, respectively, from s.v., "Culture Protestantism," *Encyclopedia of Christianity* (Grand Rapids, MI: Wm. B. Eerdmans; Leiden: Brill, 1999–2008); and Larry L. Ping, *Gustav Freytag and the Prussian Gospel: Novels, Liberalism, and History* (Bern: Peter Lang, 2006), 210–15 (at 211).

18 Blackbourn, *History of Germany 1780–1918*, 221. For a more detailed study, see Gangolf Hübinger, *Kulturprotestantismus und Politik: Zum Verhältnis von Liberalismus und Protestantismus im wilhelminischen Deutschland* (Tübingen: J. C. B. Mohr [Paul Siebeck], 1994).

19 Kalbeck, *Johannes Brahms*, 2: 236.

20 Beller-McKenna, *Brahms and the German Spirit*, 77.

"Austrian" by publishing them with a firm based in either of those states. But this comment was a red herring. As we have seen, right up until the end of 1866 he tried in vain to publish them with Simrock, then based in Bonn, in Rhenish Prussia. Moreover, in the same year in which Brahms made this comment to Reinthaler, the *Brockhaus Enzyklopädie*, a widely read reference work for educated but non-specialist German readers, and therefore an index of contemporary common knowledge, entered its article on the war of the previous year under the title "Preußisch-Deutscher Krieg," describing it, in effect, as a war between Prussia and the rest of Germany (Austria, of course, included). It is therefore difficult to see how Brahms might have fretted that *Ein deutsches Requiem* would be read by his public as *Ein preussisches Requiem*.[21] And in any case, it is not clear how removing the word "German" from the title would have affected how the cultured German bourgeoisie that was Brahms's ideal audience would have interpreted the music—as an expression of liberal *Kulturprotestantismus*. In all likelihood, in his response to Reinthaler Brahms was not worrying aloud about where he might be seen to be on the question of Prussian-Austrian or Protestant-Catholic rivalry, but rather making a rhetorical point about the work's non-dogmatic, universalist nature.

All that aside, the focus of Beller-McKenna's discussion of the *Requiem* lies on a more profound issue than its title, one that he describes in terms both religious and political. He argues that the work initiates a series of three large-scale choral compositions, later to include the *Triumphlied* and the *Fest- und Gedenksprüche*, in which Brahms "access[es] a major vein of religiously inspired political thinking of the day: the apocalyptic anticipation of the new German *Reich*."[22] In the *Requiem*, he claims, it is Brahms's treatment of time that gives rise to an apocalyptic understanding. The outer movements—the one beginning "Blessed are they who mourn"; the other, "Blessed are the dead"—form a timeless and musically detached frame. The five movements that come in between, he claims, "form a peregrination, an essay in transience, indeed, in the earthly state of transition and anticipation" that he likens to "contemporaneous apocalypticism." The two realms are not kept entirely apart from one another, however. Instead, Beller-McKenna continues, Brahms creates references between them, thereby "allowing the glimpses of the outer movements from within the inner ones to be seen

---

21 *Allgemeine deutsche Real-Enzyklopädie für die gebildeten Stände: Conversations-Lexikon*, 11th ed. (Leipzig: F. A. Brockhaus, 1867), 12: 88–94. In later editions of the encyclopedia, this article was entitled "Deutscher Krieg" (German War).

22 Beller-McKenna, *Brahms and the German Spirit*, 77.

84 &· EXCURSUS 1

as our worldly, human, and imperfect vision of a timeless world we cannot grasp."[23]

Beller-McKenna writes at greatest length about the sixth movement, whose text is largely drawn from the fifteenth chapter of Paul's First Letter to the Corinthians (vv. 51–52 and 54–55). In Paul's telling, death is understood as a "demonic cosmological power that God has defeated in Jesus Christ."[24] And this victory is painted in vivid apocalyptic images:

> Listen, I will tell you a mystery! We will not all die, but we will all be changed in a moment, in the twinkling of any eye, at the last trumpet. For the trumpet will sound, and the dead will be raised imperishable, and we will all be changed. Then the saying that is written will be fulfilled. "Death has been swallowed up in victory." "Where, O death, is your sting?"

Brahms's musical setting is powerful and effective. After a brief passage in which the chorus quietly sings a verse from Hebrews 13 by way of introduction ("For here we have no lasting city, but we are looking for the city to come"), the solo baritone steps forth to deliver the mysterious news that "we will not all die" (mm. 28ff.) The chorus picks up on this pronouncement, quiet and homophonic at first but, at the sounding of the apocalyptic last trumpet (here marked by a choir of three trombones and tuba at mm. 68ff.), quickly becoming louder and soon spilling over into a new fast section that marks the raising of the dead.

With that the solo baritone returns to take the lead once more for a moment, this time quietly announcing the fulfillment of those Old Testament sayings of Isaiah and Hosea that had foretold of death's defeat (mm. 109ff.). The chorus returns to sing the prophetic verses in question in music that grows ever more ecstatic ("Death has been swallowed up in victory. Where, O death, is your sting?" at mm. 128ff.). This eventually gives way to what Beller-McKenna calls the "apocalyptic moment," a concluding large choral fugue, sung to words of praise taken from Revelations 4:11 (mm. 208ff.). This, he writes, "belongs neither to [the] earthbound time of the inner movements] nor to [the] divine eternity [suggested in the outer ones]; it is the pure state of transition between the two." What Brahms is expressing here, he argues, is "not the Christian apocalypse but rather a deep sense of arrival that was part of the German national spirit in the years leading up to 1871."[25]

---

23   Ibid., 80, 97.

24   Mark A. Plunkett, Review of *The Defeat of Death: Apocalyptic Eschatology in 1 Corinthians*, by Martinus C. deBoer, *Journal of Biblical Literature* 111 (1992): 152–55 (here 154).

25   Beller-McKenna, *Brahms and the German Spirit*, 93, 94.

EXCURSUS 1 &♦ 85

It is true, as Klaus Vondung has argued, that German national consciousness was "suffused with apocalyptic conceptions" from its beginnings during the early nineteenth century. But the hopes that had been placed at that time in the "national spirit" were dashed by the reaction imposed by the Congress of Vienna—Napoleon's downfall had not led to the hoped-for national state—and the apocalyptic fire was nearly extinguished. It smoldered in the decades thereafter, to be sure, but only at certain moments when Germany could be seen to be threatened by a foreign adversary did it really flame up again, as it had during the Rhine Crisis of 1840 and the Schleswig-Holstein crises of 1848 and 1863–64. Apocalyptic thinking would later be used to interpret other inflection points in German history, as we shall see.[26] But we can make no similar credible linkage between art and geopolitics with respect to the composition of *A German Requiem*. The decisive war fought in the summer of 1866 between Prussia and Austria and its South German allies has no meaningful role to play in our understanding of the genesis of the work—and not only because a good portion of the *Requiem* was composed before that war had broken out or was even thought to be inevitable. Moreover, this was not a war that anyone understood in apocalyptic terms. Who, after all, would have served in the role of the Antichrist in this German War? Moreover, whatever the merits of Beller-McKenna's interpretation of Brahms's large-scale handling of time in the *Requiem* may be, and despite Brahms's decision to include in its last two movements apocalyptic passages from First Corinthians and the Book of Revelations, no convincing case can be made, in my view, of cause and effect between historical event and musical utterance. Europe's next war, and Brahms's next large-scale choral-orchestral composition, would be a different matter altogether.

---

26   Klaus Vondung, *The Apocalypse in Germany*, trans. Stephen D. Ricks (Columbia and Lincoln, MI: University of Missouri Press, 2000), 123, 154. See also the related discussion in Green, *Fatherlands*, 4–7.

Part II

Triumphlied, op. 55

Chapter Three

"A Song to Paris"

> Can this joy of victory, this patriotic elation, not be preserved in some way, expressed, as it were, on a monumental scale?[1]
>
> —Jacob Kradolfer, 1870

Brahms's *Triumphlied*, op. 55, celebrates the great historical turn that occurred in the center of Europe in the years 1870–71. With the decisive German military defeat of France at Sedan and the subsequent proclamation of King William I of Prussia as German Emperor, the German Question was at last given its definitive Prussian-dominated Smaller German solution. What mattered most to Brahms and to the liberal bourgeoisie in general, the social stratum most enthusiastic about the turn, was that Germany, the land of poets and philosophers, had at last emerged from its particularism and political impotence to become a nation-state possessed of power and influence in the world commensurate with its long-recognized achievements in the cultural sphere.

With its at times jubilant, not to say exultant, mode of expression, the *Triumphlied* seems designed to turn the page on the very idea of German political impotence. The text is taken from the apocalyptic Book of Revelation and given a powerful setting for double chorus, baritone solo, and grand orchestra, the largest array of forces to be found in any work by Brahms. Each of the three relatively short movements features a brief orchestral introduction marked by propulsive dotted rhythms and jumping octaves. The outer choruses, sharing the festive key of D major, traffic heavily in fanfare-like figures. And while the second chorus, in G major, provides tonal contrast, its most salient text, coming in the middle, is set, again, in the main key of D major and with returning fanfares in the trumpets.[2] This is

---

1 Jacob Kradolfer, "Das deutsche Volksfest: eine Anregung," *Norddeutsches Protestantenblatt* 3 (1870): 276–77 (here 276).

2 Minor has written about the work's "astounding uniformity"; Beller-McKenna, its "monochromaticism." Minor, *Choral Fantasies*, 119; and Beller-McKenna, *Brahms and the German Spirit*, 106–7.

90 ❧ CHAPTER THREE

the work that elicited Wagner's famous sneer that Brahms had dressed himself up in "Handel's Hallelujah wig"—the last movement all but quotes the "Hallelujah Chorus"—and, indeed, precedents can be found in Handel for many of the work's defining characteristics, not least the resplendent sound it makes. Yet the music is pure Brahms in its command of counterpoint, its rich harmonic language, its grand sweep and scope.[3]

The composer may have initially given thought to the idea of dedicating the work to the new imperial chancellor, Otto von Bismarck, with whom it was in any case closely associated in his mind, as we shall see. Later he hit upon the idea of prefixing two names to the score, writing, in a letter to Simrock of February 1872, that "a dedication to the Emperor and Reich Chancellor comes to mind [*liegt nah*]." This went nowhere, however, probably out of recognition that it had the potential of creating an uncomfortable clash of national symbols: Bismarck as the so-called "blacksmith of the Reich" (*Reichsschmied*); William I as the embodiment of the Hohenzollern dynasty that, as the Prussian School of Historians claimed, was destined to lead it.[4] In any case, when the score finally appeared in print, in November 1872, Bismarck's name was not to be found. The lavishly engraved title page, rich in symbols related to the Hohenzollern monarchy, reads: *Triumphlied* (*Offenbar[ung] Joh[annis] Cap[itel] 19*), op. 55. The composer originally proposed a simple formulation for the dedication page: "To the German Emperor," but in the end what appeared was, as would be expected of the occasion, rather more formal and elaborate: "To his Majesty the German Emperor William I reverently dedicated by the composer."[5]

---

3   Richard Wagner, "Über das Dichten und Komponieren," in *Gesammelte Schriften und Dichtungen*, 10 vols. (Leipzig: E. W. Fritsch, 1871–83), 10: 148. For concise discussions of the work's Handelian style, see Geiringer, *Brahms: His Life and Work*, 317–18, and Malcolm MacDonald, *Brahms* (New York: Schirmer, 1990), 207–9.

4   On the difficulties of jointly depicting Bismarck and William I in court-commissioned paintings, see Michael Courtney Quinn McGuire, "Bismarck in Walhalla: The Cult of Bismarck and the Politics of National Identity in Imperial Germany, 1890–1915" (PhD diss., University of Pennsylvania, 1993), 17–19.

5   The title and dedication pages are reproduced in *Konfrontationen. Symposium: Musik im Spannungsfeld des deutsch-französischen Verhältnisses 1871–1918. Johannes Brahms und Frankreich*, ed. Wolfgang Sandberger (Lübeck: Brahms-Institut an der Musikhochschule Lübeck; Munich: Edition Text + Kritik im Richard Boorberg Verlag, 2018), 88–89. For a detailed discussion of the dedication, see Johannes Behr and Ulrich Tadday, "Einleitung," in *Johannes Brahms, Triumphlied, Opus 55* (= *Johannes Brahms Gesamtausgabe*, series V, volume 5; hereafter JBG V/5), ed. Behr and Tadday (Munich: G. Henle Verlag, 2020), XXV–XXXII. See also Brahms's letters to his Berlin publisher

The *Triumphlied* quickly became one of Brahms's most admired large-scale compositions. As such, it was performed nearly ninety times in the years leading up to the First World War, often at large choral-orchestral festivals, mostly in German-speaking Europe, but in Holland, England, and the United States as well.[6] Originally understood as a heartfelt display of patriotism appropriate to its moment of birth, the work eventually came to be widely criticized as an embodiment of disreputable national chauvinism, especially by those for whom the German invasions of France in the two world wars of the twentieth century have greater historical resonance than any showdowns that occurred in the century before.

Yet, in my view, coming to terms with the *Triumphlied* requires us to begin by looking, not ahead in time to what came after it, but back to Brahms's own time and indeed even earlier, to a period when Napoleonic rule of much of Germany meant "ever-increasing taxation, economic exploitation, conscription, and oppression" of all kinds.[7] Even those scholars who have taken note of this broader historical context have often failed to take sufficient account of it into their considerations of the work. In what follows, I seek to fill this gap in our understanding and with that to offer a more nuanced account of Brahms's patriotism. In effect, I write in response to Barbara Eichner's recent, implicit urging to consider how and why the *Triumphlied* was "welcomed and appreciated" in its own time, not only on purely aesthetic grounds, but also because of its "uplifting message."[8]

War with the Hereditary Enemy

As the decade of the 1860s wound down, the Second French Empire under Napoleon III found itself widely distrusted and diplomatically isolated after years of adventurous foreign policy and military intervention, from Crimea

---

Fritz Simrock of February 1872, and September 6, September 22, and October 7, 1872, in *Briefwechsel*, 9, 115–17 and 125–30; and Simrock's letter to Brahms of September 20, in *Johannes Brahms und Fritz Simrock*, ed. Stephenson, 53–54. The letter of 6 September included a separate text Brahms had written for Simrock and Joseph Joachim to use in asking the emperor to accept the dedication. Simrock seems to have taken the obsequious wording found in the printed dedication from the final paragraph of that text. For an English translation, see Frithjof Haas, *Hermann Levi: From Brahms to Wagner*, trans. Cynthia Klohr (Lanham, MD: Scarecrow Press, 2012), 104.

6   Behr and Tadday, "Aufführungen," in JBG V/5: XXXII–XXXVIII.

7   Timothy Blanning, "Napoleon and German Identity," *Modern History* 48 (April 1998): 37–43 (here at 42).

8   Eichner, *History in Mighty Sounds*, 36.

92 ❧ CHAPTER THREE

to Mexico, and in Italy against Austria.[9] Had Napoleon not been reluctant to mobilize his forces yet again in 1866, he might have affected the outcome of the Austro-Prussian War on terms favorable to France. But he hesitated, and when the Prussian troops scored their rout at Königgrätz/Sadová, it was too late. Bismarck's humiliating rejection of French demands for territorial compensation for having not intervened in the conflict on Austria's behalf only made matters worse. This perceived lost opportunity fed the notion at home that it was France who had suffered defeat in 1866, and soon cries of "*revanche pour Sadova*" were widely sounded in the French press. Conflict with the new German hegemon to the east now seemed to be only a matter of time.

Four years later, on July 19, 1870, following provocations and intrigue on both sides, Napoleon III declared war against Prussia.[10] The French bore a fair share of responsibility for this development, even if it played perfectly into the hands of Bismarck. By framing the conflict as a defense of German independence from attack by its hereditary enemy (*Erbfeind*) across the Rhine, Bismarck was able to rally to the cause the various South German states that had been Austria's allies in 1866, a decisive step forward in his drive to unification on Prussian terms.[11] It was not lost on anyone at the time that France was led by Napoleon III, whose uncle, Napoleon Bonaparte, was remembered, in the vivid words of historian David Wetzel, as:

the despised monster who had reduced the states of Germany to a status of ignoble servitude, a man whom no German could ever forget, a man domi-

---

9   Roger Price, *The French Second Empire: An Anatomy of Political Power* (Cambridge: Cambridge University Press, 2001), 405–12.

10 Geoffrey Wawro, *The Franco-Prussian War: The German Conquest of France in 1870–1871* (Cambridge: Cambridge University Press, 2003), 16–40. On the war's background and causes, see David Wetzel, *A Duel of Giants: Bismarck, Napoleon III, and the Origins of the Franco-Prussian War* (Madison, WI: University of Wisconsin Press, 2001). On the diplomacy of the war, see David Wetzel, *A Duel of Nations: Germany, France, and the Diplomacy of the War of 1870–71* (Madison, WI: University of Wisconsin Press, 2012).

11 As Eichner has noted, although the English name of the conflict, "Franco-Prussian War," is diplomatically precise, the standard German appellation "Deutsch-Französischer Krieg" more accurately describes German popular sentiment at the time; see Eichner, *History in Mighty Sounds*, 9. On the enthusiasm and celebratory public opinion that broke out on both sides, see Wetzel, *A Duel of Nations*, 3–7, 67–68. For a historical overview of German-French enmity, which can be traced back to the division of the Carolingian empire in the ninth century, see Manfred Kittel, "Deutsches Nationalbewußtsein und deutsch-französischer Erbfeindmythos," in *"Heil deutschem Wort und Sang!" Nationalidentität und Gesangskultur in der deutschen Geschichte*, ed. Friedhelm Brusniak and Dietmar Klenke (Augsburg: Bernd Wißner, 1995), 47–70.

nated by an insatiable vanity and love of power, a man of inordinate touchiness, an endless vindictiveness, and an inability to forget an insult or slight, a man possessed of a thoroughgoing hatred of everything not French and a high degree of bloody-mindedness toward anyone who disagreed with him or questioned his mastery of Europe.[12]

It was not difficult to extrapolate from the singular to the plural to create a binary opposition between the German and French peoples, expressed in a nutshell as good versus bad. A rhetoric of God, king, and fatherland could be used to foster a sense of pure and wholesome German identity in the face of threatening French alterity.[13]

When, all those many years later, Napoleon III declared war on Prussia in 1870, it triggered a renewed image of the French regime, and indeed the French people themselves, of "unmitigated darkness."[14] France, it was thought, not only aimed to dominate Europe but was motivated by a "relentless determination" to subjugate the German people in particular. Under such circumstances, Francophobia ought not to be considered an entirely unforgiveable feeling. Writing to the art historian Wilhelm Lübke in June 1871, Theodor Billroth, an accomplished surgeon and professor at the Vienna Medical School who, like his good friend Brahms, was a North German immigrant in the Austrian capital, vividly articulated the national memory of the Napoleonic occupation that sustained the emotion:

> Didn't you constantly hear from your grandparents in your youth how this bestial people exploited us and our country? Wasn't your fantasy filled ... with the atrocities and brutalities the French inflicted on us? ... As a boy, didn't you and your friends wallop the French in play and vow eternal revenge and destruction? Weren't Arndt's anthems and the soldiers' songs *von anno* 1813 sung at your family gatherings! ... Did you never hear old people speak among themselves about those terrible days?[15]

---

12 Wetzel, *A Duel of Nations*, 67–68.

13 Erich Pelzer, "Die Wiedergeburt Deutschlands 1813 und die Dämonisierung Napoleons," in *"Gott mit uns": Nation, Religion und Gewalt im 19. und frühen 20. Jahrhundert*, ed. Gerd Krumeich and Hartmut Lehmann (Göttingen: Vandenhoeck & Ruprecht, 2000), 135–56; Hans Fenske, "Die Deutschen und der Krieg von 1870/71: Zeitgenössische Urteile," *Pariser Historische Studien* 29 (1990): 167–214.

14 Wetzel, *A Duel of Nations*, 6.

15 Theodor Billroth, *Briefe von Theodor Billroth*, 5th ed., ed. Georg Fischer (Hannover and Leipzig: Hannchen, 1899), 141–42. See also Clark, "The Wars of Liberation in Prussian Memory." On the patriotic songs from the time of the Wars of Liberation, see Hasko Zimmer, *Auf dem Altar des Vaterlands: Religion und Patriotismus in der deutschen Kriegslyrik des 19. Jahrhunderts* (Frankfurt am Main: Thesen Verlag, 1971), 11–70.

94 &❧ CHAPTER THREE

Brahms no doubt came by his own well-known dislike of the French through hearing tales of the same hard times experienced by his mother in occupied Hamburg. And it is not difficult to imagine that the hours on end he spent playing as a boy with his prized collection of tin soldiers involved walloping the French in the great campaign of 1813 that resulted in Napoleon's defeat in the Battle of Leipzig and the subsequent removal of the French presence east of the Rhine River.[16]

Indeed, the victorious Battle of Leipzig was etched in the German national memory, and it proved to be a wellspring of national sentiment that could be tapped when war between France and Germany broke out again fifty-seven years later.[17] On August 2, 1870, French forces crossed the German border and initiated the fighting with a series of attacks at Saarbrücken. Responding on the same day, King William I of Prussia issued a public exhortation to his troops in which he reminded them of the heroic example set by their forefathers against Napoleon Bonaparte:

> All Germany stands together in arms against a neighboring state that has declared war on us by surprise and without reason. The defense of our threatened fatherland, our honor, and our own troops is required. Today I undertake the command of the entire army and draw comfort in a battle that our fathers once gloriously won in the same situation. All Germany joins me in looking to you in full confidence. Lord God will be with our righteous cause. [18]

It is in light of this announcement of the German counterattack that we should read Brahms's comment, made in a letter to his father sent from Salzburg three days later, that he was "eagerly [waiting] for the French to get a good thrashing" and that he was only sorry that he could not "join in

---

16 Albert Dietrich's report on the young Johannes's love of playing with his toy soldiers is based on word received from the composer's mother; see Albert Dietrich, *Erinnerungen an Johannes Brahms in Briefen aus seiner Jugendzeit* (1898; Leipzig: Deutscher Verlag für Musik, 1989), 115–16. Published in a contemporaneous issue of the *Preussische Jahrbücher* that Brahms owned is a lengthy account of Germany during the Napoleonic occupation; see Rudolf Usinger, "Deutschland in der Franzözische Zeit," *Preussische Jahrbücher* 26 (1870): 297–343. Notably, Brahms also owned Carl Venturini, *Rußlands und Deutschlands Befreiungskriege von der Franzosen-Herrschaft unter Napoleon Buonaparte in den Jahren 1812–1815* (Leipzig and Altenburg: F. A. Brockhaus, 1816).

17 In this connection, recall the first stanza of Hoffmann von Fallersleben's "Die Freiwillige."

18 William's proclamation was published in newspapers throughout the German cultural sphere. I have quoted it here from the *Neue Freie Presse* (August 3, 1870).

the shooting."[19] Around the same time Brahms acquired his personal copy of Ludwig Häusser's *Deutsche Geschichte vom Tode Friedrichs des Großen bis zur Gründung des Deutschen Bundes* (German history from the death of Frederick the Great to the founding of the German Confederation), the first volume of which he inscribed "Johs. Brahms. Salzburg, 1870." More notable is the inscription found at the conclusion of the fourth and final volume: "dann kommt, Gott sei Dank, 1866 u. 1870."[20] And when he came across Ludwig Archim von Arnim's poem "Siegeslied nach Aussprüchen des Paracelsus" (Victory song based on sayings by Paracelsus, 1833), which seems to foretell a national unity to come and was published with commentary in the *Preussische Jahrbücher* in September 1870, Brahms wrote in the margins of his copy: "How prophetic."[21]

Yet Brahms had good reason to return to Vienna when war came, however much he might have wished to have been in Germany instead. He had recently come under consideration for appointment as Johann Herbeck's successor as artistic director of the concerts of the Musikverein. It quickly became evident that coming to terms on the position would not be easy. The directors were reluctant to meet Brahms's request for appointment as both artistic director and director of its choral society, thinking the combined duties to be too much for a single person to fulfill. Yet the possibility of obtaining a prestigious fixed position in a city that he had grown to

---

19   Letter of August 5, 1870, to Jakob Brahms, in *Johannes Brahms in seiner Familie: Der Briefwechsel*, ed. Kurt Stephenson (Hamburg: Ernst Hauswedell, 1973), 174–75, trans. Avins, *Johannes Brahms*, 414. Later Brahms could be quite indelicate in his humor when expressing the joy he took at the avenging of the perceived injustices and humiliation historically inflicted by France on Germany. Writing to Simrock in May 1872, the composer wryly observed that a different title page for the *Triumphlied* might need to be produced for sales in England in order not to offend against British neutrality in the Germans' recent war with France, adding, in a biting reference to a contemporaneous scandal ensuing from the summary execution in British India of several dozen Kuka Sikhs by having them blown from a cannon: "Perhaps [a title page that depicts] a cannon with a Hindu in front of the barrel would be more simpatico [to the British]." *Briefwechsel*, 9: 121–22 (at 122). On this brutal episode in colonial history, see Kim A. Wagner, "'Calculated to Strike Terror': The Amritsar Massacre and the Spectacle of Colonial Violence," *Past and Present* 233/1 (November 2016): 185–225.

20   Hofmann, *Die Bibliothek von Johannes Brahms*, 45.

21   See Karl Geiringer, "Brahms the Reader of Literature, History, and Philosophy," in *On Brahms and His Circle: Essays and Documentary Studies by Karl Geiringer*, rev. and enlarged by George S. Bozarth, published in association with the American Brahms Society (Sterling Heights, MI: Harmonie Park Press, 2006), 30–46 (at 45).

96 &❧ CHAPTER THREE

love was attractive enough to keep Brahms planted in the Austrian capital from late August through the following winter.[22] On March 5, 1871, in what amounted to an audition for the post, he conducted the first complete Viennese performance of *A German Requiem*. This was well received, but still no contract was offered. With little more to be done about things at that time, Brahms finally made for parts north. By then the war was over, and William I had accepted the title of German emperor.[23]

While cooling his heels in Vienna, Brahms kept abreast of the war reports provided in the press. The leading article in the *Neue Freie Presse* on September 3, 1870, the day following the decisive Battle of Sedan, which resulted in Napoleon's capture and the surrender of many thousands of French troops, must have offered particularly satisfying reading. This is worth quoting at some length inasmuch as its white-hot rhetoric characterizes the moment that gave birth to the *Triumphlied*:

> Attack after attack fell on the French armies. While MacMahon's army was thrown back at Beaumont and Sedan and pushed to the Belgian frontier, the East Prussian regiments at Metz drove the troops of Marshal Bazaine, who had tried a desperate breakthrough, back into the forts and trenches with bloody heads. Victory cleaves steadfastly to the German colors, and they will stream into Paris in two weeks at the latest.[24]

As the article continues, the writer goes about debunking French accusations of German violations of the accepted rules of modern warfare; more than that, it turns those accusations back on the French themselves. The first has to do with the Germans' siege of the fortified city of Strasbourg, which had begun a little more than two weeks earlier. This complaint is dismissed

---

22 On the intrigue surrounding this appointment, see Otto Biba, "Brahms und die Gesellschaft der Musikfreunde in Wien," in *Brahms-Kongress Wien 1983* (Tutzing: Hans Schneider, 1988), 45–65. Brahms broached the subject in a letter to his friend Hermann Levi written just a few days before war broke out; Levi's reply is dated July 14. Brahms's letter and a portion of Levi's long reply are given in Avins, *Brahms: Life in Letters*, 411–13. Eduard Hanslick eventually put in a public brief in support of Brahms's appointment on his own terms; see Ed. H. [Eduard Hanslick], "Musik," *Neue Freie Presse* (October 14, 1870): 1–2.

23 Kalbeck's suggestion that the directors of the Gesellschaft were reluctant to appoint a "Prussian" to the post—Brahms was, of course, a son of the Free and Hanseatic City of Hamburg—is misleading. See Kalbeck, *Johannes Brahms*, 2: 340. In 1866, Hamburg acceded to membership in the Prussian-dominated North German Confederation, but it retained a semblance of its sovereignty.

24 *Neue Freie Presse* (September 3, 1870): 1, from which the next several quotations are taken. As we shall see, Brahms would soon refer to his new work-in-progress as a "Lied auf Paris."

as an absurdity, since, when a fortress is under siege, the paper argues, the attacker cannot take into consideration which inhabitants may suffer. (The non-combatants were evacuated shortly thereafter.) This gives the writer the opportunity to complain about the earlier French shelling of the open city of Saarbrücken, on August 2, described as "an unnecessary and useless barbarism, which ... the 'great nation' regarded as its prerogative to commit." Next the writer denies outright the French accusation that German forces were guilty of the "atrocity" of shelling ambulances, and then goes on to accuse the French of willfully shooting at peace envoys in the field. "All the bravery displayed by Napoleon III's soldiers cannot wash away these stains," the article declares, "and under such circumstances the French government would do well to keep silent with its accusations, which can only bring them the mockery of the neutral powers."

At this point, the writer takes up the French demand that the Prussians treat captured members of the *francs-tireurs* (irregular volunteer militia), not as outlaws, but as prisoners of war entitled to treatment as such, or else risk retaliatory attack against the *Landwehr* and *Landsturm* (regular German military reserve forces). Once more the argument is turned back against the accuser, this time by reference to French behavior during the Napoleonic Wars of sixty years earlier:

> How did her tin god, her much-admired Napoleon I act toward the German Free Corps? Did he apply the rules of war to them? Did he not judge the captured Lützower as criminals and in Wesel shoot Schill's officers, who belonged to one of the regular troops?[25] Would the nephew [Napoleon III] have shown himself more magnanimously against the irregular troops were his army to have penetrated into Germany? No and again no. The French, who drive thousands of innocent Germans, and along with them the completely uninvolved Austrians, across their borders, insult and mistreat them, and in so doing make a mockery of international law, put the crowning touch on their mad rage by threatening not to treat the Prussian *Landwehr*, a unit of the Prussian army, as soldiers.

The article concludes with a mock attempt to mollify those whom it calls "our French friends" by claiming that the behavior of their "'great nation'" could be excused as the "stunned and bewildered [response to] the catastrophe that has befallen her." Fault is placed squarely at the feet of the country's major institutions of power and the dying system of illiberal Bonapartism that they served:

---

25   The references here are to the Lützow Free Corps, discussed earlier, which served with distinction in the anti-Napoleonic campaign of 1813, and Ferdinand Baptista von Schill, a Prussian officer who led an unsuccessful revolt against the French in 1809.

98 ✦ CHAPTER THREE

The frightful savagery, the bestiality, which here and there struck against not only the Germans but also their countrymen in France, is self-evident, as is the confusion and systematic lies coming from the leading circles within the nineteen-year-old government of that man [Napoleon III] who six weeks ago set out to humiliate Germany, and is now wandering along the Belgian frontier, listening from afar to the thunder of the guns that were crushing his soldiers.

Although this article overstated the speed with which the Germans would prevail in the war, it did not misjudge the eventual outcome. Napoleon's capitulation at Sedan was followed a few days later by a popular insurrection in Paris that led to the establishment a new Government of National Defense, the first government of the Third French Republic. By the middle of September, German troops had encircled and laid siege to the French capital. Fighting would continue sporadically for another several months, and Paris would not run up the white flag until January, but the outcome had effectively been decided.

Musica in tempore belli

The strong pro-Prussian stance taken here by Vienna's leading liberal newspaper, and in Austria's German-liberal press more generally, is not difficult to explain. In part, it reflects the ties of a shared history and culture. A passage from Eduard Hanslick's memoirs is particularly instructive on this point and, as such, is worthy of quotation *in extenso*:

The year 1870! I rejoiced over the victories of the Germans and the founding of the new Reich. That Alsace had become German again—my heart's desire since I was a boy—made me so happy it was as if I had been given a principality personally.... Yes, I triumphed day after day with the successes of the German army, although I have always been sympathetic to the French, and still am in both private and artistic life. No doubt the world would be a much duller place without the French. But under Louis Napoleon their boastfulness and arrogance toward Germany touched me just as repulsively as their childish defiance and megalomania after having received a lesson, their inability after twenty-four years to accept the unchangeable, their undying cry of revenge—"revenge" for the fact that stolen property was taken back by the owner! Austria, as is well known, was neutral between the two belligerent powers, but our German population, in contrast, was bluntly national and expressed the loudest joy at Germany's victories. The official preservation of "neutrality" in Vienna went so far that the police forbade the singing of "Die Wacht am Rhein," this harmless song, written thirty years before the German-French War. It was not allowed to be performed on any program, but it was so wildly desired by the public in every concert of our numerous male singing societies that it was sung three and four times in a row, despite the ban.[26]

Internal Austrian politics played a role in this pro-Prussian stance, too. With the Hungarians now preeminent in multinational Hungary following the Compromise of 1867, the newly empowered German liberals assumed that they would be preeminent in multinational Austria, which included more or less substantial populations of Germans, Czechs, Poles, Slovaks, Croats, Serbs, Ukrainians, Romanians, Slovenes, and Italians. Yet in 1868 the Poles and Czechs demanded arrangements similar to what the Hungarians had achieved the year before. The Poles were in fact successful in obtaining a great deal of autonomy within Galicia and in turn rewarded the Austrian government with their staunch support. The Czech question was not so easily solved, not least because of Bohemia's longstanding special relationship to Austria and German culture.[27] Francis Joseph was torn between supporting the liberal majority of the Bürger Ministry, whose anticlericalism he loathed but whose German-oriented centralism he liked, and its smaller conservative faction, whose political ideology was rather more in keeping with his own bearings, but whose ethnically driven federalist demands aroused his concern. It was a bitter disappointment for the liberals when, in April 1870, largely over their failure to solve the Czech question, the emperor installed a new cabinet, headed by the Polish count Alfred Józef Potocki, that sought to placate both Slavic and conservative Catholic interests. In the face of this defeat, standing with the Germans in their war with France served as a means for the German-Austrian liberals to take a stand against the unwelcome "anti-German" tendencies of the new Austrian government.[28]

Brahms was surely not untouched by these changing political winds as he set to work on the *Triumphlied* in the fall of 1870. In fact, they could only have served to strengthen his sense of German patriotism. The first mention of the new chorus came in the composer's letter of October 9, 1870,

---

26 Eduard Hanslick, *Aus meinem Leben*, 2 vols. (Berlin: Allgemeiner Verein für Deutsche Litteratur, 1894), 2: 108–9.

27 David S. Luft, "Austrian Intellectual History and Bohemia," *Austrian History Yearbook* 38 (2007): 108–21; David S. Luft, *The Austrian Dimension in German Intellectual History: From the Enlightenment to Anschluss* (London: Bloomsbury, 2021).

28 Peter J. Katzenstein, *Disjointed Partners: Austria and German since 1815* (Berkeley and Los Angeles: University of California Press, 1976), 93, and the references cited there; Bascom Barry Hayes, *Bismarck and Mitteleuropa* (Rutherford, Madison, and Teaneck: Fairleigh Dickinson University Press; London and Toronto: Associated University Press, 1994), 235; Blackbourn, *History of Germany 1780–1918*, 187.

100 &❧ CHAPTER THREE

to his publisher Fritz Simrock by way of a knowing reference to the Siege of Paris that had begun three weeks earlier: "If I succeed in making a song to Paris, you will have it, and I will even deliver it myself." A month later Brahms implied to another publisher, Bartholf Senff, that he was making a musical "tribute" to the year, what he called his "own hurrah." And in December he teased Reinthaler in Bremen, with whom he had corresponded at length regarding *A German Requiem*, with hints of something described as "ein gutes Te Deum," in an allusion to the title of a work for which he had the greatest admiration, Handel's *Dettingen Te Deum* of 1743, which celebrates the defeat that year of French troops at Dettingen during the War of Austrian Succession by a combined army of English and North German forces.[29]

In late February, Brahms sent Reinthaler the score of what he called "the first chorus of a Song of Triumph," thereby indicating that he now envisioned it as a part of a larger work to come. In the accompanying letter, he wrote, "It has cost me an unbelievable effort to write [it] down—one of my political reflections of this year," and he urged Reinthaler to schedule the chorus for performance, along with the previously announced *German Requiem*, in his annual Good Friday concert at the Bremen Cathedral on April 7.[30] This concert was dedicated "to the memory of those killed in battle," and, as the composer must have recognized, inclusion of his triumphant new chorus, which Brahms conducted as the concert's final number, would remind everyone that the fallen soldiers had not given their lives in vain (Figures 2 and 3).[31]

Because the *Triumphlied* as first heard in Bremen was most likely conceived as an independent piece, we would do well to consider it as such before taking up the three-movement work as a whole.[32] Marked to be

---

29 Letter to Simrock of October 9, 1870, in *Briefwechsel*, 9: 98; letter to Senff of November 11, 1870, in *Briefwechsel*, 14: 194; and letter to Reinthaler of December 12, 1870, in *Briefwechsel*, 3: 29–30.

30 Undated letter from late February 1871, in *Briefwechsel*, 3: 35–36. The press soon reported both that the new work was inspired by the Germans' triumph in the recent war with France and that the composer intended to enlarge the work with some additional movements; see "Das Charfreitagsconcert," *Weser-Zeitung* (April 5, 1871): 2–3; and *Weser-Zeitung* (April 12, 1871): 2.

31 A copy of the complete program of the Bremen performance in available at the Brahms-Institut Lübeck and is accessible for viewing through its digital archive at http://www.brahms-institut.de/web/bihl_digital/programme/abh_001_007_005_029_s_001.html.

32 Based on the discovery several years ago of the orchestral parts used in this performance, Katrin Bock and Ulrich Tadday have established that Brahms later revised the chorus substantially prior to its publication as part of Op. 55,

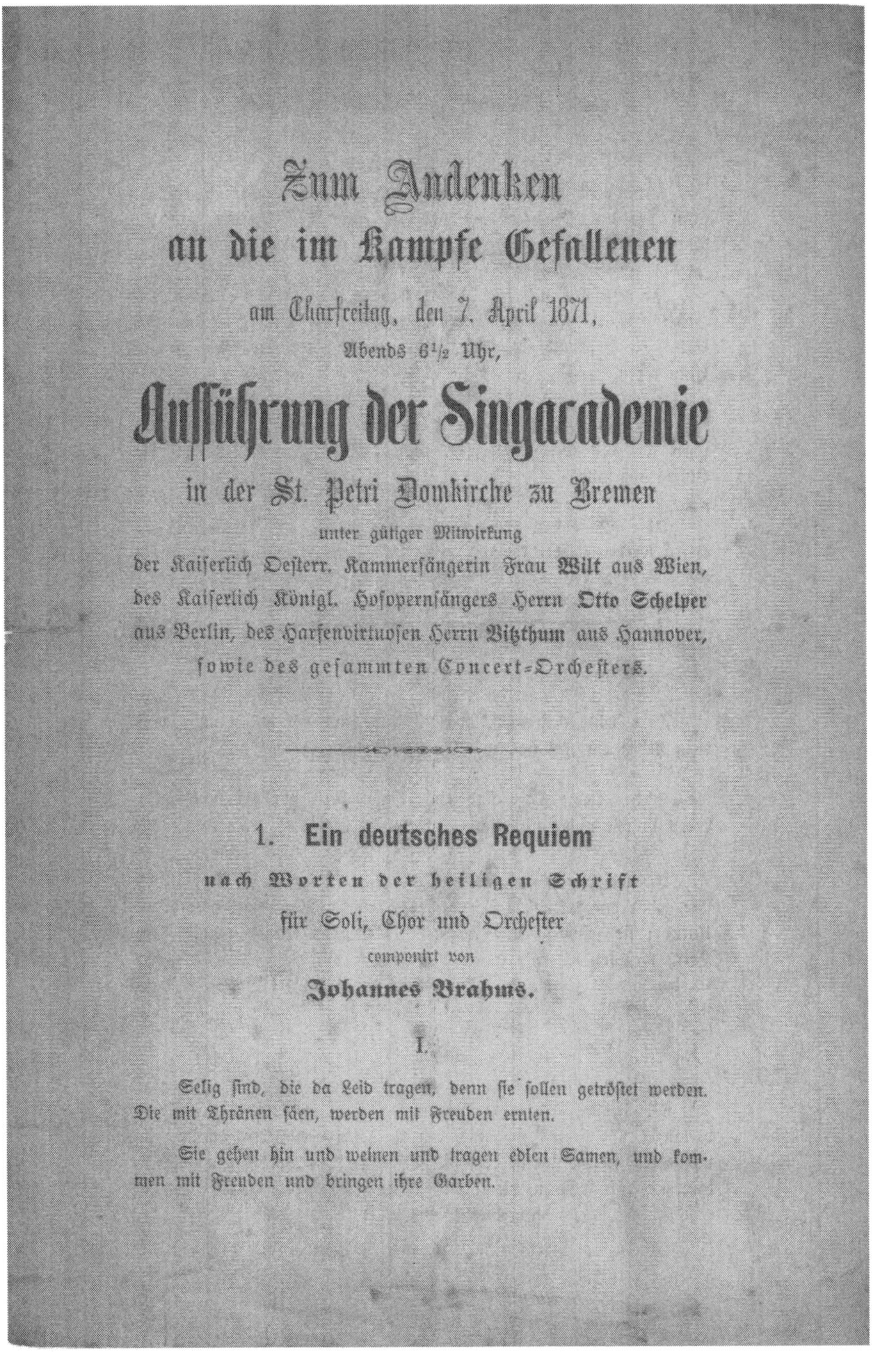

Zum Andenken
an die im Kampfe Gefallenen

am Charfreitag, den 7. April 1871,

Abends 6½ Uhr,

Aufführung der Singacademie

in der St. Petri Domkirche zu Bremen

unter gütiger Mitwirkung

der Kaiserlich Oesterr. Kammersängerin Frau Wilt aus Wien,
des Kaiserlich Königl. Hofopernsängers Herrn Otto Schelper
aus Berlin, des Harfenvirtuosen Herrn Vitzthum aus Hannover,
sowie des gesammten Concert-Orchesters.

---

1.   Ein deutsches Requiem

nach Worten der heiligen Schrift

für Soli, Chor und Orchester

componirt von

Johannes Brahms.

I.

Selig sind, die da Leid tragen, denn sie sollen getröstet werden.
Die mit Thränen säen, werden mit Freuden ernten.

Sie gehen hin und weinen und tragen edlen Samen, und kommen mit Freuden und bringen ihre Garben.

Figure 2. Program of the concert *Zum Andenken an die im Kampfen Gefallenen*, Bremen, April 7, 1871, p. 1. Reproduced with the permission of the Brahms-Institut an der Musikhochschule, Lübeck.

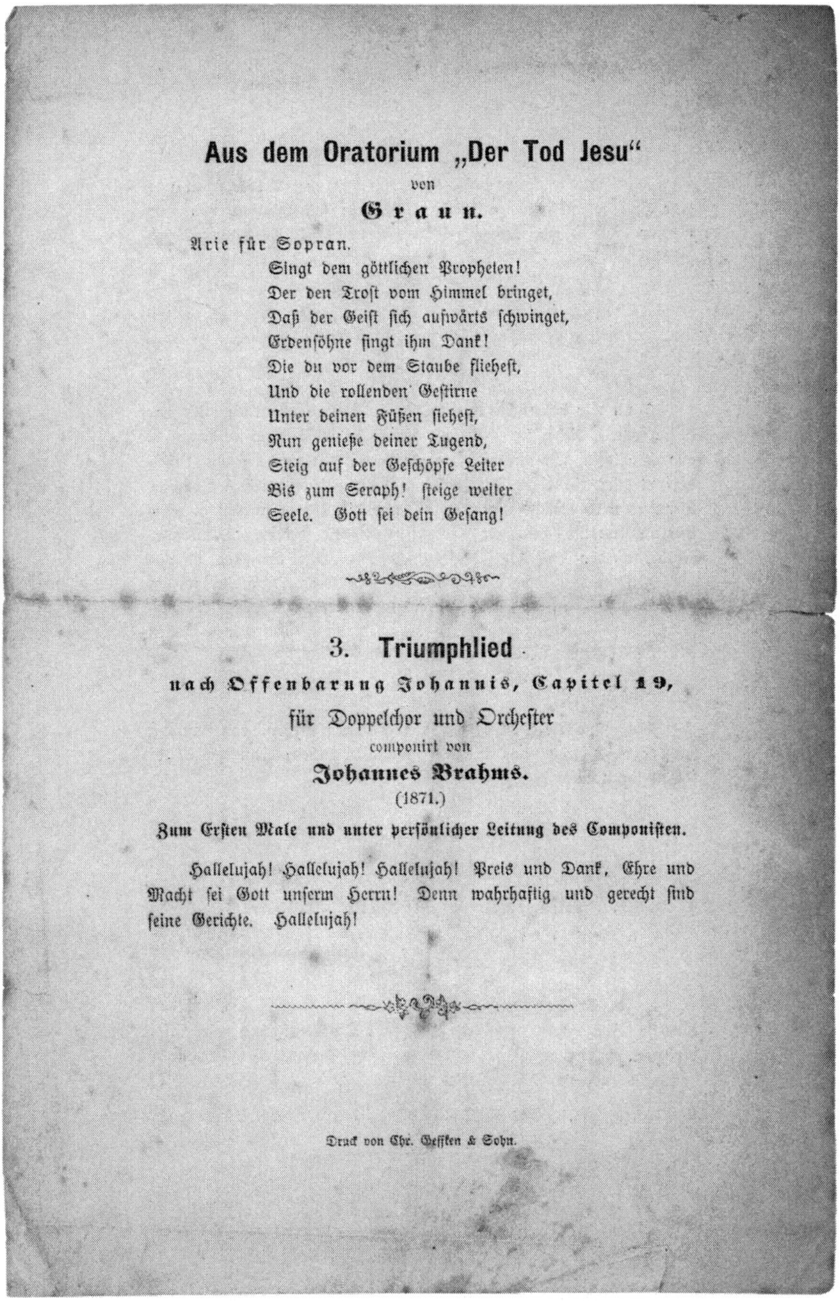

Aus dem Oratorium „Der Tod Jesu"

von

Graun.

Arie für Sopran.

Singt dem göttlichen Propheten!
Der den Trost vom Himmel bringet,
Daß der Geist sich aufwärts schwinget,
Erdensöhne singt ihm Dank!
Die du vor dem Staube fliehest,
Und die rollenden Gestirne
Unter deinen Füßen siehest,
Nun genieße deiner Tugend,
Steig auf der Geschöpfe Leiter
Bis zum Seraph! steige weiter
Seele. Gott sei dein Gesang!

---

3. Triumphlied

nach Offenbarung Johannis, Capitel 19,

für Doppelchor und Orchester

componirt von

Johannes Brahms.

(1871.)

Zum Ersten Male und unter persönlicher Leitung des Componisten.

Hallelujah! Hallelujah! Hallelujah! Preis und Dank, Ehre und Macht sei Gott unserm Herrn! Denn wahrhaftig und gerecht sind seine Gerichte. Hallelujah!

Druck von Chr. Gefften & Sohn.

Figure 3. Page 4 of the concert program of *Zum Andenken an die in Kampfen Gefallenen*, performed in Bremen, April 7, 1871, p. 4. Reproduced with the permission of the Brahms-Institut an der Musikhochschule, Lübeck.

played *Lebhaft, feierlich* (Briskly, ceremoniously), the music unfolds in a simple ternary form (ABA′) before culminating in an exhilarating coda that brings to mind the ending of the choral finale of Beethoven's Ninth Symphony.[33] The text comprises the second half of the first verse and the first half of the second verse of Revelation 19:

| 1b. Halleluja! Heil und Preis, Ehre und Kraft, sei Gott unserm Herrn! | 1b. Alleluia! Salvation and praise, glory and might be to our Lord God! |
| 2a. Denn wahrhaftig und gerecht sind seine Gerichte. | 2a. For true and righteous are his judgments. |

The outer sections of the ternary form (devoted to verse 1b) abound in pronounced dotted rhythms, quicksilver antiphonal exchanges between the two choruses, and trumpet fanfares that seemingly celebrate the recent triumph at Sedan that had brought the first phase of the war to its swift conclusion, a stunning victory worthy of shouts of Hallelujah over what had been thought to be Europe's most formidable military power.

Several early critics perceived motivic allusions in this music to the Prussian royal anthem, "Heil Dir im Siegerkranz" (Hail to you in victor's crown). The tunes are in different meters, but their similar melodic contours, not to speak of the textual resonances between them, are evident enough, even though the putative tune is never sounded openly (Example 6).[34] Ryan Minor has suggested that Brahms's allusion amounts to an endorsement of "Prussian expansionism," citing as evidence a well-known parody of the

---

shortening it by sixteen measures, making some changes in its texture and scoring, and, what is most notable, transposing it from C major into the key of D major in which it finally appeared in print. A critical edition of this early version is available as an appendix in Behr and Tadday, eds., JBG V/5. For commentary, see Katrin Bock and Ulrich Tadday, "Bericht der Fund der Bremer Fassung des Triumphliedes in C-Dur von Johannes Brahms," in *Brahms-Studien* 19, ed. Beatrix Borchard and Kerstin Schüssler-Bach (Tutzing: Hans Scheider, 2014), 153–62; and Ulrich Tadday, "Brahms' Bremer Triumphlied," in *Brahms am Werk: Konzepte-Texte-Prozesse*, ed. Siegfried Oechsle and Michael Struck with Katrin Eich (Munich: Henle, 2016), 150–69. For simplicity's sake, in the following discussion I refer to the first movement of the final version.

33 On the parallel with Beethoven's Ninth, see Beller-McKenna, *Brahms and the German Spirit*, 127.

34 See, for example, Ed. H. [Eduard Hanslick], "Concerte," *Neue Freie Presse* (December 10, 1872): 1–3 (at 3). Hermann Kretzschmar doubted that anyone but "the cleverest soothsayer" (*allerbegabtester Zeichendeuter*) would recognize the allusion, but in fact many critics took note of it. Hermann Kretzschmar, "Neue Werke von Brahms," *Musikalisches Wochenblatt* 5 (1874): 5–7, 19–21, 31–32, 43–45, 58–60, 70–73, 95–97, 107–11, 147–50, 164–66 (at 148).

Example 6. Comparison of "Heil and Preis" (Brahms, op. 55, first movement) and "Heil Dir im Siegerkranz" (unofficial Prussian national anthem).

first lines of the hymn—"Heil Dir im Siegerkranz, / Nimm', was du kriegen kannst" (Hail to you in victor's crown, plunder what you can). To use this parody to support such a claim is problematic, however, since the parodic expression appears to be of much more recent origin.[35] There is a simpler, less piquant explanation. The first stanza of the anthem equates the Prussian sovereign with a victorious military general, and since this was one of several songs performed during the short life of the North German Confederation to accompany the royal dedication of monuments and the like commemorating military conflicts of the past, up to and including the war of 1866, we need not read more into the allusion than that it may have been intended to celebrate what was widely understood to be a world-historic victory over the hereditary enemy.[36]

After all the outbursts of joy in the opening, the mood becomes soberer in the middle section when, beginning in measure 66, the two choirs unite in a homophonic intonation of the first half of the second verse, beginning on the minor subdominant and with earnest march-like rather than exuberant dotted rhythms: "For true and righteous are his judgments." These words are repeated a number of times but the second half of the verse is never sung. When sending Reinthaler the score Brahms took pains to draw his friend's attention to what was missing: "The rest of the text you will find in Chapter 19."[37] At the work's première in Bremen, he was more explicit

---

35   Minor, *Choral Fantasies*, 122–24. Minor credits Kross, *Johannes Brahms: Versuch einer kritischen Dokumentar-Biographie*, 2: 618. On the parody, see Werner Scholze-Stubenrecht and Anja Steinhauer, eds., *Zitate und Aussprüche*, 3rd. ed. (Mannheim, Leipzig, Vienna, Zurich: Dudenverlag, 2008), 237.

36   Nils Grosch, "'Heil Dir im Siegerkranz!' Zur Inszenierung von Nation und Hymne," in *Reichsgründung 1871: Ereignis–Beschreibung–Inszenierung*, ed. Michael Fischer, Christian Senkel, and Klaus Tanner (Münster: Waxman, 2010), 90–103 (at 90).

37   *Briefwechsel*, 3: 36.

in billing the chorus as *Triumphlied nach Offenbarung Johannis, Capitel 19* (Song of Triumph on the Revelation of John, Chapter 19). And he later included the same biblical source on the title page of the first edition and even wanted mention made of it in the published choral parts.[38]

Clearly Brahms was encouraging all parties to interpret this chorus within a broader context than that given only by the words he set to music. This was not lost on August Wilhelm Ambros, whose review of the first performance of the work in Vienna, on December 8, 1872, includes this key passage:

> Should the reader possess a "New Testament," I ask him to flip it open and read the second verse of the cited chapter, from which Brahms took only half, and the third verse, from which he took nothing at all, or even only the chapter heading, in order to recognize at once the connection of ideas that may have led our composer to seek his text precisely here. What he decorously left out is as significant as that which he set to music. But even the latter passages [i.e., those he did set to music] are so well selected and so clear in their relationships it would be difficult for a person to be deceived about what is meant.[39]

In nineteenth-century editions of the Luther Bible, Revelation 19 is headed by an exegetical précis (Ambros's "chapter heading") that reads: "Song of Triumph of the Elect on the fulfillment of God's judgment of the Great Whore."[40] Here we find not only the source of Brahms's title, but also, in the first three verses, the complete image he wanted his audience to bear in mind when listening to the work:

Offenbarung Johannis, Capitel 19	Revelation of John, Chapter 19
Triumphlied der Auserwählten über die Vollziehung des Gerichts Gottes, die große Hure betreffend	*Song of Triumph of the Elect on the fulfillment of God's judgment of the Great Whore*
1. Darnach hörte ich eine Stimme großer Schaaren im Himmel, die sprachen: Halleluja! Heil und Preis, Ehre und Kraft, sey Gott unserm Herrn!	1. After this I heard the voice of a great multitude in Heaven saying: Alleluia! Salvation and praise, glory and might be to our Lord God!

---

38 On the printing of the choral parts, see Brahms's letters to Simrock of February and late March 1872, in *Briefwechsel*, 9: 115, 118–19.

39 A[ugust] W[ilhlem] Ambros, "Das 'Triumphlied' von Johannes Brahms," *Wiener Zeitung* (December 11, 1872).

40 For a facsimile of the relevant page from Brahms's personal Bible, see Behr and Tadday, "Werktitel," in JBG V/5: XV.

| 2. Denn wahrhaftig und gerecht sind seine Gerichte, daß er die große Hure verurtheilet hat, welche die Erde mit ihrer Hurerei verderbet, und hat das Blut seiner Knechte von ihrer Hand gerochen. | 2. For true and righteous are his judgments, for he hath judged the great whore, which did corrupt the earth with her fornication, and hath avenged the blood of his servants at her hand. |
| 3. Und sie sprachen zum andernmal: Halleluja! Und der Rauch geht auf in ewiglich. | 3. And they said a second time: Alleluia! And the smoke will rise forever and ever. |

Max Kalbeck cast the besieged French capital as the Great Whore of Babylon who stands under Germany's "true and righteous judgment." He called Paris the modern "Babylon on the Seine" (*Seine-Babel*) and spared no adjective in describing what he claims was Brahms's attitude toward the city and her perfidies:

> He hated the sanguine [*leichtblütig*] French, all élan and temperament, and their glorious capital, upon which he never laid eyes, was to him a market-place of alien fancies and idleness, a breeding ground of perverse ideas, a pool of vices, crimes, and abominations. "Seldom has anything good come from Paris," he would say with condescension, whenever a fashionable new direction in art or literature was imported from there.[41]

Following this baroque setup (which almost certainly overstates Brahms's Francophobia outside the immediate context of the war), Kalbeck argues that as a "joke" Brahms "smuggled in" a tacit allusion to the biblical words that condemn Seine-Babel by means of a short, accented orchestral theme beginning at measure 89 that can be fitted to the text "daß er die große Hure verurteilet hat" (for he hath judged the Great Whore).[42]

---

41 Kalbeck, *Johannes Brahms*, 2: 347. Cf. Johannes Scherr, *1870–1871: Vier Bücher deutscher Geschichte*, 2 vols. (Leipzig: Otto Wigand, 1879), 2: 169, where we find both the designation of Paris as "Seine-Babel" and a moralistic judgment of the city expressed in discourse very similar to Kalbeck's own. For a more recent study, see Rupert Christiansen, *Paris Babylon: The Story of the Paris Commune* (New York: Viking, 1995).

42 Kalbeck, *Johannes Brahms*, 2: 348. Ingrid Fuchs convincingly posits that Brahms had a far more nuanced attitude toward the French than did his biographer Kalbeck. See Ingrid Fuchs, "Brahms und Frankreich—Aspekte einer Beziehung," in *Konfrontationen. Symposium: Musik im Spannungsfeld des deutsch-französischen Verhältnisses 1871–1918. Johannes Brahms und Frankreich*, ed. Wolfgang Sandberger (Lübeck: Brahms-Institut an der Musikhochschule Lübeck; Munich: Edition Text + Kritik im Richard Boorberg Verlag, 2018). 22–37.

Modern musicologists have felt obliged to comment. Although most commentators have accepted some version of Kalbeck's take, Friedhelm Krummacher dismissed it out of hand, along with the idea that it proves Brahms to be a blind nationalist.[43] As he observes, Kalbeck's discussion of the "joke" appears for the first time only in the second edition of the biography (1910), with a footnote suggesting that it was brought to his attention by the composer's friend Bernhard Scholz after the latter, presumably having read the first edition (1909), made him aware of it in a private communication. For Krummacher, this is evidence of a fabrication, whether by Kalbeck or Scholz himself.[44]

Yet there can be no question that Brahms was making irreverent mischief here. In 1926, Eusebius Mandyczewski reported that the composer's personal copy of the published score contains his handwritten addition of the words "daß er die große — —" in connection with the first incarnation of what Kalbeck called the stark, unison theme, beginning in the second half of measure 70. (The similar theme that begins at measure 89 does not fit the text nearly as well.)[45] We cannot know with certainty when Brahms conceived the idea of associating the theme with the beginning of the text he omitted, but of one thing we can be certain: the text omitted is at least as important as that which was set to music (Example 7). Assuming his listeners—at least his ideal listeners—to be imbued with the ideology of Culture

---

43   Friedhelm Krummacher, "'Eine meiner politischen Betrachtungen über das Jahr': Eschatologische Visionen im Triumphlied von Brahms," in *Studien zur Musikgeschichte: Eine Festschrift für Ludwig Finscher*, ed. Annegrit Laubenthal and Kara Kusan-Windweh (Kassel: Bärenreiter, 1995), 635–54 (at 638–39). Less skeptical accounts include Peter Petersen, "Über das 'Triumphlied' von Johannes Brahms," *Die Musikforschung* 52 (1999): 462–66; Beller-McKenna, *Brahms and the German Spirit*, 102–4; Taruskin, *Oxford History of Western Music*, 3: 712–13; and Minor, *Choral Fantasies*, 125–28.

44   Kalbeck, *Johannes Brahms*, 2: 348n.

45   *Revisionsbericht* for *Triumphlied*, in Johannes Brahms, *Sämtliche Werke* (Wiesbaden: Breitkopf & Härtel, 1926), vol. 18. That this reference occurs in measures 70–71—numbers that bring to mind the years in which the Franco-Prussian War was fought—is, in my view, mere happenstance. Brahms composed most, if not all, of this "Lied auf Paris" before the end of 1870 and before he could have known that the war would extend into January 1871. But see Klaus Häfner, "Das 'Triumphlied' Op. 55, eine vergessene Komposition von Johannes Brahms. Anmerkungen zur Rezeptionsgeschichte des Werkes," in *Johannes Brahms in Baden-Baden und Karlsruhe: Eine Ausstellung der Badischen Landesbibliothek Karlsruhe und der Brahmsgesellschaft Baden-Baden e. V.*, ed. Badische Landesbibliothek Karlsruhe unter Mitarbeit von Joachim Draheim et al. (Karlsruhe: Selbstverlag der Badischen Landesbibliothek Karlsruhe, 1983), 83–102 (at 94).

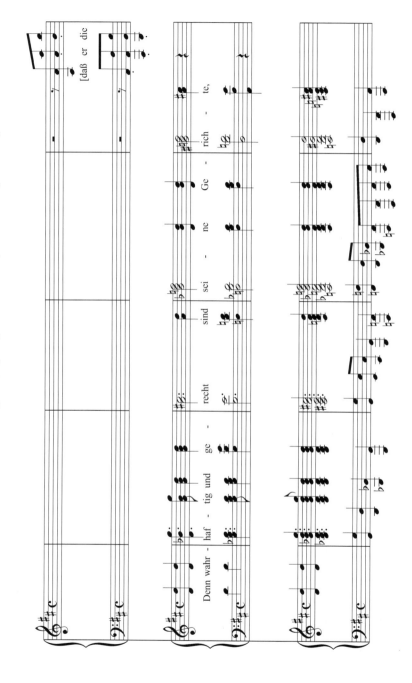

Example 7. Brahms, *Triumphlied*, op. 55, first movement, mm. 66–74 (reduction).

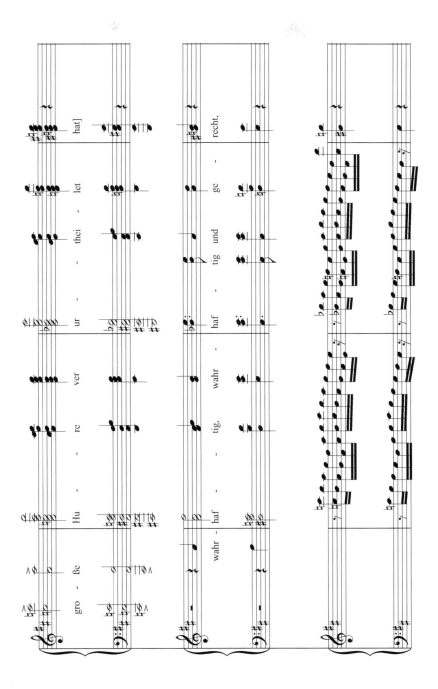

110 ❧ CHAPTER THREE

Protestantism, Brahms could count on them to recognize, with knowledge of the biblical source he made sure to give them, that in the first movement of the *Triumphlied* he was working in a rich vein of apocalyptic nationalism that would have seemed to them perfectly natural and unmarked.[46]

This way of thinking, which dates back to the Napoleonic era, was grounded in Friedrich Schiller's view that "world history is the Last Judgment" (*die Weltgeschichte ist das Weltgericht*). Schiller was not engaged in Christian eschatology; he transferred the fulfillment of human existence from the end of history, as in earlier Christian understandings of the Last Judgment, into the historical process, that is, into world history, in a way that would later influence Hegel.[47] But that did not stop Ernst Moritz Arndt, in an essay entitled "What Are the Great Powers to Do Now?" (1813), from restoring a kind of eschatological meaning to Schiller's dictum and then applying it to the historical moment at hand—the coming campaign that Arndt hoped would liberate Germany from Napoleonic occupation and lead to a unification of the nation in the wake of victory.[48]

Already at that time the Book of Revelation had been read to prophesy Napoleon's downfall. From Revelation 9:11, with its account of Abbadon,

---

46 That Brahms's confidence was not misplaced is demonstrated by a reviewer who in April 1874 characterized the music as "a successful jubilant symphony about the fall of the proud Seine-Babel, full of bursting power and the majesty of feeling" (*gelungene Jubel-Symphonie über den Fall des stolzen Seine-Babel voll strotzender Kraft und Hoheit der Empfindung*). This review, which appeared in the Bremen newspaper *Courier* on April 28, 1874, is quoted in Wolfgang Sandberger, ed., *Konfrontationen. Symposium: Musik im Spannungsfeld des deutsch-französischen Verhältnisses 1871–1918. Johannes Brahms und Frankreich* (Lübeck: Brahms-Institut an der Musikhochschule Lübeck; Munich: Edition Text + Kritik im Richard Boorberg Verlag, 2018), 86. Men of their time, Brahms—and this Bremen critic and later Kalbeck—may well have been wholly insensitive to the problematic gender implications raised by the invocation of the Whore of Babylon that now seem obvious. For a brief discussion, see Laurie McManus, "The Rhetoric of Sexuality in the Age of Brahms and Wagner" (PhD diss., University of North Carolina, Chapel Hill, 2011), 126. That is not to say, however, that Brahms, as McManus suggests, was indicting French music for its supposed immorality. The point rather seems to have been to compare the present triumphant political moment with that of the Germans in 1813 by way of shared apocalyptic nationalism.

47 Vondung, *The Apocalypse in Germany*, 109–11, 269, on which the following discussion is based. Schiller's locution appears in his poem "Resignation" (1776).

48 Ernst Moritz Arndt, "Was haben die großen Mächte jetzt zu tun?," in *Ernst Moritz Arndts Sämmtliche Werke*, vol. 10, *Geist der Zeit*, part 3 (Magdeburg: Magdeburger Verlagsanstalt, 1910).

the angel of the abyss and the king of a plague of locusts, whose name means Destruction in Hebrew, came the notion that Napoleon (easily relatable to Apollyon, the Greek name for Abbadon) was the Antichrist; his armies, the locusts; and Paris, the Great Whore of Babylon.[49] With Arndt, there was no thought of any genuine millennial kingdom of Christ. Instead, apocalyptic interpretation was rhetorical, not religious, in nature, a way of making sense of Germany's relationship with its feared neighbor to the west. The liberation and unification of Germany was seen to be an event of world-historic significance.

The conservative reaction imposed by the Congress of Vienna forestalled that event, but the outbreak of war with France in 1870 brought a new opportunity and spurred many similar apocalyptic interpretations. As Rudolf Gottschall put it: "The unanimous belief in the German national cause ... and the justified outrage at the arrogance with which France unleashed such a terrible war immediately became the Muses inspiring German national poetry."[50] Most such verses were ephemeral, but they are instructive for us here, all the same.[51] Among the first was Emmanuel Geibel's "Kriegslied" (War song), written shortly after the fighting broke out. Beginning with the apostrophe "Empor mein Volk! Das Schwert in Hand!" (Rise up, my people! Sword in hand!), the poem goes on to express the "moral earnestness and pronounced self-righteousness" that was typical of the Germans' response to what was framed, as we have seen, as French aggression.[52] Here the poet predicts that the impending battle with the hereditary enemy will prove to be nothing less than the *Weltgericht*, an apocalyptic moment, difficult and bloody but ultimately successful in uniting the Germans of north and south in a moral common cause.[53]

---

49 For images of Napoleon as the personification of the Devil in *anno 1813*, see Pelzer, "Die Wiedergeburt Deutschlands 1813 und die Dämonisierung Napoleons," 147–51.

50 [Rudolf von Gottschall], "Die Kriegslyrik von 1870," *Blätter für literarische Unterhaltung* (August 25, 1870): 556–59 (at 556); quoted in Walter Pape, "'Hurra, Germania—mir graut vor dir': Hoffmann von Fallersleben, Freiligrath, Herwegh, and the German Unification of 1870–71," in *1870/71– 1989/90: German Unifications and the Change of Literary Discourse*, ed. Walter Pape (Berlin: Walter de Gruyter, 1993), 107–18 (at 109).

51 For an early account, see [Gottschall], "Die Kriegslyrik von 1870." See also Zimmer, *Auf dem Altar des Vaterlands*, 71–149.

52 Wetzel, *A Duel of Nations*, 6. Rode [*sic*], ed., *Geibel und der Beginn der national-politischen Dichtung: Eine Sammlung politische Gedichte für Schulgebrauch* (Leipzig: Dürr'scher Buchhandlung, 1906).

53 Emanuel Geibel, *Heroldsrufe: Aeltere und neuere Zeitgedichte* (Stuttgart: Cotta, 1871), 180–82. Musical settings of this poem, and many others like it that

112 &♥ CHAPTER THREE

Later that summer came Geibel's "Am 3. September" (On the 3rd of September), in which the poet depicted the euphoria arising from the victory at Sedan.[54] Written on September 5, the poem was circulating in newspapers within a few days, and before the month was out the Leipzig music publisher Fr. Kistner had announced that Carl Reinecke's setting of it for men's chorus would soon be for sale.[55] The outer stanzas, with their imagery of rejoicing bells, mark the poem as a kind of "gutes Te Deum," to recall Brahms's description of the *Triumphlied*: "Now let the bells rejoice from tower to tower throughout the land in jubilation! The torch fans the flames, the Lord has done great things for us. Glory to God in the highest!" The fifth stanza invokes the Last Judgment on the "Antichrist" (this time the captured Napoleon III) and his "plague of locusts" (the 80,000 French soldiers taken as prisoners of war): "Then on the third day the Lord of Light raised the scales of justice, and with a clap of thunder cast down the dragon from the golden throne, into the pit of Hell. Glory to God in the Highest!"[56] And in the sixth stanza, Geibel turns his sights away from Sedan and sings a "Song to Paris," to recall another of Brahms's references to his own work: "Now trembles before God's and Germany's sword the city of scorn, the home of bloodguilt. Her illusion blazes away, How soon! into dust. And account will be taken of all her deprivations. Never again will the hereditary enemy threaten us!" In fairly obvious ways, Geibel's poem brings to mind those words from the second and third verses of Revelation 19 that Brahms left unset in the *Triumphlied*. Although we have reason to think Brahms might have taken Geibel's poem as a point of departure, whether he did or not is of little consequence. Apocalyptic interpretations were very much in the air.

---

were spawned by the outbreak of war, began to appear already in the summer and fall of 1870. At least two settings of Geibel's "Kriegslied," for example, one each by J. Felix and Friedrich Gernsheim, were published in November.

54 Geibel, *Heroldsrufe*, 249–50.

55 Geibel's poem appeared in the *Kemptner Zeitung*, for example, on September 13, 1870; Reinecke's setting was announced in the *Musikalisches Wochenblatt* ten days later. It was published by Kistner in November 1870 as the first of Reinecke's *Acht Gesänge für 4stimmigen Männerchor*, op. 103, and was probably first performed on a "Patriotic Liederabend" given by the Dresden Liedertafel on November 27, 1870; see *Die Tonhalle: Organ für Musikfreunde* (December 7, 1870): 775.

56 Translation in Ronald Speirs, "German Literature and the Foundation of the Second Empire," in *Germany's Two Unifications: Anticipations, Experiences, Responses*, ed. Ronald Speirs and John Breuilly (Houndsmill, Basingstoke, UK, and New York: Palgrave Macmillan, 2005), 185–208 (at 187–88).

Chapter Four

Sounding the Nation

Joh. Brahms is once again writing a larger composition, a "Song of Triumph" on Germany's political transformation.[1]

—*Musikalisches Wochenblatt*, 1872

Things now moved quickly. In November, the South German states of Bavaria, Württemberg, Baden, and Hesse were joined by treaty to the North German Confederation. In December, the Confederation was renamed the German Reich. On January 18, 1871, in an august ceremony held in the Hall of Mirrors of the Versailles Palace, King William I of Prussia accepted the title of German Emperor.[2] Ten days later Paris capitulated, an armistice was signed, and hostilities ceased. On February 26, the armistice was solidified through the signing of the preliminary Treaty of Versailles, and on May 10, a formal peace treaty was concluded in Frankfurt. This called for substantial reparations to be paid, but its most controversial provision required France to cede to Germany most of Alsace and a smaller portion

---

1 "Vermischte Mittheilungen und Notizen," *Musikalisches Wochenblatt* (February 16, 1872): 126. Brahms was by no means the only German composer to commemorate the events of 1870–71 in music. See also Wagner's *Kaisermarsch* (Imperial march), Max Bruch's *Das Lied vom deutschen Kaiser* (The song of the German emperor), op. 37, and August Klughardt's *Die Grenzberichtigung* (The correction of the border), op. 25.

2 Johannes Wischmeyer, "Buße, Andacht, patriotische Erhebung: Protestantische Inszenierungen der Reichsgründung 1871," in *Reichsgründung 1871: Ereignis–Beschreibung–Inszenierung*, ed. Michael Fischer, Christian Senkel, and Klaus Tanner (Münster: Waxman, 2010), 15–37. This date was not chosen idly: it coincided with the 170th anniversary of the elevation of the Duchy of Prussia to the status of a kingdom and the coronation of the Hohenzollern Frederick I as King in Prussia, the title used by the Prussian monarchs from 1701 until 1772 (when the title of King of Prussia began to be used).

114 ❧ CHAPTER FOUR

of Lorraine, regions on the west bank of the Rhine that had long been the subject of dispute.[3]

There was much for the liberals to like about the unification that their one-time nemesis Bismarck had brought about. The boundaries of the Reich were now firmly decided (at least until 1919). Germany had a constitution (largely taken over from that of the North German Confederation), with a parliament elected by universal male suffrage (although with a three-tier voting franchise in Prussia that gave disproportionate representation to large-estate owners and the wealthy) and a German chancellor (albeit one appointed by and answerable only to the emperor). Moreover, by working in concert with Bismarck, the moderate National Liberals were able to shape the foundational legislation and initial economic policies of the new state in accordance with their liberal program. As David Blackbourn has noted, by the liberals' lights, they had not "sacrificed 'liberal' values to the 'national' cause," nor had they chosen "unity over freedom." Rather they had "looked to extend freedom through unity." Strongly anticlerical, the National Liberals would soon become avid supporters of Bismarck's *Kulturkampf* (cultural struggle), a set of policies promulgated in the mid-1870s that were designed to reduce Catholic influence in Prussia and to a lesser degree elsewhere in Germany. Roman Catholicism was easy for the liberals to pillory for its "superstitions, eccentric devotional rituals, [and] pilgrimages to miraculous objects."[4] By contrast, Culture Protestantism was "eminently compatible with the culture of progress—indeed, progress was largely equated with Protestantism—and a sublimated Protestant pathos left its traces on bourgeois enthusiasm for everything from German unification to the German literary canon."[5] This enthusiasm no doubt can be registered in the enor-

---

3   The French held that the Rhine River was the country's natural border on the east; the Germans, that the Germanic dialects spoken in these regions made them a rightful part of the historic Reich. The lands had last changed hands by the terms of the Treaty of Westphalia in 1648, when Louis XIV claimed them for France. The subject of Klughardt's above-mentioned *Die Grenzberichtigung* obviously has to do with the Germans' "recovery" of Alsace and parts of Lorraine.

4   Helmut Walser Smith, *German Nationalism and Religious Conflict* (Princeton: Princeton University Press, 1995), 21. Brahms's correspondence and recorded conversations are peppered with scathing references to the Catholic clergy. (Brahms's preferred term was the pejorative *Pfaffen.*) See, for example, Ronald Knox, "Brahms as Wordsmith," *Gli spazi della musica* 5/2 (2016), at http://www.ojs.unito.it/index.php/spazidellamusica/article/view/2023.

5   Blackbourn, *History of Germany*, 195, 221. See also Williamson, "Protestants, Catholics, and Jews," 224–25.

SOUNDING THE NATION ❧ 115

mous popularity during Brahms's lifetime of both *A German Requiem* and the *Triumphlied*.

On January 25, 1871, three days before the fighting ended, Vienna's *Neue Freie Presse* shared with its readers a report from Berlin's *Spenersche Zeitung* that aimed to eliminate any fear that developments in the German Reich might bode ill for Austria:

> The situation ... is quite unlike that of the War of Liberation. At that time, we [Prussians] were able to cast off the French yoke only together with Russia and Austria, and when thereupon the rest of Germany fell back again into particularism, Prussia, being comparatively weak, was obliged willy-nilly to follow the absolutist policy of its mighty allies. Today Germany is fighting the struggle with France alone, and has already, in the midst of the war, become a unified Reich [*einheitliches Reich*]. Further development of the German spirit will be influenced by nothing other than itself, and when the Austrians see what the German governments and the Reichstag have achieved after the war of 1866 with respect to freedom and progress, they may free themselves of every worry that reaction might set in and take hold of us.[6]

Yet for the German liberals left out in Austria, things would get worse before they got better, although not on account of anything happening to the north. On February 6, 1871, Francis Joseph replaced the Potocki government with a new cabinet under the leadership of the conservative Count Karl Sigmund von Hohenwart. If the conservative direction taken by Potocki had been disconcerting, this move was greeted by the liberals with nothing short of alarm. The "essential feature" (*Grundzug*) of the new ministry, opined the *Neue Freie Presse*, was Czech and Catholic—the former, because Hohenwart had placed two ministries in the hands of Czechs; the latter, because of the minister-president's personal ultramontane tendencies.[7] Particularly galling was Josef Jireček's appointment as minister of religion and education. There was a reason, the paper implied, why no non-German, much less a Czech, had ever been given this important post. It was a core belief of German liberal identity that German was a universal culture while Czech was certainly not:

> Imagine handing over the entire educational system of Austria, all Austria, to a Jiricek [*sic*]; imagine the Academy of Sciences in the antechamber of a minister by the name of Jiricek; imagine the decision about the appointment of important Germans in the hands of a Czech minister; imagine the

---

6   *Spenersche Zeitung*, quoted in "Politische Uebersicht," *Neue Freie Presse, Abendblatt* (January 25, 1871): 1.

7   *Neue Freie Presse* (February 8, 1870): 1, from which the next two quotations are also taken.

116 ✤ CHAPTER FOUR

fate of our gymnasiums, our technical schools, our middle schools, our grade schools being dependent on the insight and love of a Jiricek ministry!

Jiriček's appointment, in short, was tantamount to inflicting "an undeserved Sedan on the German spirit in Austria."

The rhetoric may have been over-the-top, but the liberals' fear of what lay ahead for them was well grounded. Hohenwart immediately made known his willingness to accept a form of sub-Dualism, whereby considerable autonomy would be devolved to the Czech lands along the lines of the Compromise with Hungary, albeit within the existing Austrian framework. First, he dissolved the Bohemian Diet and called for new elections that he knew would ensure a majority of noble-conservative landowners at the expense of the German liberals. Then, after long negotiations, a tentative agreement was reached between the government in Vienna and the leaders of both sides of the Bohemian noble conservative-Czech nationalist alliance on a set of "fundamental articles" that would give a free hand to the Czechs in areas such as public education and the administration of justice in exchange for their willingness to accept the constitution and end their boycott of the Austrian Reichsrat. In September Francis Joseph indicated his intention to support the plan, including acceptance of the Bohemian Crown. Finally, on October 10, 1871, the new Bohemian Diet voted unanimously in favor of the Fundamental Articles with the understanding that the emperor would in turn ratify their acceptance and be crowned King of Bohemia.

Yet, once the details of the compromise became known, fierce negative reaction by nearly every group other than the Czech nationalists and their conservative federalist allies caused Francis Joseph to get cold feet, and on October 22 he announced his decision to take the side of the German liberals and their Hungarian negotiating partners. With the failure of the compromise, Hohenwart resigned his office on October 30, and a caretaker government was installed. Finally, in the following month the emperor restored the German liberals to power. Adolf von Auersperg was made minister-president; suggesting a moderation in tone, none of the leading figures who had served in the Bürger Ministry was included in the cabinet.[8]

Although the liberals had dodged a bullet, the events of the previous several months had been sobering, especially in light of the heady developments taking place under the National Liberals in the new German Reich. An ideological division soon emerged within their ranks that led, in turn, to

---

8   Jonathan Kwan, *Liberalism and the Habsburg Monarchy, 1861–1895* (Houndsmill, Basingstoke, UK, and New York: Palgrave Macmillan, 2014), 71–82; and Luther Höbelt, "Devolution Aborted: Franz Joseph I and the Bohemian 'Fundamental Articles' of 1871," *Parliaments, Estates and Representation* 32 (2012): 37–52.

SOUNDING THE NATION 117

the founding of a new daily newspaper in Vienna with an explicitly German-nationalist point of view. As Sigmund Mayer later explained: "The success against Hohenwart had emboldened the younger elements of the German Liberal party [in Austria]; they were called, in contrast to [the party's traditional leaders], the 'Young Germans.' Although it had fought against Hohenwart with unequaled verve and polish, the *Neue Freie Presse* did not satisfy them, [so] they founded the *Deutsche Zeitung*."[9]

The inaugural issue of this new organ appeared on December 17, 1871, and included a *feuilleton* entitled "Der Gott im deutschen Lager" (God in the German camp) by Ludwig Speidel.[10] This begins by celebrating Germany's triumphs in the "great world-historic year of 1870" but soon turns more reflective. After briefly touching on the outpouring of thanksgiving to the biblical god engendered by the founding of the German Reich, Speidel takes up his main purpose by describing a second god who was "in the German camp," one more in keeping with his own—and, it is fair to think, Brahms's—liberal sensibilities. This god was no divine being but was rather the secular work ethic of the Germans themselves, "a deeply moral spirit of work, an anonymous god, who rules throughout German history." This second god, which had supposedly enabled the Germans to rise from slight beginnings to great accomplishment, was not only in the camp of the citizens of the German Reich, Speidel adds, but was also in the Austrian camp. Speidel then concludes in the spirit of the new paper itself: "And this heroic and victorious god will be in the camp of the Germans of Austria and will battle for their cause, as long as they remain true to him in their sincere beliefs."

"Der Gott im deutschen Lager" speaks to a German cultural zone that took little notice of the international border that now separated Germany from Austria, something akin to what has been called, with respect to the diplomatic relations that eventually developed between the two states, a

---

9   Sigmund Mayer, *Ein jüdischer Kaufmann, 1831 bis 1911: Lebenserinnerungen* (Leipzig: Duncker & Humblot, 1911), 241. Mayer offers a concise discussion of the controversy engendered by Hohenwart's appointment written from the German-liberal point of view, ibid., 236–42. Theodor Billroth owned stock in the company and briefly served on the paper's political advisory board, along with Carl Auersperg and Karl Rechbauer, two members of the former Bürger Ministry. See Billroth's letter to Lübke of December 31, 1871, in Billroth, *Briefe*, 5th ed., 151–53. In the published edition, the letter is mistakenly dated December 31, 1872; the correct date can be ascertained by its contents.

10   L. Sp. [Ludwig Speidel], "Der Gott in der deutschen Lager," *Deutsche Zeitung* (December 17, 1871): 1–3. Speidel was the long-serving music critic for *Fremdenblatt* and would later serve as the theater critic for the *Neue Freie Presse*.

118 &❧ CHAPTER FOUR

"sphere of German nationality."[11] As it happens, this was the moment when Brahms took the decisive step of moving permanently to Vienna. In October 1871, he received word that he would be offered the position as artistic director of the Gesellschaft der Musikfreunde. On November 16 the current director, Anton Rubinstein, gave notice of his resignation at the end of the season that was just beginning. And on November 27 a formal offer was extended to Brahms for the twin positions of artistic director and director of the Choral Society. After briefly hesitating, the composer accepted early in the next month.[12] With his position now secure, on December 27 Brahms moved into an apartment at Karlsgasse 4, situated in Vienna's Fourth District within sight of the Musikverein. From this perch, which would remain his home for the remaining twenty-five years of his life, Brahms would come to inhabit the new transnational German cultural sphere in a way like no other composer. Hereafter, to borrow a notion from Celia Applegate, he "mapped out a kind of amalgamation of, even reconciliation between, Austria and the Germany of 1871."[13]

From One Chorus to Three

This brief excursus into Austrian politics in 1871 provides the context in which to understand the state of mind in which Brahms took up work again on the *Triumphlied*, one no longer marked by the apocalyptic war fever of the previous year. The first mention of his decision to expand the composition beyond the chorus first heard in Bremen, as we have seen, came in a letter to Reinthaler from late February, notably, a few weeks after Hohenwart had taken office. Shortly after that the composer's friend Billroth reported pessimistically on the Habsburg situation in a letter of March 2, 1871, to Ernst Julius Gurlt, a fellow physician in Berlin: "we Germans [here in Austria] are only tolerated; the state is becoming more and more Slavic and Hungarian. It is a matter of life and death ... that we at least maintain our scholarly connection with the German Empire."[14] And we can easily imagine that for Brahms, now hoping for a permanent position at the Musikverein, it was no

---

11 Breuilly, *Austria, Prussia, and the Making of Germany 1806–1871*, 89.

12 Letter to Levi of October 1871, in *Briefwechsel*, 7: 84–85; Biba, "Brahms und die Gesellschaft der Musikfreunde in Wien," 47–48, 50–51.

13 Celia Applegate, "Music in Place: Perspectives on Art Culture in Nineteenth-Century Germany," in *Localism, Landscape, and the Ambiguities of Place: German-Speaking Central Europe, 1860–1930*, ed. David Blackbourn and James Retallack (Toronto: University of Toronto Press, 2005), 39–59 (at 53).

14 Letter of March 2, 1871, in Billroth, *Briefe*, 5th ed., 141.

SOUNDING THE NATION & 119

less a metaphorical matter of life or death to maintain a musical as well as political connection with the unified German state to the north.

On March 20, with his performance of *A German Requiem* in Vienna behind him, the composer undertook his first visit to the new Germany, experiencing with pleasure all the national euphoria generated by the recent turn of events. He first passed through Berlin on his way home to Hamburg, and then, following concerts in Lübeck and Oldenburg, arrived in Bremen a few days before the Good Friday performances of the *Requiem* and the original incarnation of the *Triumphlied*. Catching up to him was a letter from Levi that, among other things, urged him to come celebrate in Karlrsuhe: "Allgeyer is cheerful, has eaten a dozen Frenchmen for breakfast every morning during the war, along with some articles by Treitschke, has discoursed more in the [past] six months than in the previous 40 years, and is, by the way, a splendid man who would greet you if he knew I were writing."[15] (That Brahms was a secular Protestant, Allgeyer a secular Catholic, and Levi a secular Jew shows how, within Brahms's liberal circle, this kind of heighted German pride in 1870–71 knew no sectarian divisions among the freethinkers.)

Brahms picked up on Levi's tone in his response: "You're right, I absolutely had to come to Germany. I had to take my part in the celebration. I could suffer Vienna no longer.... Long live Bismarck, in whom culminates all that has moved us beside ourselves. I'll be there in May."[16] At the same time as announcing to Clara Schumann his imminent arrival in Baden for the summer, he suggested making a trip together to nearby Alsace in order to relive the recent victory over the French, whom, in a likely reference to the widely condemned excesses of the Paris Commune (March 18–May 28, 1871), he described as "despicable" (*jämmerlich*) and more responsible than even their worst enemy for the fact that all sympathy for them had been lost.[17] Then, writing to Billroth, he expressed a child-like delight at being

---

15 Letter of March 31, 1871, in *Briefwechsel*, 7: 70. Heinrich Treitschke was a leading light of the Prussian School of history. Beginning in 1871, he served as a National Liberal member of the Reichstag.

16 Letter dated April 1871, in *Briefwechsel*, 7: 71. See also Brahms's undated letter to Reinthaler of March 1871 in which he suggests, in jest, performing a public toast to Bismarck at the Bremen performance using the words of the traditional celebratory song "Hoch soll er leben," which, in this context, might be best translated as "For he's a jolly good fellow!" (*Briefwechsel*, 3: 37).

17 Unpublished letter of April 1871, New York, Pierpont Morgan Library (MFC B8135.S392). As Heinrich August Winkler has noted, "the red revolution of the Communards" went a long way to establishing the newly founded German Reich in the eyes of the rest of Europe as "a custodian of the public order." Winkler, *Germany: The Long Road West*, 192.

120 &❧ CHAPTER FOUR

back again in Germany, where he was reading with great pleasure "surgical letters and see[ing] French prisoners."[18]

"The *Triumphlied* is sleeping at the moment," Brahms reported to Simrock upon his arrival in Lichtenthal, thus signaling that he had not yet made much, if any, progress toward expanding it beyond the single chorus heard in Bremen.[19] As his summer working holiday began, he instead went about completing a very different kind of song for chorus and orchestra, the *Schicksalslied*, op. 54, on a text from Hölderlin's *Hyperion*, which Levi and his copyists in Karlsruhe made ready for its première there under Brahms's direction on October 18, 1871. In the meanwhile, however, Levi wrote on August 11 to urge the composer, in mock-serious Latin, to get back to work on the *Triumphlied*: "Furthermore, I propose that you complete your Te Deum and dedicate it to Bismarck."[20] Whether or not the Iron Chancellor was the "secret programmatic hero" of the work, as one scholar has recently suggested, Brahms unquestionably thought of it as a tribute to what Bismarck had achieved.[21] On September 24, Brahms wrote to Simrock, quipping: "I'll be going to Vienna shortly and am hoping for [a performance] of my 'Bismarck Song' in Cologne. Once I have succeeded in extoling the man in a reasonably worthy manner, I'll become quite debauched, I promise you, and really cut loose, on music paper, of course [i.e. finish and send the score]. But that way, I can still savor my katzenjammer to the fullest. It'll be useless, all the same; for all have sinned and fall short of the glory." Here, at the end, Brahms alluded to Luther's translation of Romans 3:23; in the Pauline epistle it is humankind that falls short of the glory of God, whereas in Brahms's rather flippant take it is the metaphorically intoxicated composer himself who has fallen short of conveying the

---

18   Letter of May 1871, in *Billroth und Brahms im Briefwechsel*, ed. Otto Gottlieb-Billroth (Berlin and Vienna: Urban & Schwarzenberg, 1935), 193. At the time of this writing, Billroth's reports from the military hospitals where he had been stationed in 1870 were appearing in serialized form in the *Berliner klinischen Wochenschrift*; they were subsequently collected and published as *Chirurgische Briefe aus den Kriegs-Lazarethen in Weissenburg und Mannheim, 1870* (Berlin: August Hirschwald, 1872). The copy in Brahms's library carries Billroth's handwritten inscription: "Lieben deutschen Freunde Johannes Brahms zur Erinnerung an das Jahr 1870" (To my dear German friend Johannes Brahms in memory of the year 1870).

19   Letter of May 22, 1871, in *Briefwechsel*, 9: 102.

20   "Caeterum censeo, Te Deum esse perficiendum et Bismarckio dedicandum." *Briefwechsel*, 7: 78.

21   Schüssler-Bach, "Von Nutzen und Nachteil der Historie," 864.

glory of the Iron Chancellor's accomplishment.[22] This notably profane use of the biblical text is suggestive: for Brahms, the Luther Bible was not solely a sacred text; it was what one contemporary called the "act of creation of that which we now call our nation," and celebrating the creation of that nation was something well worth the price of a hangover.[23] Two days later Simrock responded in the same jesting manner: "I hope your *Triumphlied* will be finished soon—I am placing the greatest hopes on the debaucheries [*Ausschweifungen*] you have begun there."[24]

In the middle of October, when it still seemed likely that Francis Joseph would ratify the Fundamental Articles, Brahms wrote to Joseph Joachim, head of the new Prussian Hochschule für Musik, and used the *Triumphlied* to express his alienation from the "anti-German" compromise Hohenwart was on the verge of achieving in Austria: "I intend to come to Berlin this winter and make a proper stay of it; after all, I can hardly sing to the Bohemian [i.e. Czech] Ministers in Vienna a song I have written acclaiming Bismarck."[25] Shortly thereafter, back in the Austrian capital for the concert season, Brahms dispatched an installment of the music to Levi, asking him to arrange for the copying of the parts, and offering him, in a roundabout way, the first performance: "Have another look at the Bismarck-Lied, and if you want to perform it on Palm Sunday (or earlier), give it to the copyist [Josef Füller] and ask him to write out everything needed."[26]

---

22   "Nützen tut der doch nichts; sie sind allzumal Sünder und ermangeln des Ruhmes." Letter from Brahms to Simrock of September 24, 1871, in *Briefwechsel*, 9: 104. In the Luther Bible, Romans 3:23 reads: "Denn es ist hier kein Unterschied; sie sind allzumal Sünder und mangeln des Ruhmes, den sie bei Gott haben sollten."

23   Wilhelm Scherer, "Die deutsche Spracheinheit," in *Vortäge und Aufsätze zur Geschichte des geistigen Lebens in Deutschland und Österreich* (Berlin: Weidmannsche, 1874), 55, quoted in Smith, *German Nationalism and Religious Conflict*, 23–24.

24   Letter from Simrock to Brahms of September 26, 1871, in *Johannes Brahms und Fritz Simrock*, ed. Stephenson, 51.

25   Undated letter from Brahms to Joachim of October 1871, in Avins, *Johannes Brahms: Life and Letters*, 427. The content of this letter indicates that it was written shortly before Brahms left Baden for Vienna around October 22. I have adapted the translation here by substituting "Czech" for "Bohemian" to make the point of Brahms's complaint clear. In German usage at this time, *böhmisch* implied Czech identity; *deutschböhmisch*, German identity.

26   Letter from Brahms to Levi of October 1871, in *Briefwechsel*, 7: 84–85. Brahms must have had learned from Levi that he was planning to give a special concert on the following Palm Sunday (March 24, 1872) for which the work might be appropriate; see the discussion that follows in the text.

122 &❧ CHAPTER FOUR

The end was now in sight. From Levi's letter to Clara Schumann of November 26, we learn that on the day before Brahms had finally sent the rest of the score for copying, and that the proposed première on Palm Sunday had been confirmed.[27] Simrock made no secret of his eagerness to get his hands on the completed work, and finally, likewise on November 26, Brahms was able, in his teasing manner, to assure the impatient publisher that the orchestral and choral parts would soon be on their way: "You must be thinking of the *Triumphlied* as the latest sea serpent. It would be best if you were not convinced of its existence. But things have turned out differently, and the monster has made it to land so you can take a look at it."[28]

Nation Building in Music

Levi was in fact the first in Brahms's circle to see the monster in its final form. Expressing in no uncertain terms his approval of what Brahms had achieved, he wrote the composer on November 30 to exclaim: "All hail, praise, and thanksgiving for the hour when you were born to the nation!"[29] But what nation? Formal unification of twenty-six constituent monarchies, grand duchies and duchies, principalities, free cities, and the newly acquired imperial territory of Alsace-Lorraine did not establish universal German nation-state identity overnight. Indeed, as Helmut Walser Smith notes, strictly speaking, the Reich was not a true nation-state at all; instead it was— here he quotes from its constitution—"a 'permanent alliance' of the sovereigns of individual states for the protection of 'federal territory' and 'the care and welfare of the German people.'" Because of this, he continues, there was much work to be done before "Imperial Germany, ... rooted in the legacy of

---

27   Berthold Litzmann, *Clara Schumann, Ein Künstlerleben nach Tagebüchern und Briefen*, 3 vols. (Leipzig: Breitkopf & Härtel, 1920), 3: 265. As we have seen, in September Brahms mentioned to Simrock that he would seek a first performance in Cologne, where Ferdinand Hiller was the city's music director; he made same suggestion to Reinthaler in a letter from near the end of October; see *Briefwechsel*, 3: 40–41.

28   Letter from Brahms to Levi of October 1871, in *Briefwechsel*, 7: 84–85; letter from Brahms to Simrock of November 26, 1871, in *Briefwechsel*, 9: 107.

29   Letter from Levi to Brahms of November 30, 1871, in *Briefwechsel*, 7: 86. See also the portion of Levi's letter to Clara Schumann of November 26, quoted in translation in Minor, *Choral Fantasies*, 118, and Levi's even more enthusiastic letter to Clara of December 27, in Litzmann, *Clara Schumann, Ein Künstlerleben*, 3: 266–67.

the dynastic territorial state, [would come to] seem ... 'an objective nation' with a definitive shape."[30]

Brahms recognized at once the challenge and saw the task at hand. "We experienced the beginning together," he wrote to Senff in November 1870, in a clear reference to the founding of the North German Confederation three years earlier. "What has happened since then! May God grant that the Germans come to terms with themselves as easily and beautifully as they have with the French."[31] The challenge was in fact bigger than that. Within the Reich's boundaries were many peoples—Danes to the north, Poles to the east, and many of the newly incorporated Alsace-Lorrainers to the west— who, if asked, would have preferred not to be a part of it. And to the south, in Austria, were millions of Germans who had unwillingly been left out. Austria's expulsion, moreover, shifted Germany's sectarian divide further in favor of the Protestants (now on the order of 2:1), making the Catholics still another disgruntled minority.[32]

Yet, the National Liberals hoped that a common national identity could be inculcated by what Heinrich August Winkler has called "the hegemony of the Protestant principle in German culture, society, and state." This implied "*both* the continuing secularization of German Protestantism, making religion ideologically of very flexible utility, *and* the increased theologization of German nationalism." As noted, Culture Protestantism was essential to German bourgeois self-understanding, whereby German culture was assumed to be Protestant and Culture Protestantism was held to represent progress.[33] The second and third movements of the *Triumphlied* can be viewed productively in this light, as Brahms's contribution to the nation-building process.[34] Indeed, the completed work projects something

---

30   Helmut Walser Smith, *Germany: A Nation in Its Time: Before, During, and After Nationalism, 1500–2000* (New York: Liveright, 2020), 259–60.

31   *Briefwechsel*, 14: 194, partially translated in Minor, *Choral Fantasies*, 124.

32   Helpful here is the overview provided in Jennifer Jenkins, "Particularism and Localism," in *The Ashgate Research Companion to Imperial Germany*, ed. Matthew Jeffries (London and New York: Routledge, 2015), 195–208; and Alon Confino, *The Nation as a Local Metaphor: Württemburg, Imperial Germany, and National Memory, 1871–1918* (Chapel Hill, NC, and London: University of North Carolina Press, 1997). See also Stefan Berger, "Building the Nation among Visions of German Empire," in *Nationalizing Empires*, ed. Stefan Berger and Alexei Miller (Budapest: Central European University Press, 2014), 247–308 (at 250–60).

33   Winkler, *Germany: The Long Road West*, 1:199 (emphasis in the original); Blackbourn, *History of Germany 1780–1918*, 221.

34   Minor (*Choral Fantasies*, 123–25) also notes that the composition does nationalist work. In the same discussion, however, he overstates the nationalist

124 &❧ CHAPTER FOUR

of the confluence, as J. S. Conway has put it, of "Prussian vitality, the Hohenzollern dynasty, a 'high' culture in art, music and literature, and the morality of liberal Protestantism" that would create a set of national values, or so the founders believed, largely synonymous with "enlightened Prussian Protestantism."[35]

Let us take each of these "nation-building" movements up in turn. The second chorus (*Mäßig belebt*) unfolds in a serial tripartite form (ABC), each section of which is devoted to one of three constituent half verses (Revelation 19:5b, 6b, and 7a):

A Lobet unsern Gott, alle seine Knechte und die ihn fürchten, Kleine und Große. (Rev. 19:5b)

Praise our God, all His servants and those who fear Him, small and great;

B Halleluja! denn der allmächtige Gott hat das Reich eingenommen. (Rev. 19:6b)

Alleluia! for God Almighty reigns.

C Laß uns freuen und fröhlich sein und ihm die Ehre geben. (Rev. 19:7a)

Let us be glad and rejoice and give honor to Him.

The A and C sections, both in the key of G major, are generally quieter and more reflective in nature, although the first displays some of the same features (dotted rhythms and jumping octaves) that permeate the "victory-celebrating" opening chorus. The livelier B section (*Lebhaft*), by contrast, bursts forth in D major, the main key of the *Triumphlied*'s two outer movements, with trumpet fanfares and renewed choral exclamations of "Hallelujah." These quickly usher in a fugato setting of the linchpin words "Denn der allmächtige Gott hat das Reich eingenommen" (For God Almighty reigns).[36]

This passage cries out to be read allegorically (Example 8). By setting the salient biblical text as a fugato, a learned procedure that, with Beethoven, had become associated with monumentality, Brahms was in effect creating a national monument in tone, one in which, to borrow an apt metaphor from Kalbeck, "all the German tribes seem to participate in the polyphony, which

---

significance of the use in the published score of German rather than Italian names for the instruments. Brahms only wanted the instruments to be named consistently in one language or the other, evidently leaving the decision of which language to be made by the publisher. See the composer's letters to Simrock of October 7 and October 10, 1872, in *Briefwechsel*, 9: 129–32.

35   J. S. Conway, Review of Helmut Walser Smith, *German Nationalism and Religious Conflict: Culture, Ideology, Politics, 1870–1914*, H-Net Reviews (July 1995). http://www.h-net.org/reviews/showrev.php?id=113.

36   In his translation of Rev. 19:6b as given in the Luther Bible, Minor (*Choral Fantasies*, 144) makes a rhetorical point by leaving *Reich* in the original German ("For the almighty God has won the Reich").

Example 8. Brahms, *Triumphlied*, op. 55, second movement, mm. 110–19 (voices only, *f sempre*).

(—*continued*)

Example 8—concluded

obeys a higher unity."[37] Moreover, just as Handel, in his oratorios, had used stories of triumphant Hebrew kings to proclaim the glories of the Hanoverian monarchy, so, in the *Triumphlied*, the freethinking Brahms would seem to be using the Judeo-Christian deity as a stand-in for the Hohenzollern monarchy, now in the person of the German emperor, William I. Here, then, we can discern a slippage between altar and throne: nationalism and religion are in contact with one another in a manner characteristic of the tenets of Culture Protestantism.

The slower final section of the chorus (*Ziemlich langsam, doch nicht schleppend*) grows out of what precedes it by means of a beautiful transition back to G major that seemingly transports the listener into a suspended, timeless sphere.[38] Singing in ¼ meter, Chorus 1 sets out with the first phrase of verse 7a ("Laß uns freuen"). As Chorus 2 responds by singing the first two phrases in lilting ⁱ²⁄₈ meter ("Laß uns freuen und fröhlich sein"), the winds intone the head motive of the familiar chorale "Nun danket alle Gott" (Now thank we all our God). Later, just before the end of the movement, the pairing of the chorale head motive in the winds and the first two phrases of the verse in Chorus 2 returns (mm. 172ff.). This time, however, Brahms carries the quotation of the chorale another two measures further, not in the winds, but in Chorus 1, which brings the biblical verse to a close by singing its third and final phrase ("und ihm die Ehre geben") (Example 9).

By Brahms's time "Nun danket alle Gott" had enjoyed a long history of being sung in Germany at times of thanksgiving of all kinds, whether religious, civil, or military. It eventually came to be known in some circles as the Leuthen Chorale, after it was spontaneously sung by the army of Frederick the Great after its improbable victory in 1757 over much larger Austrian forces in the Battle of Leuthen.[39] It was later used in this fashion,

---

37   Kalbeck, *Johannes Brahms*, 2: 356. On the association of fugal procedure with monumentality, see Carl Dahlhaus, *Ludwig van Beethoven: Approaches to his Music*, trans. Mary Whittall (Cambridge: Cambridge University Press, 1991), 77–80, cited in both Beller-McKenna, *Brahms and the German Spirit*, 110, and Minor, *Choral Fantasies*, 144. See also Hans A. Pohlsander, *National Monuments and Nationalism in 19th Century Germany* (Bern: Peter Lang, 2008).

38   Both Minor (*Choral Fantasies*, 146–47) and Beller-McKenna (*Brahms and the German Spirit*, 111–14) rightly draw particular attention to this moment.

39   For useful studies, see Bernhard R. Kroener, "'Nun danket alle Gott': Der Choral von Leuthen und Friedrich der Große als protestantischer Held. Die Produktion politischer Mythen im 19. und 20. Jahrhunderts," in *"Gott mit uns: Nation, Religion und Gewalt im 19. und frühen 20. Jahrhundert,"* ed. Gerd Krumeich and Hartmut Lehmann (Göttingen: Vandenhoeck & Ruprecht, 2000), 105–34. Siegmar Keil, "Der 'Choral von Leuthen': Ein

Example 9a. Brahms, *Triumphlied*, op. 55, second movement (reduction), mm. 143–49

Example 9b. Brahms, *Triumphlied*, op. 55, second movement (reduction), mm. 172–end.

(—*continued*)

Example 9b—*concluded*

SOUNDING THE NATION &**❧** 131

often with the words changed to make them more topical, during the Wars of Liberation and the Franco-Prussian War, and it would be so used again during the First World War.[40] For Sabine Giesbrecht-Schutte, this practice suggests that the chorale's once exclusively Christian tradition eventually took on "militant-national" trappings; after 1848, she writes, the tune even approached the status of "a motto of Prussian expansionist policy." Evidently with this account in mind, Minor proposes that Brahms quoted this "war song" as a means by which to "celebrate the territorial spoils of war."[41]

Whatever one might say about the first movement of Op. 55, which after all does celebrate a great military victory, Brahms's allusion to "Nun danket alle Gott" in the second movement has nothing warlike about it. We would do well, then, to look elsewhere for an explanation of the chorale's use in the *Triumphlied*. Brahms may have taken inspiration from the Imperial Proclamation ceremony held in Versailles on January 18, 1871. This featured a lengthy consecration address (*Weiherede*) in which the Berlin court and garrison chaplain Bernhard Rogge not only asked for God's blessing on the new German Reich and the new German emperor, but prayed that the military victory over France would bring a "lasting and honorable peace," that "the German Reich [*das deutsche Reich*] might strengthen itself inwardly and outwardly into "a land of peace [*ein Reich des Friedens*]" both at home and abroad, and that "the fall of proud and mighty France [might] serve as a warning to Germany against all hubris."[42] To these petitions the congregation responded with the singing of "Nun danket alle Gott." The ending of Brahms's second chorus—which has nothing hubristic about it either—seems in keeping with precisely the sentiments expressed in Rogge's address. That Brahms tacked on an implied Amen cadence only strengthens the association of this music with the ad hoc liturgical service held in Versailles (see the final two measures of Example 9b).

---

preußisch-deutscher Mythos," *Die Tonkunst: Magazin für klassische Musik und Musikwissenschaft* 1 (2007): 442–49; and Siegmar Keil, "Eine Melodie im Wandel: Metamorphosen des Kirchenliedes 'Nun danket alle Gott,'" *Jahrbuch für Liturgik und Hymnologie* 51 (2012): 203–21.

40 Michael Fischer, s.v. "Nun danket alle Gott," *Populäre und Traditionelle Lieder: Historisch-kritisches Liederlexikon*, https://www.liederlexikon.de/lieder/nun_danket_alle_gott.

41 Giesbrecht-Schutte, "Gründerzeitliche Festkultur," 84–85; Minor, *Choral Fantasies*, 146, 147.

42 Of the many press reports easily available to Brahms in Vienna, see, for example, W. v. R., "Die Kaiser-Proclamirung in Versailles," *Neue Freie Presse* (January 24, 1871): 1–3; and "Politische Uebersicht," *Neue Freie Presse, Abendblatt* (January 25, 1871): 1, from which I have quoted here.

132 ❧ CHAPTER FOUR

Following the singing of the chorale, the Prussian king and his party gathered in a half-circle in front of the dais for Bismarck's reading of the imperial proclamation. In this address, the emperor pledged to protect the rights of the Reich and its members, to preserve the peace, support the independence of Germany, and strengthen the power of the people. He expressed hope for a lasting peace within borders that would ensure against French aggression, and he concluded by asking for God's blessing on him and his successors to the crown so that they might "at all times increase the wealth of the German Empire [i.e. Reich], not by military conquests, but by the blessings and the gifts of peace in the realm of national prosperity, liberty, and morality."[43] The brief silence that followed Bismarck's reading of the proclamation was broken when the Grand Duke of Baden cried out to salute the new German emperor, and general jubilation ensued.

This digression into the order of events in Versailles sheds light on an anecdote related by Brahms's Swiss friend Josef Viktor Widmann. On October 20, 1895, Brahms led a performance of the *Triumphlied* in Zurich by way of inaugurating the city's new *Tonhalle*. After this performance Brahms asked Widmann whether he had detected "how in the second chorus, when the melody 'Nun danket alle Gott' begins to sound, all the bells ring out victory as it were, and a festive Te Deum resonates throughout the land."[44] Since the chorale tune brings the second chorus to its quiet close, the celebratory music to which the composer referred here must be found in the third chorus.

Once again the music unfolds in a serial tripartite form:

A Und ich sahe den Himmel aufgetan; und siehe, ein weißes Pferd, und der darauf saß, hieß: Treu und Wahrhaftig, und richtet und streitet mit Gerechtigkeit. (Rev. 19:11)

And I saw heaven opened, and behold, a white horse; and he who sat upon it is called Faithful and True, and in righteousness judges and makes war.

---

43 Brahms was unquestionably familiar with this text, since the imperial proclamation was published widely in the press. Here I have quoted from "Proklamirung der deutschen Kaiserwürde," *Neues Wiener Tagblatt* (January 19, 1871): 3, and have taken my translation from the Internet History Sourcebooks Projects (https://sourcebooks.fordham.edu/mod/germanunification.asp).

44 J. V. Widmann, *Johannes Brahms in Erinnerungen* (Berlin: Gebrüder Paetel, 1898), 117; repr. (Zurich: Rotapfel-Verlag, 1980), 111. Cf. Philipp Spitta, "Johannes Brahms," in his *Zur Musik: Sechszehn Aufsätze* (Berlin: Gebrüder Paetel, 1892), 385–427 (at 413–14).

B Und er tritt die Kelter des Weins des grimmigen Zorns des allmächtigen Gottes. (Rev. 19:15b)	And he treads the winepress of the fierce wrath of Almighty God.
C Und hat einen Namen geschrieben auf seinem Kleide, und auf seiner Hüfte, also: Ein König aller Könige, und ein Herr aller Herrn. Halleluja. Amen! (Rev. 19:16)	And on his robe and on his thigh a name is written: King of Kings, and Lord of Lords. Alleluia. Amen!

Once more, the biblical text invited political allegory. In Christian eschatology, the rider on a white horse in heaven is thought to symbolize Jesus Christ; in the *Triumphlied* he can be (and was at the time) understood to be Emperor William and his successors to the crown.[45] And if the vision of John told in the biblical text has to do with the Second Coming, Brahms's musical setting concerns the establishment of the Second Reich, for which, as Gustav Freytag put it, the Germans had been waiting since the death of Emperor Frederick I (the legendary Frederick Barbarossa) at the end of the twelfth century.

Following a short introduction in D minor that rehearses the dotted rhythms of the first chorus (and those of the beginning of the second), the music turns quiet on the dominant, A, for the dramatic entry of a solo baritone in the role of John: "And I saw heaven opened, and behold, a white horse; and he who sat upon it …" Three times the soloist is interrupted by the two choruses, which echo his words in turn. The first two interruptions are quiet and only momentary. The third, by contrast, is marked by an intensification of both tempo and dynamics and a change from duple to triple meter. The choruses unite and usurp the baritone solo entirely as they complete the verse alone ("and he who sat upon it is called Faithful and True, and in righteousness judges and makes war"). The music now unfolds in D major, with hurtling triplets to illustrate the galloping of the rider's white horse.

---

45   Brahms instructed Simrock to show on the dedicatory page an image of the crown, the Prussian eagle, or the imperial coat of arms; see the letter of September 6, 1872, in *Briefwechsel*, 9: 125–27 (at 125). See also James R. Edwards, "The Rider on the White Horse, the Thigh Inscription, and Apollo: Revelation 19:16," *Journal of Biblical Literature* 137 (2018): 519–36; and McKenna, *Brahms and the German Spirit*, 118. For an early symbolic reading of the rider of the white horse as the German emperor, see Theodor Helm, "Brahms' 'Triumphlied' im ersten Gesellschaftsconcerte zu Wien," *Musikalisches Wochenblatt* 4 (1873): 10–11. A reproduction of Ferdinand Keller's painting "Apotheose Kaiser Wilhelms I" (1888), which depicts the emperor, mounted on a white horse, passing triumphantly through the Brandenburg Gate in Berlin after the victory over France in 1871, is accessible in Artstor: https://www.jstor.org/stable/community.15714656.

CHAPTER FOUR

The "fierce wrath of the Almighty God" is depicted in the ensuing B section (*Etwas lebhafter*), which is set in the new key of F♯ minor and features appropriately severe canonic writing. This soon gives way to the C section. The solo baritone makes a brief reappearance ("And on his robe and on his thigh a name is written") to prepare for the massive and resplendent concluding chorus in D major (marked *Feierlich*) ("King of kings and Lord of lords. Hallelujah"). Here we find the "festive Te Deum" of which Brahms spoke to Widmann, cloaked in a Handelian robe and practically quoting the "Hallelujah Chorus."[46] For the patriotic Brahms, and for many others of his time, the sentiments expressed in this setting seemed entirely proper, correct, and beneficial. It is no wonder, then, that the composer eventually settled on offering the dedication of the published score to the German emperor.

The First Performance

The première of the completed work took place, not on Palm Sunday, as Brahms and Levi had originally envisioned, but on June 5, 1872, as the final number in a festive concert given under Levi's direction at the Grand Ducal Theater in Karlsruhe. On May 22 Brahms wrote Billroth from nearby Lichtenthal to encourage him to make the long trip from Vienna to be in attendance: "It would be wonderful if you were among our listeners.... Because of the many singers and the extravaganza, the concert is to be given in the theater, after which there will be an opportunity to drink our toast to Bismarck." Much to his regret, Billroth was unable to be present, but under the cover of a heartfelt letter, he sent an appropriate gift to mark the grand occasion, a silver cup inscribed: "To the master of German music, Johannes Brahms, in memory of June 5, 1872":

> It was my intention to have a pre-concert drink [*vortrinken*] with you on June 5 from the enclosed beaker, and I would have chosen Alsatian wine. Unfortunately, that cannot be, and so I send cordial greetings from afar. My heart was thirsting for the refreshment of your beautiful music, but for now my thirst shall not be satisfied. When you drink from this chalice on this occasion, a thought will also fly to me, who in his unfortunately ever dwindling time for quiet reflection truly takes refuge in your art and owes so many beautiful hours to it. So, prosit![47]

---

46 For a summary of the many points of connection between the two works, see Victor Ravizza, *Brahms: Spätzeitmusik. Die sinfonische Chorwerke* (Schliengen: Edition Argus, 2008), 207.

47 Letter from Brahms to Billroth of May 22, 1872, and from Billroth to Brahms of June 1, 1872, in *Billroth und Brahms im Briefwechsel*, 196–97. For Brahms's

Viennese newspapers did not generally cover concerts given abroad, but the new *Deutsche Zeitung* made an exception when it sent Franz Gehring to report on the work from Karlsruhe. Nine months earlier Brahms had taken the lead in recruiting Gehring, a mathematician and writer on music who was then based in Bonn, to become the newspaper's first music critic. "German-minded men in Vienna and all Austria intend to found a great new German-national newspaper," as the composer explained in a letter of September 1871, and "I am asked to request whether you would be inclined under favorable conditions to relocate to Vienna and take over the position."[48] Several aspects of Gehring's lengthy review merit consideration, beginning with how the première at hand had come about.[49] The performance that Levi had originally planned for Palm Sunday, we are told, was to have been a part, notably, of a "grand musical celebration of peace" (*große musikalische Friedensfeier*). We also learn that a second performance of the work had been announced for the Lower Rhenish Music Festival in Düsseldorf that May. The siting of this festival along the Rhine River, a potent symbol of German national and cultural identity, would have made it a particularly fitting venue for the new piece, but this performance too was cancelled, in this case because the organizers refused Brahms's request to conduct it himself.

The aborted Düsseldorf performance had been in the works for a long time. In the same letter of October 1871 in which Brahms offered Levi the Palm Sunday performance, he hinted that he was quietly hoping to schedule a second performance to follow later in the spring: "Just between us, we are in a rush [to get the copying done], since there is apparently [to be] a grand performance immediately after yours, about which I can say nothing yet."[50] In December Brahms was able to be more forthcoming:

---

    moving acknowledgment of the present, see his letter to Billroth of June 9, 1872, ibid., 198, trans. in Avins, *Johannes Brahms*, 441.

48   Kurt Hofmann and Renate Hofmann, "Einige Splittern aus dem 'Faber-Nachlaß,'" in *Festschrift Otto Biba zum 60. Geburtstag*, ed. Ingrid Fuchs (Tutzing: Hans Schneider, 2008), 357–81 (at 365–70, quoted at 366). In his letter to Levi of October 1871, Brahms reported Gehring's arrival in Vienna and asked for Levi's assistance in obtaining the services of Otto Devrient, an actor and dramatist based in the Grand Ducal Theater, as a theatre correspondent; see *Briefwechsel*, 7: 85.

49   Franz Gehring, "Triumphlied auf den Sieg der deutschen Waffen," *Deutsche Zeitung* (June 11, 1872), 1–3. See also Franz Gehring, "Triumphlied (auf den Sieg der deutschen Waffen) von Johannes Brahms," *Allgemeine musikalische Zeitung* 7 (June 26, 1872): cols. 409–14.

50   *Briefwechsel*, 7: 84. See also Brahms's letter to Simrock of November 26, 1871, in *Briefwechsel*, 9: 107.

136 &❧ CHAPTER FOUR

Rubinstein is directing the [Lower Rhenish] Music Festival in Düsseldorf. He wanted to perform a piece of mine, and now this [i.e., the *Triumphlied*] is fine with him. Of course, no one has invited me to conduct it myself, and the Comité has not even written me directly. Since it is a question of an unpublished work, I may perhaps put in a case [for doing it myself]; for the time being, I'm held off by consideration of Rubinstein.[51]

As matters stood at the turn of the year, then, Levi was to conduct the première on Palm Sunday (March 24) using the relatively small forces available in Karlsruhe, and Rubinstein was to follow with a grand performance on May 21, during Pentecost, at the Lower Rhenish Music Festival. After witnessing Rubinstein's disappointing performance of the *Schicksalslied* at the Musikverein on January 21, however, Brahms came to regret his earlier tacit acquiescence to Rubinstein's decision to assign himself to conduct the *Triumphlied* at Düsseldorf. "My *Schicksalslied* went very badly on Sunday," he wrote in a letter to Levi. "Rubinstein is a middling conductor at best, and he didn't ask me to conduct, so I let the thing slide. For that reason, I'll think again about Düsseldorf and the *Triumphlied*!"[52] To be sure, Brahms was reluctant to come forward only now to insist on conducting the work himself, thinking that it would make him appear "rather foolish" to add conditions retrospectively. But he seems to have done just that. Writing to Allgeyer, he told the outcome: "Rubinstein will resign as the festival director if I direct my piece and that alone. I don't see the logic, and since the Comité has to retain him, of course my piece has been dropped—which brings me no pain."[53]

The composer evidently made the mistake of sharing with Gehring his dissatisfaction regarding Rubinstein's performance of the *Schicksalslied* in Vienna and his reluctance for this reason to allow the latter to lead the performance of the *Triumphlied* in Düsseldorf. Gehring, in turn, indiscreetly went public with the story in one of his early reports in the *Deutsche Zeitung*, in which he referred to the work in question as "Johannes Brahms' 'Triumphlied' auf den Sieg der deutschen Waffen."[54] Meanwhile Levi, after announcing his resignation from his position in Baden to become music director in Munich, postponed his performance of the *Triumphlied* from Palm Sunday so as to include it in his farewell concert to Karlsruhe on June 5.

---

51 Undated letter to Levi, in *Briefwechsel*, 7: 89.
52 Undated letter to Levi from late January 1872, in *Briefwechsel*, 7: 97.
53 Undated letters from mid-February to Levi and Allgeyer, respectively, in *Briefwechsel*, 7: 100–101; and Orel, *Johannes Brahms und Julius Allgeyer*, 76.
54 Brahms included a clipping of Gehring's report in his letter to Levi of March 1872, in *Briefwechsel*, 7: 102–5.

With that prospective performance in mind, Levi sought clarity by writing Brahms on April 7, 1872, to ask, "What is the official title of the Hallelujah?? The *Deutsche Zeitung* said something about 'Victory of German Arms'??" Brahms replied by referring in passing to "my 'Triumphlied' (as it is simply called of course)."[55] From a correspondent as elliptical as Brahms, this is about as clear an indicator as we might hope to have that the published work, for all that its first movement does extol the battlefield triumphs in France, represented much more than a celebration of a great military victory.[56] Yet, when Gehring subsequently used this mischaracterization as the title of his Karlsruhe review—"Triumphlied auf den Sieg der deutschen Waffen"—it must have seemed authoritative, and the false notion soon took hold that, as Eduard Hanslick put it in his review of the first Viennese performance, "the *Triumphlied* originally bore the subtitle 'On the Victory of German Arms.'"[57]

Writing about the Karlsruhe performance, Gehring provides a somewhat more detailed discussion of the music than one might have expected in a review of an unpublished work. He managed to do so because Brahms, in an instance that shows how cozy composers and critics could be with one another, allowed him to borrow the unpublished score.[58] What is of greater interest here, however, is Gehring's cultural analysis, his effort— directed toward a German-liberal readership in Vienna—to place Brahms and his music in the center of the momentous transformation of Germany in 1870–71: "Those who knew Brahms's *German Requiem* suspected that [the *Triumphlied*] would be something extraordinary, ... that with it the

---

55 *Briefwechsel*, 7: 110, 112. Victor Ravizza mistakenly reports that no reply to Levi's query is preserved. See Ravizza, *Brahms: Spätzeitmusik*, 196.

56 The account in Kross, *Brahms*, 624–27, takes no notice of the performance originally planned for Palm Sunday, thus erroneously suggesting that Levi had not been intended all along to lead the first performance.

57 Ed. H. [Eduard Hanslick], "Concerte," *Neue Freie Presse* (December 10, 1872): 1–3 (here 3). This mischaracterization remains alive; see, for example, Victor Ravizza, "Sinfonische Chorwerke," in *Brahms Handbuch*, ed. Wolfgang Sandberger (Stuttgart and Weimer: J. B. Metzler, 2009), 290. In his introduction to the recently published edition of Op. 55 in the *Neue Brahms-Gesamtausgabe* (JBG V/5), Johannes Behr independently debunks the idea that Brahms ever sanctioned the use of this alleged subtitle. I am grateful to Dr. Behr for sharing a pre-publication excerpt of this introduction with me in February 2020, well after I had come to the same conclusion in my own work on the piece.

58 Letter of June 17, 1872, from Brahms to Simrock, in *Briefwechsel*, 9: 122; and letter of June 18, 1872, from Simrock to Brahms, in Stephenson, ed., *Johannes Brahms und Fritz Simrock*, 52.

138 ❧ CHAPTER FOUR

deeply felt joy over the German victories would achieve true expression. The German artist [i.e., Brahms] who was to express this joy and confidence in the powerful advancement of the good German cause [also] knew how [in *A German Requiem*] to allay the mourning for the victims of the war on the part of so many Germans with his comforting sounds."[59]

As others had done when the *Requiem* first made the rounds, Gehring ties that earlier work to Robert Schumann's encomium "Neue Bahnen" (1853). But writing in 1872 he goes further by setting the work in the context of recent history. Schumann, he writes, "had predicted miraculous effects if Brahms were to direct his magic wand over the union of choir and orchestra." Those effects were evident, Gehring claims, in all the performances of the *Requiem* that came in 1870–71, in which the "consoling effect" of the music had been so compelling because both the words and tones embodied a "faithful reflection of everything that each [listener] had either personally experienced or sympathized with." The miracle could be seen in the way that a work that was not written in conjunction with the war nevertheless gave "the true full expression of those emotions and the moods that followed from them that dominated all Germans at the time."

In "Neue Bahnen" Schumann famously played the role of John the Baptist, heralding the coming of the Messiah in the figure of the unknown, twenty-year-old Brahms, who would be called "to articulate the highest expression of the time in an ideal manner." By the time of Gehring's review, of course, Brahms was a well-known composer, but the critic nevertheless continued his allusions to "Neue Bahnen" by suggesting that the recent appearance of the *Requiem* and the *Triumphlied* brought to notice a new Brahms, one hitherto unknown, who expressed the historical turn at hand in an ideal manner. In an allusion to the Sermon on the Mount (here Matthew 6:19 and 20), the first of several references to this Gospel, Gehring explains how the losses suffered through the war had served to remind the German people of the possessions of the German spirit, immortal property that neither moths nor rust could consume. More than that, through the *Requiem*, which not only comforted the mourning but embodied the immortal German spirit, the public had been introduced to the "German musician who practices his art in purity, naturalness, and sublimity, as few Germans, perhaps only one, before him. Yes, very few—let's be honest, I call out to all Germans, is not it so?"

The continuation of this passage merits quotation in full, not least because Gehring, unlike Schumann, who only proclaimed Brahms as the Messiah, goes so far as to put the words of Jesus in the composer's mouth:

---

59   This and all remaining quotations are taken from Gehring, "Triumphlied auf den Sieg der deutschen Waffen."

Is it not Brahms and he alone who has restored to our German music, to its continuity and further development, not only faith that moves mountains [allusion to Matthew 17: 20] but rather also all-inspiring love [*allbeseligende Liebe*]? Is it not Brahms alone who has dared to put up once more the age-old simple, yet so sublime, impulses of the human heart, doing so with a childlike simplicity and unassumingness, with a restraint and aversion to the great task, as possessed by only one German before him, by the name of Sebastian Bach? Verily, Brahms is an artist after the heart of God. The fact that, as such, he stands alone among the great multitude of musicians of our century, dead and living, makes him to us, his contemporaries, a hero in the field of music. Brahms is not a hero whose grandeur and power are overpowering, but a hero who can call out to us according to his deeds: Come to me, all who are weary, and I will give you comfort [quotation of Matthew 11:28]. I will show you how your sorrow will be changed into true, noble joy. I will show you your newly established human dignity.

This dignity, one presumes, was related to the Germans' gaining recognition abroad at last as members of a powerful, unified state.

As Gehring makes the point that the music of this "hero" encapsulates the heady historical moment, he also grounds that music approvingly in the present. Here again he takes off from Schumann, who penned "Neue Bahnen" as a brief against what would later be called the Music of the Future (*Musik der Zukunft*). In this way, he holds Brahms's "Music of the Present" (*Musik der Gegenwart*) to be "an expression of our time, and specifically a German expression of our time." He explains:

In political matters, we no longer think today of the future full of fear and trepidation of what it will bring because we in the present feel the power, we exercise and strengthen it, so as to be able to bear everything that the future may bring. Brahms is entirely free of that anxiety with which so many artists, and especially musicians, look into the future, wondering whether their artwork may continue to exist. And how did he gain this freedom? By offering in the music of the present that which contributes to the steeling and strengthening against all conceivable dangers of the future, by bolstering, as much as his profession is that of a musician, the German appreciation of the power that we presently possess, strengthen, and arm. Through the *German Requiem* and the *Triumphlied*, Brahms has done this for us Germans in a definitive and positive way such that no other musician before him, one can say no other artist, has dared. It was given to our time to harvest the fruits of so many endeavors and to deliver them with an energetic hand. This too has been done by Brahms in music.

Smacking of hagiography, this passage recalls in tone what others at the time were writing about Bismarck himself, who, as the *Reichsschmied*, quickly emerged as "the principal custodian of the grail of national symbols

140 &♦ CHAPTER FOUR

[and] remained unchallenged as a symbol of German national identity and interest."[60] On Gehring's account, with its slippage between nationalist and musical politics, one might even think of Brahms as though he were a Bismarck at work in a different sphere, the architect, at least in the *Requiem* and *Triumphlied*, of a salutary musical strain of the new statist-nationalism that Roger Chickering has described as a "civic religion," whereby "the national community that was to be the object of civic loyalty was coterminous with the new political entity that had emerged in the heart of Europe."[61]

Reception, Reputation, Rehabilitation

As the *Triumphlied* began to make the rounds during the 1870s, it was immediately recognized, in the words of the Leipzig critic Hermann Kretzschmar, as the musical embodiment of "the majestic jubilation and religious earnestness" that greeted "the arrival of the news of the victory of Sedan and awakened the noblest nature in all classes of our people." [62] Kretzschmar himself expressed some reservation about the unabashedly euphoric tone of the first chorus, finding it unsuited to the composer's strengths. "Jubilation and exultation," he writes, "are not among Brahms's special qualities." Articulating a concern shared by certain other critics, he claims that the many outbursts of "Hallelujah!" and "Heil und Preis" (Salvation and praise) that dominate this movement lack the originality and individuality of the composer's other large-scale choral works. They may produce a "dazzling effect" but, at least for Kretzschmar, no "lasting one." As the review continues, however, it becomes obvious that this critic, like most others at the time, held a high opinion of the work overall, and not only because of its impeccable workmanship.[63]

In light of the world-historical events that gave rise to Brahms's composition, events whose effects could be felt not only in the new German Reich,

---

60 Roger Chickering, *We Men Who Feel Most German: A Cultural Study of the Pan-German League, 1886–1914* (Boston, London, and Sydney: George Allen & Unwinn, 1984), 26.

61 Ibid.

62 Kretzschmar, "Neue Werke von Brahms," 110. For a summary discussion of the early concert reviews in the German-speaking lands, see Angelika Horstmann, *Untersuchungen zur Brahms-Rezeption der Jahre 1860–1880* (Hamburg: Karl Dieter Wagner, 1986), 199–204. For a more expansive account, see Behr and Tadday, "Rezeption," in JBG V/5: XXXVIII–XLVI.

63 Kretzschmar, "Neue Werke von Brahms," 148. See also La Mara [Marie Lipsius], *Musikalische Studienköpfe*, vol. 3: *Jüngstvergangenheit und Gegenwart* (Leipzig: Heinrich Schmidt & Carl Günther, 1883), 295–98.

but in the wider world as well, the critical reception from abroad is of particular interest. In June 1874, Maurice Kufferath, critic for the Belgian periodical *Le Guide musical*, published a substantial report on the work following its performance a few weeks earlier at the Lower Rhine Music Festival in Cologne: "The *Triumphlied*," he writes, "was composed under the direct influence of and in the aftermath of the German army's dazzling victories in 1870–71. It is a song intended to celebrate the great events of that memorable year." Notably, the Francophone Belgian critic spares no superlative in praising what Brahms had accomplished: "It is so excellent, this work, so remarkable in all respects, as inspiration, as a study of orchestration, as a work of counterpoint, so rich in novelties of all kinds, so varied, so supple and so vigorous in style, so powerful; and I believe it so superior to everything that has appeared for a long time."[64]

Kufferath was not the only foreign correspondent to be elevated by the work. The report of the same performance sent back to Britain by a critic for *The Musical Times and Singing Circular* expressed a similar reaction even more extravagantly: "So long as we have a composer living who can rise to the height of the *Triumphlied*, we need be under no apprehensions of the race of giants becoming extinct."[65] This enthusiastic critic expressed hope that Brahms's composition might soon be heard in England, and indeed August Manns evidently intended to perform it the following year at the Crystal Palace. But the challenges posed by the choral parts proved too daunting, and it would be another five years before Britain would hear the work.

By then the *Triumphlied* had been introduced in the United States, where on May 11, 1875, it opened the second biennial May Festival in Cincinnati. When an anonymous critic described the composition as "the sonorous song of the triumphs of Germany in fields of thought and action," he was surely registering the sense alluded to earlier that the German people could now be proud that the land of their birth had become a force to be reckoned with, not only in matters pertaining to the intellect and culture but also to European and indeed world political affairs.[66]

---

64   M. TH. [Maurice Kufferath], "Festival Rhénan. Deuxième et Troisième Journées," *Le Guide musical* 20 (June 4 and 11, 1874).

65   "The Lower Rhine Festival at Cologne," *Musical Times and Singing Class Circular* 16 (June 1, 1874): 509–10 (at 510, italics added).

66   "May Melodies," *Cincinnati Daily Enquirer* (May 12, 1875): 1, 4 (at 1). An earlier report in the same newspaper mentions the aborted effort to give a performance at the Crystal Palace. See "The Feast of Soul," *Cincinnati Daily Enquirer* (May 10, 1875): 8. Other reports circulating in the press at the time shared the same information.

142 ❧ CHAPTER FOUR

It is notable that this reviewer was more interested in celebrating the German thinker than the German warrior:

> Man is a fighting animal but his weapons are not simply rifles and bayonets, they are the thoughts that plan and the ready hands which execute the designs for the subjugation of nature, and the expression of all her latent resources for his honor and profit. All this is impregnated with an idea pre-eminently religious in the nobler sense of the term, and this is the true "Triumphlied," the key-note of a conquest which time itself can not [*sic*] shatter, more enduring than the Pyramids, more imperishable than brass. This inward sense of a mighty and permanent conquest must have animated the composer. Had he been but writing a paean for the fruits of one battle-field another battle-field might destroy he would have dashed at once into the clang and clamor of brass. But this was not the mete and boundary of Brahms' mind. It was as essentially religious as patriotic, and with the keen insight of poetic and emotional natures his music makes us think almost equally of the suffering of the past and the glories of the future.[67]

Four years later, on December 2, 1879, the *Triumphlied* was finally introduced in Britain at St. James's Hall, London, by Brahms's friend George Henschel.[68] *The Musical Times and Singing Circular* began its review as many others did, by characterizing the work as "a commemoration of the Franco-German War." The statement of this commonplace is then followed by a more intriguing remark: "Although Englishmen may have their own opinions as to the way the 'triumph' here celebrated was provoked"—the reference is surely to the belief that Bismarck had duplicitously tricked Napoleon III into declaring war on Prussia in the summer of 1870—"those opinions are not now dominant enough to create prejudice." Indeed, implicitly suggesting that how the war with France had come about was no longer of any import, the critic grants that "a German would naturally look at the 'world-earthquake' of 1870–71 from a German point of view" and evidently sees nothing inherently wrong with that. More problematic, he continues, is the possibility that in the third chorus, with its text "And I saw heaven opened, and behold, a white horse; and he who sat upon it is called Faithful

---

67   "May Melodies," *Cincinnati Daily Enquirer* (May 12, 1875): 4.

68   Henschel reported enthusiastically on how things had gone in a letter to the composer written the day after; see Karl Geiringer, "George Henschel," in *On Brahms and His Circle: Essays and Documentary Studies by Karl Geiringer*, revised and enlarged by George S. Bozarth, published in association with the American Brahms Society (Sterling Heights, MI: Harmonie Park Press, 2006), 338–47 (at 344–45).

and True, and in righteousness judges and makes war," Brahms intended to identify "the Apocalyptic Warrior" with the German Emperor, William I.[69]

In the *Times of London*, consternation at this possibility was expressed even more strongly, with allusion not only to the emperor but evidently also to his imperial chancellor: "It must be hoped that the composer in choosing these words did not intend any immediate reference to the charger, or indeed to the political achievements of his hero," which is to say the unification of Germany that Bismarck had engineered. The review then continues in such a way as to indict Brahms's opening chorus, too, for conflating matters religious and temporal: "Certain it is that the piece is of a warlike rather than of a devotional or mystical character, and the way also in which in the first chorus the words 'A King' are successively exclaimed by the voices in jubilant tones suggests an earthly Monarch rather than the "Lord of Lords.'"[70] Yet despite these reservations, which seem to be based in religious sensibilities rather than in any loathing of Germany's newly exercised military might, both critics are agreed, as one of them put it, that the *Triumphlied* is a "grand work" and "a masterpiece of scholarly composition" that "will ever command the respect and admiration of those who are enlightened worshippers at the shrine of art."[71]

Over the next thirty-five years the *Triumphlied* was heard several more times in Britain, a country in which large choral-orchestral works were always in demand.[72] The reviews were generally respectful and not infrequently laudatory, but by the beginning of the twentieth century, in a new context shaped by Emperor William II's controversial "Hun Speech" of July 27, 1900, with its expression of a vision of robust German imperial power, a few critics anachronistically took aim at Brahms for allegedly embracing something like this new Wilhelmine militarism. No review did so as colorfully as that which appeared in the *Manchester Guardian* on November 27, 1902: "[The *Triumphlied*] seems to us a strong, massive, enormous, over-complex, over-insistent, over-confident, unamiable, disagreeable, slightly brutal composition, in the course of which the white horse of the Apocalypse is dragged

---

69   "Herr Henschel's Concert," *Musical Times and Singing Class Circular* 21 (January 1, 1880): 20, 27 (at 27).

70   "Herr Henschel's Concert," *The Times* (London) (December 3, 1879): 10.

71   "Herr Henschel's Concert," *Musical Times and Singing Class Circular*, 27.

72   For Late Victorian and Edwardian commentary, see Louis Kelterborn, "Johannes Brahms," in *Famous Composers and Their Music: Extra Illustrated Edition of 1901*, ed. Theodore Thomas, John Knowles Paines, and Karl Klauser, 16 vols. (Boston: J. B. Millet, 1901), 4: 503–14 (at 512); J. A. Fuller-Maitland, *Brahms* (London: Methuen, 1911), 210–12; Edwin Evans, *Handbook to the Vocal Works of Brahms* (London: W. Reeves, 1912), 248–52.

144 ❧ CHAPTER FOUR

into an affair of German military swagger."[73] This sneering remark, of course, stands at a great remove from the sentiment embodied in, say, Gehring's review or the review quoted above of the first American performance, both written, as it were, during a very different historical moment. As we shall discover, it also anticipates attitudes and assumptions that would be expressed in critiques for many years to come.

Brahms's music was not especially popular in France during his lifetime or for a long while thereafter, yet by the end of the century there were at least a few important figures who championed him. One was the Belgian violinist Armand Parent, who made valiant efforts to introduce the French to the composer's chamber music. Another was Hugues Imbert, the editor-in-chief from 1894 to 1905 of the Brahms-friendly *Le Guide musical,* whose editorial office had relocated from Brussels to Paris in 1889. In 1906, the year following Imbert's death, his sympathetic biography of the composer appeared, and therein Brahms's commemoration in the *Triumphlied* of "the victories of the German armies" is acknowledged without any evident chagrin (if also without mention of whose military had been defeated).[74]

There was, of course, no question of any performance of the *Triumphlied* in France in the years that followed the events of 1870–71. Indeed, one would be hard pressed to identify any work that would seem to be more offensive to the program of the Société National de Musique, founded in February 1871 on a nationalist calling of *ars gallica.* A peevish, one-sentence mention of the work twenty-six years later in an otherwise respectful French

---

73   "The Hallé Concerts," *Manchester Guardian* (November 28, 1902): 5. On the Hun Speech, addressed to the German troops who were setting off from Bremerhaven to suppress the Boxer Rebellion in China, see Andreas Musolff, "Wilhelm II's 'Hun Speech' and its Alleged Resemiotization during World War I," *Language and Semiotic Studies* 3 (2017): 42–59.

74   Michel Stockem, "Armand Parent, Brahms et la France," *Revue belge de Musicologie/Belgisch Tijdschrift voor Muziekwetenschap* 47 (1993): 177–88; and Hugues Imbert, *Johannès Brahms, sa vie et son oeuvre,* preface by Edouard Schuré (Paris: Fischbacher, 1906), 126. Further on Brahms reception in France at this time, see Daniel Beller-McKenna, "'*Aimez-vous Brahms?*': The History of a Question," in *Rethinking Brahms,* ed. Nicole Grimes and Reuben Phillips (New York: Oxford University Press, 2022), 341–54; and Nicolas Dufetel, "'Aimez-vous Brahms ...': Zur Brahms-Rezeption in Frankreich um 1900," in *Konfrontationen. Symposium: Musik im Spannungsfeld des deutsch-französischen Verhältnisses 1871–1918. Johannes Brahms und Frankreich,* ed. Wolfgang Sandberger (Lübeck: Brahms-Institut an der Musikhochschule Lübeck; Munich: Edition Text + Kritik im Richard Boorberg Verlag, 2018), 38–54; and Marc Vignal, "Brahms und Frankreich," in *Internationaler Brahms-Kongress Gmunden 1997: Kongress Bericht,* ed. Ingrid Fuchs (Tutzing: Hans Schneider, 2001), 281–88.

obituary of Brahms suggests why: "During the winter of 1870–71 [Brahms] composed his *Chant de triomphe* at the time when Wagner wrote *Une Capitulation*." [75] The reference here is to Wagner's *Eine Kapitulation*, a farce, published in German in 1873 and in French three years later, in which Wagner takes *Schadenfreude* in the suffering of the besieged Parisians during the war's final months.[76] This would not be the last time that Brahms and Wagner, an otherwise unlikely pair, were grouped together in a French context. When, in the telling of Michel Stockem, France and Germany again went to war against one another in August 1914, the "author of a certain *Triumphlied* [would] pay the tribute of war like others, once again representing, alongside Wagner—author of a certain *Kaisersmarsch* [*sic*]—the very image of the German musician," which is to say of the "enemy musician."[77]

In Britain, too, the coming of war with Germany in 1914 had its effect on Brahms reception. At a time when some Britons were arguing that even Beethoven's music should be barred from British concert programs, there was certainly no longer any demand for performing a work like the *Triumphlied*, which could readily be thought to evoke German militarism, especially at a time when French and British soldiers were dying on battlefields not far from Sedan.[78] After the United States joined the fight in 1917, the question of whether or not to continue performing music by German composers came to the fore on the other side of the Atlantic.[79] Somewhat surprisingly, given the temper of the times, opinions there on the *Triumphlied* were mixed. On the one hand, *The Outlook*, a weekly magazine

---

75   Henry Revers and Alfred Kaiser, "Johannes Brahms," *La Revue blanche* 12 (1897): 461–66 (at 465).

76   Thomas Grey has characterized Wagner's text as a kind of Francophobic companion piece to Wagner's infamous antisemitic screed, *Jewry in Music*. See Thomas S. Grey, "'Eine Kapitulation': An Aristophanic Operetta as Cultural Warfare in 1870," in *Richard Wagner and His World*, ed. Thomas S. Grey (Princeton: Princeton University Press, 2009), 87–117 (at 93–94). Further on Wagner's farce, see Laurence Senelick, *Jacques Offenbach and the Making of Modern Culture* (Cambridge: Cambridge University Press, 2017), 68–71; and Marie-Hélène Benoit-Otis, "Richard Wagner, Louis de Fourcaud, and a Path for French Opera in the 1880s," *ACT Zeitschrift für Musik & Performance* 3 (May 2012); https://www.act.uni-bayreuth.de/en/archiv/201203/03_Benoit-Otis_Wagner/index.html.

77   Stockem, "Armand Parent, Brahms et la France," 188. On Wagner's *Kaisermarsch*, see Minor, *Choral Fantasies*, 129–62 *passim*.

78   See, for example, "National Ideals in Music: The Question of 'Enemy' Composers," *The Times* (London) (February 13, 1915): 11.

79   Jonathan Rosenberg, *Dangerous Melodies: Classical Music in America from the Great War through the Cold War* (New York: W. W. Norton, 2020), 3–124.

146 ❧ CHAPTER FOUR

that focused on social and political issues, characterized the composer of this work as a "patriot" but not one in sympathy with "Prussian ideals," by which was meant unsavory militarism, and not one, therefore, whose works should be banned. On the other hand, the *San Francisco Chronicle* urged precisely the banning of any work by a modern German composer that, like the *Triumphlied*, had been "written in celebration of German occasions."[80]

And even after the war ended and passions cooled, there was no going back as far as the *Triumphlied* was concerned. As the English critic Ralph Hill put it in the short biography of the composer he published in 1933, the centennial year of Brahms's birth: "Although Brahms was inclined to be a Germanic Jingo, in his music he wisely kept all transitory moods at arm's length. The *Triumphlied* is the one exception and the appeal of this work is necessarily a circumscribed one, in the same way as much of the music of Elgar written for ceremonial occasions and during the heat of war fever has only a limited appeal outside the emotion swayed masses."[81] A distaste for the work was no less true, if for obviously different reasons, during the postwar years of the Weimar and Austrian republics, which saw no performances of it at all, and where critical discussion, such as it was, often seemed almost sheepish in nature.[82]

The rise of National Socialism in the 1930s and the subsequent outbreak of the Second World War made performances of the *Triumphlied* abroad unthinkable. Instructive here is an article Hill published on November 1, 1940, in his role as the music editor of *Radio Times*, the BBC's weekly listings magazine. He begins by taking a stand against those who, as some had done twenty-five years earlier, would seek to "ban the music of enemy countries *in toto*," not least because, as he asserts, "with the possible exception of Wagner, the great German composers of the past would doubtless be the first to decry the present régime of oppression in Germany." All the same, given the circumstances of the moment—London was under nightly attack by the Luftwaffe and a favorable outcome of the Battle of Britain was by no

---

80 "Music and Patriotism," *The Outlook* (November 14, 1917): 407; and "The Elimination of German Music," *San Francisco Chronicle* (February 24, 1918): 8. The only documented performance of the work in the United States for more than a century after its introduction in Cincinnati in 1875 came during an all-Brahms festival held in New York in 1912. See Behr and Tadday, "Aufführungen," in JBG V/5: XXXVIII; and "Brahms Festival Opened," *New York Times* (March 26, 1912): 13.

81 Ralph Hill, *Brahms: A Study in Musical Biography* (London: Denis Archer, 1933), 180.

82 Ludwig Misch, *Johannes Brahms* (Bielefeld and Leipzig: Velhagen and Klasing, 1922), 66–68; Richard Specht, *Johannes Brahms*, trans. Eric Blom (London: Dent, 1930), 213.

means assured—he allows that it did make sense for the BBC to institute a policy of banning from its airwaves not only music by composers who were avowed Nazi sympathizers but also any "old works that [might] be interpreted in terms of modern Germany." The *Triumphlied* fell into the latter category. Hill does not doubt the musical excellence of this work, to be sure. But since it was also one in which—here he invokes his earlier characterization—"Brahms turned himself into a musical jingo," it was for the best, he held, that it be shunned at present. Surely it was no mere coincidence, then, that when Hill published an abridged version of his Brahms biography in the following year, he omitted his earlier mention of the work.[83]

In Nazi Germany, where Wagner and Bruckner were Hitler's late-nineteenth-century composers of choice, the *Triumphlied* was for all intents and purposes banned as well. Apart from five performances given in connection with the centenary celebration of Brahms's birth during the first weeks of the Nazi regime in 1933, the work was not heard there at all, not even following France's capitulation to Germany for the second time in seventy years in June 1940, an event that might well have been marked by such a performance.[84] For reasons that remain unclear—perhaps they had to do with the Nazis' difficult relationships with Christianity—the National Socialists seem to have had no more interest in appropriating a work written in celebration of the founding of the Second Reich than the BBC had in programming one that might seem instead to be glorifying the Third Reich.

Following the Second World War, the *Triumphlied*, with all its ingrained German patriotism, seemed more problematic than ever. And yet it never lacked admirers or apologists altogether. One was Karl Geiringer, a musicologist of Jewish heritage who, three years after the publication in 1935 of his still-useful life-and-works of Brahms, was forced to flee from his native Vienna following the *Anschluss*. When in 1948 Geiringer published a revised edition of the book in English, he left unchanged his original assessment of the work as a "magnificent" (*großartig*) composition.[85] Writing in the mid-1950s, the noted French critic and Brahms admirer Claude Rostand—in 1964 he was awarded the *Johannes-Brahms-Medaille* by the Hamburg Senate for his work on the city's native son—described the Franco-German War of 1870–71 as "one of the rare events" occurring in the world of national or

---

83 Ralph Hill, "Radio Music," *Radio Times* (November 1, 1940): 7; Ralph Hill, *Brahms* (London: Duckworth, 1941). Further on Hill's article in *Radio Times*, see John Vincent Morris, "Battle for Music: Music and British Wartime Propaganda 1935–1945" (PhD diss., University of Exeter, 2011), 112–13.

84 On the performances in 1933, see Behr and Tadday, "Aufführungen," in JBG V/5: XXXVIII.

85 Karl Geiringer, *Brahms: Leben und Schaffen eines deutschen Meisters* (Vienna: Rudolf M. Rohrer, 1935), 96; Karl Geiringer, *Brahms: His Life and Work*, 107.

148 &❧ CHAPTER FOUR

international politics in which "a resonance" is to be found in both Brahms's private life and his music, and he concludes, with no reproach and no allegations of anything like jingoism or chauvinism, that this exceptional work had been composed in a "patriotic delirium."

Another post-war French commentator, Jack Laufer, was no more disposed than Rostand to level charges against Brahms of anti-French jingoism. Like numerous other writers, he ties the work to "the victory of 1871" and implicitly understands the allusion in the first movement to "the old Prussian national hymn" as a marker of that victory. Yet he also notes approvingly that by restricting himself to the words of the biblical text, Brahms makes no direct reference to any wartime event. This is not to suggest any unanimity in the work's reception in France in the second half of the twentieth century. In 1984 an anonymous French record reviewer averred that no work that seemed to glorify vanquishing "corrupt France" could ever "invite us French people, even 114 years later, to savor this music in particular."[86] A similar bifurcation of opinion took place on the other side of the English Channel. If one contemporary British critic, Paul Griffiths, disparaged the work precisely on account of its "noisy and unthinking" jingoism, another, Malcolm MacDonald, not only argued that the musical merits of the *Triumphlied* transcend whatever "'nationalistic' overtones" might inhere in it, but also found nothing in the music to suggest an "endorsement of Prussian militarism."[87]

The first significant piece of revisionist writing on the work came in 1995, in the essay by Friedhelm Krummacher discussed earlier. Here Krummacher argued that Brahms's pronounced patriotism—we might in this instance say his patriotic delirium—was only in keeping with the norms of his day and that any modern understanding of the composer as a German chauvinist was owing to exaggerated descriptions by Kalbeck that tell us more about the biographer's attitudes than they do about those of the composer.[88] For Krummacher, unwarranted skittishness about Brahms's patriotic attitudes has denied the *Triumphlied* a place in today's repertoire that a work of its quality deserves. More recently, Kerstin Schüssler-Bach has urged a thoughtful, nuanced reengagement with this "*Monument für das Kaiserreich*" as a product of its own time and place, and not only in light of what followed

---

86   Claude Rostand, *Brahms*, 2 vols. (Paris: Le Bon Plaisir, 1954–55), second edition in one volume, with preface by Brigitte and Jean Massin (Paris: Fayard, 1978), 469–72 (at 470). J[ack] Laufer, *Brahms* (Paris: Scorpion , 1963), 126. Review of Johannes Brahms, *Alt-Rhapsodie, Nänie, Schicksalslied, Triumphlied* [DG 435–066–2], *La revue administrative* 37/218 (March–April 1984): 218.

87   Paul Griffiths, "A Resolute Hand for Brahms's Best and Worst," *The Times* (London) (April 30, 1983): 5; MacDonald, *Brahms*, 207.

88   Krummacher, "'Eine meiner politischen Betrachtungen,'" 640. For Kalbeck's account, see Kalbeck, *Johannes Brahms*, 2: 342–58.

it in the course of history. And for his part, Leon Botstein has suggested that Brahms's evocation of Handel, a German composer with strong ties to England, "offered the perfect foil for the liberal Brahms against Prussian conservatism." He goes so far—perhaps too far—as to speculate that Brahms was putting in a pitch here for the institution of a liberal constitutional monarchy in Germany like that of the United Kingdom with effective parliamentary power.[89]

None of this advocacy, however, has prevented what Richard Taruskin memorably characterized as the work's continuing "squeamish neglect."[90] Victor Ravizza's enumeration of its supposed sins includes "aggressive Prussianism, Francophobia, exuberant war enthusiasm, and hegemonic expansion politics." Similar concerns have been raised by Beller-McKenna (who writes that "we are repelled by its politics") and Minor (who decries the work's "overt militarism").[91] With his characteristic flair, Taruskin described

---

89   Kerstin Schüssler-Bach, "Vom Nutzen und Nachteil der Historie: Brahms' *Triumphlied* und die Signatur seiner Zeit," in *Musik-Kontexte: Festschrift für Hanns-Werner Heister*, ed. Wieland Reich and Thomas Phleps, 2 vols. (Münster: Monsenstein und Vannerdat, 2011), 2: 861–79. Leon Botstein, "The Eye of the Needle: Music as History after the Age of Recording," in *The Oxford Handbook of the New Cultural History of Music*, ed. Jane Fulcher (Oxford and New York: Oxford University Press, 2011), 523–49 (here 544). See also Leon Botstein, "Music in History: The Perils of Method in Reception History," *Musical Quarterly* 89 (2006): 1–16 (here 4).

90   Richard Taruskin, "Nationalism," Grove Music Online. Oxford Music Online. Oxford University Press, accessed March 6, 2017, http://www.oxfordmusiconline.com/subscriber/article/grove/music/50846. See also Richard Taruskin, "Some Thoughts on the History and Historiography of Russian Music," in *On Russian Music* (Berkeley and Los Angeles: University of California Press, 2009), 42. Opportunities to hear *The Triumphlied* in concert have indeed remained few and far between. The sesquicentennial of Brahms's birth in 1983 saw the first performance of the piece in fifty years. This took place in Vienna on October 16 and has since been followed by only a few others, including in Zurich (1995), New York (1997), London (2015), and Würzburg (2018).

91   Ravizza, "Sinfonische Chorwerke," 290; Ravizza, *Brahms: Spätzeitmusik*; Beller-McKenna, *Brahms and the German Spirit*, 132; Minor, *Choral Fantasies*, 126. See also Kross, *Die Chorwerke von Johannes Brahms*, 315–33, which forms the basis of discussion in Siegfried Kross, *Johannes Brahms: Versuch einer kritischen Dokumentar-Biographie*, 2 vols. (Bonn: Bouvier, 1997), 2: 612–27 and *passim*. See also Sabine Giesbrecht-Schutte, "Gründerzeitliche Festkultur: Die 'Bismarckhymne' von Carl Reinthaler und ihre Beziehung zum 'Triumphlied' von Johannes Brahms," *Die Musikforschung* 52 (1999): 70–88; Peter Petersen, "Über das 'Triumphlied' von Johannes Brahms," *Die Musikforschung* 52

150 ❧ CHAPTER FOUR

the *Triumphlied* as "the most blatant example of sacralized nationalism in the whole literature of German music"; it signals a turn from the liberal nationalism Taruskin associated with *A German Requiem* to "a more aggressive nationalism ... that not only loves but hates."[92] That's certainly enough to make one squeamish, especially for those for whom the German invasions of France in the two world wars of the twentieth century have greater historical resonance than any showdowns that occurred in the century before.

The *Triumphlied* long ago fell victim to this way of thinking. Yet, as I have suggested, seen in the context of its time, the work is better understood as a piece of "salutary," not "sacralized," nationalism. Its unabashed sense of patriotic devotion was once admired, not abhorred, because in its day it could more easily be rationalized as an understandable reaction to the threats, real or perceived, of French hegemony in Central Europe, and as a celebration of the achievement of a good—a unified German state—that was long overdue. The modern reception of this work, with its charges of overt militarism, repulsive politics, nationalism that hates, visits the sins of the sons on the father, which is to say interprets the composer's nationalism of 1870–71 from the vantage point of 1914–18 or 1933–45. The notion of a German *Sonderweg* has long since been discredited. Is it not also about time to approach the *Triumphlied* without feeling squeamish?

(1999): 462–66; Thomas Leibnitz, "'Denn wahrhaftig und gerecht sind seine Gerichte ...': Apokalypse als nationale Manifestation im *Triumphlied* op. 55 von Johannes Brahms," in *Apokalypse: Symposion 1999*, ed. Carmen Ottner (Vienna: Doblinger, 2001), 135–50; and Wolfgang Winterhager, "Text und Musik im *Triumphlied* von Johannes Brahms," in *Musik, Transfer, Kultur: Festschrift für Horst Weber*, ed. Stefan Drees, Andreas Jacob, and Stefan Orgass (Hildesheim and New York: G. Olms, 2009), 135–48.

92 Richard Taruskin, *The Oxford History of Western Music*, 6 vols. (Oxford and New York, 2005), vol. 3, *The Nineteenth Century*, 704, 712.

Excursus 2

National Holidays, Monuments, and Celebrations

> The events of the past year belong not only to us who lived through them ...; they belong to all the generations that will follow us, to whom they are to be handed down as a sacred legacy not only through the textbooks of history, but through the living transmission of the people.[1]
>
> —Franz Holtzendorff, 1871

With the founding of the German Reich came initiatives to establish an annual national holiday and to raise funds for the erection of a suitable national monument. Much of this activity originated in the overlapping spheres of Culture Protestantism and National Liberalism. Already in September 1870 the liberal Bremen pastor Jacob Kradolfer proposed an annual popular festival—what he called a youth festival (*Jugendfest*)—to be celebrated in conjunction with a church service. Through such a celebration, he hoped, the feeling of national unity engendered by the recent Battle of Sedan might be inculcated in what remained a German society divided by many social differences. Kradolfer chose this day, not, as he stressed, out of a desire to exalt German military power, but rather because he understood the capitulation of the French emperor before the Prussian king on September 2 as "as an act of divine and human justice, as the shining finger of God in world history." As such, he reasoned, it should be celebrated as a "day of joy over the salvation of our people."[2]

Kradolfer's proposal came to nothing, but the idea of establishing a festival by means of which to foster a sense of national identity was soon taken up

---

1   F[ranz] v[on] Holtzendorff, "Ein neues deutsches Volks- und Kirchenfest!," *Protestantische Kirchenzeitung für das evangelische Deutschland* (February 11, 1871): cols. 109–12 (here cols. 110–11).

2   Kradolfer, "Das deutsche Volksfest: eine Anregung," 277. In what follows I have drawn liberally from Claudia Lepp, "Protestanten feiern ihre Nation: Die kulturprotestantischen Ursprüngen des Sedantages," *Historisches Jahrbuch* 118 (1998): 201–22.

152 ❧ EXCURSUS 2

again. In early 1871 Franz von Holtzendorff, an important jurist and a committee member of the liberal *Protestantenverein* (Protestant Society), drafted an address to the emperor calling for the foundation of an annual "nationwide German popular and church festival" (*allgemeines, deutsches Volks- und Kirchenfest*), a "celebration of the resurrection of the people's and imperial Reich" (*Auferstehungsfest des Volks- und Kaiserreiches*).[3] Like Kradolfer's proposed *Volksfest*, this celebration was envisioned to be both civic and religious in nature. And here again we see evidence of the reciprocal notions of a secularized German Protestantism and a sacralized German nationalism, even in what Holtzendorff outwardly insisted must be an interdenominational affair so as to strengthen the unity of a new state that included significant numbers of Catholics and Jews.[4] Mindful that an annual celebration of the victory at Sedan might be seen as advocacy for a nationalism built on military force, he proposed instead a springtime celebration, thinking that to be the best way to signify "the immortality and resurrection of those sublime virtues of devotion which have saved and unified Germany." This, he believed, would emphasize a salutary "liberal" nationalism aimed at modernization and the liberalization of the German state, church, and society.[5]

Holtzendorff's address to the emperor was circulated for signatures in March. It gained the support, not only of men of differing classes, parties, and confessions, but of both Crown Prince Frederick William and Grand Duke Frederick I of Baden. Yet the emperor was not won over. Although he was supportive of the idea of observing some kind of a unification day, he was unwilling to impose it from above. It would be far better for this to come about, he held, not by imperial decree, but "by the German people of their own free will," citing as a precedent the annual popular festivals that could trace their origins to the Festival of All Germans (*Fest aller Deutschen*) that had been organized from below by Arndt and others and celebrated across Germany on October 18–19, 1814, to mark the first anniversary of

---

3   Holtzendorff, "Ein neues deutsches Volks- und Kirchenfest!," cols. 109–12. An early version of the text of the address appears in "Correspondenzen und Nachrichten. Berlin," *Protestantische Kirchenzeitung für das evangelische Deutschland* (March 4, 1871): cols. 196–97, from which I have quoted here.

4   Holtzendorff's correspondence from this time with Johann Caspar Blunthschli, an esteemed jurist and the president of the Protestant Association, shows this rhetoric of inclusivity to be overstated, especially with regard to the "Jesuits and ultramontanes," who could never be reconciled to their goal of creating "a national-state and national-church unification of the Germans under liberal and Protestant auspices"; see Lepp, "Protestanten feiern ihre Nation," 209–10.

5   Holtzendorf, "Correspondenzen und Nachrichten. Berlin"; Lepp, "Protestanten feiern ihre Nation," 218.

EXCURSUS 2 ❧ 153

the Battle of Leipzig. As Frederik Frank Sterkenburgh has observed, during the first years of the *Kaiserreich*, evoking the memory of the Napoleonic Wars could be seen as a strategy of integration, in that it evoked a historical period with which both conservative-monarchical and liberal-democratic elements could identify.[6]

Taking his cue from the emperor's response, Friedrich von Bodelschwingh—no liberal but rather the head of the Pietist Inner Mission—quickly undertook a campaign to urge local church and civic authorities to organize "German popular festivals" (*deutsche Volksfeste*) precisely after the example that Arndt had set in 1814, albeit with the Battle of Sedan substituting for the Battle of Leipzig as the point of reference.[7] This appeal was well received in many predominantly Protestant locales, but in the Catholic regions of the south and west and in Polish-speaking Prussia, as well as in the Protestant but Danish-speaking regions in Schleswig, calls for the new festival went largely unheeded.[8] Moreover, for the Bavarians it was not the Prussian-led Battle of Sedan but the earlier Battle of Wörth, fought on August 6, 1870, in which the Bavarian troops had played a greater role, that held the most patriotic meaning. Nor could the Alsace-Lorrainers be expected to celebrate a battle in which less than a year earlier they had been on the losing side.

Two other days for a national patriotic festival were also considered. One was May 10, the day on which the Treaty of Frankfurt was signed. This never

---

6   Frederik Frank Sterkenburgh, "Staging a Monarchical-federal Order: Wilhelm I as German Emperor," *German History* 39 (2021): 519–41 (here 529–30). See also Clark, "The Wars of Liberation in the Prussian Memory." The emperor's response to the petition, which came in late April 1871, is quoted in full in Theodor Schieder, *Das deutsche Kaiserstaat von 1871 als Nationalstaat* (Wiesbaden: Springer Fachmedien, 1961), 134–35. On the Festival of All Germans, see Hagemann, "Celebration, Contestation, and Commemoration." Similar observances occurred with some regularity thereafter. The Wartburg Celebration from 1817, discussed in the prologue to this book, was one early iteration. See also Jason Tebbe, "Revision and 'Rebirth': Commemoration of the Battle of Leipzig," *German Studies Review* 33 (2010): 618–40.

7   [Friedrich von Bodelschwingh the Elder], *Das Deutsche Volksfest: Ein Flugblatt ausgegeben vom Rheinish-Westfälischen Provinzial-Ausschuß für innere Mission in Langenberg* (Langenberg: Julius Joost, 1871); quoted in full in Schieder, *Das deutsche Kaiserstaat*, 135–45. For a thorough account, see Hartmut Lehmann, "Friedrich von Bodelschwingh und das Sedanfest: Ein Beitrag zum nationalen Denken der politisch acktiven Richtung im deutschen Pietismus des 19. Jahrhunderts," *Historische Zeitung* 202 (1966): 542–73.

8   See, for example, Pontus Hiort, "Constructing Another Kind of German: Catholic Commemorations of German Unification in Baden, 1870–1876," *Catholic Historical Review* 93 (2007): 17–46 (esp. 42–45).

154 ❧ EXCURSUS 2

gained much traction, however, evidently because of the inherent difficulty of investing an anticlimactic act of diplomacy with much emotional power.[9] The other was January 18, the day of the Imperial Proclamation in Versailles and thus, in some sense, the Reich's birthday. But this proposal, too, went nowhere. As the founding day also of the Prussian kingdom, it had little appeal as a holiday for the nation at-large; moreover, as Ute Schneider has observed, its wintertime occurrence in the calendar made it less than conducive to the staging of large outdoor public festivities.[10]

Sedan Day, the observation of the great victory over the French on September 2, did eventually become a regular, albeit controversial, fixture in German public life as a day of national celebration (*Nationalfesttag*), but it never joined the emperor's birthday as a national holiday (*Nationalfeiertag*).[11] It was never formally established or treated as a day off from work, and it was never truly national in that it held little appeal, not only for Catholics (who shunned it out of protest against Bismarck's *Kulturkampf*), but also for the socialists (who opposed the military and imperialist connotations it came to carry). And, whether as an affair dominated by veterans' groups and marked by copious consumption of alcohol, or as a day celebrated mostly in the schools, it turned out to be nothing like the day of national communion that Bodelschwingh had envisioned.

Commemoration in Stone

The early years of the German Reich also saw "a frenzy of monument-building" dedicated to the new German state. These many projects made no small contribution to the "invention of tradition" that would aid the Reich

---

9   Lepp, "Protestanten feiern ihre Nation," 206.
10   Ute Schneider, "Einheit ohne Einigkeit: Der Sedantag im Kaiserreich," in *Inszenierungen des Nationalstaats: Politische Feiern in Italien und Deutschland seit 1860/71*, ed. Sabine Behrenbeck and Alexander Nützenadel (Cologne: SH-Verlag, 2000), 27–44 (here 30).
11   For a concise, excellent overview, see Jürgen Lotterer, "Der verhinderte Nationalfeiertag: Die Sedanfeier im Deutschen Kaiserreich (1871–1918), in *Nationalismus im Kaiserreich—Der "Sedantag" in Stuttgart 1895: ein Quellen- und Arbeitsbuch für den Geschichtsunterricht*, ed. Michael Hoffmann, Jürgen Lotterer, and Günter Riederer (Stuttgart: Stadtarchiv, 1997), 4–7. See also Fritz Schellack, *Nationalfeiertage in Deutschland von 1871 bis 1945* (Frankfurt am Main: Peter Lang, 1990), 15–132; Schneider, "Einheit ohne Einigkeit"; and Jörg Koch, *Dass du nicht vergessest der Geschichte: Staatliche Gedenk- und Feiertage in Deutschland von 1871 bis heute* (Darmstadt: wbg Academic, 2020), 44–60.

EXCURSUS 2 ❧ 155

in acquiring legitimacy in the eyes of those who, as we have seen, had ample reason to be doubtful or dissatisfied or simply lacked a national consciousness.[12] Perhaps the most important was Johannes Schilling's *National-Denkmal auf dem Niederwald* (National monument on the Niederwald).[13] Already in early 1871, at the same time that efforts were first being made to establish a festival to mark the rebirth of the German Reich, there was talk in the National Liberal public sphere of building a national monument on the Rhine. Three years later Schilling's design was approved and a site selected on a hill overlooking the river at Rüdesheim. In a festive ceremony held on September 16, 1877, William I laid the cornerstone with three symbolic hammer strokes. Finally, on September 28, 1883, the monument was unveiled in a grand ceremony attended by the emperor, the German princes, and other dignitaries, together with long lines of troops, war veterans, gymnasts, and singers, and a large crowd of thousands of onlookers, all of whom were invited to join in the singing of "Nun danket alle Gott" and "Die Wacht am Rhein." Every step in the early history of the monument—from its planning to its execution to its unveiling—received extensive coverage in both the political and the illustrated popular press. Through this exposure in print even those citizens who would never experience the monument in person—the vast majority of the disparate population—could be encouraged

---

12   Patricia Mazón, "Germania Triumphant: The Niederwald National Monument and the Liberal Moment in Imperial Germany," *German History* 18 (2000): 162–92 (quoted at 162); Eric Hobsbawm, "Mass-Producing Traditions: Europe: 1870–1914," in *The Invention of Tradition*, ed. Eric Hobsbawm and Terence Ranger (Cambridge: Cambridge University Press, 1983), 263–307.

13   The literature is substantial. Among other studies, see Mazón, "Germania Triumphant"; Lutz Tittel, *Das Niederwalddenkmal* (Hildesheim: Gerstenberg, 1979); Thomas Nipperdey, "Nationalidee und Nationaldenkmal in Deutschland im 19. Jahrhundert," *Historische Zeitschrift* 206 (1968): 529–85, repr. in his *Gesellschaft, Kultur, Theorie: Gesammelte Aufsätze zur neueren Geschichte* (Göttingen: Vandenhoeck Ruprecht, 1976), 133–73; Reinhard Alings, *Monument und Nation: Das Bild vom Nationalstaat im Medium Denkmal—zum Verhältnis von Nation und Staat im deutschen Kaiserreich 1871–1918* (Berlin and New York: Walter de Gruyter, 1996), 167–76, 386–93; Esther-Beatrice Christiane von Bruchhausen, "Das Zeichen im Kostümball: Marianne und Germania in der politischen Ikonographie" (PhD diss., Martin Luther-Universität Halle-Wittenberg, 1999), 185–252; Antje Laumann-Kleineberg, *Denkmäler des 19. Jahrhunderts in Widerstreit: Drei Fallstudien zur Diskussion zwischen Auftraggebern, Planern und öffentlichen Kritiker* (Frankfurt: Peter Lang, 1989), 39–140; and Bettina Brandt, *Germania und ihre Söhne: Repräsentationen von Nation, Geschlecht und Politik in der Modern* (Göttingen: Vandenhoeck & Ruprecht, 2010), 329–36.

156 ❧ EXCURSUS 2

to imagine themselves, despite their many regional, religious, and class differences, as members in a community of nationally conscious Germans.[14]

In August 1874, *Die Gartenlaube*, a popular weekly magazine that projected a National Liberal point of view, published an extensive article about Schilling's design that included a reproduction of his model spread over two facing pages (Figure 4). Well before the monument's construction and unveiling, therefore, middle-class readers throughout the German-speaking world—including, in all probability, Brahms—were afforded a good idea of what to expect.[15] The most prominent element of Schilling's design is a towering statue of Germania, the feminine personification of the nation. Unlike the figure who had held her sword high as she watched over the proceedings at the ill-rated Frankfurt Parliament in the famous painting by Philipp Veit, Schilling's Germania does not brandish her weapon but holds it at rest. The watch on the Rhine is defensive, not warlike; the German Reich is to be understood here, as in the discourse surrounding the Imperial Proclamation, as a kingdom of peace. Standing with her back to the throne, Germania gazes into the distance as she holds the imperial crown aloft. There is no monarch in sight, and the viewer may well ask whether she intends to place the crown on her own head as the representative of the people who are referenced in the inscription that appears on her pedestal: "In memory of the unanimous and victorious uprising of the German people and of the restoration of the German Reich 1870/71" (*Zum Andenken an die einmütige und siegreiche Erhebung des deutschen Volkes und die Wiederaufrichtung des Deutschen Reiches 1870/71*). The popular "uprising" refers to the earlier Wars of Liberation, which are now linked with the recent Franco-Prussian War "in one long march toward freedom and national fulfillment."[16] There is no accounting here for the absence of Austria from this "restored" German Reich: the historical inevitability of the Smaller German solution simply goes without saying.

In contrast to the more abstract symbology of Germania, which could be read in liberal and even democratic terms, the large base underneath is covered with an array of didactic reliefs related to the recent war with France; these clearly seek to rationalize the national-monarchical, Prussian-centric solution to the German Question.[17] The victorious German armies

---

14   The classic study is Anderson, *Imagined Communities.*

15   "Das National-Denkmal auf dem Niederwald," *Die Gartenlaube* 22 (1874): 533–37.

16   Mazón, "Germania Triumphant," 177.

17   It was not the entire monument but only this large, so-called Kaiser relief, affixed to the monument's base a few days before the cermony, that was draped for the unveiling (Laumann-Kleineberg, *Denkmäler des 19. Jahrhunderts in Widerstreit*, 128).

Figure 4. Johannes Schilling's model for *Das National-Denkmal auf dem Niederwald*, reproduced in *Die Gartenlaube* 33 (1874): 534–35. Public domain.

are represented by likenesses of the reigning princes, important generals, and a few soldiers, none of whom, however, is gloating over the hereditary enemy's defeat. And the words of the iconic "Die Wacht am Rhein" that appear below the main frieze are altered in meaningful ways: in the second verse, the more general noun *Feind* (enemy) stands in place of the pejorative *Welscher* (Frenchy), and the fourth verse, which names France as the enemy, is missing altogether. These alterations give reason to question Joep Leerssen's characterization of the monument as a sign of "a Pavlovian link between anti-French warfare over the Rhine (as 'unfinished business') and

German unification."[18] The seeming contradictions embodied in the monument are characteristic of the National Liberal ideology that was ascendant in the early years of the Reich and give good cause for Patricia Mazón's claim that the Niederwalddenkmal is perhaps the "prototypical liberal monument." As Thomas Nipperdey noted, it can only "be understood politically as a striking expression of the compromise between national-democratic and national-monarchical tendencies and forces."[19]

Work on the monument was entering its final stages when, in the middle of May 1883, Brahms arrived for a summer holiday in the Rhenish city of Wiesbaden, where in the weeks that followed he wrote his Third Symphony. His lodgings were located in a former painter's studio, close by the home of his music-loving friends Rudolf and Laura von Beckerath, whom he visited nearly every day, either in town or at their vineyard estate in nearby Rüdesheim. Brahms's anticipation was high as the date of the monument's dedication approached. At least twice in August he made the short trip from Wiesbaden to Rüdesheim to have an early look at the monument, once alone and then again, on August 28, in the company of his friend Franz Wüllner. On the day following, he wrote to Billroth, who was about to embark on a Rhine journey with his wife, to encourage him to stopover in Rüdesheim so that the two of them might meet and take in the monument together, insisting that this would be far more satisfying for his friend than viewing the Germania only in passing from a ship.[20]

The dedication came on September 28, a few days before Brahms returned home to Vienna. We have reason to doubt the accuracy of Kalbeck's report that Brahms viewed the ceremony, not in person, but only from high above in the Beckeraths' garden. (As we shall see, Brahms unquestionably did pass much of the day at his friends' country home, however.) For one thing, we know that Laura von Beckerath had obtained a ticket for Brahms for the event (although, of course, that is not to confirm that he used it). Moreover, the Beckeraths' family archive preserves an anecdote about a quip Brahms made at this time "on the festival grounds" (*auf dem Festplatz*), one involving the recently ennobled August Friedrich Carl von Hergenhahn, the chief

---

18 Joep Leerssen, "The Nation and the City: Urban Festivals and Cultural Mobilisation," *Nations and Nationalism* 21 (2015): 2–20 (here 14).

19 Mazón, "Germania Triumphant," 168; Nipperdey, "Nationalidee und Nationaldenkmal," 158.

20 *Briefwechsel*, vol. 15: *Johannes Brahms im Briefwechsel mit Franz Wüllner*, ed. Ernst Wolff (1922), 108–9 (one undated letter and one postcard of August 24 from Brahms to Wüllner). Letter from Brahms to Rudolph von Beckerath of August 24, 1883, in Stephenson, *Johannes Brahms und die Familie von Beckerath*, 25. Letter from Brahms to Billroth of August 29, 1883, in *Billroth und Brahms im Briefwechsel*, 354.

of police in Frankfurt am Main, who was likely present there precisely for the unveiling.[21] Kalbeck's claim that Brahms must have experienced "unspeakable joy" as he looked down from the garden above on the procession of the emperor and his entourage, may be overwrought, but it is not entirely fanciful, even if his attempt to tie the monument to the Third Symphony (he calls it Brahms's *Germaniasinfonie*), and to explain the composer's decision to summer in Germany as an expression of his distaste for the "anti-German" politics at the moment in Austria, stretches credulity.[22] Whether Brahms was physically present for the dedication or not, there is no reason to think that he was not profoundly moved by the events of this national commemoration or that he was not stirred by the patriotic sentiments embodied in the monument itself.[23] Indeed, as we shall discover, in his next patriotic choral work, Brahms would allude to a succession of historical events very much like those to which reference is made in the inscription found on Germania's pedestal. But first we have one more celebration to consider.

A Bismarck Birthday

In the fabled German forest stands the weeping oak tree [*Trauereiche*] of the fairy tale. It is winter and the storm breeze has stripped the forest's trees. Only ice crystals hang from the trees, and the branches are thickly covered with snow. But in the middle of the forest stands the magic oak [*Zaubereiche*] in full leaf ornamentation. She is as green as on the most beautiful of spring days. This is the image of the German Chancellor, who today, greeted enthusiastically by the German people, admired by the world, is celebrating his seventieth birthday. The enchanted oak tree defies the effects of the seasons; its spring has no end. The Chancellor's iron nature defies the effects of time; the years have no power over him, and he has passed his seventieth birthday with youthful vigor.[24]

—*Neues Wiener Tagblatt*, 1885

---

21   Unpublished letter of August 15, 1883, from Laura von Beckerath (Staats- und Universitätsbibliothek Hamburg, shelfmark: BRA:Bb1:17): "Enclosed is your ticket for the dedication, which has just been sent to us" ("Anbei Ihre uns eben zugesandte Karte zur Einweihung"). Stephenson, *Johannes Brahms und die Familie von Beckerath*, 24.

22   Kalbeck, *Johannes Brahms*, 3: 400.

23   Here I differ with Beller-McKenna, who suggests that Brahms may have felt "an underlying ambivalence or uneasiness about the whole affair"; Beller-McKenna, *Brahms and the German Spirit*, 146–48 (at 148).

24   "Grün in Schnee," *Neues Wiener Tagblatt* (April 1, 1885): 1. The allusions here are to Hans Christian Andersen's "The Last Dream of the Old Oak."

160 &• EXCURSUS 2

Bismarck's seventieth birthday, on April 1, 1885, was the cause of enormous festivity throughout Germany. Congratulatory letters and telegrams addressed to the Reich Chancellor numbered in the thousands. Nearly 200 voluntary societies and other corporative bodies sent laudatory addresses. Cities bestowed certificates of honorary citizenship; universities, honorary degrees. The emperor himself presented his long-time minister with Anton von Werner's specially commissioned third version of "The Proclamation of the German Empire," in which the chancellor and the other figures in the canvas are depicted, not as they had looked in Versailles in 1871, but as they looked now, fourteen years later, in 1885. From Vienna Francis Joseph sent a life-sized portrait of himself; from other German and European princes came commemorative medals and similar tokens of esteem. Most notable perhaps among the hundreds of gifts received was the sum of nearly 2,400,000 Marks raised by public subscription in a "Bismarck Fund" whose proceeds were intended to be donated to a charity of the chancellor's choosing.

Among the contributors to this fund was Brahms, who authorized Simrock to send a contribution from his account in the amount of 100 Marks. Displaying his usual discretion in such matters, the composer asked his publisher to identify him using only his initials "J. B." But then, having heard "all manner of very bad news" (*allerei recht Unerfreuliches*) with respect to the fund—he seems to have gotten word that the organizers planned to use more than half of it, not for charity, as originally intended, but to reacquire for Bismarck ancestral lands that had been sold off by his father fifty years earlier to clear the family's debts—he wrote again three days later to ask Simrock for a report from Berlin.[25]

Public observances of the Iron Chancellor's birthday were held in many cities, including several in Austria-Hungary, but the most noteworthy events, not surprisingly, took place in Berlin. In a preliminary celebration, on the afternoon of 31 March, veterans' associations from throughout the Reich processed to the Wilhelmstraße, where, from the balcony of the Reich Chancellery, Bismarck addressed the men with words of praise for the army's work in achieving German unification in 1870–71 and for serving as a bulwark of peace thereafter. Later that evening, in what was certainly a dramatic highpoint of the festivities, came a torchlight procession that included, among the thousands of costumed students, guild workers, and other groups who filled the streets, an enormous horse-drawn chariot carrying the likeness

---

25   Otto Pflanze, *Bismarck and the Development of Germany*, 3 vols. (Princeton: Princeton University Press, 1990), 3: 185. Letters to Simrock of March 12 and 15, 1885, in *Briefwechsel*, vol. 11: *Briefe an Fritz Simrock*, ed. Max Kalbeck (1919): 91–94 (quoted at 94).

EXCURSUS 2 &❧ 161

of Germania.[26] In his remarks at the end of this demonstration, Bismarck laid stress once more on the peace that had been maintained since the establishment of the Reich, this time giving credit to the emperor as the army's commander-in-chief, whose "strong hand has kept us in peace for fourteen years and will continue to do so." [27]

Throughout the day of the anniversary itself, Bismarck received visits in the chancellery from a steady stream of well-wishers. The morning began with the arrival of the royal family. In addition to Werner's painting, William I presented Bismarck with a warm letter of appreciation, soon made public, in which he praised his "dear Prince" for his many achievements on behalf of the nation. Then came various federal councilors and ministers, representatives of the Bismarck Fund, and finally a succession of delegations from every social class and every corner of the Reich, each bearing its own testimonials to the chancellor. Not for nothing did the *Neue Freie Presse* liken the celebration to "a ceremonial all-German pilgrimage from the emperor to the simple peasant."[28]

Newspaper coverage was extensive, and Brahms followed it closely. In addition to its own reporting, the Viennese political press reprinted excerpts from its counterpart in Berlin. The *Neue Freie Presse*, for example, published several excerpts from the reporting found in the *Vossische Zeitung* and *Berliner Tageblatt*, both of which supported the new left-liberal *Deutsche Freisinnige Partei* (German Liberal Party), as well as the more conservative, Bismarck-friendly *National-Zeitung*, which reflected the National Liberal point of view, and the *Norddeutsche Allgemeine Zeitung*, which functioned as Bismarck's semi-official organ.[29] The last-named publication, presum-

---

26 Herein lies some irony. Bismarck later explained his unwillingness to attend either the laying of the foundation stone or the unveiling of the Niederwald Monument as a reaction to his distaste for the idea of representing the new nation-state with the feminine figure of Germania, indicating that he would have preferred an image of Charlemagne. See Tittel, *Das Niederwalddenkmal*, 109.

27 "Festzug," *Norddeutsche Allgemeine Zeitung* (April 1, 1885): 1; and "Der Fackelzug," ibid., 1–2. I have quoted Bismarck from "Bismarck-Feier," *Neue Freie Presse* (April 1, 1885): 7–8 (at 8). Bismarck's record of maintaining peace since 1871 as Europe's dominant statesman was noted approvingly in nearly all the reporting on the events, both foreign and domestic.

28 "Bismarck-Feier," *Neue Freie Presse* (April 2, 1885): 8.

29 On the various liberal parties during the *Kaiserreich*, see Dieter Langewiesche, *Liberalism in Germany*, trans. Christiane Banerji (Princeton: Princeton University Press, 2000), 121–249; and Gary Bonham, *Ideology and Interests in the German State* (1991; repr. ed., Abingdon, UK: Routledge, 2014), 60–74. Both Langewiesche (p. 164) and Bonham (p. 72) translate *Deutsche Freisinnige Partei* as German Radical Party, but "freisinnig" (free-thinking) is to be understood here as implying "left-liberalism." See Frank Lorenz Müller, *Our Fritz: Emperor Frederick*

162 &· EXCURSUS 2

ably alluding to Josef Viktor von Scheffel's *Ekkehard* (1855), a popular historical novel whose eponymous hero overcomes his enemies to become the trusted advisor to the emperor, lauded the chancellor as "the faithful Eckart of the Emperor and the Reich and as an honest broker and bold social-political reformer." [30] But even the newspapers who supported the left-liberals, whom Bismarck had characterized as "enemies of the Reich" (*Reichsfeinde*), were of one mind in recognizing his enormous national significance.

Meanwhile, from Simrock came a parcel of Berlin newspapers, probably including some or all of those just mentioned: "Thank you for the newspapers," Brahms wrote on April 4, "but they are a poor substitute [*quader Ersatz*]. I should have been clever and visited you on April 1! How magnificent and delightful it must have been just strolling up and down the streets to enjoy it." As Brahms goes on, he seems transported by the moment in which he was living: "But we are experiencing and beholding figures, circumstances, and people such as have never before been seen in history. How will this chapter appear in a later world history! The writer must feel like a Homer, and his real-life story like fairy tales and legends!"[31]

Of the many descriptions of the Berlin celebrations available to Brahms, a leading article in the *Berliner Tageblatt* may be the most extraordinary of all. Through Bismarck, the author observes, German liberalism could finally claim its vindication: "Truly, the history of the last thirty years ... must prove to even the most blinded that the ideals that rule a people finally leave their mark on the course of world-historical development." And in a striking peroration, the author proclaims:

This Bismarck Day will forever symbolize the attitudes that are flooding the German nation these days. When tomorrow we resume the struggle over domestic questions brought to a halt by this jubilation, and ... continue to stand up for those values we consider to be the highest for the well-being of the Fatherland, then hopefully the words of the poet [Friedrich Theodor] Vischer in honor of the nation and of the acclaimed will also be accepted as the full truth:

III and the Political Culture of Imperial Germany (Cambridge, MA, and London: Harvard University Press, 2011), 162. See also Daniele Carimani, *The Societies of Europe: Elections in Western Europe since 1815, Electoral Results by Constituencies* (London: Macmillan, 2000), 396–400 (here 398).

30 "Der 70. Geburtstag des Fürsten Bismarck," *Norddeutsche Allgemeine Zeitung* (April 1, 1885): 1. A copy of the second edition of Scheffel's novel (1862) is preserved in Brahms's library.

31 Letter of April 4, 1885, from Brahms to Simrock, in *Briefwechsel*, 11: 94–95 (at 94). Brahms's reference to "fairy tales and legends" may have been prompted by the above-quoted leading article from the *Neues Wiener Tagblatt* (April 1, 1885).

The great man is idolized
By the good one who can make nothing himself.
The great man is despised
By the scoundrel who can see nothing great.
The great man is honored without restraint
By the man who can make something himself.[32]

Although Brahms's admiration for Bismarck is common currency, it has perhaps not been stressed sufficiently in the musicological literature that what really mattered for him was what the Iron Chancellor had facilitated during the 1860s and 1870s. These were the years, as we have seen, when Bismarck accomplished unification, gave the new nation-state a constitutional framework (limited though it was), and instituted no small number of liberal reforms in domestic policy. More problematic is determining what Brahms may have thought about Bismarck after the "great turn" of 1878–79, which initiated, in the words of Heinrich August Winkler, a transition from "leftist to rightist nationalism." Bismarck now broke with the committed free-trade ideology of the traditional liberals to support economic protectionism, ended the *Kulturkampf* and began working with the Catholic Center Party, and promulgated an antisocialist law while introducing welfare and social security programs in the hope of discouraging the working class from embracing social democracy.[33]

By now fully a Viennese, Brahms left more traces of his political attitudes during these later years to matters pertaining to Austria, the country that he had long called home. Austria, too, experienced a turn to the right in 1879, when the German liberals lost the hold on political power they had enjoyed

---

32   "Zum Bismarcktage," *Berliner Tageblatt* (April 1, 1885): 1. Vischer's original reads: "Blind verehrt einen großen Mann / Der Gute, der selbst nichts schaffen kann. / Nicht verehrt einen großen Mann / Der Wicht, der nichts Großes sehen kann. / Frei verehrt einen großen Mann / Der Mann, der selbst etwas schaffen kann." The last couplet is taken from the Epilogue, Scene 5, of Vischer's *Faust: Der Tragödie dritter Teil*, a parody of Goethe's *Faust: The Second Part of the Tragedy*, published in 1862 under the pseudonym Deutobold Symbolizetti Allegoriowitsch Mystifizinsky. The six-line adaptation that appears in the *Berliner Tageblatt* was published under the title "Verehrung" (Veneration) in *Fels zum Meer: Spemann's illustrierte Zeitschrift für das deutsche Haus* 2 (April–September 1885): 142. Vischer later included it in the enlarged second edition of his *Lyrische Gänge* (Lyrical passageways) (Stuttgart, Leipzig, Berlin, and Vienna: Deutsche Verlag-Anstalt, 1888), 178–79, as one of a group of "Ein- und Ausfälle" (Inspirations and diversions).

33   Winkler, *Germany: The Long Road West*, 213–23. On the "great turn," see Jonathan Steinberg, *Bismarck: A Life* (Oxford: Oxford University Press, 2011), 315; and Feuchtwenger, *Bismarck: A Political History*, 200–211.

164 ❧ EXCURSUS 2

for most of the constitutional era to Count Eduard von Taaffe and his conservative, pro-Slavic Iron Ring.[34] Yet evidence of Brahms's oppositional attitudes with respect to this new power arrangement in Austria—and in particular with respect to the perceived threats it posed to the preeminent status of the German language in public discourse in the multilingual state—suggests what Brahms must have thought about one of Bismarck's public policies in the 1880s. In a tendentious and markedly illiberal speech before the Lower House of the Prussian Diet on January 28, 1886, Bismarck, in his role as Prussian Chancellor, announced his determination to strengthen Germanization efforts in heavily Catholic, Polish-speaking East Prussia. Ending a short note to Simrock three days later with what can only have been an approving reference to this speech, Brahms wrote: "By the way, long live Bismarck!"[35]

All this aside, political orientation mattered very little during the national celebration of Bismarck's seventieth birthday. To the *Berliner Tageblatt* Bismarck was "the mighty hero who finally helped to make the aspirations and yearnings of all liberal patriots a tangible reality"; he was, indeed, a long-awaited "national Messiah" who had to be given his due for achieving German unification.[36] And that signal achievement would hereafter never be far from mind as Brahms, a man who "could make something himself," continued not only to honor but practically to idolize the "great man" freely.

---

34 William A. Jenks, *Austria under the Iron Ring* (Charlottesville, VA: University Press of Virginia, 1965). On Brahms's embrace of German liberalism as practiced in Late Habsburg Austria, see Brodbeck, *Defining Deutschtum*, 143–98 *passim*, 290–91; and Margaret Notley, *Lateness in Brahms: Music and Culture in the Twilight of Viennese Liberalism* (New York: Oxford University Press, 2007), 15–35, 204–20.

35 Matthew P. Fitzpatrick, "Poles and the Demographic Threat in Prussia, 1881–1887," in his *Purging the Empire: Mass Expulsions in Germany, 1871–1914* (Oxford: Oxford University Press, 2015), 93–122. Letter of January 31, 1886, *Briefwechsel*, 11: 113. A substantial portion of Bismarck's speech is given in English translation by Richard S. Levy in "Bismarck and the 'Polish Question'"; https://networks.h-net.org/node/35008/pages/60770/bismarck-and-polish-question.

36 "Zum Bismarcktage," *Berliner Tageblatt* (April 1, 1885): 1. Brahms could be forgiven if this characterization of Bismarck made him think of what Schumann had said about him twenty-two years earlier in "Neue Bahnen."

Part III
Fest- und Gedenksprüche,
op. 109

Chapter Five

"Words quite lovely and for us Germans uplifting"

Let us thank Master Johannes Brahms, for this beautiful, patriotic gift![1]
—Hugo Riemann, 1889

On May 23, 1889, Brahms received a telegram from Carl Petersen, the mayor of Hamburg. This brought word of the Hamburg Parliament's decision to confer on him the right of honorary citizenship (*Ehrenbürgerrecht*). The composer gratefully acknowledged receipt of this news by return wire and then, on May 30, followed up with Petersen in a heartfelt letter of gratitude.[2] Playing a discreet role behind the scenes was Hans von Bülow, a long-time friend and champion of Brahms who was then serving as the conductor of the city's *Abonnement Concerte*. In late March the archivist of the Hamburg Senate, Otto Beneke, prepared a memorandum of recommendation for that body's consideration—likely ghostwritten by Bülow—in which he vouched for Brahms's artistic significance by referring to his sterling reputation in the leading music journals and encyclopedias of the day and suggested that the conferral of an honorary citizenship might induce the composer to write a new work specifically for the inauguration of the city's new city hall, which was then in the early stages of construction. On April 26,

---

1   Unpublished program note; see below, footnote 25.
2   For Brahms's telegraphic reply, see Avins, *Johannes Brahms: Life and Letters*, 663. For his letter to Petersen, see Kurt Hofmann, "Brahmsiana der Familie Petersen: Erinnerungen und Briefe," *Brahms-Studien* 3 (1979): 69–105 (here 85). Bibliographical details regarding both sides of the Brahms-Petersen correspondence are available online in the *Brahms-Briefwechsel-Verzeichnis*, maintained by the Brahms-Institut, Musikhochschule Lübeck, https://www.brahmsinstitut.de/index.php?cID=316.

168 & CHAPTER FIVE

the Senate submitted its formal nomination to the Hamburg Parliament.[3] Word of this soon leaked in both the political and musical press, and on May 8 the *Neue Zeitschrift für Musik* published the text of the nomination in full.[4] It was from the latter report that another of Brahms's conductor friends, Franz Wüllner, learned the news. Knowing how much this would mean to the composer, who had long felt underappreciated by his native city—twice he had been passed over in the 1860s for appointment as conductor of the Hamburg Philharmonic—Wüllner wrote immediately to share his opinion that the honorary citizenship would surely be "worth more than all the medals in the world."[5] On May 22, the Parliament voted its approval. The deluxe, leather-bound *Ehrenbürgerbrief* (diploma of honorary citizenship), dated June 14, 1889, was prepared during the summer and presented to Brahms in a ceremony held at Petersen's country home outside Hamburg on September 14. It was subsequently put on public display for four weeks in the Hamburg Kunsthalle before eventually being hand-delivered to the composer in Vienna in late October.[6]

---

3   Passages from Beneke's memorandum, dated March 29, 1889 (Staatsarchiv Hamburg, Senat Cl. VII Lit. Bc Nr. 7a 3 Fasc. 10, p. 5), are published in Kalbeck, *Johannes Brahms,* 4: 181; Joachim Mischke, "Johannes Brahms: ein 'werther Sohn' der Hansestadt," *Hamburger Abendblatt* (June 21, 2014); https://www.abendblatt.de/hamburg/magazin/article129325879/Johannes-Brahms-Ein-werther-Sohn-der-Hansestadt.html, accessed April 9, 2022; and (in translation) in Minor, *Choral Fantasies,* 168. The Senate's memorandum is reproduced in *Verhandlungen zwischen Senat und Bürgerschaft im Jahre 1889* (Hamburg: Lücke & Wulff, 1890), 216.

4   See, for example, *Neue Freie Presse* (April 30, 1889) and *Neues Wiener Tagblatt* (May 1, 1889); *Neue Zeitschrift für Musik* 56 (May 8, 1889): 9.

5   Letter of May 11, 1889, from Wüllner to Brahms, in *Briefwechsel,* 15: 157–58. In 1887 Brahms was awarded Prussia's medal *Pour le Mérite for the Sciences and Arts.* And yet another medal would soon be forthcoming. On June 6, 1889, in part on the recommendation of Hanslick, Brahms was named to receive the Knight's Cross of the Austrian Imperial Order of Leopold; see the notice in the *Wiener Zeitung* (June 20, 1889): 1.

6   The memorandum of the Parliament's approval is reproduced in *Verhandlungen zwischen Senat und Bürgerschaft im Jahre 1889,* 285; the diploma of honorary citizenship, in "Hamburgs großer Sohn," in *"… in meinen Töne spreche ich." Für Johannes Brahms 1833–1897 (anläßlich der Ausstellung im Museum für Kunst und Gewerbe Hamburg 5. September–2. November 1897),* ed. Otto Biba and Jürgen Neubacher (Heidelberg: Edition Braus, 1997), 152–63 (at 161). See also Petersen's letters to Brahms of September 10 and October 21, 1889, and Brahms's letter to Petersen of late October, in Hofmann, "Brahmsiana der Familie Petersen," 86–89.

"WORDS QUITE LOVELY AND FOR US GERMANS UPLIFTING" ᾧ 169

Bülow waited until after Petersen had informed Brahms of the honor to send along his own congratulations. Word of this came in a letter of May 24. Remaining quiet at this stage about his involvement behind the scenes, Bülow gave full credit to Petersen for bringing the honor about. In the same letter the conductor also explained that he was organizing a three-day music festival for early September as part of the Hamburg Trade and Industrial Exhibition for which he intended to program music by the city's newest honorary citizen on every concert.[7] With his reply of May 30, Brahms sent a parcel containing a new work he thought might be particularly appropriate for performance on the festival: "They are three short, hymn-like *Sprüche* [biblical passages] for eight-part choir *a cappella*," he explained, "which are almost intended for days of national celebration and commemoration, and in connection with which those days of Leipzig, Sedan, and the Imperial Coronation could even be mentioned expressively, as far as I am concerned. (But better not!)"[8] Writing two days later to the choral conductor Julius Spengel, whose Hamburg *Cäcilienverein* would serve as the core of the choral forces used in the festival, Brahms characterized the *Sprüche* similarly

---

7   Hans von Bülow, *Die Briefe an Johannes Brahms*, ed. Hans-Joachim Hinrichsen (Tutzing: Hans Schneider, 1994), 66–67; translation in *Hans von Bülow's Letters to Johannes Brahms: A Research Edition*, ed. Hans-Joachim Hinrichsen, trans. Cynthia Klohr (Lanham, MD: Scarecrow Press, 2012), 56–57. On the exhibition, see Oliver Korn, *Hanseatische Gewerbeausstellungen im 19. Jahrhundert: Republikanische Selbstdarstellung, regionale Wirschaftsförderung und bürgerliches Vergnügen* (Opladen: Leske + Budrich, 1999), 115–37; and Steinmeister, *Im Weltgarten zu Hamburg*, 327–49.

8   Letter from Brahms to Bülow of 30 May 1889, in Bülow, *Die Briefe an Johannes Brahms*, 129; I have adapted my translation from Avins, *Johannes Brahms: Life and Letters*, 664–65. Avins translates *Sprüche* as "epigrams." Minor translates it as "sayings," but generally retains the collective title in German; see Minor, *Choral Variations*, 165. Beller-McKenna simply uses the original German title throughout, as I will also do. What seems to have escaped notice hitherto is the likelihood that Brahms called his pieces *Sprüche* to indicate that the texts he had chosen are significant biblical passages that are intelligible in and of themselves. See under "SPRUCH, m.," *Deutsches Wörterbuch von Jacob Grimm und Wilhelm Grimm*, digitalized version in the Wörterbuchnetz des Trier Center for Digital Humanities, Version 01.21, https://www.woerterbuchnetz.de/DWB?lemid=S37531, accessed January 23, 2022. The most notable antecedent in this respect is probably Felix Mendelssohn-Bartholdy's *Sechs Sprüche* for eight-part chorus, op. 79, although these were liturgical works composed for use at the Berlin Cathedral.

170 ❧ CHAPTER FIVE

as "hymn-like" works written "expressly for days of national celebration" (*Nationalfesttage*).[9]

This characterization is significant. By the later years of the nineteenth century, newly composed hymns might take various designs, but because they aimed, as Hugo Riemann put it, to achieve a "grandiosity of effect," they nearly always entailed singing by large choirs and were often accompanied by brass instruments. Moreover, and this is key, they typically contained "both sacred and secular content."[10] Riemann's account fits Brahms's *Sprüche* perfectly, right down to the *ad libitum* use of brass accompaniment. "The pieces are not very difficult," Brahms told Bülow, adding "I wouldn't mind if the wind players joined in."[11] The secular content of these settings of sacred texts have to do with three red-letter dates in the annals of the German national movement, all of which have drawn our attention before: the Battle of Leipzig on October 16–19, 1813, in which Napoleon Bonaparte's troops were defeated and finally forced to begin their withdrawal from Germany; the Battle of Sedan on September 1–2, 1870, in which the allied forces of the North German Confederation and the South German states defeated the French army and forced the capitulation of Napoleon III himself; and the ceremonial Imperial Proclamation in the Hall of Mirrors at Versailles on January 18, 1871. If the *Triumphlied* had embodied Brahms's sense of wonder and exaltation at the defeat of French military might and the subsequent rebuilding of the German Reich, the *Fest- und Gedenksprüche* (Festive and Commemorative *Sprüche*), op. 109, for eight-part double choir *a cappella*, may be said in part to embody the determination to preserve for Germany what had thereby been gained. Once more Brahms drew his texts from the Luther Bible. Once more the texts he selected could be understood to have political connotations. And once more, as we shall see, those connotations have at least in part to do with historical Franco-German enmity.

---

9   Annemari Spengel, ed., *Johannes Brahms an Julius Spengel: Unveröffentlichte Briefe aus den Jahren 1882–1897* (Hamburg: Gesellschaft der Bücherfreunde zu Hamburg, 1959), 31; trans. in Avins, *Johannes Brahms: Life and Letters*, 668, where "*Nationalfesttage*" is translated as "national holidays."

10   Hugo Riemann, *Musik-Lexikon* (Leipzig: Verlag des Bibliographischen Instituts, 1884), 409–10. Beller-McKenna cites this passage from Riemann in a different translation and to a different end; Beller-McKenna, *Brahms and the German Spirit*, 231n. As we shall see, the *Sprüche* also show historical links to the festive music of the seventeenth century, especially to the multi-voiced choral music of Giovanni Gabrielli and Heinrich Schütz.

11   Letter of May 30, 1889, in Avins, *Johannes Brahms: Life and Letters*, 664–65. I am aware of no early performance of the pieces that included brass, however. That Brahms did not include the option in the published score suggests that he finally decided against it.

In a letter of June 4, Bülow responded enthusiastically to what he characterized as Brahms's "strikingly grandiose new piece" and expressed his hope that Spengel would have time enough to prepare it for performance in September before his chorus broke off its rehearsals for the summer. Here, at last, the conductor also seems to have hinted that he, not Petersen, had been the one to instigate the process leading to the honorary citizenship, writing, in his inimitable style, "I am … sending a [H]anseatic document that pertains to you, but for which I refuse to take responsibility, as they say." Although we cannot determine with certainty what this document was, we may reasonably assume it had to do with the testimonial Bülow had probably supplied for Beneke in March, in which the suggestion was made that Brahms might respond to the honor with a new work written expressly for Hamburg. With the new *Sprüche* ready to be programmed in September, such a work was in effect already at hand.[12]

Whatever the case may be, Brahms contacted Simrock straightaway to arrange for the immediate printing of the parts.[13] From this correspondence we discover that he thought of the *Sprüche* as a collective work in three movements (*"Ich gebe die 3 Chöre als ein Werk"*)—this is an important point to which we shall return—and that he was uncertain about what to call it: "The title will be something like 'Deutsche Fest- und Gedenksprüche,' and I'm tempted, just in case, to suggest that you give a second title for other countries (Switzerland, England): 'National' etc. Would that be possible?" Simrock's reply is lost. It cannot have been encouraging, however, for the composer soon wrote again to acknowledge the impracticality of publishing the *Sprüche* under two different titles. The question of what the title *should* be, however, seems to have remained open in his mind until the end of the year.[14] At any rate, in its announcement that summer of the forthcoming music festival in Hamburg, the *Musikalisches Wochenblatt*, presumably acting on information provided by Bülow's office, gave the title of the still-unpublished pieces as *Deutsche Fest- und Gedenksprüche*.[15]

That same month Brahms was in touch with Petersen again, this time to share his hope of personally expressing his "venerating gratitude" for the honorary citizenship when he came to Hamburg in September. As for

---

12   Bülow, *Die Briefe an Johannes Brahms*, 67; trans. in *Hans von Bülow's Letters to Johannes Brahms*, 58.

13   As we have seen, the lack of printed parts for "Geleit" had precluded the possibility of a performance of this new choral song at the Vienna *Volksfest* in August 1863.

14   Letters from Brahms to Simrock of June 7, 11, and 15, 1889, in *Briefwechsel*, 11: 219–21 (here 220), 222, and 224, respectively; and undated letter of November 1889 from Brahms to Wüllner, in *Briefwechsel*, 15: 164.

15   *Musikalisches Wochenblatt* 20 (June 20, 1889): 313.

a public expression of thanks, this, he implied, would first come, as noted, in the form of a new choral work to be performed at Bülow's music festival, one whose words are "quite lovely and, for us Germans, uplifting."[16] Later would come a second: when, in February 1890, the new choruses were published under the title *Fest- und Gedenksprüche*, op. 109, they carried the dedication "To his Magnificence the Mayor Dr. Carl Petersen in Hamburg."[17]

Kross, once again seeking to inoculate the composer against charges of German nationalism, argued that the use of this pared-down, nationally indifferent title should encourage us to "strip [the music] of its national pathos."[18] To do so would be grossly misleading. For one thing, when Brahms wrote Petersen to ask permission to dedicate the music to him, he wryly noted that, had he not recently become acquainted with the mayor, he would have dedicated the music to Bismarck or Moltke, both of whom had been named honorary citizens of Hamburg in 1871 for their services in bringing about "the unity of the reborn German fatherland."[19] Notable, too, in this connection is Brahms's correspondence with Billroth, to whom he sent the autograph score to enjoy on his sixtieth birthday, on April 26, 1889, before learning of the Hamburg distinction to come. The letter that accompanied the score included a subtle hint about the music's patriotic meaning that Brahms presumably thought his fellow North German émigré in Vienna would not miss: "You must be reading a lot of nice things about yourself these days; that is a public hurrah in which I heartily and happily join. Perhaps, however, you would like to have a rest from words for once

---

16 Letter from Brahms to Petersen of June 1889, in Hofmann, "Brahmsiana der Familie Petersen," 85. On this visit, see Toni Petersen's "Erinnerungen an Brahms," in Hofmann, "Brahmsiana der Familie Petersen," 76–83 (here 77–79).

17 This is not to suggest that the *Sprüche* were in fact *composed* in response to receiving the Hamburg distinction. For a partial listing of the many scholars who have erroneously made this assumption, see Minor, *Choral Fantasies*, 239n. On the dedication, see Andrea Hammes, *Brahms gewidmet: Ein Beitrag zu Systemaktik und Funktion der Widmung in der zweiten Hälfte des 19. Jahrhunderts* (Göttingen: V & R unipress, 2015), 115–16.

18 "Man soll sie getrost heute ihres nationalen Pathos entkleiden, wie das ja eigentlich schon mit der Auslassung des Hinweises darauf im Titel vorgezeichnet ist." Kross, *Die Chorwerke von Johanns Brahms*, 453. Beuerle espouses a similar take; see Beuerle, *Johannes Brahms: Untersuchungen zu den A-cappella-Komposition*, 127.

19 Letter of October 1889 from Brahms to Petersen, in Hofmann, "Brahmsiana der Familie Petersen," 88–89 (at 88). *Verhandlungen zwischen Senat und Bürgerschaft im Jahre 1871* (Hamburg: Th. G. Meißner, 1872), 123–24 (quoted at 124).

and hear the hurrah in tones. The enclosed may be suitable for this. I wish I could have you awakened with it on the 26th—although of course other days are meant."[20]

Unlike Billroth, the broader public, as Bülow must have sensed, would require some guidance in discerning the work's grounding in patriotic history. Ignoring the composer's ironic expression of hesitation in the matter ("But better not!"), Bülow took steps to ensure that his public would be informed about the music's national touchstones. It was surely his doing, for example, that readers of the *Hamburgische Musikzeitung* learned in July that the city's forthcoming music festival would include the first performance of three new choruses by "our newest honorary citizen, ... 'commemorative *Sprüche*' [that] are related to the great events of the Wars of Liberation and the founding of the German Reich," and in particular to the Battle of Leipzig (the first chorus), the Battle of Sedan (the second), and the Imperial Coronation in Versailles, "the birthday of the German Reich" (the third).[21] By including all the texts in full (albeit without their biblical citations), the author of the unsigned article invited the readers—an imagined Culture Protestant readership—to draw the biblical-patriotic connections for themselves:

I [Die Schlacht bei Leipzig]	I [The Battle of Leipzig]
(*Psalm 22:5–6*)	
Unsere Väter hofften auf dich;	Our fathers trusted in you;
Und da sie hofften, halfst du ihnen aus.	Because they trusted, you delivered them.
Zu dir schrien sie, und wurden errettet,	To you they cried, and were saved;
Sie hofften auf dich, und wurden nicht zu Schanden.	In you they trusted, and were not put to shame.
(*Psalm 29:11*)	
Der Herr wird seinem Volk Kraft geben,	The Lord will give strength to his people,
Der Herr wird sein Volk segnen mit Frieden.	The Lord will bless his people with peace.

---

20   *Billroth und Brahms in Briefwechsel*, 444–45.

21   *Hamburgische Musikzeitung* (July 7, 1889): 2. The movement titles I have supplied in square brackets are taken from the description of the music in this article.

II [Die Schlacht bei Sedan]	II [The Battle of Sedan]
(*Luke 11:21*)	
Wenn ein starker Gewappneter	When a heavily armed man guards
seinen Palast bewahrt, So bleibet	his palace,
das Seine mit Frieden.	His possessions are secure.
(*Luke 11:17*)	
Aber: ein jeglich Reich,	But: every kingdom
So es mit ihm selbst uneins wird,	divided against itself
Das wird wüste,	Is brought to desolation,
Und ein Haus fallet über das andere.	and house falls upon house.
III [Der Tag von Versailles, der	III [The Day of Versailles, the
Geburtstag des Deutschen Reiches]	Birthday of the German Reich]
(*Deuteronomy 4:7*)	
Wo ist ein so herrlich Volk,	For what great people is there
Zu dem Götter also nahe sich tun	That has a God so near to it
Als der Herr, unser Gott,	As the Lord our God is to us,
so oft wir ihn anrufen.	whenever we call upon him.
(*Deuteronomy 4:9*)	
Hüte dich nur und bewahre deine	Take heed, and keep your soul
Seele wohl,	diligently,
Daß du nicht vergesset der Geschichte,	Lest you forget the history that
Die deine Augen gesehen haben,	your eyes have seen,
Und daß sie nicht aus deinem	And lest it departs from your heart
Herzen komme alle dein Lebenlang.	all the days of your life.
Und sollt deinen Kindern und	And make it known to your children
Kindeskindern kund tun.	and your children's children.

If the patriotic concerns of the work are bound up with the German-national movement that was born during the Napoleonic era, its polychoral medium is rooted in a more distant historical period. During the years when the *Sprüche* were composed, Brahms was closely engaged with the music of Heinrich Schütz (1585–1672), a one-time student of the Venetian polychoral master Giovanni Gabrieli (ca. 1554/57–1612), and the composer who was arguably most responsible for establishing depth and craftmanship as the hallmarks of the German style. (These are, of course, the hallmarks of Brahms's own style, too.) The composer's interest in Gabrieli and Schütz had been sparked during the course of his intense self-tuition in the music of the past that began during the 1850s, but it took on a particular intensity in later years.[22] Between 1885 and 1894 Schütz's collected works were published in sixteen volumes in an edition by the composer's friend Philipp

---

22 Virginia Hancock, *Brahms's Choral Compositions and His Library of Early Music* (Ann Arbor, MI: UMI Research Press, 1983); Virginia Hancock, "The Growth of Brahms's Interest in Early Choral Music, and Its Effect on His Own Choral Compositions," in *Brahms: Biographical, Documentary and*

Spitta. Brahms acquired each as it became available. The second and third volumes, which together contain Schütz's *Psalmen Davids* for eight-part chorus and continuo (1619), appeared in 1886–87. Brahms's exemplars show signs of a scrupulous study that paid dividends when, soon thereafter, he set to work on the *Fest- und Gedenksprüche*. None of his own polychoral settings is modeled after any single work by Schütz, to be sure, but general similarities of style abound.[23]

The "grandiosity of effect" Brahms seems to have intended in this work is achieved in no small measure through his skillful handling of the polychoral idiom. Particularly in the first two movements, the paired choruses frequently engage one another in block-like choral exchanges in a slow harmonic rhythm; passages such as these seem especially well suited for performance by large choirs in large spaces and with the wind doubling that Brahms half-heartedly authorized. Elsewhere, especially in the last movement, the voices of the two choirs come together as one united community. These uses of eight-voice musical texture help to create settings that are, in the apt words of Malcolm MacDonald, "forthright, public and sonorously collective in their utterance," a fitting musical dress for the patriotic topics taken up in the work.[24] There are other contributing factors as well. Each of the three short movements—together they have a performance time of only about ten minutes—unfolds an easily recognizable, if subtly executed, tripartite form. That major keys and diatonic harmonies predominate throughout likewise contributes to the uplifting public ethos of the music.

On September 9, 1889, the new work, as yet unpublished and still billed as *Deutsche Fest- und Gedenk-Sprüche* [*sic*], was performed *a cappella* with a chorus of some four hundred voices under Spengel's direction in the opening concert of Bülow's music festival on a program that also featured music by Beethoven, Wagner, and Mendelssohn (Figure 5). In an unsigned program note for this concert, Hugo Riemann offered a brief but insightful account of the music itself, and also, notably, rehearsed the music's patriotic reference points. In Riemann's slightly emended telling of what had first appeared in the *Hamburgische Musikzeitung*, the first and second movements refer, respectively, to the battles of Leipzig and Sedan, as before; but now the third movement not only "celebrates the magnificence of the new German

---

    Analytical Studies, ed. Robert Pascall (Cambridge: Cambridge University Press, 1983), 27–40.

23   Hancock, *Brahms's Choral Compositions and His Library of Early Music*, 91–93, 135–46; Ravizza, *Brahms: Spätzeitmusik*, 214–15.

24   MacDonald, *Brahms*, 328. MacDonald was of the mistaken belief that Brahms was commemorating Hamburg's bestowal on him of freedom of the city, not historical events of German-national significance, but that does not invalidate his description of the music's basic character.

Hamburgische Gewerbe- und Industrie-Ausstellung 1889.

Erstes Fest-Concert

unter gütiger Leitung des Herrn

Dr. Hans von Bülow

Montag, den 9. September, Abends 7½ Uhr in der Festhalle.

Solisten:

Frau **Marie Wilhelmj**, Concertsängerin aus Wiesbaden (Sopran).

Frau **Ernestine Heink-Rössler** vom Hamburg. Stadttheater (Alt).

Herr **Carl Dierich**, Grossherzogl. Mecklenb. Kammersänger aus Schwerin (Tenor).

Herr **Franz Schwarz**, Grossherzogl. Sächs. Hof-Opernsänger aus Weimar (Bass).

Chor ca. 400 Damen und Herren. — Orchester 116 Musiker.

PROGRAMM.

I.

1. **L. v. Beethoven:** Kyrie und Gloria a. d. Missa solemnis für Solistinnen, Chor und Orchester op. 123 (1823).

II.

2. **Joh. Brahms:** Deutsche Fest- und Gedenk-Sprüche für Chor a capella op. 109 (Manuscript).

    Unter gef. Leitung des Herrn Director Julius Spengel.

3. **R. Wagner:** Huldigungsmarsch. König Ludwig II. von Bayern gewidmet (1864).

III.

4. **F. Mendelssohn:** „Lobgesang". Symphonie-Cantate für Solostimmen, Chor und Orchester op. 52 (1840).

    Symphonie: Allegretto maestoso e vivace — Allegretto agitato — Adagio religioso.

Figure 5. Concert program, *Hamburgische Gewerbe- und Industrie-Ausstellung 1889*, Hamburg, September 9, 1889. Reproduced with permission of the British Library, London.

"WORDS QUITE LOVELY AND FOR US GERMANS UPLIFTING" ❦ 177

Reich" but, in a recollection of the sentiments expressed in the court and garrison chaplain Rogge's prayer during the Imperial Proclamation ceremony eighteen years earlier in Versailles, "cautions [the Germans of the new state] against arrogance."[25]

Brahms was pleased with what Riemann had written, and when the two happened to sit together during one of the last rehearsals in Hamburg, he "took the opportunity of thanking the younger man for making him 'come out smelling sweet' in the program book."[26] This is strong evidence that the composer was not unhappy that the national content of the music had been revealed to the public despite his eventual decision to omit any overt reference to it in the published score. We can assume, therefore, that neither would Brahms have been cross with a review like that of Paul Mirsch, who likewise pointed out the patriotic touchstones, and who concluded thus: "Popularity in the ordinary sense of the word will not be granted to the *Deutsche Fest- und Gedenksprüche*: with his most noble art ... Johannes Brahms has offered *his consecration on the altar of the fatherland* to all cultured and knowing people [*allen Gebildeten und Verständigen*], a lasting landmark of the highest ability and noblest sentiments."[27] This explicitly German-patriotic reading of the *Sprüche* was soon taken up by Louis Kelterborn and can be seen in the English-language reception of the work through the years preceding the outbreak of war in 1914.[28]

What, then, are we to make of Brahms's downplaying of patriotic sentiments in his letter to Bülow of May 30, 1889? In my view, it is—as so often the case—the composer's laconic style of writing that has created a good deal of confusion on this point. Kross believed Brahms took back his linkage of the pieces to the three specific historical events named above so that no one would mistake the music as a "glorification" (*Verherrlichung*) of those

---

25 The complete program booklets for all three festival concerts are preserved in the British Library, Abonnement Concerte, Hamburg (1886–1894) 1609/3137, Volume 2 (1889–90). Riemann's work was unsigned. Here I have quoted from vol. 2, p. 20.

26 [Carl Mennike], "Einleitung: Hugo Riemann, eine biographische Skizze nebst einem Verzeichnis seiner Werke," in *Riemann-Festschrift: Gesammelte Schriften*, ed. Carl Mennike (Leipzig: Max Hesses Verlag, 1909), VII–XXIV (here XX–XXI): "Brahms nahm noch Gelegenheit, Riemann zu danken dafür, daß er ihn im Programmbuch 'in so guten Geruch gebracht habe.'"

27 P[aul] Mirsch, "Hamburgische Gewerbe- und Industrie-Ausstellung. I. Festkonzert," *Hamburger Nachrichten, Abend-Ausgabe* (September 10, 1889): [1] (emphasis added), https://www.europeana.eu/de/item/9200338/BibliographicResource_3000119017471.

28 Kelterborn, "Johannes Brahms," in *Famous Composers and Their Music*, 4: 512; Evans, *Handbook to the Vocal Works of Brahms*, 470–71.

178 ⇚ CHAPTER FIVE

events, even if they had in fact been in Brahms's mind as he composed the choruses.[29] Beller-McKenna and Minor offer explanations of this "retraction" of their own. Both assume that Brahms, through his use of the locution "days of national celebration and commemoration," was referring to "national festivals," and in particular to those that were supposedly held in conjunction with three "national holidays." Beller-McKenna seeks to distance the composer at once from the displays of "military pomp and imperial aggrandizement" that marked state-sponsored festivals—he does not identify which ones—as well as from what he describes as the increasingly *völkisch* enthusiasms of *fin-de-siècle* popular festivals staged by the *Turnervereine* and *Schützenvereine* (and presumably also by the *Sängervereine*). Brahms's soft-pedalling of the ties with Leipzig, Sedan, and Imperial Coronation evinces a fear, Beller-McKenna holds, that his opus might become associated with the "dubious position the national festivals occupied by 1889."[30] For his part, Minor holds that Brahms's fleeting use in the first movement of a *Männerchor* texture is evidence to the contrary (mm. 29–36). Indeed, he argues that, by combining the male voices of the two choirs in this way while temporarily excluding the female voices, the composer intended to allude to the *völkisch* organizations that supposedly participated in these festivals, even if, at the same time, he had no desire that performances of the *Sprüche* should be limited to such venues.[31]

All this may be doubted, and not only because Brahms showed no discomfort when, on multiple occasions in 1889, the patriotic reference points of the three choruses were made public. Significantly, Brahms never characterized the music as being suitable for singing at "national festivals" (*nationale Feste*), that is, at the large public, often multi-day, commemorative gatherings that Minor seems to have in mind when he refers to "the festive culture of Brahms's *Kaiserreich*."[32] As we have seen, in correspondence pertaining to this music with Bülow and Spengel, he referred to *nationale Fest- und Gedenkstage* and *nationale Festtage*, respectively. And when he first mentioned the new choruses to Clara Schumann, he noted that they might well be sung on "national holidays [*nationale Feiertage*] such as Sedan, etc."[33] These are not distinctions without difference, even if Brahms's use

---

29   Kross, *Die Chorwerke von Johannes Brahms*, 437–38.

30   Beller-McKenna, *Brahms and the German Spirit*, 148.

31   Minor, *Choral Fantasies*, 173, 182–84.

32   Ibid., 165.

33   Letter to Clara Schumann dated "End of June 1889," in *Clara Schumann Johannes Brahms: Briefe aus den Jahren 1853–1896*, ed. Berhold Litzmann, 2 vols. (Leipzig: Breitkopf & Härtel, 1927), 2: 384–85 (here 385). As we have seen, strictly speaking, the only national holiday was the emperor's birthday. Sedan Day was, rather, a *Nationalfesttag* and treated as a regular work day.

"WORDS QUITE LOVELY AND FOR US GERMANS UPLIFTING" ❧ 179

in his letter to Clara Schumann of the term national holiday to characterize any day other than the emperor's birthday was, strictly speaking, incorrect.

Moreover, there were to my knowledge no large festivals held to celebrate the Imperial Coronation. Even in Prussia, where January 18 held longstanding significance as the anniversary of Prussia's elevation to the status of a kingdom, this day was not officially celebrated as a holiday with imperial connotations until 1896.[34] And it is also the case that celebrations of the victory over Napoleon at Leipzig dwindled after the founding of the German Reich, at least until the centenary of that victory in 1913.[35] It appears that the state-sponsored "festivals" to which Beller-McKenna refers were not national festivals at all but were instead the annual military maneuvers that William I used after 1871 "to celebrate the new nation and its new imperial monarchy." This was all the more important, as Frederik Frank Sterkenburgh observes, because the emperor refused to designate Sedan Day as "an annual German-national celebration."[36] To be sure, local celebrations of Sedan Day (occasionally even billed as "national festivals") were a common, if controversial and by no means universal, feature of German public life for the nationally minded bourgeoisie, in the schools, and among the veterans' associations. But the musical ambition of such events rarely exceeded the singing of familiar patriotic songs such as "Die Wacht am Rhein," "Das Deutschlandlied," and "Heil Dir im Siegerkranz," all standard fare well before the rise of the *völkisch* movement. There was simply no place in these events for performance of a musical work of the scope and difficulty of the *Fest- und Gedenksprüche*, not even in elaborately staged national festivals such as those that held in 1890 and 1895, the twentieth and twenty-fifth anniversaries, respectively, of the Battle of Sedan.[37]

The really salient point here, however, is that nowhere did Brahms ever suggest that his works were appropriate to be sung at "national festivals."

34   Wolfgang Hardtweg, "Bürgertum, Staatsymbolik und Staatsbewußtsein im Deutschen Kaiserreich 1871–1914," *Geschichte und Gesellschaft* 16/3 = *Bürger—Kleinbürger—Nation* (1990): 269–95 (here 291).

35   Tebbe, "Revision and 'Rebirth,'" 623–26; Ute Schneider, "Nationalfeste ohne politisches Zeremoniell? Der Sedantag (2. September) und die Erinnerung an die Befreiungskriege (18. Oktober) im Kaiserreich," in *Das politische Zeremoniell im Deutschen Kaiserreich 1871–1918*, ed. Andreas Biefang, Michael Epkenhans, and Klaus Tenfelde (Düsseldorf: Droste, 2008), 163–87 (here 178–79).

36   Frederik Frank Sterkenburgh, "Staging a Monarchical-Federal Order: Wilhelm I as German Emperor," *German History* 39 (2021): 519–41 (here 528).

37   *Pace* Minor, who holds that the *Sprüche*, while not intended exclusively for national festivals, were tailor-made to be performed in them (*Choral Fantasies*, 265). See, for example, the discussion in *Nationalismus im Kaiserreich—Der*

180 &❧ CHAPTER FIVE

In fact, Brahms evidently never envisioned performances of the *Sprüche* elsewhere than in standard, well-rehearsed performances in concert and church settings. These might take place in non-national choral festivals of all kinds. The Hamburg music festival held in September 1889 in connection with the city's *Gewerbe- und Industrie-Ausstellung* was one example; a festival held in August 1891 in Bern to celebrate the 700th anniversary of the Swiss city's founding was another.[38] None of this is to suggest that Brahms would have disapproved of *concert* performances given on days that carried patriotic meaning. On the contrary, he seems to have hoped for such performances in Germany at least, albeit as an integrated whole comprising "3 choruses as one work." Consider his letter from September 30, 1889, to Paul Limberger, the chairman of the board of the Leipzig Gewandhaus Orchestra. Limburger had attended the première of the *Sprüche* a few weeks earlier in Hamburg and subsequently wrote to the composer to inquire about arranging a performance of the still-unpublished pieces in Leipzig on the Gewandhaus's annual New Year's Day concert. Brahms replied with as much tact as he could muster to discourage this idea:

> The choruses are really only possible or permissible for your concerts under certain conditions. Thus I would like to ask you to wait for their appearance [in print] (about which I cannot say anything definite). Perhaps later it would seem appropriate to have them sung occasionally (notably on national birthdays) [*nationale Geburtstage*], in the church, and even the Gewandhaus. I cannot recommend them just now as the latest concert novelty.[39]

To understand why Brahms sought to dissuade Limburger—and why this had nothing to do with any "national question"—we must turn our attention back to the summer of 1889, when Brahms and Wüllner went over the score together in Bad Ischl, the Upper Austrian spa town the composer

---

"Sedantag" in Stuttgart 1895: ein Quellen- und Arbeitsbuch für den Geschichtsunterricht, ed. Michael Hoffmann, Jürgen Lotterer, and Günter Riederer (Stuttgart: Stadtarchiv, 1997), 17–21, 40.

38 *Die 700jährige Gründungsfeier der Stadt Bern, 1191–1891* (Bern: Schmid, Francke & Cie., 1891): 73.

39 This letter was first published in Johannes Forner, *Johannes Brahms in Leipzig: Geschichte einer Beziehung* (Leipzig: Edition Peters, 1987), 91–92. For an earlier English translation, which gives Brahms's locution "nationale Geburtstage" as "national holidays" and omits the composer's plea to Limburger to wait for the publication of the works before programming them, see Minor, *Choral Fantasies,* 174.

"WORDS QUITE LOVELY AND FOR US GERMANS UPLIFTING" ❧ 181

favored for summer holidays in his later years.[40] The director of both the *Musikhochschule* in Cologne and the city's Gürzenich Orchestra concerts, Wüllner was an experienced choral conductor whose judgment in such matters Brahms took seriously. It appears that after studying the score Wüllner made some suggestions for improvements. But since Spengel had already begun rehearsals for his performance at the forthcoming Hamburg trade show using parts produced by Simrock in accordance with Brahms's original score, there was nothing to be done before the première in September. These circumstances suggest why Brahms tried to deter Limburger: he presumably wanted no more public performances of the pieces until he had heard the Hamburg première, had made revisions, and had the final version of the score and parts published.

Meanwhile, probably during his summertime visit with the composer in Ischl, Wüllner expressed an interest in performing the new choruses himself during the coming season in Cologne, and with that in mind Brahms hoped that Wüllner might be able to run through the work in a pre-publication rehearsal in December to try out any revisions the composer might wish to make after the performance in Hamburg.[41] At first he thought Wüllner could employ, with only minor adjustments, the specially printed parts that Spengel had used in Hamburg. But in a letter of November 3 he wrote to ask the conductor to await delivery of a new set of parts from Simrock and of a full score that he would prepare himself, both of which incorporated more extensive changes than had originally been anticipated, including a complete rewriting of the ending of the first number.[42]

Brahms was not present in Cologne when, on 19 December, Wüllner rehearsed the revised work with his choir, but the conductor wrote a week later to assure him that the *Sprüche* "had been sung quite well and [given]

---

40   On Minor's differing take, see *Choral Fantasies*, 173–74. The narrative presented in this paragraph and the next is pieced together from Brahms's correspondence with Wüllner in the fall of 1889; see *Briefwechsel*, 15: 160–67 *passim*. See also Brahms's letter to Simrock of November 4, 1889, in *Briefwechsel*, 12: 10–12.

41   Kalbeck's supposition that Wüllner had rehearsed the pieces already by mid-June 1889 is not credible. *Briefwechsel*, 11: 224n. When, in his letter to Simrock of June 15 Brahms reports that he had received "a lovely telegram" from Cologne with 79 signatures, he was probably alluding to a telegram received from Wüllner's choristers sent in congratulations on Brahms's honorary citizenship, not, as Kalbeck supposed, in response to their having rehearsed his *Sprüche*. Ibid., 224.

42   For a transcription of the original ending of op. 109, no. 1, see the *Revisionsbericht* for *Fest- und Gedenksprüche*, in Brahms, *Sämtliche Werke*, vol. 21.

182 &» CHAPTER FIVE

great pleasure to the participants and listeners alike," adding, "they are magnificent pieces and ... sound excellent."[43] Considering that Wüllner would not even be able to try out the revised pieces until mid-December, it is no wonder that Brahms would not want to give the go-ahead to the Leipzig performance a short time later. As he explained to Simrock in mid-November, a performance in Leipzig on New Year's Day would be quite impossible because the *Thomaner* would have no time [for rehearsals] during the holiday season." In the event, Rust's concert performance, using the combined forces of the St. Thomas Choir and the *Akademischer Chorverein Arion*, went forward against Brahms's wishes, probably with the use, as Virginia Hancock has plausibly suggested, of parts pirated from Simrock's firm.[44] Rust led a second performance in a service held at St. Thomas Church on January 11, and thereafter the *Fest- und Gedenksprüche* were a fixture in the choir's repertoire. Perhaps with Brahms's suggestion to Limburger in mind, *complete* performances of the set during the Wilhelmine era were often performed on or very near to September 2, that is, Sedan Day, which, despite the controversy that had originally surrounded it, came to be accepted as the Reich's "national birthday." As for the first public performance of the *Sprüche* in their final, revised form, this came on March 13, 1890, when Wüllner performed the pieces with his choir in Cologne. Brahms attended and was by all accounts delighted.[45]

Brahms's correspondence with Billroth establishes late April 1889 as the *terminus ad quem* of the completion of the *Sprüche* as heard in the pre-publication performance in Hamburg; similarly, his correspondence with Wüllner establishes November 1889 as the *terminus ad quem* of the revised version that saw print in March 1890. The date of the work's origin is far more difficult to determine. When did Brahms first give thought to composing these biblical passages? When did he in fact compose them? And how did his musical settings of biblical texts project a patriotic message? It is to these questions that we turn in the two chapters that follow.

---

43   Letter from Wüllner to Brahms of December 26, 1889, in *Briefwechsel*, 15: 165–67.

44   Virginia Hancock, "Pre-Publication Performances and Brahms's Revisions of the *Fest-und Gedenksprüche*, Op. 109," unpublished paper given at the Annual Meeting of the American Musicological Society (Kansas City, MO, November 1997).

45   For the correspondence between the two in the lead up to this performance, see *Briefwechsel*, 15: 172–76.

Chapter Six

The Stuff of Tragedy?

As 1870, the year of German victories, gave birth to the *Triumphlied*, so 1888, the Year of Three Emperors, the year of German mourning, gave birth to the Commemoration *Sprüche*.[1]

—Max Kalbeck

On March 9, 1888, Emperor William I died in Berlin just two weeks shy of his ninety-first birthday. He was followed on the throne by the moderately liberal Crown Prince Frederick William. As everyone had known for months, the new German emperor, who took the regnal name Frederick III, was not well. Already deep in the throes of throat cancer, he was unable even to speak, and on June 15 he died after reigning for only ninety-nine days. Thereupon his twenty-nine-year-old eldest and decidedly non-liberal son became Emperor William II.[2]

Kalbeck supposed that Brahms "sought to find comfort" at this time of "distress and affliction" by giving musical expression to the words of the *Fest- und Gedenksprüche*.[3] Beller-McKenna expands this tragedy trope to take in a far broader context than Kalbeck intended. Attributing a personal piety to the composer that strikes me as unfounded, he proposes that Brahms offers in the work a series of national prayers for Germany at a time of what he calls "ominous divisions in the *Kaiserreich*" between those who viewed the German state in terms of top-down dynastic patriotism and those who viewed it in terms of bottom-up *völkisch* nationalism. Without citing hard

---

1   Kalbeck, *Johannes Brahms*, 4: 186.

2   Müller, *Our Fritz*, 149–242; John C. G. Röhl, *Young Wilhelm: The Kaiser's Early Life, 1859–1888*, trans. Jeremy Gaines and Rebecca Wallach (Cambridge: Cambridge University Press, 1998), 773–825; and John C. G. Röhl, *Wilhelm II: The Kaiser's Personal Monarchy, 1888–1900*, trans. Sheila de Bellaigue (Cambridge: Cambridge University Press, 2004), 1–72. The crown prince's cancer diagnosis had been made public on November 12, 1887; see Müller, *Our Fritz*, 204.

3   Kalbeck, *Johannes Brahms*, 4: 187.

184 &❧ CHAPTER SIX

evidence that Brahms saw things thus, Beller-McKenna asserts that Brahms had by 1888 come to hold a "conflicted attitude toward his own patriotism" that is revealed in the *Fest- und Gedenksprüche*. In his view, the largely positive images conveyed in its outer movements of a people delivered by God and of a God who remains near to his people, surround what he calls the "dark core" of the entire opus, coming in the dead center of the middle movement, which presents a "troubled image of [a] *Reich*" divided against itself.[4]

We have reason to doubt this claim. To begin with, as Jan Markert has noted, when William I died, the Hohenzollern monarchy was "at the peak of its popularity, political legitimacy, and stability." The divide to which Beller-McKenna seems to be alluding did not take hold, as we shall see, until the 1890s, after Bismarck had left office.[5] Moreover, the tone of the *Sprüche*—characterized by bright-sounding, largely diatonic harmony in major keys—scarcely fits with a mood of national mourning or consolation and seems far more in keeping with the three uplifting national events that Brahms would later mention to Bülow in connection with the Hamburg première.[6] Indeed, the composer first gave thought to composing the biblical texts already in the later 1870s, during the early years of the Bismarckian Reich, at a time when National Liberalism was at its strongest and when, with William I by then approaching his eightieth birthday and his eldest son in good health, there was no reason to think that the liberal crown prince would not eventually enjoy a long reign.

The earliest evidence of Brahms's engagement with these texts is found in a small, upright notebook he maintained of biblical citations for possible use

---

4   Beller-McKenna, *Brahms and the German Spirit*, 78, 143–51, and 163–64 (quoted at 143 and 163).

5   Jan Markert, "'Wer Deutschland regieren will, muß es sich erobern.' Das deutsche Kaiserreich als monarschisches Projekt Wilhelms I.," in *Einigkeit und Recht, doch Freiheit: Das Deutsche Kaiserreich in der Demokratiegeschichte und Erinnerungskultur*, ed. Andreas Braune et al. (Stuttgart: Franz Steiner Verlag, 2021), 11–37 (at 31); Pieter M. Judson, "Nationalism in the Era of the Nation State, 1870–1945," in *Oxford Modern German History*, ed. Helmut Walser Smith (Oxford: Oxford University Pres, 2011), 499–526.

6   Jürgen Heidrich also notes the incongruence between Kalbeck's tragedy trope and Brahms's linking of the pieces to celebrations of the German nation. See Jürgen Heidrich, "'der getreue Eckart des über alles geliebten Vaterlandes'? Johannes Brahms, das 'Dreikaiserjahr' und die 'Fest- und Gedenksprüche' op. 109," in *Spätphase(n)? Johannes Brahms' Werke der 1880er und 1890er Jahre: Internationales musikwissenschaftliches Symposium Meiningen 2008*, ed. Maren Goltz, Wolfgang Sandberger, and Christiane Wiesenfeldt (Munich: Henle Verlag, 2010), 88–95 (at 89–90).

THE STUFF OF TRAGEDY? ❧ 185

in musical compositions (hereafter: biblical notebook).[7] This source originally comprised twenty-four leaves, the first twelve and last two of which were subsequently torn out. What remains is one omnibus gathering of relatively short verses written in lead pencil (on fols. 13r–15r), followed by another, likely made later, that is written in black ink and comprises relatively lengthier passages (on fols. 15v–19r). Let us for now focus attention on the inscriptions made on fols. 13r–14r, among which are two passages that were used in the motet "Warum ist das Licht gegeben dem Mühlseligen," op. 74, no. 1 (James 5:11 and Lamentations 3:41); two that were used in "Ich aber bin elend" (Psalm 69:30 and Exodus 34:6–7), the first of the Three Motets, op. 110; and all four of the passages used in the *Fest- und Gedenksprüche*. The proximity of all these texts within the notebook establishes 1877, the year in which "Warum" was completed, as the probable *terminus ante quem* of this set of notebook entries.[8]

Relevant to the question too is evidence provided by another notebook, one in which the composer, beginning in March 1877 and evidently continuing into the next decade, wrote out 112 poems for possible use as song texts.[9] Brahms's musical settings of several of these poems date from the mid-1880s. Among these is his setting of Friedrich Rückert's "Gestillte Sehnsucht," which he composed in the summer of 1884 and published later that year as the first of the Two Songs for Alto, Viola, and Piano, op. 91. Notably, in the right-hand margin of the leaf containing Rückert's poem (fol. 12r) is the complete biblical text of op. 109, no. 1 (Psalm 22), and cross-references to the texts of op. 109, nos. 2 and 3 (Luke 11:21 and 17, and Deuteronomy 4:7 and 9).[10] In view of how closely the succession of movements in op. 109 as characterized by Brahms to Bülow tracks with the pedestal inscription of Schilling's *Germania* ("Leipzig–Sedan–Imperial

---

7   The notebook is preserved in the Wienbibliothek im Rathaus under the shelf-mark H.I.N. 55 733. See George S. Bozarth, "Brahms's Lieder Inventory of 1859–60 and Other Documents of His Life and Works," *Fontes Artis Musicae* 30 (1983): 98–117 (at 109–10); and Beller-McKenna, *Brahms and the German Spirit*, 53–57.

8   Brahms's quotation of Exodus 34:6–7 is ascribed to the motet op. 110, no. 2 ("Ach, arme Welt") in Bozarth, "Brahms's Lieder Inventory of 1859–60," 109.

9   This source is preserved in the Wienbibliothek im Rathaus under the shelf-mark H.I.N. 55 731. See Bozarth, "Brahms's Lieder Inventory of 1859–60," 111–12; and McCorkle, *Brahms Werkverzeichnis*, 744.

10   Also found, crossed out in the lower right-hand margin, is the text for Job 9:11: "Siehe, er gehet vor mir über, ehe ichs gewahr werde, und verwandelt sich ehe ichs merke" (Behold, he passes before me before I am aware of it, and changes before I realize it).

186 ❧ CHAPTER SIX

Coronation" = "In memory of the unanimous and victorious uprising of the German people and of the restoration of the German Reich 1870–1871"), we must consider the possibility that the *Fest- und Gedenksprüche* stands as a sonic manifestation of the Small German conception of history already given concrete expression in the Niederwald Monument, which, as we know, Brahms visited in September 1883.[11]

None of this is to say that Brahms gave no thought in 1888 to memorializing the recently deceased emperors. But those thoughts almost certainly did not come to fruition, contrary to general understanding, in the *Fest- und Gedenksprüche*, or, for that matter, in any other surviving musical composition by Brahms.

A Musical Commemoration?

On the day of William I's death, Brahms wrote from Vienna to Simrock in Berlin: "How strangely solemn it must be. I always wish I were in Germany at such great, cheerful, or serious moments, one has the desire to feel it more fully." That same day his friend Elisabeth von Herzogenberg shared her feelings with the composer at the end of a long letter begun several weeks earlier: "The emperor's death was a great shock to us.... Now he is [gone] and the poor crown prince as good as dead. How terrible to enter into such an inheritance in his condition! To have spent a lifetime in expectation of this moment, and then to be unable to say "Tarry awhile!" It's one of the saddest things the world has ever seen." Brahms replied immediately: "I have, of course, been much affected by the shattering events in Germany. It is all on a scale—a tragic scale at present—unparalleled in history."[12]

By June, Brahms was in Switzerland, beginning a lengthy composing holiday in Thun, close to the home of Joseph Viktor Widmann, a writer, critic, and journalist to whom we shall return. Shortly upon his arrival there, word of Frederick's passing was received. This death lies at the heart of the "imperial tragedy" Kalbeck had in mind when writing about the emotional impact

---

11 As we have seen, on September 16, 1877, the cornerstone of the monument was laid in well-reported ceremonies in Rüdesheim presided over by the emperor. This event thus took place at around the time when Brahms, whose motet "Warum" was composed that summer, seems to have entered the texts he would eventually use in Op. 109 in his biblical notebook.

12 *Briefwechsel*, 11: 178; *Briefwechsel*, vols. 1–2: *Johannes Brahms im Briefwechsel mit Heinrich und Elisabeth von Herzogenberg*, ed. Max Kalbeck (1908), 2: 173–81 (at 180), 181–83 (at 183). Herzogenberg alluded in her letter to the famous line from Part I of Goethe's *Faust*: "Verweile doch, du bist so schön" (Tarry awhile, you are so fair!).

THE STUFF OF TRAGEDY? ❧ 187

on Brahms of the *Dreikaiserjahr*.[13] William I, after all, had lived to be a nonagenarian; his passing was something to be mourned, but it was not the stuff of tragedy. The death of the fifty-seven-year-old Frederick hit harder. For he was a figure on whom many liberals had long pinned their hopes for the future. Registering the impact of the loss on Brahms was the poet Klaus Groth, who was visiting the composer in Thun at the time: "When we heard the news we went straight to a shop to buy black crepe, in order to show the English colony in particular how German men felt the loss."[14]

A month later, Simrock sent Brahms a copy of Heinrich von Treitschke's essay *Zwei Kaiser. 15. Juni 1888*, a short panegyric to the two recently deceased emperors.[15] The exemplar preserved in the composer's library contains a small number of markings that merit some consideration. Some are written in blue pencil; others, in lead pencil. Since the majority are vertical lines drawn in the margin or else underlining of short passages in the text, it is difficult to determine which may have been made by Simrock and which by Brahms. Circumstantial evidence, however, allows us to make some educated guesses in this regard. In particular, annotations written in blue pencil appear to have been made by the publisher before he sent the pamphlet to Brahms, while most if not all of those written in lead pencil were the work of the composer.

The first annotation, a nota bene ("NB") written in Brahms's hand, highlights a passage found on page 8: "durch die Kaiserkrönung im Bourbonensaale von Versailles ward alles überboten, was die Kämpfer von 1813 einst von dem ersehnten dritten Punischen Kriege erhofft hatten. Die Preußen erkannten dankbar, daß ihre Verfassung unter diesem starken Königtum besser denn je gesichert war" (through the coronation of the Emperor in the Bourbon Hall at Versailles, everything that the fighters of 1813 had once hoped could come from the longed-for Third Punic War was

---

13 Kalbeck, *Johannes Brahms*, 4: 187.

14 Letter of June 22, 1888, from Klaus Groth to Charlotte Finke, quoted in *Johannes Brahms—Klaus Groth: Briefe der Freundschaft*, ed. Dieter Lohmeier (Heide, 1997), 119. On Frederick's liberalism, see Müller, *Our Fritz*, 63–104. On the tragic fate of Frederick and his wife Victoria ("Vicky"), the Royal Princess of the United Kingdom, who was a more committed liberal even than her husband, see Thomas A. Kohut, *Wilhelm II and the Germans: A Study in Leadership* (New York and Oxford: Oxford University Press, 1991), 19–29. The region around Lake Thun was popular with English summer tourists, whose curiosity about the musical celebrity in their midst was, according to Kalbeck, a source of some annoyance to Brahms. See Kalbeck, *Johannes Brahms*, 4: 149.

15 Heinrich Treitschke, *Zwei Kaiser. 15 Juni 1888. Abdruck aus dem 62. Bande der Preußischen Jahrbücher* (Berlin: Georg Reimer, 1888).

188 &❧ CHAPTER SIX

surpassed. The Prussians gratefully recognized that their constitution was better secured than ever under this strong kingdom). Why Brahms's attention might be drawn to this passage is not difficult to understand: it presents the same Smaller-German historical narrative as that carved into the stone of the Niederwald Monument and represented in the succession of the three movements of his *Fest- und Gedenksprüche*.

Other markings are more intriguing. The last six lines of page 15 are highlighted with a vertical line in the margin written in lead pencil; similar highlighting in blue pencil is found on pages 16–17 (Figure 6). At the beginning of this passage, Treitschke refers almost patronizingly to Frederick William's strong public stances—what to the historian were signs of his political naïveté—not only against the racial antisemitism that had emerged in Germany around 1880, but also to displays of national chauvinism:

> He was the first in the line of Prussian heirs to the throne to be academically educated, and with pride he wore the purple coat of the rector of the old Albertina. But in the quiet life he led for so long, the crown prince sometimes lost touch with the powerfully emerging times and was no longer able to follow its new ideas. The antisemitic movement, the cause of which lay solely in the arrogance of the Jews, he thought he could dismiss with a few words of angry rebuke, and he even warned the Königsberg students of the dangers of chauvinism—a sentiment that, after two centuries of cosmopolitanism, is as foreign to the Germans as is its Frenchy name ...[16]

Then, after discussing the mishandling of the late emperor's medical care at the hands of an English doctor favored by his wife rather then follow the approach (the correct one, as it turned out) of a team of German physicians, Treitschke goes on to praise the superiority of monarchical government over republicanism on account of its durability. And so he laments that the very short-term government of Frederick III "could only become a sad episode in national history," not only "through the nameless sufferings of the noble

---

16 Treitschke, *Zwei Kaiser*, 15–16. In a series of remarks made in 1879–81, the crown prince had become the only member of the royal family to speak openly against antisemitism. Frank Lorenz Müller describes his reaction as "public, courageous, and unequivocal." Müller, *Our Fritz*, 74–75. The term chauvinism was originally used to characterize the fanatical devotion to all things military embraced after Napoleon's fall by some of the veterans of his armies; it is derived from the name of one such veteran, Nicolas Chauvin. The text of the speech in Königsberg was published in the *Vossische Zeitung, Abend-Ausgabe* (June 5, 1885): 1, and elsewhere. Brahms, who had returned to Vienna from his summer holiday in Mürzzuschlag on September 20, would surely, at the very least, have read the coverage provided in any of several Viennese newspapers, including the *Neue Freie Presse, Abendblatt* (June 5, 1885): 2.

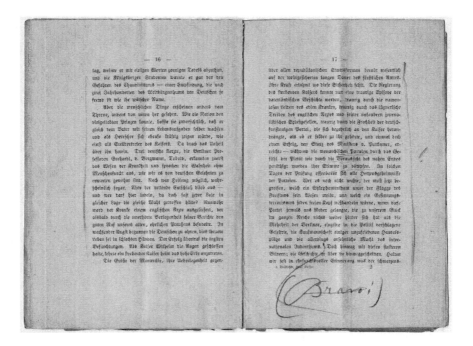

Figure 6. Heinrich von Treitschke, *Zwei Kaiser, 15. Juni 1888*, pp. 16–17. Reproduced with permission of the Archive of the Gesellschaft der Musikfreunde, Vienna.

sick man" and "the mendacious goings-on of the English doctor and his unclean journalistic henchmen," but also owing "to the insolence of the German Liberal Party [*Frechheit der Deutsch-freisinnigen Partei*]." In this last comment, Treitschke aims his attack on the left-liberals for attempting to hijack the emperor for their own cause at the very moment of his greatest suffering. Although the historian shudders at the thought that such a party might ever come to power, he takes comfort in believing this to be unlikely, since the purveyors of this "ideological terrorism" (*Gesinnungsterrorismus*) had "nothing more behind [them] in the entire Reich than the majority of Berliners, individual scholars who have been drawn into politics, the merchants of a few dissatisfied trading centers, and the admittedly considerable power of international Jewry."[17]

What would Brahms have made of all this? In the following chapter, we shall find strong evidence that at this stage of his life he essentially agreed with Treitschke on the merits of durable monarchical government. This is

---

17   Treitschke, *Zwei Kaiser*, 17.

190 &❧ CHAPTER SIX

not entirely surprising. Gustav Jenner, who studied with Brahms beginning around this time, reported that he often heard the composer praise "dauerhafte Musik" (durable music), by which he meant "music that is rooted in the deep underground of the spirit of music and nowhere contradicts it."[18] This attitude, this reverence of deep and abiding tradition, may not be incompatible with a preference for deeply rooted monarchical governance.

Whether Brahms shared Treitschke's total abhorrence of the left-liberals is uncertain. What is certain is the strong exception he took to Treitschke's well known antisemitism.[19] As he wrote to Simrock when acknowledging receipt of the pamphlet on July 21, 1888: "The Treitschke has just arrived, and I am very much looking forward to it. But I will hardly write such a simple Bravo as you do. Precisely at the point where your Bravo is written, the lie is really too outrageous." [20] From this cryptic remark we may safely conclude that the "Bravo!" entered in blue pencil in the bottom margin of page 17 of Brahms's exemplar and connected back to the Treitschke's condemnation of "international Jewry" (*internationales Judenthum*) was Simrock's annotation. It was surely Brahms, then, who struck out that annotation in lead pencil.[21]

Four years earlier, in May 1884, Hanslick had placed in Brahms's hands for authentication the recently discovered copyist scores of Beethoven's early, previously unknown *Cantata on the Death of Joseph II*, WoO 87, and *Cantata on the Accession of Leopold II*, WoO 88 (both 1790). Following up with Hanslick, Brahms not only vouched for the authenticity of the compositions, but wrote in noteworthy terms about how Beethoven's music had captured something of what the German nation had lost with the death of the liberal reformer Joseph II ("still remembered and never replaced," as he put it).[22] Perhaps Brahms had something like this in mind as he and Groth mourned Frederick III's death so early in his reign in June 1888. After all, as Maciej Janowski notes, the traditions of "enlightened absolutism" of Joseph

---

18   Gustav Jenner, *Johannes Brahms als Mensch, Lehrer und Künstler: Studies und Erlebnisse* (Marburg: N. G. Elwert'sche Verlagsbuchhandlung, 1905), 74.

19   Heinrich von Treitschke, *Ein Wort über unser Judenthum* (Berlin: G. Reiner, 1880).

20   *Briefwechsel*, 11: 193–94 (at 194).

21   Since it was Simrock who made the inscription "Bravo!," it seems probable that the marginal lines that were made in blue pencil on pages 16–17, if not also the marginal line made in lead pencil next to the last six lines on page 15, were made by the publisher as well.

22   Brahms's letter to Eduard Hanslick of May 1884, in Avins, *Johannes Brahms: Life and Letters*, 612–14. Avins rightly draws attention to the importance of this letter in revealing Brahms's humanitarian and, by extension, his political views. Ibid., 613n.

THE STUFF OF TRAGEDY? 🙟 191

II in Austria and of Frederick the Great in Prussia were commonly "invoked by the liberals as their own."[23] Brahms would have had good reason to think that Frederick III would have ruled with an equally if not greater liberal spirit.[24]

A Path Not Taken

Whatever these speculations may amount to, we have reason to believe that in the "tragic" summer of 1888 Brahms culled his Luther Bible anew for texts suitable for an envisioned musical memorial to the two deceased emperors. To explore this possibility, let us return to his notebook of biblical citations, directing our attention now to the texts written out in black ink on fols. 15v–16v (Table 1).[25]

Circumstantial evidence suggests these undated entries were written out in 1888. The first citation, for example, may well have been prompted by a suggestion made to Brahms by Elisabeth von Herzogenberg in a letter of March 28 of that year. Undoubtedly recalling the dedication sixteen years earlier of the *Triumphlied* ("To his Majesty the German Emperor William I reverently dedicated by the composer"), Herzogenberg now proposed that Brahms should "write something dear for the dear *departed* emperor, so that *once again* a worthy sound will sound in his honor."[26] The text of 1 Kings 6:11–14 was eminently suitable for this purpose. It allowed Brahms to liken the late, beloved William I, the founding head of the first nation-state of the German people, to King Solomon, the builder of the First Temple of the Jews—a symbolic pairing if ever there were one.[27]

---

23 Maciej Janowski, "Wavering Friendship: Liberal and National Ideas in Nineteenth Century East-Central Europe," *Ab Imperio* 3–4 (2000): 69–90 (at 71), quoted in Oskar Mulej, "National Liberals and Their Progeny: Approaching the Peculiar Developments in Central European Liberal Party Traditions, 1867–1918," *Acta Poloniae Historica* 111 (2015): 57–81 (at 60–61).

24 On the left-liberals and the crown prince, and on Bismarck's fight to prevent any effective alliance between the two, see Müller, *Our Fritz*, 149–90.

25 For a more detailed tabular presentation of all the biblical texts touched on in the discussion that follows, given in German and in English translation, see Nicole Grimes, *Brahms's Elegies: The Poetics of Loss in Nineteenth-Century German Culture* (Cambridge: Cambridge University Press, 2019), 184–89 (Table 4.1).

26 *Briefwechsel*, 2: 188 (emphasis added).

27 Beller-McKenna also notes the suitability of this biblical text for a work pertaining to William I. See Beller-McKenna, *Brahms and the German Spirit*, 63.

Table 1. Brahms's biblical notebook, fols. 15v–16v.

Fol. 15v	1 Kings 6:11–14	Now the word of the Lord came to Solomon. "Concerning this house that you are building, if you will walk in my statutes and obey my ordinances and keep all my commandments and walk in them, then I will establish my word with you, which I spoke to David your father. And I will dwell among the children of Israel and will not forsake my people Israel." So Solomon built the house and finished it.
	Ecclesiasticus 41:1–4	O death, how bitter is the thought of you to the one at peace among possessions, who has nothing to worry about and is prosperous in everything, and still is vigorous enough to enjoy food! O death, how sweet you are to one who is old and failing in strength, worn down by age and has nothing better to hope for or expect.
Fol. 16r	Ecclesiastes 3:18–22	I said in my heart with regard to the children of man that God is testing them that they may see that they themselves are but beasts: For what happens to the children of man and what happens to the beast is the same: as one dies, so dies the other. They all have the same breath, and man has not advantage over the beasts, for all is vanity. All go to one place. All are from the dust, and to dust all return. Who knows whether the spirit of man goes upward and the spirit of the beast goes down into the earth? So I saw that there is nothing better than that a man should rejoice in his work, for that is his lot. Who can bring him to see what will be after him?
Fol. 16v	Ecclesiastes 4:1–4, *beginning of v. 5*	Again I saw the oppressions that are done under the sun. And behold, the tears of the oppressed, and they had no one to comfort them! On the side of their oppressors there was power, and there was no one to comfort them. And I thought the dead who are already dead more fortunate than the living who are still alive. But better than both is he who has not yet been and has not seen the evil deeds that are done under the sun. Then I saw that all toil and all skill in work come from a man's envy of his neighbor. This also is vanity and striving after wind. *Do not fear death.*

THE STUFF OF TRAGEDY? ❦ 193

Next in the notebook are three deeply pessimistic ruminations on death: Ecclesiasticus 41:1–4 (bottom of fol. 15v); Ecclesiastes 3:18–22 (fol. 16r); and Ecclesiastes 4:1–4 (fol. 16v).[28] It is not obvious what these texts may have to do thematically with the passage from 1 Kings that precedes them.[29] Yet the relationship may not be one of overarching theme, however, but of similar occasions—in the one case, the death of William I and in the other, the death of Frederick III. As suggested, of the two recent imperial deaths, the tragic one, especially for German liberals, was that of Frederick. It is plausible, therefore, that Brahms chose the citations from Ecclesiasticus and Ecclesiastes with an eye toward composing a work connected with that demoralizing, if not unexpected, loss.

Later Brahms added an annotation in lead pencil on the bottom of fol. 16v: "NB Weisheit Solomonis / Kap. 8 [*recte* 9] 'Gebet eines Königs.'" (NB Wisdom Chap. 8 [*recte* 9] "Prayer of a King").[30] This biblical passage speaks in the person of King Solomon, offering a prayer to God for wisdom (*Gebet zu Gott um Weisheit*, as the heading in the Luther Bible explains). Brahms substitutes a more generalized description for the chapter, characterizing it as "Prayer of a King." This is telling. If the citation of 1 Kings 6:11–14 allowed Solomon to be treated as a metaphor for William I, in "Prayer of a King," Solomon is re-envisioned as the young William II. Kalbeck even argued that Brahms "wanted to use his art to aid the young emperor, to hold up a classical 'regent's mirror'" before him."[31]

The biographer is presumably making an unacknowledged reference here to Johann Balthazar Schupp's mid-seventeenth-century treatise *Salomo, oder Regenten-Spiegel / Vorgestellt aus denen eilff ersten Capitulen des ersten Buchs der Königen. Andern Gottsfürchtigen und Sinnreichen Politicis auszuführen und genauer zu elaboriren überlassen* (Solomon, or Regent's Mirror, presented from the first eleven chapters of the first Book of Kings, to convey to other God-fearing and astute governors [how] to execute and elaborate [their duties] correctly, 1657). As Joachim Whaley astutely observes, this treatise complicates our understanding of the Lutheran injunction to obey authority at all costs, an injunction that is often seen as a contributing factor to supposed German susceptibility to authoritarianism. Schupp does not abide rebellion, to be sure. But by aiming to instill in the Christian ruler a

---

28 Although Brahms's marginal inscription for the first citation reads: "Sirach [Ecclesiasticus] 41:1–4," the beginning of the fifth verse is also written out. The marginal inscription for the last citation reads: "Prediger Salomo [Ecclesiastes] 4:1–4," but only the first three verses are written out.

29 For one attempt to draw a thematic connection, see Beller-McKenna, *Brahms and the German Spirit*, 57–64.

30 For a reproduction of fol. 16v, see Grimes, *Brahms's Elegies*, 190 (Figure 4.1a).

31 Kalbeck, *Johannes Brahms*, 4: 444–45.

194 ❧ CHAPTER SIX

sense of obligation to assist in a "reformation of society" he seeks to render rebellion unnecessary.[32] Thus, in a typically oblique manner, Kalbeck is implicitly arguing for the composer's embrace at this stage of his life of enlightened monarchical rule, perhaps of precisely the kind Brahms so admired in the Habsburg Joseph II. Brahms would have had good reason to expect that of Frederick III; of the brash and untested William II, he could not be sure.

This supposition finds support in a trail of evidence that begins with the exemplar Brahms owned of Gottfried Büchner's widely used *Biblische Real- und Verbal-Hand-Concordanz*. First published in 1740, this exegetical-homiletical lexicon is represented in Brahms's library in an edition published in 1859. To Büchner's original entry for the keyword *Volk*, Heinrich Leonhard Heubner, who edited the editions that appeared beginning in 1840, added three sentences that bespeak a *Vormärz* conservative's fear of the shifting political winds. Brahms not only set this passage off with brackets; he also underlined Heubner's striking reference to "mindless constitutional goings-on" (*blindes constitutionelle Treiben*):

> To become a people of God is the supreme task for any people, infinitely more than to become a people of a constitution. Indeed, <u>mindless constitutional goings-on can remove the higher</u> purpose from view so completely that in the end the people no longer knows what it means to be a people of God! Only where Christ rules and unites the minds does a people of God come into being; Christocracy is the only redeeming constitution.[33]

In Jan Brachmann's view, Brahms's markings in this passage give evidence, on the one hand, that he understood the establishment of the Reich as a sign of God's grace on the Germans as a new people of God, and, on the other, that he knew this gift could easily be forfeited were the German people to forget whence it had come. "Liberal constitutionalism, modern etatism does not reflect such thinking at all," he writes. And though Brachmann rightly hastens to distance Brahms from the clerical opponents of modernity, he claims that the composer's inscriptions reveal "the alleged 'heretic and free spirit' to be rather a subversive advocate of a Christocracy," adding, "Brahms evidently did not conceive of the 'people' as an entity merely of the state,

---

32 Joachim Whaley, "Obedient Servants? Lutheran Attitudes to Authority and Society in the First Half of the Seventeenth Century: The Case of Johann Balthasar Schupp," *The Historical Journal* (1992): 27–42.

33 *M. Gottfried Büchner's Biblische Real- und Verbal-Hand-Concordanz oder exegetisch-homiletisches Lexicon*, 11th ed., ed. Heinrich Leonhard Heubner (Braunschweig: C. A. Schwetschke und Sohn, 1859), 1064, §3. On Brahms's annotations elsewhere in this biblical concordance, see Beller-McKenna, *Brahms and the German Spirit*, 35–37.

THE STUFF OF TRAGEDY? ❧ 195

but above all of the spirit." As such, its basic law "should not be a 'constitution,' but a different code: the Bible."[34]

Is this too simple an explanation? Brachmann leaves unmentioned the cross-reference made at the point where Brahms's marginal bracket ends, which moves us further along the evidentiary trail. Here Heubner directs the reader to a passage from the second volume of the *Vermischte Schriften* (Miscellaneous writings) of Georg Christoph Lichtenberg (1742–99).[35] Lichtenberg was a physicist and mathematician, but his posthumous fame rests largely on his work as an aphorist. First published in the decade following his death, these terse writings, over 1,000 in number, show the author to be one of the wittiest of German satirists, and, as a radical nonconformist, one whose barbs were frequently aimed at all forms of organized religion.[36] In the passage to which Heubner refers, Lichtenberg grants the teachings of Christ their due (once they are "cleansed of the accursed scribblings of priests and suitably adopted to our mode of expression") as the most expedient, albeit not the only, means "for the promotion of peace and happiness in the world." Yet Lichtenberg quickly asserts that "there is another system proceeding wholly from pure reason and leading to the same result"; but that system is of necessity suitable only for "practiced thinkers and not at all for man in general." Even if Christ had conceived a system of pure reason with an appeal to the philosopher, he continues, the people at large would never have understood it, "and was such a thing as that supposed to serve to guide and lead the human race and sustain it in the hour of death?" Indeed not, he adds, since "that which is to guide men must be true but also universally understandable."[37]

Brahms owned the *Vermischte Schriften* in an enlarged second edition published in 1844 and 1853. Given his interest in Heubner's addition to the entry *Volk* in Büchner's biblical concordance, it is inconceivable that he would not have wanted to look into the cross-reference made there to Lichtenberg. Whether he found it or not is uncertain, since the page in

---

34 Brachmann, *Kunst–Religion–Krise*, 199.

35 *Georg Christoph Lichtenberg's Vermischte Schriften*, ed. Ludwig Christian Lichtenberg and Friedrich Kries, 9 vols. in 8 (Göttingen: Dietrich, 1800–1806), vol. 2 (1801): 32–34.

36 Lichtenberg was admired by the likes of Goethe, Kierkegaard, Schopenhauer, and Nietzsche; see Roger Kimball, "G. C. Lichtenberg: A 'Spy on Humanity,'" *New Criterion* 20/9 (May 2002): 20, https://newcriterion.com/issues/2002/5/g-c-lichtenberg-a-ldquospy-on-humanityrdquo, accessed April 12, 2022.

37 I have taken my translation from Georg Christoph Lichtenberg, *The Waste Books*, trans. with introduction and notes by R. J. Hollingdale (New York: New York Review of Books, 2000), 137–38.

196 ❧ CHAPTER SIX

Brahms's exemplar containing the aphoristic writing in question contains no annotations.[38] We can be confident, however, that it would have appealed to the "alleged 'heretic and free spirit,'" who may have rejected Christianity's dogmatic claims but embraced its ethical vision. And in keeping with Lichtenberg's line of reasoning, we might think of Brahms's large-scale compositions to biblical texts— not only the *Fest- und Gedenksprüche*, but *Ein deutsches Requiem* and the *Triumphlied* as well—as efforts to impart that vision to everyday "unpracticed thinkers," to the German people at large as gathered in the bourgeois concert space.

In the end, Brahms decided not to compose the text from 1 Kings that would have made a fitting musical memorial to William I. Nor did he compose or even initially write out the text from Wisdom of Solomon—the "Prayer of a King"—that Kalbeck would later liken to a regent's mirror to be set before the young William II.[39] He did, however, provide music for the three gloomy citations from Ecclesiasticus and Ecclesiastes, albeit not until some years later, near the end of his life, when, as he confided to Clara Schumann in February 1895, he was no longer writing music "for the public, but only for himself."[40]

These settings come as the first three of the *Vier ernste Gesänge* (Four Serious Songs), op. 121, for bass with piano accompaniment (Table 2). The first song uses the second of the three citations in Brahms's biblical notebook (Ecclesiastes 3:18–21, with v. 18 omitted); the second, the third citation (Ecclesiastes 4:1–4); and the third, the first citation (Ecclesiasticus 41:1–4, with the fragment of v. 5 omitted). The text of the fourth song, selected from the thirteenth chapter of Paul's First Letter to the Corinthians, stands in every respect at a great remove from the somber verses used in the first three. (Malcolm MacDonald aptly described it as an "apostrophe" of love.[41]) That it was inscribed in Brahms's biblical notebook but set off

---

38 George Christoph Lichtenberg, *Vermischte Schriften*, 8 vols. (Göttingen: Dieterich'schen Buchhandlung, 1844–1853), vol. 1 (1853): 67–68. The only markings in Brahms's hand are found in vols. 7 and 8.

39 *Pace* Michael Heinemann, who holds that in the second movement of the *Fest- und Gedenksprüche* Brahms pays his respect to the young emperor while simultaneously sounding "some words of warning." See Michael Heinemann, "Geistliche Chorwerke a cappella," in *Brahms Handbuch*, ed. Wolfgang Sandberger (Stuttgart and Weimer: J. B. Metzler, 2009), 303–13 (at 303). I take up the musical setting of Op. 109 in the following chapter.

40 Reported in Kalbeck, *Johannes Brahms*, 4: 390, and ibid., 4: 441. Kalbeck appears to be conflating details of two different visits to Schumann's home in Frankfurt am Main, occurring in November 1894 and February 1895, although this makes no difference to the point he wants to make.

41 MacDonald, *Brahms*, 376.

from what comes before by an empty leaf may indicate a later date of entry, perhaps in 1895, as Nicole Grimes has argued.[42] Yet it should be observed that this Pauline text is followed in the notebook by most of the "Prayer of a King" (viz., Wisdom of Solomon 9:1–5, 7, and 10–12). Taking note of the verses the composer chose not to write out and of the square brackets and parentheses he added to some that he did write out, Kalbeck makes the reasonable inference that Brahms gave serious thought to how he might compose the text, although there is no evidence that he ever did.[43] What is important to note here is that the "Prayer of a King" would not have had the same currency in the mid-1890s as it had during the Year of the Three Emperors. This raises the possibility, then, that both texts copied onto fols. 17v–19r of Brahms's biblical notebook may date from around 1888 or a little later, but not as late as 1895. On the basis of the extant documentary evidence, we simply cannot settle the matter one way or the other.

Irrespective of the question of when the Pauline text of op. 121, no. 4, was inscribed, whether in 1888 or 1895 or at any time in between, the *Vier ernste Gesänge* as we know them were composed in the spring of 1896.[44] The autograph manuscript is inscribed "Wien Mai 96." Kalbeck recalled that when Brahms showed him the manuscript at this time he told him that the songs had been composed as a birthday present for himself. (On May 7, the composer marked his sixty-third birthday.) On 8 May, Brahms reported similarly to Simrock, and with typical irony, that he had just composed "a few tiny little songs" (*ein paar kleine Liederschen*) for his birthday.[45] All this was happening in the midst of Clara Schumann's final illness. Her death would come on May 20, following a pair of strokes on March 26 and May 16. Upon learning the news, Brahms rushed to Germany to be in attendance at her internment in Bonn next to the grave of her husband Robert. He may have carried with him the score of the new songs and in any case a few days

---

42 Grimes, *Brahms's Elegies*, 165–72, 182–202 (at 183).

43 Kalbeck, *Johannes Brahms*, 4: 444n. For Kalbeck's insightful, if not entirely credible, account, see ibid., 441–60; translated as Max Kalbeck, "Brahms's *Four Serious Songs*, op. 121 (1914)," trans. William Miller, introduced and annotated by Kevin C. Kearns, in *Brahms and His World*, rev. ed., ed. Walter Frisch and Kevin C. Kearns (Princeton: Princeton University Press, 2009), 267–86. Hereafter in this discussion I will cite this English translation.

44 Kalbeck seems to have been the first to observe that a sketch leaf found in the composer's personal effects at the time of his death contains notations for, among other things, a possible orchestral setting of op. 121, no. 4. Kalbeck, "Brahms's *Four Serious Songs*," 272–79. For a more recent, thoughtful discussion, see Grimes, *Brahms's Elegies*, 195–201.

45 Kalbeck, "Brahms's *Four Serious Songs*," 268; letter to Simrock of May 8, 1896, in *Briefwechsel*, 12: 195–96 (at 195).

198   ❧   CHAPTER SIX

Table 2. Brahms's biblical notebook, fols. 15v–19r.

fol. 15v		
1 Kings 6:11–12	William I	Not composed
Ecclesiasticus 41:1–4	Frederick III	Not composed in 1888; composed in 1896 as op. 121, no. 3
fol. 16r		
Ecclesiastes 3:18–22	Frederick III	Not composed in 1888; composed in 1896 as op. 121, no. 1 (except v. 18)
fol. 16v		
Ecclesiastes 4:1–4	Frederick III	Not composed in 1888; composed in 1896 as op. 121, no. 3
Notation: *"NB Wisdom Chap. 8* [recte 9] *('Prayer of a King')"*	William II	Text not written or composed
fol. 17r		
Empty		
fols. 17v–18r		
1 Corinthians 13		Composed in 1896 as op. 121, no. 4
fols. 18v–19r		
Wisdom 9:1–12 ("Prayer of a King")		Not composed

later gave an impromptu performance for those who had gathered for the funeral. Then, on July 7, he wrote to Schumann's daughter Marie to inform her that she would be receiving a copy of the score upon its imminent publication, adding that, even though he had not dedicated the songs to her, they "indeed concern you quite personally. I wrote them during the first weeks of May. I have often been preoccupied with similar words." Recognizing that the songs might be too painful for the mourning daughter to hear just yet, he concluded by asking her simply "to view them as a funeral offering for your beloved mother, and then to put them aside."[46]

---

46   Avins, *Johannes Brahms: Life and Letters*, 737–38. Kalbeck mistakenly reports that this letter was addressed to both Marie and Eugenie Schumann; see Kalbeck, "Brahms's *Four Serious Songs*," 270. Brahms dedicated Op. 121 to the Leipzig artist Max Klinger (1857–1920) as a token of appreciation for

It was probably not mere coincidence, and especially so since Brahms acknowledged that he had long been preoccupied with such texts, that the first three *Serious Songs* were composed to the same dark biblical verses that, as I have argued, Brahms had thought to use in memorializing Frederick III in 1888.[47] Yet, as Grimes has argued, the set may be something richer and more complex than memorial music. She brings into the interpretative mix Nietzsche's *Der Antichrist*, written—and this certainly was a mere coincidence—in the year of Frederick's death, although not published until 1895. By early February Brahms had obtained a copy, the numerous annotations in which bespeak a very close reading.[48] There was much for the free-thinking composer to agree with in Nietzsche's controversial tract. Yet he apparently reacted negatively, on Grimes's reading, to the philosopher's indictment of Luther, "the German monk" whom he held responsible for restoring the Church in the face of Renaissance Humanism, and especially to Nietzsche's complaint that, because of this restoration, the Germans would be to blame "if we never get rid of Christianity." This last reproach, Grimes holds, "would have struck at the heart of Brahms's patriotic, cultural, and artistic

---

Klinger's magnificent *Brahms-Phantasie* (1894), recently published in a beautiful facsimile edition as Max Klinger, *Brahms-Phantasie op. XII: Einundvierzig Stiche. Radierungen und Steinzeichnungen zu Compositionen von Johannes Brahms. Leipzig Selbstverlag 1894*, numbered facsimile edition, ed. Johannes-Brahms-Gesellschaft Hamburg (Hamburg: Ellert & Richter, 2017). For a thoughtful account in the musicological literature, see Kevin C. Karnes, "Brahms, Max Klinger, and the Promise of the *Gesamtkunstwerk*," in *Brahms and His World*, ed. Walter Frisch and Kevin C. Karnes, rev. ed. (Princeton: Princeton University Press, 2009), 167–91.

47   Kalbeck rightly notes that the *Four Serious Songs* could just as easily be thought to memorialize Elisabeth von Herzogenberg (who died in 1892) and Hans von Bülow and Theodor Billroth (who died in 1894) as they were thought to memorialize Schumann. See Kalbeck, "Brahms's *Four Serious Songs*," 270. That the texts of the first three songs were inscribed in Brahms's biblical notebook in connection with an envisioned memorial to Frederick III, however, has gone unnoticed before.

48   Friedrich Nietzsche, *Der Fall Wagner. Götzen-Dämmerung. Nietzsche Contra Wagner. Der Antichrist. Gedichte* (Leipzig: C. G. Naumann, 1895); letter from Brahms to Simrock of February 6, 1895, in *Briefwechsel*, 12: 163–64. For discussion, see Grimes, *Brahms's Elegies*, 165–72. *Der Antichrist* is not catalogued in Hofmann, *Die Bibliothek von Johannes Brahms*. That Brahms owned this book was, to my knowledge, first reported in Mark Peters, "Introduction to and Catalogue of Brahms's Library" (MA thesis, University of Pittsburgh, 1999).

200 ❧ CHAPTER SIX

identity."[49] And though, we ought to add, the Christianity Brahms valued was not of any kind that Luther would have recognized, the Luther Bible was central to the ideology of the Culture Protestantism of the nineteenth century that decidedly did play a meaningful role in his liberal worldview.

Our concern here, however, is not with what Brahms did or did not compose in 1896 but instead with what he did or did not compose in 1888. Why were the biblical citations that can so easily be associated with the three German emperors who reigned in 1888 left without a musical setting at that time? Why instead did Brahms to choose to set the biblical texts he had originally copied in the 1870s and to publish those settings as the *Fest- und Gedenksprüche*? As we shall discover, this change in plans coincides suggestively with certain developments taking place in the world of international affairs during the first months of the reign of William II. We consider those developments next.

---

49   Grimes, *Brahms's Elegies*, 171, quoting Nietzsche's text from Friedrich Nietzsche, *Twilight of the Idols and The Antichrist*, trans. R. J. Hollingdale (London: Penguin, 1990), 197.

Chapter Seven

Revanche and Response

> The national festival [Sedan Day], which ... inscribes the cultivation of national duties and virtues in the heart of the people, ... will, with its inevitable and ever-renewing impression on the overall life of the German people, awaken and stir all the forces whose full content we would need if ever again the independence and unity of the dear Fatherland were to be threatened from without.[1]
>
> —*Norddeutsche Allgemeine Zeitung*, 1875

Although Bismarck had used a series of three wars to bring about national consolidation in 1871 under Prussian leadership, he sought to avoid military conflict thereafter, understanding that only peace and stability could ensure the Reich's security. Above all, it was paramount in his calculations for Germany to avoid being squeezed by its hereditary enemy, France, in the west, and a hostile Russian Empire in the east. To that end, he engineered a series of alliances designed at once to isolate France and to encourage the other Great Powers to grow dependent on Berlin so as to mitigate the possibility of the formation of any effective anti-German coalition. This approach was generally successful at first—indeed, relations between France and Germany improved remarkably between 1877 and 1885—but by the mid-1880s a state of permanent crisis was becoming the norm.[2]

Consider the fate of the Three Emperors' Agreement of 1881. This accord stipulated that Russia and Austria-Hungary would remain neutral

---

1   "Politischer Tagesbericht," *Norddeutsche Allgemeine Zeitung* (August 31, 1875).

2   Katharine Anne Lerman, "Bismarckian Germany," in *Imperial Germany 1871–1918*, ed. James Retallack (Oxford: Oxford University Press, 2008), 18–39 (at 26–31); Nathan N. Orgill, "Between Coercion and Conciliation: Franco-German Relations in the Bismarck Era, 1871–1890," in Carine Germond and Henning Türk, eds., *A History of Franco-German Relations in Europe: From "Hereditary Enemies" to Partners* (New York: Palgrave Macmillan, 2008), 49–59.

should Germany become involved in a war with France. As long as this agreement held, Germany was spared the prospect of fighting a two-front war. Ongoing tensions between Russia and Austria-Hungary over the Balkans proved insuperable, however, and the alliance collapsed in 1887. Bismarck was able to salvage Russo-German cooperation only by negotiating the top-secret Reinsurance Treaty with St. Petersburg, thus staving off German vulnerability to attack from the east and preventing the formation of a French-Russian alliance.

Meanwhile, to the west, in France, the dashing minister of war, General Georges Boulanger, was beginning his meteoric rise to fame on the basis of a bellicose determination to restore French national grandeur through a platform of nationalism, militarism, and a revanchism that demanded return of Alsace and Lorraine. In April 1887, Boulanger conflated a short-lived, insignificant episode involving German allegations of French spying along the German-French border into an affront to French national honor. The war scare that came about from this proved to be an embarrassment to the French government, and the general soon lost his ministerial position. Yet, his populist credentials only grew as he became the face of French revanchism and the subject of a great number of *chants patriotiques*, with titles such as "C'est Boulanger qu'il nous faut" (It's Boulanger whom we need), "A bas Bismarck ... et vive Boulanger" (Down with Bismarck and long live Boulanger), and "Le général revanche" (General Revenge). Especially salient for our purposes is the title page of "Boulanger, maître d'école en Alsace" (Boulanger, schoolmaster in Alsace), on which the general is depicted overseeing a teacher who is showing his pupils where on a map of France the "stolen" regions of Alsace and Lorraine are located (Figure 7).[3]

---

3   For a concise account of what he calls the "Boulanger Menace" of 1886–89, see Robert Gildea, *Children of the Revolution: The French, 1799–1914* (London: Allen Lane, 2008), 260–65. See also Orgill, "Between Coercion and Conciliation," 55–57. Useful is Matthew P. Fitzpatrick, "French Revanchism and the Boulangist Threat in Alsace-Lorraine," in his *Purging the Empire: Mass Expulsions in Germany, 1871–1914* (Oxford: Oxford University Press, 2015), 207–28. For a longer study, see William D. Irvine, *The Boulanger Affair Reconsidered: Royalism, Boulangism, and the Origins of the Radical Right in France* (New York and Oxford: Oxford University Press, 1989). On the chansons, see Georges Grison, *Le général Boulanger jugé par ses partisans et ses adversaires (janvier 1886–mars 1888* (Paris: Librairie Illustrée, 1888), 430–37, 551–57. See also Jann Pasler, *Composing the Citizen: Music as Public Utility in Third Republic France* (Berkeley, Los Angeles, and London: University of California Press, 2009), 495–501.

Figure 7. Title page, "Boulanger Maître d'Ecole en Alsace." Public domain.

204 &❧ CHAPTER SEVEN

A dispatch from Berlin, published in the *New York Times* on April 17, 1888, captures perfectly the tension felt all around:

> This prospect of an immediate and sweeping change in the Government of Germany is linked in every mind with the even more sinister threat of Governmental chaos in France. Either the death of Emperor Frederick or the meteor-like rise of Gen. Boulanger would have been in itself enough powerfully to affect Europe. The two things apparently coming together dazzle the imagination.... There are now prophesies that out of such a crash as this anything may come. General Boulanger's immense [popularity] means a good many such things, but the chief of these is that the French crowd is tired of having wordy lawyers and editors run things and are willing to give men of action a chance. The purely military power, made up of all sorts of incongruous political elements, thus comes to the front with the wild impetus of a plebiscite. Nothing could invest this with more terrible significance than the fact that simultaneously the military party in Germany steps also into power. Men may well be frightened at the sudden looming up of these two sable, sulphureous clouds in the sky.[4]

It is obvious why the impending death of Frederick would be viewed as a dark cloud hanging over Europe. He had not only proven himself as a steady leader on the field of battle in all three of the Wars of Unification. He was also thought by some, as we have seen, to be committed to making liberal reforms—perhaps even to leading Germany to emulate the constitutional monarchy of the United Kingdom—and to be unlikely to take Germany into further military conflicts with its neighbors. Crown Prince William, by contrast, was untested on the world stage and was known to be under the influence of the German "military party," led by the reactionary Alfred von Waldersee, chief of the Imperial German General Staff. Meanwhile, in France, the populist cult surrounding Boulanger continued to grow. He had recently made his entry into elective politics and was beginning to win a series of plebiscite-like by-elections throughout France. And though he eventually lost his nerve, or perhaps only his interest, by early 1889 he seemed poised to enact a coup d'état.

In this midst of this turbulence in France came Frederick's death and the accession of William II. The new emperor, young and ambitious, was, as Winkler observes, "the precise opposite of his father in nearly all important aspects." Winkler continues with a devastating portrait of a monarch who was

> no man of liberal convictions, but rather profoundly authoritarian; at times closely allied with leading representatives of the anti-Semitic movement

---

4   "Frederick's Illness and Boulanger's Triumph," *New York Times* (April 17, 1888).

REVANCHE AND RESPONSE   205

like the court chaplain, [Adolph] Stoecker; widely talented but superficial; a vain, pomp-loving blusterer, who sought to compensate for inner insecurity and a physical defect—his left arm had been crippled since birth—with tough talk. That he would clash with Bismarck was clear from the outset.[5]

It did not take long for Wilhelminian tough talk to cause a stir. While visiting Berlin in June 1888 to attend Frederick's funeral, the deceased's brother-in-law, Albert Edward, Prince of Wales, waded into the minefield of German politics by making known his opinion that, among other things, the Imperial Territory of Alsace-Lorraine ought to be returned to France. Before long the rumor flew that Frederick himself, before he died, had agreed with this proposition. That William II rejected the idea root and branch became evident from brief remarks he made at the end of a speech given on August 16, 1888. That morning he travelled east by train from Berlin to the city of Frankfurt an der Oder. The occasion was the unveiling of a monument in commemoration of the late Prince Frederick Karl, who on that date eighteen years earlier had successfully led the Prussian Second Army over French forces in the Battle of Vionville. William's brief visit concluded with a luncheon held in the city hall. As they were first reported in the press, the young emperor's remarks, an early instance of the blustery rhetorical style that would characterize his public pronouncements throughout his reign, read in part as follows:

> There are people who have the impudence to maintain that my father wanted to give up what he, together with the late Prince, won on the field of battle. But we knew him too well to be able to tolerate such an insult to his memory, even for a single instant. He held the view, as We do, that nothing of what was gained in those great days can be surrendered. I believe that every one of us ... in the army knows that there can be only one opinion on this matter, namely, that we would rather have all eighteen of our army corps and all forty-two millions of our inhabitants laid out in a row [*auf der Strecke liegen lassen*] than surrender a single stone of what my father and Prince Frederick Karl gained.[6]

William's final sentence makes an unmistakable reference to Jules Favre's famous assertion in the days following the defeat at Sedan: "Nous ne cèderons ni un pouce de notre territoire, ni une pierre de nos forteresses" (We shall not give up one inch of our territory nor one stone of our fortresses), an assertion to which Bismarck soon responded with the Germans'

---

5   Winkler, *Germany: The Long Road West*, 233.

6   "Die Enthüllungsfeier des Prinz Friedrich-Karl-Denkmals," *National-Zeitung, Beiblatt* (August 17, 1888). For a discussion of this speech, see Röhl, *Wilhelm II: The Kaiser's Personal Monarchy*, 73–77.

206 & CHAPTER SEVEN

demand for Alsace and Lorraine, recognizing the security concerns of the neighboring South German states and assuming that the French were likely to seek revenge for their defeat whether they were to lose any territory or fortresses or not.[7]

The response to William's speech in the *Vossiche Zeitung* registers what we may take to be widespread German popular sentiment, including that of Brahms:

> The Emperor's words are a serious warning to any power that might wish to disturb Germany's peace. They announce the determination of the whole nation to defend its honor and unity against everyone…. That the Emperor has expressed this attitude right now … may be seen as a sign that anxiety remains concerning our restless neighbors' thirst for adventure. The German nation, however, will not give up the hope that this cold stream of water will heal the chauvinism beyond its borders. In [his] speech Emperor William II repeatedly reaffirmed his love of peace. He spoke in the spirit of all his people. He will always be able to count on his people if an open attack on the German Reich and the peace of [our] nation's part of the world should push the sword into the hand.[8]

Soon thereafter, on August 19, Brahms's friend Widmann published an opinion piece in the liberal Swiss newspaper *Der Bund* entitled "Forty-Two Million Germans Laid Out in a Row." Here he criticized as morally repugnant William's use of the huntsman's expression—laid out in a row, that is, like animals killed in the hunt—to express his determination to go to any length necessary in order not to surrender Alsace-Lorraine to France.[9]

Widmann's article drew a sharp response the following day in the Berlin *National-Zeitung*: "The *Bund* stands out in the European press for its spitefulness. One is used to encountering [there] hostile and vile language against Germany…. The insults which the *Bund* allowed against Emperor William with regard to the Frankfurt speech can scarcely be enumerated…. This behavior can only be described as most regrettable."[10]

Undoubtedly familiar with all this earlier reporting, Brahms quickly followed up with Widmann in a letter that can only be described as scathing:

---

7   Feuchtwanger, *Bismarck: A Political History*, 172–73.

8   *Vossische Zeitung, Abend-Ausgabe* (August 17, 1888).

9   w. [Joseph Victor Widmann], "Zweiundvierzig Millionen Deutsche auf der Strecke," *Der Bund* (August 19, 1888); reprinted in *Gottfried Keller und J. V. Widmann Briefwechsel*, ed. Max Widmann (Basel and Leipzig: Rhein-Verlag, 1922), 27–29; and Josef Viktor Widmann, *"Ein Journalist aus Temperament"*: *Ausgewählte Feuilletons*, ed. Elspeth Pulver and Rudolf Käser (Bern: Zytglogge, 1992), 89–90.

10   *National-Zeitung, Abend-Ausgabe* (August 20, 1888).

"When I read the imperial speech ... I quietly turned the page and wished that not every word would have been spoken or reproduced exactly. I regret your harsh comments about it. But that's the way everything coming out of Germany is criticized."[11] The composer complains about what he sees as Widmann's double standard in criticizing the German emperor for expressing a sentiment he would have praised had it come instead from Giuseppe Garibaldi, the great Italian nationalist, or Léon Gambetta, the leading voice among the French revanchists in the first years following the Franco-Prussian War. He sarcastically explains that if either of those men had spoken about Alsace as William had done in his speech, the newspapers would report something like this: "These are not words, they are living flames which cannot be extinguished! These are weapons, which cannot be withstood! Return the Alsace; not mere justice, but fervor such as this demands and compels it."

What follows is significant: "The [emperor's] precise wording is not certain, only the sentiment, which is shared by the whole nation." Indeed, on August 18, the imperial gazette had printed its official version of William's remarks, and here the indelicate huntsman's phrase "auf der Strecke" was replaced with something more anodyne: "We would rather see all eighteen of our army corps and all forty-two millions of our inhabitants perish on the battlefield [*auf der Wahlstatt*] than surrender a single stone of what my father and Prince Frederick Karl gained."[12] The difference in tone is not negligible, and the composer clearly wanted to give the young emperor the benefit of the doubt, writing to Widmann: "I don't wish to have greeted him at the beginning of his great and far-reaching reign as you—on the basis and with the evidence of a single fleeting and uncertain word."[13]

Widmann's criticism of William's Frankfurt speech had struck a nerve with Brahms, who throughout the letter gives unequivocal evidence of his firm embrace of the Prussian School of History and its monarchical, dynastic, and teleological version of the German past.[14] This is not to say that

---

11   Letter of August 20, 1888, in Avins, *Johannes Brahms*, 660–61, from which the next several quotations from this letter are taken.

12   *Deutscher Reichs-Anzeiger und Königlich-Preußischer Staats-Anzeiger* (August 18, 1888); translation from Röhl, *Wilhelm II*, 73. This version of the speech was widely reprinted the following day in a number of newspapers that we know Brahms regularly read, including the *Norddeutsche Allgemeine* and the *National-Zeitung*.

13   The revised reporting on what the emperor said in Frankfurt an der Oder has gone unnoticed in earlier musicological accounts of the incident.

14   Frank Lorenz Müller, "The Prince, the Crypt, and the Historians: Kaiser Friedrich III and the Continuities of Monarchical *Geschichtspolitik* in Imperial Germany," *German Studies Review* 35 (2012): 521–40.

208 ❧ CHAPTER SEVEN

Brahms could not recognize William's foibles. In effect, he acknowledged to Widmann that the young emperor had not chosen his words carefully in Frankfurt an der Oder; in later years he would even belittle him for his vanity with nasty humor. Rather, Brahms's angry response to Widmann's opinion piece in the *Bund* must be read in the light of what he considered to be Widmann's insufficient appreciation for the Prussian royal family as an institution. He scolds his friend, for example, for "confer[ing] honour and respect on the individual great person—but not on a lineage like the Hohenzoller[n]s with Fr[ederick] II and W[illiam] I," and for showing "respect for every young man who, well prepared, strives towards a far-off goal—but not for a youthful new Emperor of the German people [*Kaiser des deutschen Volkes*], who has surely prepared himself earnestly and with dignity for his high and difficult office, who may well still fulfil all kinds of hopes."[15]

According to Widmann, Brahms went so far as to accuse him of Germanophobia (*Deutschenhass*). Widmann, in turn, was troubled by what he characterized as Brahms's "*fanatical* overbearing Germanomania" (*Deutschtümelei*) and his "unimaginably chauvinistic German point of view," and he even suggested that the composer had felt no loss upon the death of the moderately liberal Frederick III, a position clearly at odds with what we know about Brahms's response from Klaus Groth and his annotations in Treitschke's *Zwei Kaiser*.[16] In a heated moment, there was miscommunication all around. Yet this led to no permanent rift in the friendship, in part because the men agreed to steer clear of the topic of politics and to carry on as before. In fact, it was not long until Brahms felt comfortable enough to begin teasing Widmann for his republican views.[17]

---

15   Also useful in this connection is Giloi, *Monarchy, Myth, and Material Culture*, 330–34.

16   Letter from Widmann to Henriette Feuerbach of October 10, 1888, in Josef Viktor Widmann, *Briefwechsel mit Henriette Feuerbach und Ricarda Huch*, ed. Charlotte von Dach (Zurich: Artemis, 1965), 105–9 (at 107). Widmann also opened up about the matter with Gottfried Keller, Friedrich Hegar, and Richard Heuberger. See *Keller Widmann Briefwechsel*, 27–33, 125–31; and Richard Heuberger, "Briefe Joseph Victor Widmanns," *Der Merker* 3/2 (January 1912): 59–63 (at 62).

17   See the discussion in Avins, *Johannes Brahms*, 661–62, 775. Letters to Widmann of September 7, 1888, September 9, 1888, and January 24, 1891, in *Briefwechsel*, 8: 91, 91, and 112–14 (at 114).

The Musical Setting in Context

From this tense colloquy between Brahms and Widmann, which unfolded against a backdrop formed by the words and actions of the revanchist French general and the tempestuous German emperor, we turn, at last, to Brahms's musical setting of the *Fest- und Gedenksprüche*. The carefully selected biblical texts unfold a narrative that is remarkably similar to that inscribed on the pedestal of Schilling's *Germania*. Just as in Schilling's monument there is no gloating at France's misfortune, so there is none in the composer's *Sprüche*, as even Widmann would implicitly have to acknowledge, as we shall see. Indeed, we might be forgiven for thinking of Brahms's musical settings of these biblical texts—"forthright, public and sonorously collective in their utterance"—as a demonstration to his friend that one could be a fervent German patriot without embracing chauvinism or Germanomania.

Given Brahms's terse programmatic description to Bülow, there is little doubt that the fathers about whom the choruses sing at the outset of the first movement (F major, $\frac{3}{2}$) are the faithful heroes of the Battle of Leipzig, the turning point in the Wars of Liberation: "Our fathers trusted in you; because they trusted, you delivered them." In an opening series of polychoral exchanges, Chorus 2 leads the way with a disjunct arpeggiation of the tonic harmony in unison and octaves on the words "Unsere Väter" (Our fathers); Chorus 1 responds with dovetailed, elaborated, and slightly extended iterations of the same material in four-part harmony (Example 10). After both choruses come together to produce a full cadence in the tonic, the polychoral exchanges pick up again, more animated than before, to begin the middle section (mm. 15–29): "To you they cried and were saved. In you they trusted and were not put to shame." The music eventually appears to be headed toward a cadence in the key of the relative minor, only to slip away at the last moment, with a change to common time at measure 27, into an attenuated cadence in the tonic, F major. The third and final section (mm. 29–51) turns forthright again in expression and develops the arpeggiated tonic harmony with which the piece began, now, however, not only in the newly established quadruple meter but in an utterly new texture as well. In place of the earlier *cori spezzati* scoring, Brahms introduces the intrinsically patriotic sounds of a *Männerchor* made up of the unified male voices of both choruses. Soon the female voices join in, and the two choruses are integrated into one to bring the movement to its close with the words "The Lord will give strength to his people. The Lord will bless his people with peace."

Example 10. Brahms, *Fest- und Gedenksprüche*, op. 109, first movement, mm. 1–15.

(—*continued*)

Example 10—concluded

212 ❧ CHAPTER SEVEN

In the polychoral exchanges that characterize much of this opening movement, Beller-McKenna detects a number of binary distinctions—between simplicity and elaboration, low and high, mystical *Volk* and the educated bourgeoisie. This is in keeping with his understanding that the music was composed at a time, not, as I have argued, of heightened tensions between Germany and France, but instead one of ominous internal divisions. He asserts that it was Brahms's fear of this dissension over the very nature of the Reich that lay behind his decision to provide the two choruses, contrasting though they may be at times, with musical materials that at least show enough "common identity [and] underlying unity" to raise the possibility of a "reconciliation" between the two sides of the national divide. Picking up on Beller-McKenna's suggestion, Minor holds that Brahms used the *cori spezzati* scoring "to present *obstacles* to unification," understood here in the sense of national or political, not purely musical, unity.[18]

But why should we not take Brahms at his word that this music alludes in some way to the unifying catharsis experienced when the Germans defeated the forces of Napoleon in the Battle of Leipzig? Let us reflect for a moment on something that Theodor Billroth, in the immediate afterglow of Germany's unification in 1871, had written to a friend who, like Brahms, had experienced an upbringing in *Vormärz* Germany similar to that of Billroth: "Weren't Arndt's anthems and the soldiers' songs *von anno* 1813 sung at your family gatherings!" Soldiers' songs are not exactly the same thing as settings of sober biblical texts, of course. Yet it is easy enough to hear Chorus 2, singing in one firm voice at the outset in the role of a paterfamilias set on instructing his sons and daughters about the course of national history, and Chorus 1, with its slightly wayward variations, as his descendants, learning that history and coming to an appreciation of what it had brought them. Indeed, when the two choruses are integrated to bring the piece to a close the righteous hopes of *anno 1813* seem fulfilled.

No part of the *Fest- und Gedenksprüche* has drawn more speculation about its meaning than the second movement: "When a heavily armed man guards his palace, his possessions are secure [Luke 11:21]. But: every kingdom divided against itself is brought to desolation, and house falls upon house [Luke 11:17]." In his review of the Hamburg première, the music critic Paul Mirsch, taking his lead from Hugo Riemann's program notes, accepts at face value the composer's suggestion to Bülow that this chorus relates somehow to Sedan.[19] Indeed, he reads the A section of the ternary form almost as

---

18   Beller-McKenna, *Brahms and the German Spirit*, 151–53 (quoted at 151, 152). Minor, *Choral Fantasies*, 179–84 (quoted at 180, emphasis added).

19   Mirsch, "Hamburgische Gewerbe- und Industrie-Ausstellung. I. Festkonzert," [1].

though it were a literal retelling of the great battle that had changed the course of German history nineteen years earlier:

Biblical text	Mirsch's gloss
A (C major; ¾, Lively and determined)	
Luke 11:21	Mm. 1–28
When a heavily armed man guards his palace	"The beginning advances pugnaciously and with firm confidence in victory, like the unfaltering steps of the German army columns clattering with arms."
His possessions are secure.	"The continuation rises to a full comforting effect."

By contrast to the opening movement, here the *cori spezzati* move in lockstep with one another, trading the same disjunct "pugnacious" material back and forth, first in strict imitation (Example 11) and then in somewhat freer imitation. Following a half cadence in the tonic in measure 12, the polychoral exchange continues with a version of the disjunct motive in F major that initiates a passage which gradually rises to a peak on the note a^2 in the sopranos of chorus 1 and then gradually descends, as the two choruses come together for the first time in a homophonic texture and produce the "full comforting effect" of a perfect authentic cadence on the words "his possessions are secure" (mm. 13–28).

Yet the comfort provided by this moment of surety is immediately disturbed when all eight voices combine to intone the word "but" (*aber*) on two measures of a dominant harmony that seems posed to lead to anywhere other than back to the tonic. Where it in fact leads is to the remarkable B section of the ternary form (C minor, C). No commentator fails to take note of the tone-painting in which Brahms engages here. The tenors of Chorus 1 are assigned to sing the words "A kingdom divided against itself," but almost immediately the sopranos and altos of the same chorus intrude with a syncopated line that seems all too eager to make clear the unfortunate outcome of that internal division (mm. 31–33). Yet that outcome is withheld for a moment longer while the forces of Chorus 2 rehearse the same material in invertible counterpoint (mm. 33–35). Only then is the divided house—the divided chorus—"brought to desolation." The dynamics suddenly change dramatically from *forte* to *piano* on a German-sixth chord that fails to resolve in normal fashion and instead sets off a succession of chromatic, hollow-sounding chords. Emerging from this quiet moment of utter devastation and ruin is a contrapuntal *tour de force*. Beginning at measure 41, the words "and house falls upon house" are sung in turn by the two choruses in a tight four-voice canon based on a series of descending triads whose entries come at a distance of only one quarter note (Example 12). Then, in a symbolic

Example 11. Brahms, *Fest- und Gedenksprüche*, op. 109, second movement, mm. 1–7.

Example 12. Brahms, *Fest- und Gedenksprüche*, op. 109, second movement, mm. 41–50.

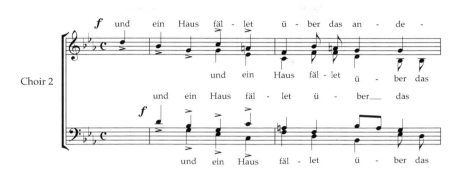

(—*continued*)

Example 12—concluded

depiction of the all-encompassing tumbling walls, Brahms dispenses with the polychoral disposition and provides an eight-part canonic stretto made up almost entirely of downward melodic gestures that generates great rhythmic confusion. Passing quickly by descending fifths from C to D♭, the music, seemingly representing the ruined remains of the house, comes to rest on G, the dominant of the home key of C minor.

Beller-McKenna and Minor both read this passage as a musical depiction of what lay in store should the Reich decide to go to war with itself, a prospect, in both scholars' view, that Brahms feared might happen. (Beller-McKenna goes so far as to suggest that Brahms was invoking prayer here to help ensure that it did not.)[20] Mirsch sees things quite differently. If, in his opinion, the A section had symbolized the Germans' victory on the battlefield at Sedan, the B section suggests that France had only its own hubris and internal divisions to blame for the catastrophe. And when the ensuing A' section gradually emerges at measure 51 out of the middle section, with six iterations of the words "when a heavily armed man," it is, as Mirsch puts it, as though "the good German rings out in the chaos of French instability":

Biblical text	Mirsch's gloss
B (C minor, ₵)	
Luke 11:17	Mm. 31–35
But: every kingdom divided against itself	"The following measures unfold a picture of unsteady hesitation, out of which individual boastful words sound to no avail."
	Mm. 36–40
Is brought to desolation	"A strangely hollow-sounding harmony lies coldly, frighteningly on the listener's chest."
	Mm. 41–50
And house falls upon house.	"The eight choral voices tumble over one another in extremely tight voice-leading."
A' (C major), ₵, changing to ¾	
Luke 11:21	Mm. 51–86
When a heavily armed man guards his palace his possessions are secure.	"Brightly challenging, jubilantly victorious, the good German rings out in the chaos of French instability."

Brahms was never given to musical story-telling, and there is no reason to think that Mirsch's account tells us very much about the composer's intentions. But the critic's patriotic narrative is valuable, all the same, because it

---

20   Beller-McKenna, *Brahms and the German Spirit*, 153–57; Minor, *Choral Fantasies*, 187–91. For the location "a Reich at war with itself," see Minor, *Choral Fantasies*, 188.

218 &❧ CHAPTER SEVEN

provides us with an on-the-ground glimpse of how those for whom the victory at Sedan and the foundation of the Reich were vivid living memories may have processed and made sense of a work that still, after all, carried the title "German Festive and Commemorative *Sprüche*."

Brahms's likening of the movement to Sedan is therefore not to be discounted. The key to understanding why may be found, not in Mirsch's review, however, but in the chapter heading for Luke 11 in the Luther Bible: "Formel und Kraft des Gebets, Austreibung des Satans, Zeichenforderung, Gast- und Strafpredigt Christi" (Formula and Power of Prayer, Exorcism of Satan, Demand for Signs, Christ's Guest and Punitive Sermon). The second unit in this series—Exorcism of Satan—has to do with Luke 11:14–23, the larger passage from which the biblical verses used in Brahms's movement are extracted and reordered. (In the quotations that follow, the verses Brahms set to music are highlighted in italic type.) This begins as Jesus has healed a man who had previously been unable to speak by casting out the demon who had held him in its grip. The people are understandably amazed when they hear the man speaking, but some of those present—Pharisees, as we know from a version of the same story told in Matthew 12:22–30—deny that this exorcism might have been done through any Messianic power and urge the crowd to accept that it could only have been done through the agency of Beelzebub, the prince of demons. To quell their doubts, the people test Jesus by asking for another sign from heaven (vv. 14–16). Implicit in the Pharisees' claim is the idea that the Devil would work to destroy his own forces.[21] To demonstrate the absurdity of this idea, Jesus asks the Pharisees if their own exorcists—Jewish exorcisms are reported in the Hebrew Bible— were similarly empowered by Beelzebub:

> *Every kingdom divided against itself is brought to desolation and house falls upon house.* And if Satan is divided against himself, how will his kingdom stand? For you say that it is by Beelzebub that I drive out demons. And if I cast out demons by Beelzebub, by whom do your sons cast them out? But if it is by the finger of God that I cast out demons, then the kingdom of God has come upon you. (vv. 17–20)

---

21 The figure of Beelzebub has long been a source of debate among New Testament scholars. See, among several recent discussions of the so-called Beelzebul Controversy, Todd Klutz, "Beelzebub, Beelzebul. II. New Testament," in *The Encyclopedia of the Bible and Its Reception*, ed. Hans-Josef Klauck et al., 19 vols. to date (Berlin: Walter de Gruyter, 2009–), vol. 3 (2011): 742–43; and Czire Szabolcs, "The Beelzebul Controversy—A Mediterranean Cultural Reading," in *Hellenistischer und Judaistischer Hintergrund des Neuen Testaments*, ed. György Szabolcs (Szeged: JATE Press, 2018), 69–81.

Jesus' claim is that his powers of exorcism constitute a victory of cosmic proportions against the Kingdom of Darkness and herald the arrival of God's eschatological reign and salvation.[22] This point is driven home with a parable:

> When a heavily armed man guards his palace, his possessions are secure. But when one stronger than he attacks and overcomes him, he takes away the armor on which he relied and distributes the spoils. Whoever is not with me is against me, and whoever does not gather with me scatters. (vv. 21–23)

It is through the idea of the exorcism of Satan by Jesus, by the one is who is stronger than the strongly armed man, that we can associate these verses with Sedan. As we have seen, during the years of Napoleonic domination in Central Europe, nationally minded Germans viewed the French emperor as something akin to the Devil Incarnate. (Recall Arndt's "Lied der Rache" [Song of revenge] of 1812.) And as the wealth of apocalyptic poetry generated by the outbreak of war with France in 1870 suggests, the second French emperor, Napoleon III, was not considered to be all that different. And in that sense, Napoleon III's unconditional surrender to William I in Sedan can be understood metaphorically as something like the "exorcism of Satan."

That is not the end of the story, however. In a letter to Widmann of March 19, 1890, Brahms asked: "Did you not even notice the theological, even Jesuitical sophistry of the second of the *Sprüche*? I've always wanted to ask you whether something like that is allowed. (Luke 11:21 and 17.) Take a look at it for fun."[23] Brahms was clearly inviting discussion of the matter with his friend, a fellow Christian atheist and devoted student of the Luther Bible, not as divine revelation, but as cultural patrimony.[24] The two men, their hard feelings of the previous summer patched up, were about to embark on a tour of Italy, during which Brahms, indeed, was uncharacteristically eager to speak about his music. Widmann's explication of the composer's handling of the biblical verses thus bears a certain degree of authoritativeness.[25]

In Luke's Gospel, as Widmann rightly notes, the realm divided against itself is the Kingdom of Darkness and the heavily armed man who watches over that realm is Satan. The subversive sophistry in Brahms's work is the

---

22 Klutz, "Beelzebub, Beelzebul. II. New Testament," 743.

23 *Briefwechsel*, 8: 104–5.

24 On Brahms, Widmann, and their shared religious skepticism and reverence for the Bible, see Grimes, *Brahms's Elegies*, 177–80. Grimes takes the apt expression "Christian atheism" from Max Widmann, *Josef Viktor Widmann: Ein Lebensbild. Zweite Lebenshälfte* (Leipzig: Frauenfeld, 1924), 68.

25 On Op. 109, see Widmann, *Johannes Brahms in Erinnerungen*, 96–97.

220   *&*   CHAPTER SEVEN

reversal of those "bad" things into "good" things: the Kingdom of Darkness becomes the prosperity and well-being of Germany, and the heavily armed man represents, not Satan, but the military power needed to ensure the Reich's security—and, we might add, its self-perceived territorial integrity, including Alsace-Lorraine—in what felt like a world made unsafe by the rise of Boulangism.[26]

As Widmann continues his recollection, he briefly takes up the outer movements:

> From the opening words, "Our fathers trusted in you" to the admonishing words at the close, "Take heed and keep your soul diligently, lest you forget the history that your eyes have seen, and lest it departs from your heart all the days of your life, and make it known to your children and your children's children"—this free handling of the biblical words is but a fresh proof of [Brahms's] anxious, "faithful Eckart" frame of mind.... And if Brahms had particularly solemn sounds for "the history that your eyes have seen, lest it depart from your heart," he himself set a good example in this regard.[27]

Indeed, the passage singled out here from the final movement ("Imperial Coronation"), indulgent, as Minor notes, in suspensions and rich, bass-heavy sonorities, does sound particularly Brahmsian (Example 13).[28] As Widmann explains: "When Brahms set patriotic thoughts to music, it was not festive occasions that guided him, but rather the feelings that lived everlastingly within him and belonged to the core of his masculine nature."

---

26   Ibid., 101–2. Other commentators have likened the strong man specifically to Bismarck. See Kalbeck, *Johannes Brahms*, 4: 189; Beller-McKenna, "Fest- und Gedenksprüche, for Eight-Part Chorus, Opus 109," in *The Compleat Brahms*, ed. Leon Botstein (New York: Norton, 1997), 360–63 (here 362); and Minor, *Choral Fantasies*, 184–86 (at 186). Brahms was delighted when he learned that the *Fest- und Gedenksprüche* had been put on the schedule for performance in Bern in August 1891 since he knew this would afford Widmann, who lived in the city, the chance to hear the *Sprüche* in person. In the end, Brahms decided not to make the trip himself to hear this performance, but he let Widmann know that he was eager to have his report. Letter of July 21, 1891, from Brahms to Eusebius Mandyczewski, quoted in Karl Geiringer, *Essays and Documentary Studies*, ed. George S. Bozarth (Sterling Heights, MI: Harmonie Press, 2006), 246–47; letter to Widmann of August 18, 1891, in *Briefwechsel*, 8: 118. No reply to Brahms's letter has been preserved.

27   Widmann, *Johannes Brahms in Erinnerungen*, 96–97.

28   Minor, *Choral Fantasies*, 191.

Example 13. Brahms, *Fest- und Gedenksprüche*, op. 109, third movement, mm. 43–67.

(—*continued*)

Example 13—continued

(—continued)

Example 13—concluded

224 ❧ CHAPTER SEVEN

It was with good reason, therefore, that Widmann described Brahms's patriotic feelings by invoking the "faithful Eckart," the legendary model of Teutonic rectitude and reliabdility, the loyal protector, the "strong man armed" who stands guard on the Rhine.[29] For, despite Beller-McKenna's assertions, Brahms's patriotic feelings were true, not conflicted. Nor should we think of the *Sprüche* as national prayers to a Heavenly Father. They can be better understood as a patriotic freethinker's call to strengthen and preserve the national fathers' legacy. All this—the anxiety in the face of threats from abroad, the determination to meet those threats head on—brings to mind the reporting quoted earlier from the *Vossische Zeitung* in which young William II's controversial speech in August 1888 was characterized as a signal to the world that a German nation made anxious by the revanchist designs of Boulanger in France would surely respond if necessary to defend its territorial integrity. Here is the contemporary political development in which to understand the music that Brahms composed as his *Deutsche Fest- und Gedenksprüche*, with their memories of German fathers, evocations of the German people, and admonishments against division within the new German Reich. And as Widmann himself tacitly acknowledged in the end, the expression of German national sentiment of this kind ought not to be equated with an unimaginably chauvinistic point of view.

---

29   As we have seen, this is a description used by the *Neues Wiener Tagblatt* in 1885 to characterize Bismarck on his seventieth birthday.

Epilogue

An Old Man's Political Disillusionment

He reads a lot of history; but in his mind all history is made by strong individuals. He immerses himself continually in German history; every significant account of it (Treitschke, Carlyle, especially Sybel's *Foundation of the German Reich*) captivates him—as though it were a heroic poem. He sees history in a series of great figures who stride through the ages in his mind's eye: the giants of the Renaissance, Cromwell and Frederick of Prussia, down to his living hero, Bismarck. For him, the whole story is a deadly serious combat sport between heroes and the powers that oppose them. As the enemy of his hero, whoever is against Bismarck is the embodiment of evil.[1]

—Otto Gottlieb-Billroth

On May 16, 1890, Brahms traveled from Vienna to Bad Ischl for his annual summer holiday. Packed in his bags that day were the first two volumes of Heinrich von Sybel's *Die Begründung des Deutschen Reiches durch Wilhelm I.* (The foundation of the German Reich by William I).[2] These books were a birthday present from Laura von Beckerath, whose inscription is found on the flyleaf of the first volume: "May 7, 1890. In grateful memory of beautiful times in the past."[3] As Brahms would discover, Sybel's project was, in effect, a history of Bismarck's foreign policy during the period 1850–70.[4] The first five volumes, published in 1889–90, make extensive use of

---

1 *Billroth und Brahms im Briefwechsel*, 45–46. Otto Gottlieb-Billroth was the son-in-law of Brahms's close friend Theodor Billroth, whose family name he eventually added to his own as a sign of respect.

2 Heinrich von Sybel, *Die Begründung des Deutschen Reiches durch Wilhelm I.*, 7 vols. (Munich and Leipzig: R. Oldenbourg, 1889–94). All seven volumes are preserved in Brahms's library.

3 Quoted in Hofmann, *Die Bibliothek von Johannes Brahms*, 114.

4 Paul Bailleu, "Sybel, Heinrich von," in *Allgemeine Deutsche Biographie* 54 (1908), 645–67 [online version], https://www.deutsche-biographie.de/pnd118620223.html#adbcontent.

226 ❧ EPILOGUE

privileged materials in the registry of the Prussian Foreign Ministry, exclusive access to which Bismarck had granted Sybel in 1881 for the purpose of writing an account of recent German and Prussian history.[5] These volumes advance the story to Prussia's victorious showdown with Austria in the summer of 1866. Publication of volumes 6 and 7, which cover the history of the North German Confederation and the lead up to the war with France, did not come until November 1894, for reasons to be discussed below. These too Brahms would receive as a gift from Laura von Beckerath, whom he thanked in a letter of December 5, 1894: "It is especially nice that the volumes of our imperial history always come to me from the Niederwald. And this time I had to think, with the greatest pleasure, of the great festival day [in 1883] that I experienced so happily in your charming home! But I am not in the least impatient for the [18]70 volume! Of [18]66–70 Sybel can never tell me enough."[6]

As it turned out, Sybel would have no more to tell Brahms. Eight months later the historian died without completing, or perhaps even beginning, a culminating volume on *Anno 70*.

The scope and ambition of Sybel's *magnum opus* had been made evident already in the critical reception that greeted the publication of volumes 1 and 2 in 1889. Vienna's *Neue Freie Presse* and *Neues Wiener Abendblatt* published substantial two-part reviews. We may take it for granted that Brahms was familiar with both.[7] The unnamed author of the latter (identified as W. L.) begins by taking note of Sybel's Prussian and National Liberal convictions only to assure his readers that "the Austrian, too, will be able to follow [the historian's] description without taking offense." One reason for this, we are told, is that unlike his fellow National Liberal historian Treitschke, Sybel does not try "to give the impression that the first and last aim of world history was the transfer of the German imperial dignity to the House of Hohenzollern." Rather than finding "stupidity, malice, and deceit in the non-Prussian camp," he seeks to understand and explain the non-Prussian standpoint in accordance with the historical premises that gave rise to it. This reviewer is pleased that Sybel favors the close relation that had developed

---

5   Already in 1875 Bismarck had placed Sybel in charge of the Prussian State Archive (*Preussisches Geheimes Staatsarchiv*).

6   Letter from Brahms to Beckerath of December 5, 1894, quoted in Stephenson, *Johannes Brahms und die Familie von Beckerath*, 61. See also Brahms's letter to Simrock of November 30, 1894, in *Briefwechsel*, 12: 157.

7   –j.—e., "Die Begründung des Deutschen Reiches durch Wilhelm I.," *Neue Freie Presse* (December 3, 1889): 1–4, and ibid. (December 4, 1889): 1–3; and W. L., "Die Begründung des Deutschen Reiches durch Wilhelm I.," *Neues Wiener Abendblatt* (December 2, 1889): 1–2; and W. L., "Sybel über Bismarck," ibid. (December 9, 1889): 1–2.

EPILOGUE 🔊 **227**

between Austria and Prussia in the years since 1866 and agrees with him that "today one could talk about Königgrätz just as unbiasedly as about Kolin and Beuthen." Here Königgrätz refers to the great Prussian defeat of the Austrian military in 1866; Kolin/Kolín and Beuthen/Bytom, to towns that had figured prominently in the three Silesian Wars of the mid-eighteenth century, fought between Frederick the Great's Prussia and Maria Theresa's Austria.[8] The implication is that the once-warring brothers now stood side-by-side in a mutual accord, one that extended well beyond the confines of the Dual Alliance into which they had entered in 1879.[9]

W. L. closes out the first installment of his review by quoting Sybel's assessment of where things stood at mid-century by way of preparing the introduction of the real hero of his account: "'Whoever wanted the German federal state without Austria had to be determined to go to war with Austria; this was the issue owing to a centuries' long development.'[10] But to think such a thought with cold-bloodedness and to carry it out with ruthless determination was reserved for Bismarck, whose powerful personality, given sharp delineation by Sybel, now comes to the fore." The entire second installment of the review, published one week later, is, at bottom, a panegyric to Bismarck.

Both parts of this review would have resonated with Brahms. Over the course of time, he had developed a strong attachment to Austria, indeed warm feelings of *Heimat* for Vienna, but he remained, at heart, a patriotic North German and an admirer of Bismarck.[11] And so with his appetite whetted, he plunged into his reading of Sybel's first two volumes during his next *Sommerfrische*. "I am traveling to Ischl today," began his thank-you note to

---

8　Kolin had been the site of an Austrian victory over Prussia in 1757 in the Third Silesian War.

9　W. L., in *Neues Wiener Abendblatt* (December 2, 1889): 1–2 (at 1), from which the next several quotations are taken.

10　Sybel, *Die Begründung des Deutschens Reiches*, 1: 330.

11　For the most straightforward expression of Brahms's feeling for Austria and for the Germans of Austria, see his letter to Hanslick of June 1883, quoted in Eduard Hanslick, "Johannes Brahms: The Last Days, Memories and Letters," trans. Susie Gillespie, Andrew Holman, and Caroline Homan, in *Brahms and His World*, ed. Walter Frisch and Kevin C. Karnes, rev. ed. (Princeton: Princeton University Press, 2009), 307–35 (at 327). See also Helene Hecht, *Unsere Reise nach Kleinasien und Griechenland im Frühjahr 1891* (Munich: Knorr & Hirth, 1891), 18–19; undated letter to Philipp Spitta from the summer of 1893, in *Briefwechsel*, vol. 16: *Johannes Brahms im Briefwechsel mit Philipp Spitta*, ed. Carl Krebs (1920): 92–93; Brodbeck, *Defining Deutschtum*, 158–61, 174–77; Brodbeck, "Politics and Religion," 266–67; and the composer's letter to Simrock of March 10, 1897, in *Briefwechsel*, 12: 214.

228 & EPILOGUE

Beckerath of May 16, 1890. "How often have I changed around the books that are supposed to make me happy on beautiful summer days? Then along come your two thick volumes; this couldn't have been better, more opportune." He continued:

> Only one little sigh since the story won't go on—but two more volumes have already been reserved to be sent to Ischl, and now it's good that for the time being it won't go on, because otherwise one would definitely reach for the last and forget the first ones. Now I'll start cozily from the beginning, and how happy the whole person will feel when the last volume and the great year [18]70 comes![12]

Brahms's summer reading that year encompassed not only the two thick volumes received for his birthday, but also, as indicated, two more installments and eventually a third that appeared in the first half of 1890. Writing to Eduard Hanslick from Salzburg on 28 May, Theodor Billroth reported that he had recently spent two pleasant hours with the composer in Ischl, adding "He [is] deep in Sybel's 'Foundation of the German Reich,' three thick volumes with the fourth to come."[13] Two days later, in a letter to Simrock, Brahms drew an implicit contrast between Sybel's work and another new publication, *Rembrandt als Erzieher* (Rembrandt as educator), an idiosyncratic attack on modernity by August Julius Langbehn that had taken the German-speaking world by storm that spring: "Rembrandt doesn't entice me. I'm reading Sybel's imperial history, by contrast, with passion."[14]

---

12   Quoted in Stephenson, *Johannes Brahms und die Familie von Beckerath*, 58.

13   Letter from Billroth to Hanslick of May 28, 1890, in *Briefe von Theodor Billroth*, ed. Georg Fischer, 7th ed. (Hannover and Leipzig: Hahnschen Buchhandlung, 1906), 475. Brahms obviously had the third and fourth volumes in hand by the end of May, and he seems to have acquired the fifth shortly after its publication in June. He frequently asked Simrock, who managed his finances, to draw on his accounts to make such purchases for him.

14   Letter from Brahms to Simrock of May 30, 1890, in *Briefwechsel*, 12: 24. Ein Deutscher [Julius Langbehn], *Rembrandt als Erzieher* (Leipzig: C. L. Hirschfeld, 1890). Langbehn's book appeared anonymously at first; it quickly went through more than seventy printings before eventually falling into obscurity. The classic account in English is Fritz Richard Stern, *The Politics of Cultural Despair: A Study in the Rise of the Germanic Ideology* (Berkeley and Los Angeles: University of California Press, 1961), 97–182. For more recent discussions, see Bernd Behrendt, "August Julius Langbehn, der 'Rembrandtdeutsche,'" in *Handbuch zur "Völkischen Bewegung" 1871–1918*, ed. Uwe Puschner, Walter Schmitz, and Justus H. Ulbricht (Munich, New Providence, London, and Paris, 1996), 94–113; Anja Lobenstein-Reichmann, "Julius Langbehns 'Rembrandt als Erzieher': Diskursive Traditionen und begriffliche Fäden eines nicht ungefährlichen Buches," in *Identitätsentwürfe*

EPILOGUE ❧ 229

Whether or not Brahms ever acquired a copy of Langbehn's polemic—none is preserved in his library—he would have been familiar with its outlines from the widespread cultural scuttlebutt it generated. Among its targets of attack was the "false Germanness" (*falsches Deutschtum*) perpetrated, in Langbehn's view, by contemporary scholarship and its avatar, the German professoriate.[15] As Augustinius P. Dierick put it:

> The main theme of Langbehn's book, and the one which is meant to unite the rambling main sections dealing with German art, science, politics, education, and humanities, is that German culture had been destroyed by science, intellectualism, rationalism, and is in great need of regeneration through art, and primarily through great artistic individuals who could be held up as models. The dominant features of modern German life—positivism, skepticism, dogmatism and specialization—have to be counterbalanced by art, creativity, energy and mystery.[16]

That such a book had no attraction for Brahms is unsurprising.[17] He had always placed the highest value, after all, on learning and numbered many university professors and other distinguished members of the

---

in der Kunstkommunikation: Studien zur Praxis der sprachlichen und multimodalen Positionierung im Interaktionsraum "Kunst," ed. Marcus Müller (Berlin and Boston: Walter de Gruyter, 2012), 295–318; and Ulrich Sieg, "'Radikaler Konservatismus' im Deutschen Reich," in Einigkeit und Recht, doch Freiheit: Das Deutsche Kaiserreich in der Demokratiegeschichte und Erinnerungskultur, ed. Andreas Braune et al. (Stuttgart: Franz Steiner Verlag, 2021), 249–65 (at 257–58).

15 I take the characterization of "false Germanness" from one early review that Brahms almost certainly read: Karl v. Thaler, "Rembrandt als Erzieher," *Neue Freie Presse* (March 29, 1890): 1–3.

16 Augustinius P. Dierick, "Julius Langbehn's 'Rembrandt als Erzieher': Politics and Cultural Esthetics," *Mosaic: An Interdisciplinary Critical Journal* 21/1 (Winter 1988): 25–35 (at 28). See also Carl Niekerk, "Mahler, Rembrandt, and the Dark Side of German Culture," in *Legacies of Modernism: Art and Politics in Northern Europe, 1890–1950*, ed. Patricia C. McBride, Richard W. McCormick, and Monica Žagar (New York: Palgrave Macmillan, 2007), 29–40 (at 31–34); and Carl Niekerk, *Reading Mahler: German Culture and Jewish Identity in Fin-de-siècle Vienna* (Rochester, NY: Camden Books, 2010), 141–47.

17 Margaret Notley assumes that Simrock sent the book to Brahms, who declined to read it. See Notley, *Lateness and Brahms*, 204. Since Simrock's side of the correspondence at this point has not been preserved, and since, as noted, no copy of Langbehn's book is preserved in the composer's library, we cannot rule out the possibility that Brahms may have sought out a library copy. He held as one of the attractions of living in Vienna that whenever he wanted to

230 & EPILOGUE

Bildungsbürgertum among his friends. (Pride of place here goes to Hanslick and Billroth, but there were numerous others, including Adolf Exner [1841–94], jurist and professor of law at the University of Vienna, and Theodor Engelmann [1843–1909], physiologist and professor at the universities of Utrecht and Berlin.)[18] By contrast, Sybel's National Liberal historiography and its uniformly positive appraisal of Bismarck appealed to Brahms most strongly, not only because it validated views he had come to embrace in the years since 1866, but precisely because of its unimpeachable scholarship and command of the sources.

Brahms was thus hugely disappointed when publication of *Die Begründung des Deutschen Reiches* stalled in 1890, following the conclusion of what the *Neue Freie Presse* called "only the first and less important half of the unified structure to which the name of William I will be tied for all time."[19] As Brahms would eventually learn, this delay came about as fallout from a power struggle between the imperious, seventy-five-year-old Bismarck and William II, the ambitious, thirty-year-old emperor whom he had served since the summer of 1888. To put the matter in brief, when Bismarck lost this struggle and with it his powerful governmental positions, Sybel lost the access he had enjoyed as Bismarck's protégé to the privileged material that had given the first five volumes of his study their unmatched authority. Forced thereafter to work under vastly different conditions, using information supplied by living historical agents, including Bismarck, but without essential archival material, Sybel would be unable to publish the next two volumes of his study, as noted, until 1894. Nor would he be able to complete this "second and more important half" of his "unified structure" before his death the following year. In view of Brahms's interest in Sybel—and, of course, in Bismarck himself—the events surrounding this matter thus warrant some discussion.

---

read a book right away, he need only look for it in the city's public libraries. See Hecht, *Unsere Reisen nach Kleinasien und Griechenland*, 18.

18   On the composer's intellectual interests, see the following chapters from *Brahms in Context*, ed. Natasha Loges and Katy Hamilton (Cambridge: Cambridge University Press, 2019): Natasha Loges, "Literature" (269–76); Nicole Grimes, "Philosophy" (277–85); William Vaughan, "Visual Arts" (286–95); and Myles W. Jackson and Katy Hamilton, "Science and Technology" (296–304). See also Michael Musgrave, *A Brahms Reader* (New Haven and London: Yale University Press, 2000), 151–84; and Leon Botstein, "Time and Memory: Concert Life, Science, and Music in Brahms's Vienna," in *Brahms and His World*, ed. Walter Frisch and Kevin C. Karnes, rev. ed. (Princeton: Princeton University Press, 2009), 3–25.

19   –j.—e., in *Neue Freie Presse* (December 4, 1889): 3.

Bismarck's Dismissal

Although tension between Bismarck and William II had been building for years, the proximate cause of their decisive dispute was a difference over how to deal with the Social Question. The chancellor wanted to extend the controversial anti-socialist law, hoping to provoke the workers into an overreaction that could be used to justify harsh repression. The emperor wanted to avoid the notoriety that would come with any such outbreak of domestic violence so early in his reign. He favored tackling the problem by employing an approach that Bismarck himself had once used by pushing for extensive new social legislation with an eye toward wooing the workers away from socialism and into his own camp of supporters.[20] Matters quickly came to a head. On March 18, 1890, Bismarck, accustomed to getting his way with policy, offered his resignation in writing, not quite believing that it would be accepted. He had used this stratagem successfully many times before with the emperor's grandfather, William I. But the new sovereign, itching to exercise what he considered his rightful leadership role, was only too happy to call Bismarck's bluff. (By ensuring that the office of the Reich Chancellor would be responsible solely to the Kaiser, not to the Reichstag, Bismarck was ultimately hoisted with his own petard.) In the first of two letters delivered to the Reich Chancellor's residence on 20 March, duplicitously written to suggest to the public that Bismarck had asked to step down for reasons of his health, the emperor accepted the resignation "with a sad heart but in the firm confidence that the granting of your request will help to preserve and sustain your life and strength, which are irreplaceable for the fatherland, for as long as possible." In the second letter, in what was obviously meant to soften the blow, William conferred on Bismarck the dignity of the Dukedom of Lauenburg and made him colonel-general with the rank of field marshal.[21]

Brahms was in Frankfurt, fresh off Wüllner's performance of the *Fest- und Gedenksprüche* in Cologne, when word of the resignation was made public. On March 21, 1890, the *Frankfurter Zeitung* reprinted the texts of both of William's letters to Bismarck from the day before. Not only did Brahms clip this article; he eventually inserted it between pages 142 and 143 of the second volume of *Die Begründung des Deutschen Reiches*. By using the clipping

---

20 On the tension between Bismarck and Wilhelm II, see Christopher Clark, *Kaiser Wilhelm II: A Life in Power* (London: Penguin, 2009), 35–66.

21 *Deutscher Reichs-Anzeiger und Königlich-Preußischer Staats-Anzeiger*, No. 72 (March 20, 1890). On Bismarck's downfall, see Pflanze, *Bismarck and the Development of Germany*, 3: 350–77; Röhl, *Wilhelm II: The Kaiser's Personal Monarchy*, 272–305; Feuchtwanger, *Bismarck: A Political History*, 240–52; and Steinberg, *Bismarck: A Life*, 425–65.

232 &❧ EPILOGUE

to mark the passage in which Bismarck first appears in Sybel's narrative, Brahms in effect highlighted for himself the extraordinary length and importance of a career that had, by 1890, seemingly run its course.[22]

In Sybel's telling, Bismarck's appointment as the Prussian envoy to the Federal Diet in Frankfurt in 1851 had signaled the beginning of something momentous: "In the Federal Diet ... the king appointed the former dike captain Otto von Bismarck-Schönhausen to replace [Theodor] von Rochow.... With the presentation of his credentials to the Federal President on August 29, 1851, [Bismarck] took the first step on a career of world-historical significance."[23]

Sybel goes on to describe a man who already then was a figure larger than life:

> Bismarck was now in his thirty-sixth year, in the full bloom of his vigorous manhood. A tall and imposing figure, which towered by a whole head above the generality of the children of men, a face glowing with every sign of health, a glance enlivened with intelligence, in his mouth and chin the expression of an inflexible will—such he appeared to his contemporaries, enlivening every conversation with original thoughts, brilliant figures, and striking phrases, manifesting a charming affability in social life, and in business affairs a consummate superiority.[24] He has been for the most part self-taught.... He was afterwards, in the light of his broad experience, accustomed to say that for every statesman a properly-directed course of study in history was the most important element in the foundation of his knowledge.

This fulsome delineation is one of numerous passages in *Die Begründung des Deutschen Reiches* that Brahms highlighted for emphasis. Together they confirm that Brahms shared Sybel's assessment that Bismarck was "the central, heroic figure in German unification."[25]

On the basis of this achievement, Bismarck began to take on the status of a living legend even during his years in office. (Recall the story of the ageless magic oak recounted in Excursus 2.) But if Bismarck's masterful steering of Germany's foreign policy was widely appreciated throughout his long tenure, that was by no means the case, as we have seen, with respect

---

22 "Der offizielle Abschied des Fürsten Bismarck," *Frankfurter Zeitung, Zweites Morgenblatt* (March 21, 1890): 2.

23 Sybel, *Die Begründung des Deutsches Reiches*, 2: 142, from which the following quotation is taken.

24 One is immediately struck by parallels between this passage and the description of Brahms's attitude toward Bismarck and other "heroic" figures from history quoted as the epigraph of this chapter.

25 Burford, "Brahms's Sybel," 431.

EPILOGUE & 233

to domestic policy.[26] By 1890, not only Bismarck's so-called *Reichsfeinde*, but many other Germans as well, were happy to see him go.[27] The selfsame *Frankfurter Zeitung*, in the leading article of its evening edition of March 21, put it thus: "The nation is quiet; not without movement, but without fear of the future the German people see the mighty man depart from the power in which he had become an internal obstacle…. May it also be said of him that what has gone before will not return; the nation will soon count March 18, 1890, as one of those days that will be remembered with joy."[28]

It was decidedly not a day that Bismarck would remember with any joy. On March 29 the deposed chancellor left the German capital for his country manor in Friedrichsruh an embittered man.[29] Still, the enthusiastic and appreciative sendoff he received from the public along the short route to the train station for the journey home suggested that it would not be difficult for him to shape public opinion to his liking. Indeed, when two years later he made a grand tour of Germany that took him to Vienna for his son Herbert's wedding to the daughter of a prominent member of the Magyar nobility, he was not only cheered at every stop on his way, he was celebrated throughout his week in the Austrian capital—just as William had feared when he made it known to the German ambassador in Vienna that he should ignore Bismarck's presence in the city, and when he wrote to ask the Habsburg emperor-king not to receive him.[30]

As Otto Pflanze noted, such popular displays gave evidence of the "need for additional psychological bonds capable of reinforcing the solidarity of a young nation-state still doubtful about its internal cohesion and external power." (One can view Brahms's Op. 109 as an early attempt to provide such reinforcement in music.) Thus from the ashes of his dismissal, Bismarck quickly rose to become the most revered of all German statesmen, the very symbol of *Deutschtum*. Devotion to the Iron Chancellor became a cornerstone of German identity, even that of the German population in Habsburg Austria, whose traditional hegemonic status in the multinational state had been sorely weakened by the empowerment of the Czechs and other nationalities, and even, through what Pflanze describes as an act of selective

---

26   Feuchtwanger, *Bismarck*, 180–82, 254–57.

27   Ibid., 240–45.

28   "Politische Uebersicht," *Frankfurter Zeitung, Abendblatt* (March 21, 1890): 1. Since Brahms clipped an article from one of the earlier editions of this newspaper that day, we have reason to think he would have seen this article as well.

29   On March 24, Brahms traveled home from Frankfurt to Vienna, where he would have read the reports of Bismarck's departure in the local newspapers; see, for example, "Fürst Bismarck's Abreise nach Friedrichsruhe," *Neue Freie Presse* (March 30, 1890): 7.

30   Pflanze, *Bismarck*, 3: 395–98; Steinberg, *Bismarck: A Life*, 455–56.

memory, for many of those, even "enemies of the Reich," who had once opposed Bismarck when he was in power. Throughout German-speaking Central Europe, Bismarck was less now a man than a myth.[31]

With the compliant *Hamburger Nachrichten* and Maximilian Harden's Berlin weekly *Die Zukunft* serving as his mouthpieces in the press, Bismarck soon undertook a resentful, contemptuous campaign in opposition to the emperor who had let him go and to the chancellor who replaced him, Leo von Caprivi.[32] He welcomed countless groups for visits to Friedrichsruh and used these encounters to shape his image. And he became a rallying point for Germans generally who were disenchanted with their government. Notably, whereas he had once embodied a conception of German nationalism in which responsibility for defining and defending the national interest was rooted in the top-down authority of the nation-state, in retirement, insofar as it served his own political interests, he allowed his name to be associated with various non-parliamentary interest groups, some of them *völkisch* in orientation, that practiced a type of populist politics of national opposition that he had always worked to keep under control while in power.[33]

The evidence of Brahms's immediate reaction to Bismarck's dismissal is surprisingly slim. His preserved correspondence from the period is silent on the subject, even with Simrock, to whom he wrote in the week after Bismarck stepped down.[34] For most of April 1890, as we have seen, the composer was on holiday in Italy with Widmann. It is inconceivable that the topic of Bismarck's departure did not come up in their discussions, but we have no indication from Widmann's recollections what Brahms had to say about it. Moreover, though it was during the weeks of this Italian holiday that Bismarck began his open attack on Caprivi's "New Course," it is not likely that from afar Brahms could have made himself fully informed about that development.

---

31 Pflanze, *Bismarck*, 3: 444–47. See also Chickering, *We Men Who Feel Most German*, 23–73; Richard E. Frankel, *Bismarck's Shadow: The Cult of Leadership and the Transformation of the German Reich, 1898–1945* (Oxford and New York: Berg, 2005), 19–47; Robert Grewarth, *The Bismarck Myth: Weimar Germany and the Legacy of the Iron Chancellor* (Oxford: Oxford University Press, 2005), 11–18; and Steinberg, *Bismarck: A Life*, 425–64.

32 Pflanze, *Bismarck*, 3: 381–95.

33 Among such groups were the Pan-German League (*Alldeutscher Verband*, founded in 1891), the Agrarian League (*Bund der Landwirte*, 1893), and the German Eastern Marches Association (*Deutscher Ostmarkenverein*, 1894); later, after Bismarck's death, would come others, most prominently the *Deutsche Flottenverein* (German Navy League, 1898).

34 Two letters of March 26, 1890, in *Briefwechsel*, 12: 20–21.

EPILOGUE ❧ 235

The topic of Bismarck's dismissal finally did come up in the preserved correspondence several weeks later, albeit only obliquely. On June 8, 1890, Heinrich von Herzogenberg sent word to the composer about his recent visit with their mutual friend Friedrich Chrysander, the great Handel scholar, who lived close to Bismarck in Friedrichsruh and whose son was the ex-chancellor's private secretary and personal physician. From Chrysander, he wrote, "we gleaned the freshest and most reliable news about his great neighbor and understood less and less the latest turning point in world history and the good Lord who permitted it." Although Herzogenberg referred here to a matter of the greatest national and political interest, Brahms, in his reply six days later, said nothing about it.[35]

Not until the following year do we have any written indication that Brahms disapproved of Bismarck's sacking. This comes in a letter to Laura von Beckerath of May 13, 1891. It appears that Beckerath had recently written Brahms to express her regret that she could not, as she had done the previous year, present him with any more volumes of Sybel's *Begründung* for his birthday. "I heard it was ready for printing," Brahms wrote in reply, "but unfortunately it's being held back because the moment isn't right. If we regret [not] having the pleasure of seeing the beautiful work completed and of enjoying it, we must surely regret even more that this should be forbidden for such a reason."[36] It seems clear that Brahms had by then learned that publication of Sybel's study had grounded to a halt because of Bismarck's forced resignation.

Brahms's Bismarck

On 11 December 1890, only nine months after Bismarck gave up his chancellorship, Brahms announced his own retirement from composition. "With this scrap of paper," he wrote to Simrock, "you can take your farewell from my music—because it really is time to stop."[37] Yet Brahms's voluntary retirement would prove to be no more permanent than Bismarck's forced retirement was quiet. Still to come were four masterful essays in the sonata

---

35 Letter to Brahms of June 8, 1890, in *Briefwechsel*, 2: 235–37 (at 237). Letter from Brahms to Herzogenberg of June 14, 1890, in *Briefwechsel*, 2: 238.

36 Quoted in Stephenson, *Johannes Brahms und die Familie von Beckerath*, 59.

37 *Briefwechsel*, 12: 35–36 (here 35). The reference here is to a manuscript containing the ending of the first movement of the four-hand arrangement of the String Quartet in G major, op. 111. Five months later, Brahms entrusted Simrock with his newly written last will, the so-called "Ischl Testament," later the subject of considerable legal wrangling.

236 &❧ EPILOGUE

style, each featuring the warm sound of Richard Mühlfeld's clarinet; four books of exquisite *Klavierstücke*; the profound *Vier ernste Gesänge* on biblical texts; and the posthumously published set of eleven *Chorale Preludes* for organ, drenched in the manner of the German Baroque but imbued with Romantic harmonic sensibilities. All this music—not to speak of the seven books of *Deutsche Volkslieder*, WoO 33, that Brahms gathered for publication in 1894—was German through-and-through. But none of it bears any trace of the national-political sentiment evident in the works explored in this book—nothing like the five *Männerchöre*, with their call for a constitutional "Greater German" nation-state; the *Triumphlied*, with its celebration of Bismarck's achievement of a "Lesser German" nation-state; and the *Fest- und Gedenksprüche*, with their dedication to the preservation of that nation-state in peace and security.

It is from Brahms's autumnal years, nevertheless, that we have the most substantial body of evidence regarding his patriotism in general and of his admiration of Bismarck in particular. Significantly, he shared no truck with the predominantly antisemitic *völkisch* groups that tied themselves to Bismarck in their quest to remake older notions of German nationalism.[38] Brahms's abiding attachment to the German chancellor was not transactional but worshipful; it reflected, at a time of growing pessimism about what was becoming of German Central Europe, a desire to honor and revel in what the Iron Chancellor had achieved a quarter of a century earlier.

Matters were different with respect to William II. To be sure, Brahms had come forcefully to the young emperor's defense during his kerfuffle with Widmann in the summer of 1888, although in that instance the cause of his defense was the Hohenzollern dynasty as an institution more than it was the hotheaded monarch himself.[39] And during the final weeks of his life, he was pleased by William's decision to project a forceful stance in the Eastern Mediterranean in February 1897 with regard to a serious dispute between the Ottoman Empire and Greece over the status of the island of Crete.[40] But after Bismarck's rift with William II became a matter of public knowledge, he never failed to take sides in favor of the Iron Chancellor. One example came in the spring of 1892, following rumors of a possible reconciliation between the two men and of the ensuing battle of wills over which of the two would risk a loss of face by taking the first step to make

---

38 Brahms's attitude toward racialist antisemitism in the German Reich, mentioned in passing in Chapter 8, can be inferred from his well-documented attitude toward the same social pathology in *fin-de-siècle* Vienna. See Brodbeck, "Politics and Religion," 266–68; and Notley, *Lateness in Brahms*, 204–7.

39 See Brahms's letter to Widmann of August 20, 1888, discussed in Chapter 7.

40 Röhl, *William II*, 938–44; Kalbeck, *Johannes Brahms*, 4: 504.

this possible. On May 15, around the time when Brahms departed Vienna for his summer holiday in Ischl, the *Neue Freie Presse* reported: "Herbert Bismarck, contrary to what is reported in the papers, does not intend to enter the civil service. His re-entry would only be possible if a reconciliation between the emperor and Prince Bismarck were to take place, which Caprivi prevented. Influential members of the Prussian ministry, however, consider the reconciliation to be absolutely necessary."[41] The news of this aborted attempt at peace gave *Der Floh*, one of Vienna's satirical weeklies, cause to make light of the situation in its edition of May 22 through its assurance that "Bismarck passionately denies the rumors that he might be reconciled with Kaiser Wilhelm. Does the Prince think that his offenses are such that the German Kaiser could never forgive them?" It was probably this remark to which Brahms referred in a letter to Simrock sent from Ischl later that same day: "The papers here are teaming with bad jokes like the one enclosed. Unfortunately, your emperor has never given such sad and serious reasons for bad jokes."[42]

Later, Brahms himself retold witticisms at the expense of "Simrock's emperor."[43] One had to do with a four-voice male part-song entitled "Sang an Ägir," a panegyric to the divine personification of the sea in Norse mythology whose pseudo-Wagnerian text has been interpreted as an example of the "aesthetic antisemitism" that circulated freely in the Wilhelmine court.[44] Although the authors of the text and music were likely the emperor's friends Philipp Eulenberg and Kuno von Moltke, respectively, the piece

---

41   "München, 14. Mai," *Neue Freie Presse* (May 15, 1892): 7. Herbert Bismarck, who had served as German Foreign Minister from 1886 to 1890, resigned shortly after his father's dismissal.

42   *Der Floh* (May 22, 1892): 2; *Briefwechsel*, 12: 68–69 (at 68).

43   It is inconceivable that Brahms would have spoken of William II's grandfather in similar terms. According to Kalbeck, the composer's patriotic devotion to the first German emperor was something "heartfelt and stubbornly devoted [*trotzig-gläubig*], almost childlike." Kalbeck, *Johannes Brahms*, 4: 110. On William I's image in the popular imagination in the later nineteenth century as a figure of "modesty and legendary 'aversion to the ostentations trappings of the royal office,'" and of "endearing kindheartedness, ... gentle earnestness, [and] trusting candor," see Giloi, *Monarchy, Myth, and Material Culture*, 298. The personal qualities listed align very much with Brahms's own.

44   John C. G. Röhl, *The Kaiser and His Court: Wilhelm II and the Government of Germany*, trans. Terence F. Cole (Cambridge: Cambridge University Press, 1994), 190–212; Röhl, *Wilhelm II*, 134–37, 230, 315, 465, 466–67; Norman Domeier, *The Eulenburg Affair: A Cultural History of Politics in the German Empire*, trans. Deborah Lucas Schneider (Rochester, NY: Camden House, 2015), 141–205.

238 &❧ EPILOGUE

was published and passed off as William's own.[45] Introduced in Berlin in June 1894, "Sang an Ägir" was subsequently performed twice in Vienna before the year's end. Whether Brahms was in attendance at either performance—by the Vienna Men's Choral Society on November 10 and the Vienna Commercial Choral Society on December 6—is unknown, but he was certainly familiar with the publicity that surrounded what he was amused to call the "Kaiserschmarrn" (Emperor's mess), after the popular Viennese dessert of the same name. And we can be sure that he would have taken devilish delight in the review that appeared in the *Arbeiter Zeitung* after the first Viennese performance:

> Nine-tenths of the audience did not dare to applaud, obviously out of sheer reverence. Yet Choral Master Kremser, who had come to the Sophiensaal with the unshakable decision to have the work of his imperial patron sung twice, was quick to comply with the wish for a repetition by the tenth-tenth, which had not called for it all that urgently. Hopefully he will receive a Prussian Order for this, for which already today we congratulate him.[46]

Shortly after this performance Brahms wickedly characterized Germany as the "most musical state" because "the emperor composes and the ministers go down the drain" (*der Kaiser komponiert und die Minister flöten gehen*).[47] Here Brahms was referring not only to William's supposed composition, which begins with the words "O Ägir, Herr der Fluthen" (O Aegir, Lord of billows), but also to his recent dismissal of both the Reich Chancellor Caprivi, with whom he had long been on the outs, and the Prussian Minister-President Botho zu Eulenburg.[48] That Brahms delighted in retelling these jokes is suggestive of the personal disdain in which he had come to hold the increasingly authoritarian German emperor, not to speak of the antisemitism

---

45   Giles MacDonogh, *The Last Kaiser: The Life of Wilhelm II* (New York: St. Martin's, 2001), 201–3; Domeier, *The Eulenburg Affair*, 170; and Florian Heesch, "Volkstümlichkeit und Pathos: Bemerkungen zur Musik des 'Sang an Aegir' von Wilhelm II.," in *"Sang an Aegir": Nordische Mythen um 1900*, ed. Katja Schulz and Florian Heesch (Heidelberg: Universitätsverlag Winter, 2009), 31–43.

46   "Sang an Aegir," *Arbeiter-Zeitung* (November 20, 1894): 2.

47   Letter to Simrock of November 30, 1894, in *Briefwechsel*, 12: 157; Richard Heuberger, *Erinnerungen an Johannes Brahms*, 2nd ed., rev. and improved, ed. Kurt Hofmann (Tutzing: Hans Schneider, 1976), 165 (entries for December 1, 1894, and January 6, 1895). The humor lies in the homonymic use of the verb *flöten* (meaning to pipe but used here as part of the idiom *flöten gehen* [go down the drain]), and the plural noun *Flöten* (flutes).

48   Röhl, *Wilhelm II*, 610–19.

the emperor tolerated and abetted.[49] Brahms was not alone in holding this attitude. Indeed, the Viennese performances of *Sang an Ägir* came at a moment when the emperor's popularity in Germany had reached a nadir.[50]

A Bismarck Fan Club

Humor of a different kind, playful rather than wicked, is on display in Brahms's relationship with Sophie Charlotte von Sell (1864–1941), a young woman who presided over a group of Bismarck admirers founded in Berlin in the early 1890s. Calling itself the *Verein "zur Ausspannung der Pferde"* (Association for the Unhitching of the Horses), this group was founded with the mission of paying the discharged Bismarck proper respect upon his hoped-for return to the capital someday by unhitching his horses and drawing his carriage through the city's streets themselves.[51] The Association ultimately failed to realize its *raison d'être*. When Bismarck finally returned to Berlin for a brief and, as it turned out, inconsequential reconciliation visit with the emperor on January 26, 1894, he was met at the station and escorted to the palace by Prince Heinrich, accompanied by a unit of cuirassier guards charged precisely with preventing any group from disrupting the procession by unharnessing the horses.[52] Nevertheless, the organization lived on until Bismarck's death in 1898 as a kind of fan club.

Brahms learned of its existence during a visit to Berlin for a concert with Joseph Joachim on January 25, 1895. Indeed, it was probably through Joachim, who had joined the Association three years earlier, that Brahms

---

49 Notley cites these jokes as a sign that Brahms was only willing to go so far in his embrace of *fin-de-siècle* German nationalism. See Notley, *Lateness and Brahms*, 215.

50 Röhl, *Wilhelm II*, 560–65, 700–13.

51 Sophie Charlotte von Sell, *Johannes Brahms: Ein deutscher Künstler* (Stuttgart: J. F. Steinkopf, 1931), 78–81. The daughter of a military officer from a prominent Prussian family, Sell became a prolific author mostly of fiction. Of her two works of non-fiction, one is this biography of Brahms; the other, a biography of Bismarck's wife, Johanna (which reads much like a biography of Bismarck himself). See Sophie Charlotte von Sell, *Fürst Bismarcks Frau: Lebensbild* (Berlin: Trowitzsch & Sohn, 1914). Something of the woman's independent streak is evident in the description of her in the recent memoirs of one of her nieces. See Sibylle Sarah Niemöller, Baroness von Sell, *Crowns, Crosses, and Stars: My Youth in Prussia, Surviving Hitler, and A Life Beyond* (West Lafayette, IN: Purdue University Press, 2012), 24–25.

52 Pflanze, *Bismarck and the Development of Germany*, 3: 404–6.

240 ❧ EPILOGUE

came into contact with Sell.[53] Brahms teased her with the fictitious news that word of her organization had reached the Habsburg capital and that her photograph, with the inscription "President of the Z. A. d. P.," could be seen on display on the Am Graben. Playing along, Sell suggested that Brahms should found a Viennese branch and accept its honorary presidency. Brahms, in turn, continued the charade by accepting this office on the condition that she provide him with a suitable large-format diploma (*auf großem Bogen*). When in short order this was produced, Sell sent it to Brahms under the cover of a letter dated February 5, 1895 (Figure 8).[54]

Correspondence between the two continued in the spring, when Sell reported to Brahms on the pilgrimage that she and two other members of the group had made to Friedrichsruh for an audience with Bismarck on 5 May.[55] There the visitors presented the old man, who had recently turned eighty, with a lighthearted, illuminated address that recounted the Association's history, under which the names of all the members, including Brahms, were listed, together with a floral arrangement modeled, by way of representing the Association's founding purpose, on a Roman quadriga. Sell made sure to note that Bismarck, having noticed Brahms's name among the other members, had asked about the composer. In reply Brahms, who was put off by all forms of lionization, wrote: "Forgive me for having a little pity for the celebrated man! But it was beautiful nonetheless, and really I envy you."[56]

Brahms never attempted to meet Bismarck himself, although this could easily have been arranged for him through his friend Chrysander. Instead he was content to immerse himself in books on recent German political history,

---

53 Joachim's membership card, dated May 13, 1892, and signed by Sell, is preserved in Berlin, Staatliches Institut für Musikforschung, SM 12/1957–4142.

54 Unpublished letter from Sell to Brahms of February 5, 1895, in Vienna, Gesellschaft der Musikfreunde, Brahms-Nachlass (Briefe Sophie von Sell an Johannes Brahms, 314, 1).

55 Pflanze estimates that from the time of his dismissal through his eightieth birthday, in 1895, Bismarck received some 150 visiting delegations at Friedrichsruh. Pflanze, *Bismarck and the Development of Germany*, 3: 407–13.

56 Unpublished letter from Sell to Brahms of May 10, 1895, in Vienna, Gesellschaft der Musikfreunde, Brahms-Nachlass (Briefe Sophie von Sell an Johannes Brahms, 314, 2). The short passage quoted here from Brahms's reply reads: "Verzeihen Sie, wenn sich ein wenig Mitleid mit dem Gefeierten dazu drängt! Aber schön war es doch und eigentlich beneide ich Sie" (Sell, *Johannes Brahms*, 81). Transcriptions and translations of all extant letters from Sell to Brahms, each of which pertains to the Bismarck Association, are provided in the Appendix.

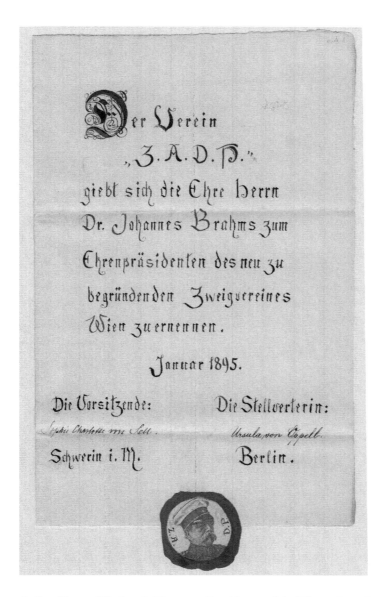

Figure 8. Certificate of Brahms's Honorary Presidency of the Vienna branch of the Association for the Unhitching of the Horses. Reproduced with permission of the Archive of the Gesellschaft der Musikfreunde, Vienna.

242 &▶ EPILOGUE

in which Bismarck of course featured prominently.[57] When the last two volumes of Bismarck's collected parliamentary speeches appeared in 1891, Brahms made sure to obtain them.[58] That same year he also arranged for Simrock to send him a copy of the *Bismarckiade fürs deutsche Volk*.[59] This curious volume, "a humorous heroic poem in ten songs that are as original as can be, a 'Sybel' in doggerel, in which humor and seriousness alternate most successfully," was intended to preserve the achievements of the Iron Chancellor in the collective memory of the general public.[60] Enjoying a comical Sybel was no substitute for reading the real thing, however, and so, as noted, Brahms was greatly cheered when, in December 1894, Laura von Beckerath sent him the last two volumes of the *Begründung* that would ever appear. And five months later, in a conversation with Richard Heuberger during a late-night walk in Vienna's Prater, Brahms enthused about the recent publication of new volume of Bismarck's speeches and letters: "And most of them extempore. Perhaps a sentence polished here or there, but on the whole improvised. An enormous intellect! And eighty-years old!"[61]

It was probably this volume to which Rudolf von der Leyen later referred when claiming that Brahms liked to pack "a volume of Bismarck's speeches or letters" when traveling. We are well advised to assume poetic license in

---

57   Some of the volumes discussed can be found in Brahms's library; others cannot. But, as noted, the composer was a regular user of Vienna's public libraries.

58   Alfred Dove, *Fürst Bismarck als Redner: Vollständige Sammlung der parlamentarischen Reden Bismarcks seit dem Jahre 1847* (Stuttgart: Union Deutsche Gesellschaft, [1885–1891]), vol. 15: *Polenfrage, Kirchenfriede, Septennat* (1891); vol. 16: *Die letzten Zeiten im Amt* (1891). Both volumes found a place in his library next to a collection of Bismarck's letters from the years 1844–70 that had probably been acquired earlier: [Otto von Bismarck,] *Bismarckbriefe 1844–1870: Originalbriefe Bismarcks an seine Gemahlin, seine Schwester und Andere* (Bielefeld and Leipzig: Verlhagen & Klasing, 1876).

59   [Rudolph Genée], *Die Bismarckiade fürs deutsche Volk* (Berlin: A. Hoffmann, 1891). The booklet was originally published anonymously. Brahms thanked Simrock in a letter postmarked May 1, 1891; see *Briefwechsel*, 12: 44–45.

60   Brahms may have seen the booklet's description as "highly recommended" (*bestens empfohlen*) in the Viennese humor weekly *Figaro* (April 18, 1891): 3. My characterization is taken from an advertisement in *Kladderadatsch* 51/35 (August 28, 1898), unnumbered supplementary page.

61   Heuberger, *Erinnerungen an Johannes Brahms*, 82; trans. in Notley, *Lateness and Brahms*, 215. The reference here is presumably to *Bismarcks Reden und Briefe, nebst einer Darstellung des Lebens und der Sprache Bismarcks* (Bismarck's speeches and letters, with an account of Bismarck's life and language), ed. Otto Lyon (Leipzig: B. G. Teubner, 1895). Lyon's foreword is dated March 20, 1895; Brahms's conversation with Heuberger took place during a walk in Vienna's Prater on May 1, 1895, that ran well past midnight.

EPILOGUE ❧ 243

the telling, however, when considering von der Leyen's further claim that Brahms had spoken to him of using Bismarck's thoughts to resolve his political doubts: "What *he* says to me is enough; that is what I believe."[62] After all, what Brahms valued most highly about Bismarck were the early years of the chancellor's tenure and above all his achievement of unification. This holds especially true for Brahms as his life drew to a close. Between November 1896 and March 1897, for example, the composer ordered no fewer than three copies of *Krieg und Sieg 1870–71*, a richly illustrated two-volume history of the Franco-Prussian War with contributions by generals and other officers who had served in it, keeping one for himself and presumably making presents of the other two.[63] And as he explained to Arthur Faber three weeks before his death: "I only want to read about Bismarck. Send me the book by Busch, *Bismarck and His Men*."[64] It is unlikely that Brahms ever got his hands on Busch's study, an account of Bismarck's activities in France in 1870–71. But Simrock saw to it that he did receive two final volumes on related topics, Wilhelm Oncken's *Unser Heldenkaiser*, published on the occasion of the centenary of the birth of William I, and the final issue of the *Bismarck-Jahrbuch* that was to appear in his lifetime.[65]

---

62 Rudolf von der Leyen, *Johannes Brahms als Mensch und Freund* (Düsseldorf and Leipzig: Karl Robert Langewiesche, 1905), 29–30, translated in Michael Musgrave, *A Brahms Reader* (New Haven and London: Yale University Press, 2000), 174.

63 *Krieg und Sieg 1870–71*, 2 unnumbered vols., ed. Julius Albert Georg von Pflugk-Hartung (Berlin: Schall & Grund 1895–96); vol. 1: *Ein Gedenkbuch*, vol. 2: *Kulturgeschichte*. One copy of each is found in Brahms's library. See Brahms's letters to Simrock of November 15, 1896, December 3, 1896, December 19, 1896, and March 4, 1897, in *Briefwechsel*, 12: 206–14 *passim*. Brahms's unusual interest in this set may have been motivated by knowledge that the proceeds from sales were earmarked for the support of the new *Kaiser-Wilhelm-Nationaldenkmal auf dem Kyffhäuser* (Emperor Wilhelm National Monument on the Kyffhäuser) in Thuringia.

64 Moritz Busch, *Graf Bismarck und seine Leute während des Kreiges mit Frankreich, nach Tagebuchblättern*, 2 vols. (Leipzig: Fr. Wilh. Grunow, 1878). Brahms's conversation with Faber is recounted in Hanslick, "Johannes Brahms: The Last Days, Memories and Letters," 327.

65 Wilhelm Oncken, *Unser Heldenkaiser: Festschrift zum hundertjährigen Geburttage Kaiser Wilhelms des Grossen* (Berlin: Schall & Grund, 1897); *Bismarck-Jahrbuch*, vol. 4, 1st issue, ed. Horst Kohl (Leipzig: G. J. Grölschen-Verlag, 1897). See Brahms's letter to Simrock of March 13, 1897, in *Briefwechsel*, 12: 214–15. Only the latter is preserved in Brahms's library.

244 &❧ EPILOGUE

Bleak Days at the End

The era of Wilhelmine Germany was one of rapidly advancing prosperity (after 1893) and growing pessimism. Writers and artists deprecated the growth of materialism and philistinism in the upper social strata. Critical journalists and commentators never ceased to deplore what they perceived as a dearth of effective political leadership in the parliament and government. The self-satisfaction of a bourgeoisie steadily growing in numbers and wealth was accompanied by a deep-seated fear of an alienated proletariat attracted in ever-increasing numbers to the Social Democratic Party. Had Marx been right in his conviction that capitalism would self-destruct? Was the rising of the masses that would speed the collapse of the bourgeoisie an immediate prospect? As the fears grew, Bismarck's genius seemed all the more apparent, his dismissal all the more tragic, the void he left behind all the more gaping. In this environment the Bismarck cult flourished.[66]

Otto Pflanze's cogent characterization of the temper of the times in Wilhelmine Germany at the *fin de siècle* offers clues to making sense, not only of Brahms's unwavering devotion to Bismarck, but also of the melancholy that increasingly weighed on him during the twilight of his life in Vienna. To be sure, many of the sources of Brahms's discontent had nothing to do with politics. The death of Clara Schumann, following on those of Elisabeth von Herzogenberg, Hans von Bülow, and Theodor Billroth, not to speak of the liver cancer with which he suffered for several months before succumbing to death on April 3, 1897— all were reason enough to bring him low. Moreover, as Notley has discussed, Brahms could not escape the feeling that, in his life's calling as a composer, he was outdated and out of step with the changing times.[67]

Still, the larger social, cultural, and political matters that have been my concern in this book loomed large for Brahms right up to the end. Consider Max Kalbeck's diary entry for February 22–23, 1897, which records one of his last intimate conversations with the composer, coming during an afternoon in which the two men visited the large Schubert exhibition mounted in the Vienna Künstlerhaus in conjunction with the centenary of Schubert's birth:

> Remarkable conversation in the coach. Our shared pessimism and the bleak future of humankind. Interest-group economics and clerical rule [*Interesenwirtschaft und Pfaffenherrschaft*]. The Social Problem. Impossibility of rescuing the masses through education [*Bildung*]. The miserable aver-

---

66 Pflanze, *Bismarck and the Development of Germany*, 3: 445.
67 Notley, *Lateness and Brahms*, 10–11.

age nature of mankind. Degeneration leads back to the type of apes. (My thought.) The ruling and noble families.[68]

Kalbeck acknowledges that it was he who introduced into the conversation the topic of degeneration theory, the subject of an influential recent book by Max Nordau on the deleterious effects of modernity on culture.[69] It is clear, nevertheless, that Brahms, who must have known that his days were numbered, was pessimistic, not only about the direction in which music was headed, but about the state of the world he would soon be leaving behind, one in which the elite German liberal milieu in which he had won a position of respect had yielded its seat of power to another dominated by the newer populist politics of Social Democracy (with its class-based economics) and antisemitic Christian Socialism (support for which had first come from Austria's lower Catholic clergy).

Shortly thereafter came one last letter from Sophie Charlotte von Sell. This contained word that the Association for the Unhitching of the Horses had recently voted to send a laurel wreath to Bismarck on his birthday each year "for as long as we are allowed to call him ours." She added, in closing, and obviously misinformed, that she had recently learned from friends in Berlin that Brahms had been ill but was now "in full possession of [his] health again."[70] In fact, the composer's prognosis was dire, and when Simrock visited him in Vienna for the last time on March 20, he was shocked by the deterioration in his friend's condition that had occurred since their last meeting, five months earlier, when he had joined Hanslick and Brahms one morning for breakfast in Vienna's Imperial Hotel.[71] Simrock returned home to Berlin the next day, just ahead of the unveiling, on March 22, of the *Kaiser-Wilhelm-Nationaldenkmal* (Emperor Wilhelm National Monument) outside the Berlin Palace.[72] The publisher does not seem to

---

68   "Denkwürdig das Gespräch im Wagen. Unser gemeinsamer Pessimismus u. die trübe Zukunft der Menschheit. Interessenwirtschaft u. Pfaffenherrschaft. Das sociale Problem. Unmöglichkeit die Massen durch Bildung zu befreien. Die miserable Durchschnittsnatur der Menschen. Degeneration führt zu dem Typus der Affen zurück. (Mein Gedanke.) Die Herrscher- u. Adelsfamilien." I am grateful to Sandra McColl for sharing with me her transcription of this passage from Kalbeck's complete diary for 1897 (which remains in private hands). Kalbeck emended the original somewhat when he quoted the passage in Kalbeck, *Johannes Brahms*, 4: 504.

69   Max Nordau, *Entartung* (Berlin: C. Dunder, 1892).

70   Unpublished letter of March 15, 1897, in Vienna, Gesellschaft der Musikfreunde, Brahms-Nachlass (Briefe Sophie von Sell an Johannes Brahms, 314, 3).

71   Kalbeck, *Johannes Brahms*, 4: 507, based on his diary entry of March 20.

72   The monument was one manifestation of William II's determined effort to create a cult of Wilhelm der Große, by which to elevate his grandfather to a

246 ❧ EPILOGUE

have been present for the ceremonies, which William II conducted with characteristic ostentation.[73] Still, the event left its impression on him, and on March 24 he shared his thoughts about it with Brahms in what turned out to be his next-to-last letter to his old friend: "With the conclusion of the military pageantry, speeches, torchlight processions, patriotic binges, the waves of 'national enthusiasm' now break again in the sands of the Mark Brandenburg—and what remains is the quarrelling in the Reichstag about the naval demands and a lot of miserable gossip. I have kept quiet at home. But the monument is really a beautiful and impressive work of art."[74]

The emptiness Simrock felt is palpable. The composer's reply, if any was written, is lost. But we can be sure that Simrock would have found in his old friend a like-minded soul receptive to his pessimism. After all, he had only recently received one of Brahms's last letters, in which the composer lamented the outcome of the Austrian Reichsrat elections earlier that month, the first to include a new fifth curia with universal male suffrage, an obvious reflection of the new mass politics. The returns, as anticipated, brought decisive losses for the traditional German liberals and corresponding gains by the more populist parties of left and right. Depressed by what he called the "unbelievable Reichsrat election results," Brahms ended this brief note: "I'm more and more miserable!" (*Mir geht es immer miserabler!*)[75] The composer, who was never given to self-pity, nevertheless was probably referring to the steadily declining state of his health. But his assessment offers an apt description as well of the state of the world—at least as Brahms saw it from his death bed—that he would soon leave behind. The composer breathed his last on April 3. Two and a half weeks later, the populist demagogue and antisemite Karl Lueger was sworn in as the mayor of Vienna.

---

pantheon of warrior-kings alongside Frederick the Great and, before him, the Great Elector. This was a means by which William II fought to counteract the growing influence of the Bismarck Cult. See Giloi, *Monarchy, Myth, and Material Culture in Germany*, 294. Another was the production and mass distribution of Oncken's *Unser Heldenkaiser*.

73 For a detailed first-person account of the unveiling of the monument, with a criticism of the monument itself as being too intricate and noisy, see "Unveiled by Wilhelm II. Monument and Loggia to 'Wilhelm der Grosse,' Near the Berlin Palace, Exposed to the Public. Parades and Illuminations," in *New York Times* (April 11, 1897): 19. The unsigned article carries the dateline "Berlin, March 24." See also Schellack, *Nationalfeiertage in Deutschland*, 33–43.

74 Letter from Simrock to Brahms of March 24, 1897, in Stephenson, *Brahms und Simrock*, 232.

75 Letter from Brahms to Simrock of March 10, 1897, in *Briefwechsel*, 12: 214.

Appendix

Correspondence from Sophie Charlotte von Sell to Johannes Brahms

1. Archiv der Gesellschaft der Musikfreunde in Wien, Brahms-Nachlass, Briefe Sophie v. Sell an Johannes Brahms 314, 1.

Berlin, 5. Februar 1895

Hochverehrter Herr Doktor.

Bevor ich nach Schwerin zurückkehre, muß ich Ihnen als Vereinsvorstand das Diplom—wie bestellt "auf großem Bogen"—übersenden. Wenn Sie nur hätten sehen können, wie viel Freude es meiner Freundin und mir gemacht hat es anzufertigen! Und wie schön wird es sein, wenn wir unserm verehrten Fürsten Bismarck zum 80. Geburtstag gratulieren und auch den Zweigverein Wien mit aufführen können!

Nehmen Sie noch herzlichen Gruß und Dank. Ich habe mir's stets gewünscht, Ihnen einmal persönlich danken zu dürfen für all' die schönen Stunden, die mir ihre Musik bereitet hat und immer auf's Neue bereitet. Sei es, indem ich sie höre; sei es, indem ich mich selbst mit Ihren herrlichen Liedern beschäftige. Und neulich habe ich Ihnen von alledem kein Wort zu sagen vermocht! So geht es mir immer. Sie zeigten aber über den Bismarckverein ein so wunderbares Wissen,— vielleicht haben sie auch ein wenig von dem gemerkt, was ich auszusprechen nicht den Mut fand! Und seien Sie nicht böse, dass ich es schriftlich versuche. Ein Versuch bleibt es freilich. Vielleicht kann man nur Gott, der den Menschen die Macht gegeben Anderen so hohe Freuden zu bereiten, in rechter Weise für dieselben danken.

Verzeihen Sie! Ich bin eine schriftliche Plaudertasche.—Hoffentlich einmal auf Wiedersehen in Berlin oder sonst irgendwo in der schönen, weiten Welt, mein verehrter Herr Ehrenpräsident!

Ihre
Sophie Charlotte von Sell.

APPENDIX

ak ak ak

Berlin, February 5, 1895

Highly esteemed Herr Doctor,

Before I return to Schwerin, I must send you the diploma—in a "large format" as ordered—in my capacity as chairman of the association. If only you could have seen how much pleasure it gave my friend and me to make it! And how nice it will be when we can congratulate our honored Prince Bismarck on his 80th birthday and also list the Vienna Branch!

Please accept our warmest greetings and thanks. I have always wanted to thank you personally for all the wonderful hours your music has given me and continues to give me. Be it by listening to it; be it by occupying myself with your wonderful songs. And the other day I was not able to tell you a word about all this! That's how I always feel. But you showed such a wonderful knowledge about the Bismarck Association; perhaps you also noticed a little of what I did not find the courage to say! And don't be angry with me for trying to do it in writing. Of course, it remains an attempt. Perhaps only God, who gave mankind the power to give others such high pleasures, can be thanked in the right way for the same.

Forgive me! I am a chatterbox by letter. I hope to see you again in Berlin or somewhere else in the beautiful, wide world, my esteemed Herr Honorary President.

Your Sophie Charlotte von Sell

2. Archiv der Gesellschaft der Musikfreunde in Wien, Brahms-Nachlass, Briefe Sophie v. Sell an Johannes Brahms 314, 2.

Schwerin i[n] M[ecklenburg], 10. Mai 1895

Hochverehrter Herr Doktor.

Der Vorstand des Vereins Z. A. d. P. möchte nicht verfehlen den Herrn Ehrenpräsidenten unseres Wiener Zweigvereins geziemend in Kenntniß zu setzen, daß am letzten Sonntag, den 5. Mai, drei Abgesandtinnen des Vereins die Ehre hatten dem Fürsten Bismarck persönlich die Glückwünsche zum 80. Geburtstage darzubringen. Die Glücklichen waren die Vorsitzende und 2 Fräulein Witte aus Hamburg. Wir überreichten eine Adresse, welche mit Hülfe eines malenden Mitgliedes sehr hübsch hergestellt war und ein Blumenarrangement, in Form einer sehr zierlichen, römischen Quadriga angefertigt, welches dem Fürsten als Emblem des Vereins "zum Ausspannen der Pferde" viel Vergnügen machte.

Auf Wunsch fast sämmtlicher Mitglieder waren alle Namen derselben unter die Adresse gesetzt und natürlich auch der Zweigverein Wien aufgeführt. Wir glaubten dies auch ohne besondere Erlaubnis thun zu dürfen, da wir uns in den Gesinnungen für den verehrten Helden mit dem dortigen Vertreter unsres Vereins einig wissen. Der Fürst freute sich sehr über den Zweigverein und erkundigte sich in seiner liebenswürdigen Weise nach dem Herrn Ehrenpräsidenten.

Wir hatten die Freude dem auf den unsern folgenden Empfang der Ostfriesen beiwohnen zu dürfen und später mit zur Frühstückstafel geladen zu werden, wobei die Vorsitzende die Ehre hatte neben dem Fürsten zu sitzen. Es waren unvergessliche Stunden.

Mit herzlicher Empfehlung bleibe ich, mein sehr verehrter Herr Ehrenpräsident,

Ihre ergebene
Sophie Charlotte von Sell,
Vorsitzende des Vereins Z. A. d. P.

🦋 🦋 🦋

Schwerin i[n] M[ecklenburg], May 10, 1895

Highly esteemed Herr Doctor.

The Board of the Z. A. d. P. would not fail to inform the Honorary President of our Viennese branch that last Sunday, May 5, three delegates of the Association had the honor of personally congratulating Prince Bismarck on his 80th birthday. The lucky ones were the chairwoman and two Misses Witte from Hamburg. We presented an address, which was very nicely made with the help of a painting member, and a flower arrangement, made in the form of a very dainty Roman quadriga, which gave the prince much pleasure as an emblem of the Association "To Unhitch the Horses."

At the request of almost all members, all names of the same were placed under the address and, of course, the Vienna branch was also listed. We believed we were allowed to do this without special permission, since we know that we are in agreement with the local representative of our association in the sentiments for the honored hero. The prince was very pleased about the branch association and inquired in his amiable way about the honorary president.

We had the pleasure being permitted to attend the reception of the East Frisians that followed ours and later to be invited to the breakfast table, where the chairwoman had the honor to sit next to the prince. These were unforgettable hours.

With hearty recommendation I remain, my very honored Herr Honorary President,

Your devoted
Sophie Charlotte von Sell,
Chairwoman of the Association Z. A. d. P.

250 &❧ APPENDIX

3. Vienna, Wienbibliothek im Rathaus, J.N. 165.603

Schwerin i[n] M[ecklenburg], 2 Landreiterstr.

24.3.1896

Hochverehrter Herr Doktor.

Der Verein Z. A. d. P. will nicht verfehlen seinen Ehrenpräsidenten des Zweigvereins Wien geziemend in Kenntniß zu setzen, daß der Verein auf Anregung verschiedener Mitglieder beschlossen hat, dem Fürsten von Bismarck zu seinen diesjährigen Geburtstagen einen Lorbeerkranz zu übersenden. Die Mitglieder begründeten ihren Antrag damit, daß wohl jeder den Wunsch habe dem Helden, solange er noch unter uns weile, seine Liebe und Verehrung zu bezeigen. Und in seinem hohen Alter solle man dazu nicht noch einen beson-deren Abschnitt, wie es der 80. Geburtstag war, abwarten. Der Vorstand hat deshalb eine Vereinssteuer von 50 Pfennigen pro Kopf ausgeschrieben. Zahlung in Briefmarken / auch in oestreichischen [sic], wird von der Vorsitzenden entgegengenommen.

Ich freue mich dieser Gelegenheit Ihnen, sehr verehrter Herr Präsident, für die liebenswürdigen Zeilen zu danken, die Sie mir im vorigen Mai auf meinen Bericht von unsrer Expedition nach Friedrichsruh schrieben.

Dies Mal werden wir aber unseren Glückwunsch der Post anvertrauen. So groß die Versuchung wäre—man darf doch nicht zu unbescheiden werden.

Das will ich auch nicht gegen Sie und darum schnell schließen als Ihre sehr ergebene

Sophie Charlotte von Sell

❧ ❧ ❧

Schwerin i[n] M[ecklenburg], 2 Landreiterstr.

March 24, 1896

Highly esteemed Herr Doctor.

The Association Z. A. d. P. does not want to fail to inform its Honorary President of the Vienna Branch that the Association, at the suggestion of various members, has decided to send a laurel wreath to Prince von Bismarck on his birthday this year. The members justified their request with the fact that probably everyone has the desire to show the hero, as long as he is still among us, his love and reverence. And at his high age one should not wait for a special time as in the case of his 80th birthday. The board has therefore announced a club tax of 50 Pfennigs per head. Payment in stamps / also in Austrian, will be accepted by the chairwoman.

I am pleased to take this opportunity to thank you, dear Mr. President, for the kind lines you wrote me last May in response to my report of our expedition to Friedrichsruh.

This time, however, we will entrust our congratulations [to Bismarck] to the mail. As great as the temptation would be, one must not become too immodest.

Nor do I want to be too immodest toward you, and therefore I will close quickly as your very devoted
Sophie Charlotte von Sell

4. Archiv der Gesellschaft der Musikfreunde in Wien, Brahms-Nachlass, Briefe Sophie v. Sell an Johannes Brahms 314, 3

Schwerin i[n] M[ecklenburg], 15. März 1897

Mein verehrter Herr Ehrenpräsident.

Der Verein Z. A. D. Pf. hat mit Stimmenmehrheit beschlossen dem Fürsten Bismarck nunmehr zu jedem 1. April—so lange wir ihn noch uns ernennen dürfen—einen Lorbeerkranz zu übersenden und erbittet dazu wiederum von seinen Mitgliedern einen Beitrag von 50 Pfennigen pro Kopf. Ich erlaube mir den Wiener Zweigverein hiervon geziemend in Kenntniß zu setzen.

Anfangs des Winters lernte ich Ihre "ernsten Lieder" kennen und sie sind mir—wie rechte Freunde—immer lieber geworden, je näher ich mit ihnen bekannt wurde. Mit warmem Anteil hörte ich fast gleichzeitig, daß der Componist krank sei. Gebe Gott daß die Besserung, von der mir Ihre Berliner Freunde zu meiner Freude berichten konnten, von Dauer war und Sie jetzt wieder im Vollbesitz ihrer Gesundheit sind! Ich hörte seit Januar nichts darüber. Nehmen Sie die herzlichsten Wünsche für ihr Ergehen von Ihrer ergebenen
Sophie Charlotte von Sell.

ご ご ご

Schwerin i[n] M[ecklenburg], March 15, 1897

My esteemed Mr. Honorary President.

The Z. A. D. Pf. Association has decided by majority vote to send Prince Bismarck a laurel wreath every April 1—for as long as we may still call him ours—and again requests a contribution of 50 Pfennigs per head from its members. I take the liberty of duly informing the Vienna branch of this.

At the beginning of the winter, I became acquainted with your *Ernste Lieder* [op. 121] and they became dearer and dearer to me—like true friends—the closer I became acquainted with them. With warm sympathy I

252 ❧ APPENDIX

heard almost simultaneously that the composer was ill. God grant that the recovery of which your Berlin friends were able to report to my delight was lasting and that you are now in full possession of your health again! Since January I have heard nothing about it. Please accept the most sincere wishes for your condition from your devoted

Sophie Charlotte von Sell

Bibliography

Published Correspondences

Avins, Styra, ed. *Johannes Brahms: Life and Letters*. Translated by Josef Eisinger and Styra Avins. Oxford and New York: Oxford University Press, 1997.

Avins, Styra, and Josef Eisinger. "Six Unpublished Letters from Johannes Brahms." In *For the Love of Music: Festschrift in Honor of Theodore Front on his 90th Birthday*, edited by Darwin F. Scott, 105–36. Lucca: Antigua, 2002.

Billroth, Theodor. *Briefe von Theodor Billroth*. Edited by Georg Fischer. 5th ed. Hannover and Leipzig: Hannchen, 1899.

Billroth, Theodor. *Briefe von Theodor Billroth*. Edited by Georg Fischer. 7th ed. Hannover and Leipzig: Hahnschen Buchhandlung, 1906.

Billroth und Brahms im Briefwechsel. Edited by Otto Gottlieb-Billroth. Berlin: Urban & Schwarzenberg, 1935.

Bülow, Hans von. *Die Briefe an Johannes Brahms*. Edited by Hans-Joachim Hinrichsen. Tutzing: Hans Schneider, 1994.

Bülow, Hans von. *Hans von Bülow's Letters to Johannes Brahms: A Research Edition*. Edited by Hans-Joachim Hinrichsen. Translated by Cynthia Klohr. Lanham, MD: Scarecrow Press, 2012.

Clara Schumann–Johannes Brahms: Briefe aus den Jahren 1853–1896. Edited by Berhold Litzmann. 2 vols. Leipzig: Breitkopf & Härtel, 1927.

Gottfried Keller und J. V. Widmann Briefwechsel. Edited by Max Widmann. Basel and Leipzig: Rhein-Verlag, 1922.

Johannes Brahms an Julius Spengel: Unveröffentlichte Briefe aus den Jahren 1882–1897. Edited by Annemari Spengel. Hamburg: Gesellschaft der Bücherfreunde zu Hamburg, 1959.

Johannes Brahms Briefwechsel. 19 vols. to date. Consisting of 16 orig. vols. Rev. eds., Berlin: Deutsche Brahms-Gesellschaft, 1912–22. Reprint, Tutzing: Hans Schneider, 1974. *Neue Folge* consisting of 3 vols. Tutzing: Hans Schneider, 1991–95.

Johannes Brahms in seiner Familie: Der Briefwechsel. Edited by Kurt Stephenson. Hamburg: Ernst Hauswedell, 1973.

Widmann, Josef Viktor. *Briefwechsel mit Henriette Feuerbach und Ricarda Huch*. Edited by Charlotte von Dach. Zurich: Artemis, 1965.

254 &❧ BIBLIOGRAPHY

Wiesefeldt, Christiane. "Johannes Brahms im Briefwechsel mit Eduard Hanslick." In *Musik und Musikforschung: Johannes Brahms im Dialog mit der Geschichte*, edited by Wolfgang Sandberger and Christiane Wiesenfeldt, 275–348. Kassel: Bärenreiter, 2007.

Books, Articles, and Dissertations

Aaslestad, Katherine. *Place and Politics: Local Identity, Civic Culture, and German Nationalism in North Germany during the Revolutionary Era.* Leiden and Boston: Brill, 2005.

Aegidi, Ludwig. "Erinnerung an und von Emanuel Geibel." *Deutsche Revue über das gesamte nationale Leben der Gegenwart* 23/1 (January–March 1898): 6–24.

Alings, Reinhard. *Monument und Nation: Das Bild vom Nationalstaat im Medium Denkmal—zum Verhältnis von Nation und Staat im deutschen Kaiserreich 1871–1918.* Berlin and New York: Walter der Gruyter, 1996.

Allgemeine deutsche Real-Enzyklopädie für die gebildeten Stände: Conversations-Lexikon. 11th ed. Leipzig: F. A. Brockhaus, 1867.

Altgeld, Wolfgang. "Religion, Denomination and Nationalism in Nineteenth-Century Germany." In *Protestants, Catholics and Jews in Germany, 1800–1914*, edited by Helmut Walser Smith, 49–65. Oxford: Oxford University Press, 2001.

Anderson, Benedict. *Imagined Communities: Reflections on the Origin and Spread of Nationalism.* Rev. ed. London and New York: Verso, 2006.

Anonymous [Dr. F.], "Die Fahnenweihe des Wiener Gesangvereines: 'Biedersinn.'" *Die Liedgenossen* 2/4 (October 1862): 26–27.

Anonymous. "Das National-Denkmal auf dem Niederwald." *Die Gartenlaube* 22 (1874): 533–37.

Anonymous. "The Lower Rhine Festival at Cologne." *Musical Times and Singing Class Circular* 16 (June 1, 1874): 509–10.

Anonymous. "Herr Henschel's Concert." *Musical Times and Singing Class Circular* 21 (January 1, 1880): 20, 27.

Anonymous. "Music and Patriotism." *The Outlook* (November 14, 1917): 407.

Anonymous. Review of Johannes Brahms, *Alt-Rhapsodie, Nänie, Schicksalslied, Triumphlied*, DG 435–066–2. *La revue administrative* 37/218 (March–April 1984): 218.

Applegate, Celia. "Music in Place: Perspectives on Art Culture in Nineteenth-Century Germany." In *Localism, Landscape, and the Ambiguities of Place: German-Speaking Central Europe, 1860–1930*, edited by David Blackbourn and James Retallack, 39–59. Toronto: University of Toronto Press, 2005.

BIBLIOGRAPHY ❧ 255

Applegate, Celia. "The Building of Community through Choral Singing." In *Nineteenth-Century Choral Music*, edited by Donna DaGrazia, 1–20. New York and London: Routledge, 2013.

Applegate, Celia. *The Necessity of Music: Variations on a German Theme.* Toronto, Buffalo, and London: University of Toronto Press, 2017.

Arndt, E[rnst] M[oritz]. *Lieder der Teutsche.* N.p.: Im Jahr der Freiheit 1813.

Arndt, Ernst Moritz. "Was haben die großen Mächte jetzt zu tun?" In *Ernst Moritz Arndts Sämmtliche Werke*, vol. 10, *Geist der Zeit*, part 3. Magdeburg: Magdeburger Verlagsanstalt, 1910.

Avins, Styra. Review of Daniel Beller-McKenna, *Brahms and the German Spirit. Music and Letters* 87 (2006): 136–41.

Bailleu, Paul. "Sybel, Heinrich von." In *Allgemeine Deutsche Biographie* 54 (1908), 645–67. https://www.deutsche-biographie.de/pnd118620223.html#adbcontent.

Barker, Andrew. "Setting the Tone: Austria's National Anthems from Haydn to Haider." *Austrian Studies* 17 (2009): 12–28.

Baumgarten, Hermann. *Der deutsche Liberalismus: Eine Selbstkritik.* Berlin, 1866. Edited and enlarged by Adolf M. Birke. Frankfurt, Berlin, and Vienna: Ullstein, 1974.

Behrendt, Bernd. "August Julius Langbehn, der 'Rembrandtdeutsche.'" In Puschner, Schmitz, and Ulbricht, *Handbuch zur "Völkischen Bewegung" 1871–1918*, 94–113.

Beller-McKenna, Daniel. "5 Lieder, for Four-Part Men's Chorus, Opus 41." In Botstein, *The Compleat Brahms*, 342–44.

Beller-McKenna, Daniel. "Fest- und Gedenksprüche, for Eight-Part Chorus, Opus 109." In Botstein, *The Compleat Brahms*, 360–63.

Beller-McKenna, Daniel. "How 'deutsch' a Requiem? Absolute Music, Universality, and the Reception of Brahms's 'Ein deutsches Requiem,' op. 45." *19th-Century Music* 22 (1998): 3–19.

Beller-McKenna, Daniel. "The Scope and Significance of the Choral Music." In Musgrave, *The Cambridge Companion to Brahms*, 171–94.

Beller-McKenna, Daniel. *Brahms and the German Spirit.* Cambridge, MA, and London: Harvard University Press, 2004.

Beller-McKenna, Daniel. "'Aimez-vous Brahms?': The History of a Question." In Grimes and Phillips, *Rethinking Brahms*, 341–43.

Beller, Steven. "Hitler's Hero: Georg von Schönerer and the Origins of Nazism." In *In the Shadow of Hitler: Personalities of the Right in Central and Eastern Europe*, edited by Rebecca Haynes and Martyn Rady, 38–54. London: Taurus, 2011.

Beller, Steven. *The Habsburg Monarchy 1815–1918.* Cambridge: Cambridge University Press, 2018.

BIBLIOGRAPHY

Benoit-Otis, Marie-Hèléne. "Richard Wagner, Louis de Fourcaud, and a Path for French Opera in the 1880s." *ACT Zeitschrift für Musik & Performance* 3 (May 2012). https://www.act.uni-bayreuth.de/en/archiv/201203/03_Benoit-Otis_Wagner/index.html.

Berger, Stefan. "Building the Nation among Visions of German Empire." In *Nationalizing Empires*, edited by Stefan Berger and Alexei Miller, 247–308. Budapest: Central European University Press, 2014.

Bernstein, Paul. "The Economic Aspect of Napoleon III's Rhine Policy." *French Historical Studies* 1 (1960): 335–47.

Berry, Paul. *Brahms among Friends: Listening, Performance, and the Rhetoric of Allusion*. Oxford and New York: Oxford University Press, 2014.

Berry, Paul. "Brahms, Johannes." In *The Oxford Encyclopedia of the Bible and the Arts*, edited by Timothy Beal. 2 vols., 1: 5–19. Oxford: Oxford University Press, 2015.

Beta, Ottomar. "Gespräche mit Adolph Menzel." *Deutsche Revue über das gesamte nationale Leben der Gegenwart* 23/2 (April–June 1898): 45–58.

Beuerle, Hans Michael. *Untersuchungen zu den A-cappella-Kompositionen: Ein Beitrag zur Geschichte der Chormusik*. Hamburg: K. D. Wagner, 1987.

Biba, Otto. "Brahms und die Gesellschaft der Musikfreunde in Wien." In *Brahms-Kongress Wien 1983*, edited by Susanne Antonicek and Otto Biba, 45–65. Tutzing: Hans Schneider, 1988.

Biba, Otto, and Jürgen Neubacher, eds. *"... in meinen Töne spreche ich." Für Johannes Brahms 1833–1897 (anläßlich der Ausstellung im Museum für Kunst und Gewerbe Hamburg 5. September–2. November 1897)*, 152–63. Heidelberg: Edition Braus, 1997.

Billing, Heinrich v[on]. *Neunter Jahresbericht des Wiener Männer-Gesang-Verein für das Vereinsjahr von 1. Oktober 1862 bis 1. Oktober 1863*. Vienna: Friedr[ich] und Moritz Förster, 1863.

Bismarck-Jahrbuch. Edited by Horst Kohl. Vol. 4, issue 1. Leipzig: G. J. Grölschen-Verlag, 1897.

Bismarck, Otto von. *Bismarckbriefe 1844–1870: Originalbriefe Bismarcks an seine Gemahlin, seine Schwester und Andere*. Bielefeld and Leipzig: Verlhagen & Klasing, 1876.

Bismarck, Otto von. *Bismarcks Reden und Briefe, nebst einer Darstellung des Lebens und der Sprache Bismarcks*. Edited by Otto Lyon. Leipzig: B. G. Teubner, 1895.

Blackbourn, David. *History of Germany 1780–1918: The Long Nineteenth Century*. 2nd ed. Malden, MA: Blackwell, 2003.

Blanning, Timothy. "Napoleon and German Identity." *Modern History* 48 (April 1998): 37–43.

Bock, Alfred. "Erinnerungen an Clara Simrock und Johannes Brahms." *Zeitschrift für Musik* 97 (1931): 477–78.

Bock, Katrin, and Ulrich Tadday. "Bericht der Fund der Bremer Fassung des Triumphliedes in C-Dur von Johannes Brahms." In *Brahms-Studien 19*, edited by Beatrix Borchard and Kerstin Schüssler-Bach, 153–62. Tutzing: Hans Scheider, 2014.

Bonham, Gary. *Ideology and Interests in the German State*. 1991. Reprint ed. Abingdon, UK: Routledge, 2014.

Botstein, Leon, ed. *The Compleat Brahms*. New York: Norton, 1997.

Botstein, Leon. "Music in History: The Perils of Method in Reception History." *Musical Quarterly* 89 (2006): 1–16.

Botstein, Leon. "Time and Memory: Concert Life, Science, and Music in Brahms's Vienna." In Frisch and Karnes, *Brahms and His World*, 3–25.

Botstein, Leon. "The Eye of the Needle: Music as History after the Age of Recording." In *The Oxford Handbook of the New Cultural History of Music*, edited by Jane Fulcher, 523–49. Oxford and New York: Oxford University Press, 2011.

Bozarth, George S. "Brahms's Lieder Inventory of 1859–60 and Other Documents of His Life and Works." *Fontes Artis Musicae* 30 (1983): 98–117.

Bozarth, George S. "Brahms and the Breitkopf & Härtel Affair." *Music Review* 60 (1994): 202–13.

Brachmann, Jan. *Kunst–Religion–Krise: Der Fall Brahms*. Kassel, Basel, London, New York, Prague: Bärenreiter, 2003.

Brachmann, Jan. "Brahms zwischen Religion und Kunst." In Sandberger, *Brahms Handbuch*, 128–33.

Brahms, Johannes. *Des jungen Kreislers Schatzkästlein: Aussprüche von Dichtern, Philosophen und Künstlern*. Edited by Carl Krebs. Berlin, 1909. English translation as *The Brahms Notebooks: The Little Treasure Chest of the Young Kreisler*. Translated by Agnes Eisenberger. Annotations by Siegmund Levarie. Hillsdale, NY: Pendragon Press, 2003.

Brahms, Johannes. *Zwei Lieder für Männerstimmen a cappella*. Edited by Helmut Lauterwasser. Wiesbaden: Breitkopf & Härtel, 2010.

Brandt, Bettina. *Germania und ihre Söhne: Repräsentationen von Nation, Geschlecht und Politik in der Modern*. Göttingen: Vandenhoeck & Ruprecht, 2010.

Braune, Andreas, Michael Dreyer, Markus Lang, and Ulrich Lappenküper, eds. *Einigkeit und Recht, doch Freiheit: Das Deutsche Kaiserreich in der Demokratiegeschichte und Erinnerungskultur*. Stuttgart: Franz Steiner Verlag, 2021.

258 ❧ BIBLIOGRAPHY

Breuilly, John. *Austria, Prussia, and the Making of Germany, 1806–1871.* 2nd ed. Harlow, UK: Pearson, 2011.

Breuilly, John. "Revolution to Unification." In *Nineteenth-Century Germany: Politics, Culture and Society, 1780–1918,* edited by John Breuilly. 2nd ed., 123–42. London: Bloomsbury Academic, 2020.

Breuilly, John, and Iorwerth Prothero. "The Revolution as Urban Event: Hamburg and Lyon during the Revolutions of 1848–49." In Dowe et al., *Europe in 1848,* 371–98.

Brinkman, James M. "The German Male Chorus at the Beginning of the Nineteenth Century." *Journal of Research in Music Education* 18 (1970): 18–24.

Brinkmann, Reinhold. "Zeitgenossen: Feuerbach, Böcklin, Klinger und Menzel." In *Johannes Brahms: Quellen—Text—Rezeption—Interpretation: Internationaler Brahms Kongress Hamburg 1997,* edited by Freidhelm Krummacher and Peter Petersen, 71–94. Munich: G. Henle, 1999.

Brodbeck, David. "Brahms as Editor and Composer: His Two Editions of Ländler by Schubert and His First Two Cycles of Waltzes, opp. 39 and 52." PhD diss., University of Pennsylvania, 1984.

Brodbeck, David. "Dance Music as High Art: Schubert's Twelve Ländler, Op. 171 (D. 790)." In *Schubert: Critical and Analytical Studies,* edited by Walter Frisch, 30–47. Lincoln, NE: University of Nebraska Press, 1986.

Brodbeck, David. "Brahms, the Third Symphony, and the New German School." In Frisch and Karnes, *Brahms and His World,* 95–116.

Brodbeck, David. *Defining Deutschtum: Liberal Ideology, German Identity, and Music-Critical Discourse in Liberal Vienna.* New York: Oxford University Press, 2014.

Brodbeck, David. "Notes from the Lives of Two Viennese Composers." *The American Brahms Society Newsletter* 32/1 (2014): 1–5.

Brodbeck, David. "Politics and Religion." In Loges and Hamilton, *Brahms in Context,* 259–68.

Brodbeck, David. "Settling for Second Best: Brahms's Männerchor-Lieder in Context." In Grimes and Phillips, *Rethinking Brahms,* 56–69.

Brophy, James M. "The Rhine Crisis of 1840 and German Nationalism: Chauvinism, Skepticism, and Regional Reception." *Journal of Modern History* 85 (March 2013): 1–35.

Brown, A. Peter. "Brahms' Third Symphony and the New German School." *Journal of Musicology* 2 (1983): 434–52.

Bruchhausen, Esther-Beatrice Christiane von. "Das Zeichen im Kostümball: Marianne und Germania in der politischen Ikonographie". PhD diss., Martin Luther-Universität Halle-Wittenberg, 1999.

BIBLIOGRAPHY ❧ 259

Brusniak, Friedhelm. "Der Deutsche Sängerbund und das 'deutsche Lied.'" In *Nationale Musik im 20. Jahrhunder: kompositorische und soziokulturelle Aspekte der Musikgeschichte zwischen Ost- und Westeuropa: Konferenzbericht Leipzig 2002*, edited by Helmut Loos and Stefan Keym, 409–21. Leipzig: Gudrun Schröder, 2004.

Brusniak, Friedhelm, and Dietmar Klenke, eds. *"Heil deutschem Wort und Sang!": Nationalidentität und Gesangskultur in der deutschen Geschichte.* Augsburg: Wißner, 1995.

Brusniak, Friedhelm, and Dietmar Klenke. "Sängerfeste und die Musikpolitik der deutschen Nationalbewegung." *Die Musikforschung* 52 (1999): 29–54.

Burford, Mark. "Brahms's Sybel: The Politics and Practice of German Nationalist Historiography." *Nineteenth-Century Music Review* 16 (2019): 417–39.

Busch, Moritz. *Graf Bismarck und seine Leute während des Kreiges mit Frankreich, nach Tagebuchblättern.* 2 vols. Leipzig: Fr. Wilh. Grunow, 1878.

Busch, Werner. *Adolph Menzel: The Quest for Reality.* Translated by Carola Kleinstück-Schulman. Los Angeles: Getty Research Institute, 2017.

Buschmann, Nikolaus. *Einkreisung und Waffenbruderschaft: Die öffentliche Deutung von Krieg und Nation in Deutschland 1850–1871.* Göttingen: Vandenhoeck & Ruprecht, 2003.

Carimani, Daniele. *The Societies of Europe: Elections in Western Europe since 1815, Electoral Results by Constituencies.* London: Macmillan, 2000.

Chickering, Roger. *We Men Who Feel Most German: A Cultural Study of the Pan-German League, 1886–1914.* Boston, London, and Sydney: George Allen & Unwin, 1984.

Christiansen, Rupert. *Paris Babylon: The Story of the Paris Commune.* New York: Viking, 1995.

Clark, Christopher. "The Wars of Liberation in Prussian Memory: Reflections on the Memorialization of War in Early Nineteenth-Century Germany." *Journal of Modern History* 68 (1996): 550–76.

Clark, Christopher. *Iron Kingdom: The Rise and Fall of Prussia, 1600–1947.* Cambridge, MA: Belknap Press of Harvard University Press, 2006.

Clark, Christopher. *Kaiser Wilhelm II: A Life in Power.* London: Penguin, 2009.

Clark, Christopher. *Revolutionary Spring: Europe Aflame and the Fight for a New World, 1848–49.* New York: Crown, 2023.

Clive, Peter. *Brahms and His World: A Biographical Dictionary.* Latham, MD: Scarecrow Press, 2006.

Cohen, Gary B. *The Politics of Ethnic Survival: Germans in Prague, 1861–1914.* 2nd ed., rev. West Lafayette, IN: Purdue University Press, 2006.

260 &❧ BIBLIOGRAPHY

Confino, Alon. *The Nation as a Local Metaphor: Württemburg, Imperial Germany, and National Memory, 1871–1918.* Chapel Hill, NC, and London: University of North Carolina Press, 1997.

Conway, J. S. Review of Helmut Walser Smith, *German Nationalism and Religious Conflict: Culture, Ideology, Politics, 1870–1914.* H-Net Reviews (July 1995). http://www.h-net.org/reviews/showrev.php?id=113.

"Culture Protestantism." *Encyclopedia of Christianity.* Grand Rapids, MI: Wm. B. Eerdmans; Leiden: Brill, 1999–2008.

Dahlhaus, Carl. *Ludwig van Beethoven: Approaches to his Music.* Translated by Mary Whittall. Cambridge: Cambridge University Press, 1991.

Dencker, Berit Elisabeth. "Popular Gymnastics and the Military Spirit in Germany, 1848–1871." *Central European History* 34 (2001): 503–30.

Dennis, David B. "Johannes Brahms's Requiem eines Unpolitischen." In *Searching for Common Ground: Diskurse zur deutschen Identität 1750–1871,* edited by Nicholas Vazsonyi, 283–98. Cologne: Böhlau, 2000.

Deutsches Wörterbuch von Jacob Grimm und Wilhelm Grimm. Digitalized version in the Wörterbuchnetz des Trier Center for Digital Humanities, Version 01.21. https://www.woerterbuchnetz.de/DWB?lemid=S37531.

Die 700jährige Gründungsfeier der Stadt Bern, 1191–1891. Bern: Schmid, Francke & Cie., 1891.

Die Armee Friedrichs des Grossen in ihrer Uniformirung, gezeichnet und erläutert von Adolph Menzel. 3 vols. Berlin: L. Sachse, 1851–57.

Dierick, Augustinius P. "Julius Langbehn's 'Rembrandt als Erzieher': Politics and Cultural Esthetics." *Mosaic: An Interdisciplinary Critical Journal* 21/1 (Winter 1988): 25–35.

Dietrich, Albert. *Erinnerungen an Johannes Brahms in Briefen aus seiner Jugendzeit.* [1898]. Leipzig: Deutscher Verlag für Musik, 1989.

Domeier, Norman. *The Eulenburg Affair: A Cultural History of Politics in the German Empire.* Translated by Deborah Lucas Schneider. Rochester, NY: Camden House, 2015.

Dove, Alfred. *Fürst Bismarck als Redner: Vollständige Sammlung der parlamentarischen Reden Bismarcks seit dem Jahre 1847.* Stuttgart: Union Deutsche Gesellschaft, 1885–91.

Dowe, Dieter, Heinz-Gerhard Haupt, Dieter Langewiesche, and Jonathan Sperber, eds. *Europe in 1848: Revolution and Reform.* Translated by David Higgins. New York and Oxford: Berghahn Books, 2001.

Drinker, Sophie. *Brahms and His Women's Choruses.* Merion, PA: Sophie Drinker, under the auspices of Musurgia Publishers, A. G. Hess, 1952.

Düdling, Dieter. *Organisierter gesellschaftlicher Nationalismus in Deutschland (1808–1847): Bewegung und Funktion der Turner- und Sängervereine für die deutsche Nationalbewegung.* Munich: Oldenbourg, 1984.

BIBLIOGRAPHY ❧ 261

Dufetel, Nicolas. "'Aimez-vous Brahms …': Zur Brahms-Rezeption in Frankreich um 1900." In Sandberger, *Konfrontationen. Symposium: Musik im Spannungsfeld des deutsch-französischen Verhältnisses 1871–1918. Johannes Brahms und Frankreich*, 38–54.

Dwyer, Philip. *Citizen Emperor: Napoleon in Power.* New Haven and London: Yale University Press, 2013.

Eckhard, John, and David Robb. *Songs for a Revolution: The 1848 Protest Song Tradition in Germany.* Rochester, NY: Camden House, 2020.

Ed. H. [Eduard Hanslick], "Oesterreichische Componisten und Musikverleger," *Oesterreichische Wochenschrift* 2 (1864): 1031–41. Reprinted in *Eduard Hanslick Sämtliche Schriften. Historisch-kritische Ausgabe*, vol. 1, no. 7: *Aufsätze und Rezensionen 1864–1865*, edited by Dietmar Strauß, with Bonnie Lomnäs, 235–48. Vienna, Cologne, and Weimer: Böhlau Verlag, 2011.

Edwards, James R. "The Rider on the White Horse, the Thigh Inscription, and Apollo: Revelation 19:16." *Journal of Biblical Literature* 137 (2018): 519–36.

Ehrmann, Alfred von. *Brahms: Weg, Werk und Welt.* Leipzig: Breitkopf & Härtel, 1933.

Eichner, Barbara. *History in Mighty Sounds: Musical Constructions of German National Identity 1848–1914.* Woodbridge, UK, and Rochester, NY: Boydell Press, 2012.

Elben, Otto. *Der volksthümliche deutsche Männergesang: Geschichte und Stellung im Leben der Nation" der deutsche Sängerbund und seine Glieder.* 2nd ed. 1887. Reprint ed., edited by Friedhelm Brusniak and Franz Krautwurst. Wolfenbüttel: Möseler, 1991.

Evans, Edwin. *Handbook to the Vocal Works of Brahms.* London: W. Reeves, 1912.

Evans, Richard J. *Death in Hamburg: Society and Politics in the Cholera Years, 1830–1910.* New York: Penguin, 2005.

Fenske, Hans. "Die Deutschen und der Krieg von 1870/71: Zeitgenössische Urteile." *Pariser Historische Studien* 29 (1990): 167–214.

Festschrift zur Feier des 50jährigen Gestandes des Wiener Kaufmännischen Gesangvereines am 5. und 6. Januar 1912. Vienna: Verlag des Wiener Kaufmännischen Gesangvereines, 1912.

Feuchtwanger, Edgar. *Bismarck: A Political History.* 2nd ed. London and New York: Routledge, 2014.

Fichte, Johann Gottlieb. *Fichte: Addresses to the German Nation.* Edited by Gregory Moore. Cambridge: Cambridge University Press, 2008.

262 ❧ BIBLIOGRAPHY

Fischer, Michael. s.v. "Nun danket alle Gott." *Populäre und Traditionelle Lieder: Historisch-kritisches Liederlexikon.* https://www.liederlexikon.de/lieder/nun_danket_alle_gott.

Fischer, Michael, Christian Senkel, and Klaus Tanner, eds. *Reichsgründung 1871: Ereignis–Beschreibung–Inszenierung.* Münster: Waxman, 2010.

Fitzpatrick, Matthew P. *Purging the Empire: Mass Expulsions in Germany, 1871–1914.* Oxford: Oxford University Press, 2015.

Flaig, Herbert. "The Historian as Pedagogue of the Nation." *History: The Journal of the Historical Association* 59 (1974): 18–32.

Forner, Johannes. *Johannes Brahms in Leipzig: Geschichte einer Beziehung.* Leipzig: Edition Peters, 1987.

Forster-Hahn, Françoise. "Adolph Menzel's 'Daguerrotypical' Image of Frederick the Great: A Liberal Bourgeois Interpretation of German History." *Art Bulletin* 59 (1977): 242–61.

Forster-Hahn, Françoise. "Adolph Menzel: Readings between Nationalism and Modernity." In *Adolph Menzel, 1815–1905: Between Romanticism and Impressionism,* edited by Claude Keisch and Marie Ursula Riemann-Reyher, 103–12. New Haven and London: Yale University Press, in association with the National Gallery of Art, Washington, 1996.

Frandsen, Steen Bo. "Denmark 1848: The Victory of Democracy and the Shattering of the Conglomerate State." In Dowe et al., *Europe in 1848,* 289–311.

Frankel, Richard E. *Bismarck's Shadow: The Cult of Leadership and the Transformation of the German Reich, 1898–1945.* Oxford and New York: Berg, 2005.

Freiligrath, Ferdinand. *Neuere politische und soziale Gedichte.* 2 vols. Cologne: Selbstverlag der Verfassers; Düsseldorf: W. H. Scheller, 1849; and Düsseldorf: Selbstverlag der Verfassers, 1851.

Freytag, Gustav. *Aus dem Mittelalter.* Vol. 1 of *Bilder aus der deutschen Vergangenheit.* 5th ed. Leipzig: S. Hirzel, 1867.

Freytag, Gustav [GF]. "Krieg oder Frieden?" *Die Grenzboten* 25/2 (April 1866): 64–69.

Frisch, Walter, and Kevin C. Karnes, eds. *Brahms and His World.* Rev. ed. Princeton: Princeton University Press, 2009.

Fuchs, Ingrid. "Brahms und Frankreich—Aspekte einer Beziehung." In Sandberger, *Konfrontationen. Symposium: Musik im Spannungsfeld des deutsch-französischen Verhältnisses 1871–1918. Johannes Brahms und Frankreich,* 22–37.

Fulbrook, Mary. *A Concise History of Germany.* 3rd ed. Cambridge: Cambridge University Press, 2019.

Fuller-Maitland, J. A. *Brahms.* London: Methuen, 1911.

BIBLIOGRAPHY 👁 263

Gaedertz, Karl Theodor. *Die plattdeutsche Komödie im neunzehnte Jahrhundert.* Berlin: A. Hofmann, 1884.

Garratt, James. *Music, Culture, and Social Reform in the Age of Wagner.* Cambridge: Cambridge University Press, 2010.

Geering, Hermann. "Tagesereignisse im Spiegel des Hamburger Volks- und Garten-Theater: Ein Beitrag zur Geschichte des Hamburger Volkstheaters im Mittel des 19. Jahrhundert." *Beiträge zur deutschen Volks- und Altertumskunde* 15 (1971): 69–96.

Gehring, Franz [F. G.]. s.v. "Liedertafel." *A Dictionary of Music and Musicians,* edited by George Grove. 4 vols. London: Macmillan, 1879–89. Vol. 2 (1880).

Gehring, Franz. "Triumphlied (auf den Sieg der deutschen Waffen) von Johannes Brahms." *Allgemeine musikalische Zeitung* 7 (June 26, 1872): cols. 409–14.

Geibel, Emanuel. *Heroldsrufe: Aeltere und neuere Zeitgedichte.* Stuttgart: Cotta, 1871.

Geiringer, Karl. "Brahms the Reader of Literature, History, and Philosophy." In Bozarth, *On Brahms and His Circle,* 30–46.

Geiringer, Karl. "George Henschel." In Bozarth, *On Brahms and His Circle,* 338–47.

Geiringer, Karl. *Brahms: Leben und Schaffen eines deutschen Meisters.* Vienna: Rudolf M. Rohrer, 1935. English translation as *Brahms: His Life and Work.* 3rd ed. New York: Da Capo, 1982.

Geiringer, Karl. *On Brahms and His Circle: Essays and Documentary Studies by Karl Geiringer.* Revised and enlarged by George S. Bozarth. Published in association with the American Brahms Society. Sterling Heights, MI: Harmonie Park Press, 2006.

Genée, Rudolph. *Die Bismarckiade fürs deutsche Volk.* Berlin: A. Hoffmann, 1891.

Giesbrecht-Schutte, Sabine. "Gründerzeitliche Festkultur: Die 'Bismarckhymne' von Carl Reinthaler und ihre Beziehung zum 'Triumphlied' von Johannes Brahms." *Die Musikforschung* 52 (1999): 70–88.

Gildea, Robert. *Children of the Revolution: The French, 1799–1914.* London: Allen Lane, 2008.

Giloi, Eva. *Monarchy, Myth, and Material Culture in Germany 1750–1950.* Cambridge: Cambridge University Press, 2011.

Gottschall, Rudolf von. "Die Kriegslyrik von 1870." *Blätter für literarische Unterhaltung* (August 25, 1870): 556–59.

Göttsche, Dirk. "Nationalism, Regionalism, and Liberalism in the Literary Representation of the Anti-Napoleonic 'Wars of Liberation.'" In *Nationalism before the Nation State: Literary Constructions of Inclusion, Exclusion, and Self-Definition (1756–1871)*, edited by Dagmar Paulus and Ellen Pilsworth, 147–70. Leiden and Boston: Brill, 2020.

Green, Abigail. *Fatherlands: State-Building and Nationhood in Nineteenth-Century Germany.* Cambridge: Cambridge University Press, 2001.

Green, Abigail. "Political and Diplomatic Movements, 1850–1870: National Movement, Liberal Movement, Great-Power Struggles, and the Creation of the German Empire." In *Germany 1800–1870*, edited by Jonathan Sperber, 69–90. Oxford and New York: Oxford University Press, 2004.

Grewarth, Robert. *The Bismarck Myth: Weimar Germany and the Legacy of the Iron Chancellor.* Oxford: Oxford University Press, 2005.

Grey, Thomas S. "'Eine Kapitulation': An Aristophanic Operetta as Cultural Warfare in 1870." In *Richard Wagner and His World*, edited by Thomas S. Grey, 87–117. Princeton: Princeton University Press, 2009.

Grimes, Nicole. *Brahms's Elegies: The Poetics of Loss in Nineteenth-Century German Culture.* Cambridge: Cambridge University Press, 2019.

Grimes, Nicole. "Philosophy." In Loges and Hamilton, *Brahms in Context*, 277–85.

Grimes, Nicole, and Reuben Phillips, eds. *Rethinking Brahms.* Oxford: Oxford University Press, 2022.

Grison, Georges. *Le général Boulanger jugé par ses partisans et ses adversaires (janvier 1886–mars 1888).* Paris: Librairie Illustrée, 1888.

Grosch, Nils. "'Heil Dir im Siegerkranz!' Zur Inszenierung von Nation und Hymne." In Fischer, Senkel, and Tanner, *Reichsgründung 1871: Ereignis–Beschreibung–Inszenierung*, 90–103.

Haas, Frithjof. *Hermann Levi: From Brahms to Wagner.* Translated by Cynthia Klohr. Lanham, MD: Scarecrow Press, 2012.

Habermas, Jürgen. *The Structural Transformation of the Public Sphere: An Inquiry into a Category of Bourgeois Society.* Translated by Thomas Burger. Cambridge, MA: MIT Press, 1989.

Häfner, Klaus. "Das 'Triumphlied' Op. 55, eine vergessene Komposition von Johannes Brahms. Anmerkungen zur Rezeptionsgeschichte des Werkes." In *Johannes Brahms in Baden-Baden und Karlsruhe*, 83–102.

Hagemann, Karen. "Francophobia and Patriotism: Anti-French Images and Sentiments in Prussia and Northern Germany during the Anti-Napoleonic Wars." *French History* 18 (2004): 404–25.

Hagemann, Karen. "Occupation, Mobilization, and Politics: The Anti-Napoleonic Wars in Prussian Experience, Memory, and Historiography." *Central European History* 39 (2006): 580–620.

Hagemann, Karen. "Celebration, Contestation and Commemoration: The Battle of Leipzig in German Memories of the Anti-Napoleonic Wars." In *War, Demobilization and Memory: The Legacy of War in the Era of Atlantic Revolutions*, edited by Alan Forrest, Karen Hagemann, and Michael Rowe, 335–52. New York: Palgrave Macmillan, 2016.

Hammes, Andrea. *Brahms gewidmet: Ein Beitrag zu Systemaktik und Funktion der Widmung in der zweiten Hälfte des 19. Jahrhunderts*. Göttigen: V & R unipress, 2015.

Hancock, Virginia. *Brahms's Choral Compositions and His Library of Early Music*. Ann Arbor, MI: UMI Research Press, 1983.

Hancock, Virginia. "The Growth of Brahms's Interest in Early Choral Music, and Its Effect on His Own Choral Compositions." In *Brahms: Biographical, Documentary and Analytical Studies*, edited by Robert Pascall, 27–40. Cambridge: Cambridge University Press, 1983.

Hancock, Virginia. "Pre-Publication Performances and Brahms's Revisions of the Fest-und Gedenksprüche, Op. 109." Unpublished paper given at the Annual Meeting of the American Musicological Society. Kansas City, MO, November 1997.

Hanslick, Eduard. *Aus meinem Leben*. 2 vols. Berlin: Allgemeiner Verein für Deutsche Litteratur, 1894.

Hanslick, Eduard. "Johannes Brahms: The Last Days, Memories and Letters." In Frisch and Karnes, *Brahms and His World*, 307–35.

Hardtweg, Wolfgang. "Bürgertum, Staatsymbolik und Staatsbewußtsein im Deutschen Kaiserreich 1871–1914." *Geschichte und Gesellschaft 16/3 = Bürger—Kleinbürger—Nation* (1990): 269–95.

Hartung, Günter. "Völkische Ideologie." In Puschner, Schmitz, and Ulbricht, *Handbuch zur "Völkische Bewegung" 1871–1918*, 22–41.

Hayes, Bascom Barry. *Bismarck and Mitteleuropa*. Rutherford, Madison, and Teaneck: Fairleigh Dickinson University Press; London and Toronto: Associated University Press, 1994.

Hecht, Helene. *Unsere Reise nach Kleinasien und Griechenland im Frühjahr 1891*. Munich: Knorr & Hirth, 1891.

Heesch, Florian. "Volkstümlichkeit und Pathos: Bemerkungen zur Musik des 'Sang an Aegir' von Wilhelm II." In *"Sang an Aegir": Nordische Mythen um 1900*, edited by Katja Schulz and Florian Heesch, 31–43. Heidelberg: Universitätsverlag Winter, 2009.

266 ❧ BIBLIOGRAPHY

Heidrich, Jürgen. "'der getreue Eckart des über alles geliebten Vaterlandes'? Johannes Brahms, das 'Dreikaiserjahr' und die 'Fest- und Gedenksprüche' op. 109." In *Spätphase(n)? Johannes Brahms' Werke der 1880er und 1890er Jahre: Internationales musikwissenschaftliches Symposium Meiningen 2008*, edited by Maren Goltz, Wolfgang Sandberger, and Christiane Wiesenfeldt, 88–95. Munich: Henle Verlag, 2010.

Heinemann, Johann. *Johann Meyer, ein schleswig-holsteinischer Dichter: Festschrift zum 70. Geburtstag.* 3 vols. (Hamburg: Boysen, 1899–1900), vol. 3: *Johann Meyer als dramatischer Dichter* (1900): 45.

Heinemann, Michael. "Geistliche Chorwerke a cappella." In Sandberger, *Brahms Handbuch*, 303–13.

Heinzen, Jasper. *Making Prussians, Raising Germans: A Cultural History of Prussian State-Building after Civil War, 1866–1935.* Cambridge: Cambridge University Press, 2017.

Hermand, Jost. "On the History of the "Deutschlandlied."" In *Music and German National Identity*, edited by Celia Applegate and Pamela Potter, 251–68. Chicago and London: University of Chicago Press, 2002.

Hermann, Ulrich. "Was ist des Deutschen Vaterland?" *Die Zeit Online* (December 4, 1987), https://www.zeit.de/1987/50/was-ist-des-deutschen-vaterland/seite-3 (accessed July 6, 2020).

Herwegh, Georg. *Gedichte eines Lebendigen.* 9th printing. Stuttgart: G. J. Göschen, 1871.

Heuberger, Richard. "Briefe Joseph Victor Widmanns." *Der Merker* 3/2 (January 1912): 59–63.

Heuberger, Richard. *Erinnerungen an Johannes Brahms.* 2nd ed., revised and improved. Edited by Kurt Hofmann. Tutzing: Hans Schneider, 1976.

Hewitson, Mark. *Nationalism in Germany, 1848–1866: Revolutionary Nation.* New York: Palgrave Macmillan, 2010.

Hill, Ralph. *Brahms: A Study in Musical Biography.* London: Denis Archer, 1933.

Hill, Ralph. "Radio Music." *Radio Times* (November 1, 1940): 7.

Hill, Ralph. *Brahms.* London: Duckworth, 1941.

Hiort, Pontus. "Constructing Another Kind of German: Catholic Commemorations of German Unification in Baden, 1870–1876." *Catholic Historical Review* 93 (2007): 17–46.

Höbelt, Luther. "Devolution Aborted: Franz Joseph I and the Bohemian 'Fundamental Articles' of 1871." *Parliaments, Estates and Representation* 32 (2012): 37–52.

Hobsbawm, Eric. "Mass-Producing Traditions: Europe: 1870–1914." In *The Invention of Tradition*, edited by Eric Hobsbawm and Terence Ranger, 263–307. Cambridge: Cambridge University Press, 1983.

Hoffmann von Fallersleben, August Heinrich, ed. *Politische Gedichte aus der deutschen Vorzeit.* Leipzig: Wilhelm Engelmann, 1843.

Hoffmann von Fallersleben, [August Heinrich]. *Mein Leben.* 6 vols. Hannover: Carl Rümpler, 1868.

Hoffmeister Monatsberichte. September 1863.

Hofmann, Kurt. *Die Bibliothek von Johannes Brahms: Bücher- und Musikalienverzeichnis.* Hamburg: Karl Dieter Wagner, 1974.

Hofmann, Kurt. "Brahmsiana der Familie Petersen: Erinnerungen und Briefe." *Brahms-Studien* 3 (1979): 69–105.

Hofmann, Kurt. "Brahms the Hamburg Musician, 1833–1862." In Musgrave, *The Cambridge Companion to Brahms,* 3–30.

Hofmann, Kurt, and Renate Hofmann. "Einige Splittern aus dem 'Faber-Nachlaß.'" In *Festschrift Otto Biba zum 60. Geburtstag,* edited by Ingrid Fuchs, 357–81. Tutzing: Hans Schneider, 2008.

Hofmann, Michael, Jürgen Lotterer, and Günter Riederer, eds. *Nationalismus im Kaiserreich—Der "Sedantag" in Stuttgart 1895: ein Quellen- und Arbeitsbuch für den Geschichtsunterricht.* Stuttgart: Stadtarchiv, 1997.

Hofmann, Renate, and Kurt Hofmann. *Johannes Brahms: Zeittafel zu Leben und Werk.* Tutzing: Hans Schneider, 1983.

Hofmann, Renate, and Kurt Hofmann. *Johannes Brahms in Baden-Baden.* Baden-Baden: Brahmsgesellschaft Baden-Baden; Karben: CODA, 1996.

Hofmann, Rudolf. *Der Wiener Männergesangverein: Chronik der Jahre 1843 bis 1893.* Vienna: Verlag des Wiener Männergesangvereines, 1893.

Holst, Karl Heinz. *Die Stellung Hamburgs zum inneren Konflikt in Preussen, 1862–1866.* Wismar: Albert Sander, 1932.

Holtzendorff, F[ranz] v[on]. "Ein neues deutsches Volks- und Kirchenfest!" *Protestantische Kirchenzeitung für das evangelische Deutschland* (February 11, 1871): cols. 109–12.

Holtzendorff, F[ranz] v[on]. "Correspondenzen und Nachrichten. Berlin." *Protestantische Kirchenzeitung für das evangelische Deutschland* (March 4, 1871): cols. 196–97.

Hornstein, Robert von. *Memoiren.* Munich: Süddeutsche Monatsheft, 1908.

Horstmann, Angelika. *Untersuchungen zur Brahms-Rezeption der Jahre 1860–1880.* Hamburg: Karl Dieter Wagner, 1986.

Hübbe, Walter. *Brahms in Hamburg.* Hamburg: Lütcke & Wulff, 1902.

Hübinger, Gangolf. *Kulturprotestantismus und Politik: Zum Verhältnis von Liberalismus und Protestantismus im wilhelminischen Deutschland.* Tübingen: J. C. B. Mohr [Paul Siebeck], 1994.

268 &❧ BIBLIOGRAPHY

Hurd, Madeleine. "Oligarchs, Liberals, and Mittelstand: Defining Civil Society in Hamburg, 1858–1862." In *Paradoxes of Civil Society: New Perspectives on Modern Germany and British History,* edited by Frank Trentmann, 283–305. New York: Berghahn Books, 1999.

Hurd, Madeleine. *Public Spheres, Public Mores, and Democracy: Hamburg and Stockholm, 1870–1914.* Ann Arbor, MI: University of Michigan Press, 2000.

Imbert, Hugues. *Johannès Brahms, sa vie et son oeuvre.* Preface by Edouard Schuré. Paris: Fischbacher, 1906.

Irvine, William D. *The Boulanger Affair Reconsidered: Royalism, Boulangism, and the Origins of the Radical Right in France.* New York and Oxford: Oxford University Press, 1989.

Jackson, Myles W., and Katy Hamilton. "Science and Technology." In Loges and Hamilton, *Brahms in Context,* 296–304.

Jenkins, Jennifer. "Particularism and Localism." In *The Ashgate Research Companion to Imperial Germany,* edited by Matthew Jeffries, 195–208. London and New York: Routledge, 2015.

Jenks, William A. *Austria under the Iron Ring.* Charlottesville, VA: University Press of Virginia, 1965.

Jenner, Gustav. *Johannes Brahms als Mensch, Lehrer und Künstler: Studies und Erlebnisse.* Marburg: N. G. Elwert'sche Verlagsbuchhandlung, 1905.

Johannes Brahms—Klaus Groth: Briefe der Freundschaft. Edited by Dieter Lohmeier. Heide, 1997.

Johannes Brahms in Baden-Baden und Karlsruhe: Eine Ausstellung der Badischen Landesbibliothek Karlsruhe und der Brahmsgesellschaft Baden-Baden e. V. Edited by Badische Landesbibliothek Karlsruhe unter Mitarbeit von Joachim Draheim et al. Karlsruhe: Selbstverlag der Badischen Landesbibliothek Karlsruhe, 1983.

Johannes Brahms und Fritz Simrock: Weg einer Freundschaft. Edited by Kurt Stephenson. Hamburg: J. J. Augustin, 1961.

Judson, Pieter M. *Exclusive Revolutionaries: Liberal Politics, Social Experience, and National Identity in the Austrian Empire, 1848–1914.* Ann Arbor, MI: University of Michigan Press, 1996.

Judson, Pieter M. "Nationalism in the Era of the Nation State, 1870–1945." In *Oxford Modern German History,* edited by Helmut Walser Smith, 499–526. Oxford: Oxford University Pres, 2011.

Kalbeck, Max. *Johannes Brahms,* rev. ed., 4 vols. in 8. Berlin: Deutsche Brahms-Gesellschaft, 1915–21. Reprint, Tutzing: Hans Schneider, 1976.

Kalbeck, Max. "Brahms's Four Serious Songs, op. 121 (1914)." Translated by William Miller. Introduced and annotated by Kevin C. Kearns. In Frisch and Karnes, *Brahms and His World,* 267–86.

BIBLIOGRAPHY &♦ 269

Karnes, Kevin C. "Brahms, Max Klinger, and the Promise of the Gesamtkunstwerk." In Frisch and Karnes, *Brahms and His World*, 167–91.

Katzenstein, Peter J. *Disjointed Partners: Austria and German since 1815.* Berkeley and Los Angeles: University of California Press, 1976.

Keil, Siegmar. "Der 'Choral von Leuthen': Ein preußisch-deutscher Mythos." *Die Tonkunst: Magazin für klassische Musik und Musikwissenschaft* 1 (2007): 442–49.

Keil, Siegmar. "Eine Melodie im Wandel: Metamorphosen des Kirchenliedes 'Nun danket alle Gott.'" *Jahrbuch für Liturgik und Hymnologie* 51 (2012): 203–21.

Kelterborn, Louis. "Johannes Brahms." In *Famous Composers and Their Music. Extra Illustrated Edition of 1901*, edited by Theodore Thomas, John Knowles Paines, and Karl Klauser. 16 vols, 4: 503–14. Boston: J. B. Millet, 1901.

Kimball, Roger. "G. C. Lichtenberg: A 'Spy on Humanity.'" *New Criterion* 20/9 (May 2002): 20.

Kittel, Manfred. "Deutsches Nationalbewußtsein und deutsch-französischer Erbfeindmythos." In *"Heil deutschem Wort und Sang!" Nationalidentität und Gesangskultur in der deutschen Geschichte*, edited by Friedhelm Brusniak and Dietmar Klenke, 47–70. Augsburg: Bernd Wißner, 1995.

Klenke, Dietmar. "Nationalkriegerisches Gemeinschaftsideal als politische Religion: Zum Vereinsnationalismus der Sänger, Schützen und Turner am Vorabend der Einigungskriege." *Historische Zeitschrift* 260 (1995): 395–448.

Klenke, Dietmar. *Der singende 'deutsche Mann': Gesangvereine und deutsches Nationalbewußtsein von Napoleon bis Hitler.* Münster: Waxmann, 1998.

Klinger, Max. *Brahms-Phantasie op. XII: Einundvierzig Stiche. Radierungen und Steinzeichnungen zu Compositionen von Johannes Brahms.* Leipzig Selbstverlag 1894. Numbered facsimile edition. Edited by the Johannes-Brahms-Gesellschaft Hamburg. Hamburg: Ellert & Richter, 2017.

Klutz, Todd. "Beelzebub, Beelzebul. II. New Testament." In *The Encyclopedia of the Bible and Its Reception*, edited by Hans-Josef Klauck et al. 19 vols. to date. Berlin: Walter de Gruyter, 2009–, vol. 3 (2011): 742–43.

Knox, Ronald. "Brahms and His Religion." *Il Saggiatore musicale* 22 (2015): 215–49.

Knox, Ronald. "Brahms as Wordsmith." *Gli spazi della musica* 5/2 (2016). http://www.ojs.unito.it/index.php/spazidellamusica/article/view/2023.

Koch, Jörg. *Dass du nicht vergessest der Geschichte: Staatliche Gedenk- und Feiertage in Deutschland von 1871 bis heute.* Darmstadt: wbg Academic, 2020.

Kohut, Thomas A. *Wilhelm II and the Germans: A Study in Leadership.* New York and Oxford: Oxford University Press, 1991.

270 ❧ BIBLIOGRAPHY

Korn, Oliver. *Hanseatische Gewerbeausstellungen im 19. Jahrhundert: Republikanische Selbstdarstellung, regionale Wirschaftsförderung und bürgerliches Vergnügen.* Opladen: Leske + Budrich, 1999.

Kradolfer, Jacob. "Das deutsche Volksfest: eine Anregung." *Norddeutsches Protestantenblatt* 3 (1870): 276–77.

Kral, Eduard. *Taschenbuch für Deutsche Sänger.* Vienna: Hoffmann & Ludwig, 1864.

Kreissle von Hellborn, Heinrich. "Franz Schubert in seinem Verhältniss zu mehrstimmigen, insbesondere Männergesang." In Eduard Kral, *Taschenbuch für Deutsche Sänger*, 323–30. Vienna: Hoffmann & Ludwig, 1864.

Kreissle von Hellborn, Heinrich. *Franz Schubert.* Vienna: G. Gerold's Sohn, 1865. Reprint ed., Hildesheim: Georg Olms, 1978.

Kretzschmar, Hermann. "Neue Werke von Brahms." *Musikalisches Wochenblatt* 5 (1874): 5–7, 19–21, 31–32, 43–45, 58–60, 70–73, 95–97, 107–11, 147–50, 164–66.

Kretzschmar, Hermann. *Gesammelte Aufsätze über Musik und Anderes.* Edited by Alfred Heuss. Leipzig: Breitkopf & Härtel, 1910.

Krieg und Sieg 1870–71. Edited by Julius Albert Georg von Pflugk-Hartung. 2 unnumbered vols. Berlin: Schall & Grund, 1895–96.

Kroener, Bernhard R. "'Nun danket alle Gott': Der Choral von Leuthen und Friedrich der Große als protestantischer Held. Die Produktion politischer Mythen im 19. und 20. Jahrhunderts." In Krumeich and Lehmann, *"Gott mit uns,"* 105–34.

Kross, Siegfried. *Die Chorwerke von Johannes Brahms.* 2nd ed. Berlin: Max Hesses Verlag, 1963.

Kross, Siegfried. *Johannes Brahms: Versuch einer kritischen Dokumentar-Biographie.* 2 vols. Bonn: Bouvier, 1997.

Krumeich, Gerd, and Hartmut Lehmann, eds., *"Gott mit uns": Nation, Religion und Gewalt im 19. und frühen 20. Jahrhundert.* Göttingen: Vandenhoeck & Ruprecht, 2000.

Krummacher, Friedhelm. "'Eine meiner politischen Betrachtungen über das Jahr': Eschatologische Visionen im Triumphlied von Brahms." In *Studien zur Musikgeschichte: Eine Festschrift für Ludwig Finscher*, edited by Annegrit Laubenthal and Kara Kusan-Windweh, 635–54. Kassel: Bärenreiter, 1995.

Kufferath, Maurice [M. TH.]. "Festival Rhénan. Deuxième et Troisième Journées." *Le Guide musical* 20 (June 4 and 11, 1874).

Kugler, Franz. *Geschichte des Friedrichs des Grossen, mit 400 Illustrationen von Adolph Menzel.* Leipzig: Mendelssohn, 1867.

Kwan, Jonathan. *Liberalism and the Habsburg Monarchy, 1861–1895.* Houndsmill, Basingstoke, UK, and New York: Palgrave Macmillan, 2014.

Kwan, Jonathan. "Politics, Liberal Idealism and Jewish Life in Nineteenth-Century Vienna: The Formative Years of Heinrich Jacques (1831–1894)." *Leo Baeck Institute Yearbook* 64 (2019): 197–218.

La Mara [Marie Lipsius]. *Musikalische Studienköpfe.* Vol. 3, *Jüngstvergangenheit und Gegenwart.* Leipzig: Heinrich Schmidt & Carl Günther, 1883.

Landormy, Paul. *Brahms.* [Paris]: Librairie Félix Alcan, 1920.

Langbehn, Julius [Ein Deutscher]. *Rembrandt als Erzieher.* Leipzig: C. L. Hirschfeld, 1890.

Langewiesche, Dieter. *Liberalism in Germany.* Translated by Christiane Banerji. Princeton: Princeton University Press, 2000.

Langewiesche, Dieter. "Revolution in Germany: Constitutional State–Nation State–Social Reform." In Dowe et al., *Europe in 1848,* 120–43.

Laufer, J[ack]. *Brahms.* Paris: Scorpion, 1963.

Laumann-Kleineberg, Antje. *Denkmäler des 19. Jahrhunderts in Widerstreit: Drei Fallstudien zur Diskussion zwischen Auftraggebern, Planern und öffentlichen Kritiker.* Frankfurt: Peter Lang, 1989.

Lauterwasser, Helmut. "'Von seinen Jugendstreichen bewahrt man nicht gern die sichtbaren Zeichen': Johannes Brahms' älteste erhaltene Kompositionen im Stadtarchiv Celle entdeckt." *Brahms-Studien* 16 (2011): 101–12.

Leerssen, Joep. "The Nation and the City: Urban Festivals and Cultural Mobilisation." *Nations and Nationalism* 21 (2015): 2–20.

Lehmann, Hartmut. "Friedrich von Bodelschwingh und das Sedanfest: Ein Beitrag zum nationalen Denken der politisch acktiven Richtung im deutschen Pietismus des 19. Jahrhunderts." *Historische Zeitung* 202 (1966): 542–73.

Leibnitz, Thomas. "'Denn wahrhaftig und gerecht sind seine Gerichte …': Apokalypse als nationale Manifestation im Triumphlied op. 55 von Johannes Brahms." In *Apokalypse: Symposion 1999,* edited by Carmen Ottner, 135–50. Vienna: Doblinger, 2001.

Lemcke, Carl. *Lieder und Gedichte.* Hamburg: Hoffmann und Campe, 1861.

Lepp, Claudia. "Protestanten feiern ihre Nation: Die kulturprotestantischen Ursprüngen des Sedantages." *Historisches Jahrbuch* 118 (1998): 201–22.

Lerman, Katharine Anne. "Bismarckian Germany." In *Imperial Germany 1871–1918,* edited by James Retallack, 18–39. Oxford: Oxford University Press, 2008.

Lesaffer, Randall. "1864." In *Oxford Public Law International,* https://opil.ouplaw.com/page/545/1864.

Leyen, Rudolf von der. *Johannes Brahms als Mensch und Freund.* Düsseldorf and Leipzig: Karl Robert Langewiesche, 1905.

Lichtenberg, Georg Christoph. *Vermischte Schriften.* 8 vols. Göttingen: Dieterich'schen Buchhandlung, 1844–53.

BIBLIOGRAPHY

Lichtenberg, Georg Christoph. *The Waste Books.* Translated, with an introduction and notes, by R. J. Hollingdale. New York: New York Review of Books, 2000.

Lichtenberg, Ludwig Christian, and Friedrich Kries, eds. *Georg Christoph Lichtenberg's Vermischte Schriften.* 9 vols. in 8. Göttingen: Dietrich, 1800–1806.

Litzmann, Berthold. *Clara Schumann: Ein Künstlerleben, nach Tagebücher und Briefen.* 3 vols. Leipzig: Breitkopf & Härtel, 1923–25. Reprint ed., Hildesheim and New York: G. Olms, 1971.

Lobenstein-Reichmann, Anja. "Julius Langbehns 'Rembrandt als Erzieher': Diskursive Traditionen und begriffliche Fäden eines nicht ungefährlichen Buches." *In Identitätsentwürfe in der Kunstkommunikation: Studien zur Praxis der sprachlichen und multimodalen Positionierung im Interaktionsraum "Kunst,"* edited by Marcus Müller, 295–318. Berlin and Boston: Walter de Gruyter, 2012.

Loges, Natasha. *Brahms and His Poets: A Handbook.* Woodbridge, UK: Boydell Press, 2017.

Loges, Natasha. "Literature." In Loges and Hamilton, *Brahms in Context,* 269–76.

Loges, Natasha, and Katy Hamilton, eds. *Brahms in Context.* Cambridge: Cambridge University Press, 2019.

Loos, Helmut. "Franz Schubert im Repertoire der deutschen Männergesangvereine: Ein Beitrag zur Rezeptionsgeschichte." *Archiv für Musikwissenschaft* 57 (2000): 113–29.

Lott, R. Allen. *Brahms's A German Requiem: Reconsidering Its Biblical, Historical, and Musical Contexts.* Rochester, NY: University of Rochester Press, 2020.

Lotterer, Jürgen. "Der verhinderte Nationalfeiertag: Die Sedanfeier im Deutschen Kaiserreich (1871–1918)." In *Nationalismus im Kaiserreich— Der "Sedantag" in Stuttgart 1895: ein Quellen- und Arbeitsbuch für den Geschichtsunterricht,* edited by Michael Hoffmann, Jürgen Lotterer, and Günter Riederer, 4–7. Stuttgart: Stadtarchiv, 1997.

Luft, David S. "Austrian Intellectual History and Bohemia." *Austrian History Yearbook* 38 (2007): 108–21.

Luft, David S. *The Austrian Dimension in German Intellectual History: From the Enlightenment to Anschluss.* London: Bloomsbury, 2021.

M. Gottfried Büchner's Biblische Real- und Verbal-Hand-Concordanz oder exegetisch-homiletisches Lexicon. 11th ed. Edited by Heinrich Leonhard Heubner. Braunschweig: C. A. Schwetschke und Sohn, 1859.

MacDonald, Malcolm. *Brahms.* New York: Schirmer, 1990.

BIBLIOGRAPHY & 273

MacDonogh, Giles. *The Last Kaiser: The Life of Wilhelm II.* New York: St. Martin's, 2001.

Markert, Jan. "'Wer Deutschland regieren will, muß es sich erobern.' Das deutsche Kaiserreich als monarschisches Projekt Wilhelms I." In Braune et al., *Einigkeit und Recht, doch Freiheit*, 11–37.

Maxwell, Alexander. "Hungaro-German Dual Nationality: Germans, Slavs, and Magyars during the 1848 Revolution." *German Studies Review* 39 (2016): 17–39.

May, Florence. *The Life of Brahms.* 2 vols. London: Edward Arnold, 1905.

Mayer, Sigmund. *Ein jüdischer Kaufmann, 1831 bis 1911: Lebenserinnerungen.* Leipzig: Duncker & Humblot, 1911.

Mazón, Patricia. "Germania Triumphant: The Niederwald National Monument and the Liberal Moment in Imperial Germany." *German History* 18 (2000): 162–92.

McColl, Sandra. "A Model German." *Musical Times* 138 (1997): 7–12.

McCorkle, Margit L. *Johannes Brahms: Thematisch-bibliographisches Werkverzeichnis*, published following joint preliminary work with Donald McCorkle. Munich: Henle, 1984.

McGuire, Michael Courtney Quinn. "Bismarck in Walhalla: The Cult of Bismarck and the Politics of National Identity in Imperial Germany, 1890–1915." PhD diss., University of Pennsylvania, 1993.

McManus, Laurie. "The Rhetoric of Sexuality in the Age of Brahms and Wagner." PhD diss., University of North Carolina, Chapel Hill, 2011.

McMillan, Daniel A. "Energy, Willpower, and Harmony: On the Problematic Relationship between State and Civil Society in Nineteenth-Century Germany." In *Paradoxes of Civil Society: New Perspectives on Modern German and British History*, edited by Frank Trentmann, 176–95. New York: Berghahn, 1999.

Meischein, Burkhard. "Weltliche Chorwerke A Cappella." In Sandberger, *Brahms Handbuch*, 314–29.

Mennike, Carl. "Einleitung: Hugo Riemann, eine biographische Skizze nebst einem Verzeichnis seiner Werke." In *Riemann-Festschrift: Gesammelte Schriften*, edited by Carl Mennike, VII–XXIV. Leipzig: Max Hesses Verlag, 1909.

Minor, Ryan. *Choral Fantasies: Music, Festivity, and Nationhood in Nineteenth-Century Germany.* Cambridge: Cambridge University Press, 2012.

Misch, Ludwig. *Johannes Brahms.* Bielefeld and Leipzig: Velhagen and Klasing, 1922.

Morris, John Vincent. "Battle for Music: Music and British Wartime Propaganda 1935–1945." PhD diss., University of Exeter, 2011.

Mulej, Oskar. "National Liberals and Their Progeny: Approaching the Peculiar Developments in Central European Liberal Party Traditions, 1867–1918." *Acta Poloniae Historica* 111 (2015): 57–81.

Müller, Frank Lorenz. "The Spectre of a People in Arms: The Prussian Government and the Militarisation of German Nationalism, 1859–1864." *English Historical Review* 122 (2007): 82–104.

Müller, Frank Lorenz. *Our Fritz: Emperor Frederick III and the Political Culture of Imperial Germany.* Cambridge, MA, and London: Harvard University Press, 2011.

Müller, Frank Lorenz. "The Prince, the Crypt, and the Historians: Kaiser Friedrich III and the Continuities of Monarchical Geschichtspolitik in Imperial Germany." *German Studies Review* 35 (2012): 521–40.

Musgrave, Michael. *Brahms: A German Requiem.* Cambridge: Cambridge University Press, 1996.

Musgrave, Michael. *The Cambridge Companion to Brahms.* Cambridge: Cambridge University Press, 1999.

Musgrave, Michael. *A Brahms Reader.* New Haven and London: Yale University Press, 2000.

Musolff, Andreas. "Wilhelm II's 'Hun Speech' and Its Alleged Resemiotization during World War I." *Language and Semiotic Studies* 3 (2017): 42–59.

Naegele, Verena. "Brahms und die Politik." In *"Hoch aufm Berg, tief im Thal …": Die Schweizer Inspirationen von Johannes Brahms,* edited by Sibylle Ehrismann, 49–77. Zurich: Musik Hug, 1997.

Niekerk, Carl. "Mahler, Rembrandt, and the Dark Side of German Culture." In *Legacies of Modernism: Art and Politics in Northern Europe, 1890–1950,* edited by Patricia C. McBride, Richard W. McCormick, and Monica Žagar, 29–40. New York: Palgrave Macmillan, 2007.

Niekerk, Carl. *Reading Mahler: German Culture and Jewish Identity in Fin-de-siècle Vienna.* Rochester, NY: Camden Books, 2010.

Niemann, Walter. *Brahms.* Berlin: Schuster & Loeffler, 1920.

Niemöller, Sibylle Sarah Baroness von. *Crowns, Crosses, and Stars: My Youth in Prussia, Surviving Hitler, and A Life Beyond.* West Lafayette, IN: Purdue University Press, 2012.

Nietzsche, Friedrich. *Der Fall Wagner. Götzen-Dämmerung. Nietzsche Contra Wagner. Der Antichrist. Gedichte.* Leipzig: C. G. Naumann, 1895.

Nipperdey, Thomas. "Nationalidee und Nationaldenkmal in Deutschland im 19. Jahrhundert." *Historische Zeitschrift* 206 (1968): 529–85, repr. in his *Gesellschaft, Kultur, Theorie: Gesammelte Aufsätze zur neueren Geschichte,* 133–73. Göttingen: Vandenhoeck Ruprecht, 1976.

Nordau, Max. *Entartung.* Berlin: C. Dunder, 1892.

BIBLIOGRAPHY & 275

Notley, Margaret. *Lateness in Brahms: Music and Culture in the Twilight of Viennese Liberalism.* New York: Oxford University Press, 2007.

Oncken, Wilhelm. *Unser Heldenkaiser: Festschrift zum hundertjährigen Geburttage Kaiser Wilhelms des Grossen.* Berlin: Schall & Grund, 1897.

Orel, Alfred. *Johannes Brahms und Julius Allgeyer: Eine Künstlerfreundschaft in Briefen.* Tutzing: Hans Schneider, 1964.

Orgill, Nathan N. "Between Coercion and Conciliation: Franco-German Relations in the Bismarck Era, 1871–1890." In *A History of Franco-German Relations in Europe: From "Hereditary Enemies" to Partners,* edited by Carine Germond and Henning Türk, 48–59. New York: Palgrave Macmillan, 2008.

Pape, Walter. "'Hurra, Germania—mir graut vor dir': Hoffmann von Fallersleben, Freiligrath, Herwegh, and the German Unification of 1870–71." In *1870/71–1989/90: German Unifications and the Change of Literary Discourse,* edited by Walter Pape, 107–18. Berlin: Walter de Gruyter, 1993.

Pascall, Robert. "Brahms and Schubert." *Musical Times* 124 (1983): 286–90.

Pasler, Jann. *Composing the Citizen: Music as Public Utility in Third Republic France.* Berkeley, Los Angeles, and London: University of California Press, 2009.

Pelzer, Erich. "Die Wiedergeburt Deutschlands 1813 und die Dämonisierung Napoleons." In Krumeich and Lehmann, *"Gott mit uns,"* 135–56.

Petersen, Peter. "Über das 'Triumphlied' von Johannes Brahms." *Die Musikforschung* 52 (1999): 462–66.

Peterson, Brent O. *History, Fiction, and Germany: Writing the Nineteenth-Century Nation.* Detroit: Wayne State University Press, 2005.

Pflanze, Otto. *Bismarck and the Development of Germany.* 3 vols. Princeton: Princeton University Press, 1990.

Phillips, Reuben. "Between Hoffmann and Goethe: The Young Brahms as Reader." *Journal of the Royal Musical Association* 146 (2021): 455–89.

Phillips, Reuben. "Brahms as Reader." PhD diss., Princeton University, 2019.

Pietsch, L[udwig]. *Adolph Menzel's Illustrationen zu den Werken Friedrich des Großen, Jubiläums-Ausgabe.* 2 vols. Berlin: R. Wagner, 1886.

Ping, Larry L. *Gustav Freytag and the Prussian Gospel: Novels, Liberalism, and History.* Bern: Peter Lang, 2006.

Ping, Larry L. "Gustav Freytag's Bilder aus der deutschen Vergangenheit and the Meaning of German History." *German Studies Review* 32 (2009): 549–68.

Plunkett, Mark A. Review of *The Defeat of Death: Apocalyptic Eschatology in 1 Corinthians,* by Martinus C. DeBoer. *Journal of Biblical Literature* 111 (1992): 152–55.

276 &❧ BIBLIOGRAPHY

Pohlsander, Hans A. *National Monuments and Nationalism in 19th Century Germany*. Bern: Peter Lang, 2008.

Porter, Cecilia Hopkins. "The Rheinlieder Critics: A Case of Musical Nationalism." *Musical Quarterly* 63 (1977): 74–98.

Press, Steven Michael. "False Fire: The Warburg Book-Burning of 1817." *Central European History* 42 (2009): 621–46.

Price, Roger. *The French Second Empire: An Anatomy of Political Power*. Cambridge: Cambridge University Press, 2001.

Puschner, Uwe, Walter Schmitz, and Justus H. Ulbricht, eds. *Handbuch zur "Völkische Bewegung" 1871–1918*. Munich: K. G. Saur, 1996.

Ravizza, Victor. *Brahms: Spätzeitmusik. Die sinfonische Chorwerke*. Schliengen: Edition Argus, 2008.

Ravizza, Victor. "Sinfonische Chorwerke." In Sandberger, *Brahms Handbuch*, 279–302.

Reimann, Hugo. *Musik-Lexikon*. Leipzig: Verlag des Bibliographischen Instituts, 1884.

Retallack, James. "From Pariah to Professional? The Journalist in German Society and Politics, from the Late Enlightenment to the Rise of Hitler." *German Studies Review* 16 (1993): 175–223.

Rode [sic], ed. *Geibel und der Beginn der national-politischen Dichtung: Eine Sammlung politische Gedichte für Schulgebrauch*. Leipzig: Dürr'scher Buchhandlung, 1906.

Röhl, John C. G. *The Kaiser and His Court: Wilhelm II and the Government of Germany*. Translated by Terence F. Cole. Cambridge: Cambridge University Press, 1994.

Röhl, John C. G. *Young Wilhelm: The Kaiser's Early Life, 1859–1888*. Translated by Jeremy Gaines and Rebecca Wallach. Cambridge: Cambridge University Press, 1998.

Röhl, John C. G. *Wilhelm II: The Kaiser's Personal Monarchy, 1888–1900*. Translated by Sheila de Bellaigue. Cambridge: Cambridge University Press, 2004.

Rosenberg, Jonathan. *Dangerous Melodies: Classical Music in America from the Great War through the Cold War*. New York: W. W. Norton, 2020.

Rostand, Claude. *Brahms*, 2 vols. Paris: Le Bon Plaisir, 1954–55. 2nd ed. in one volume. Preface by Brigitte and Jean Massin. Paris: Fayard, 1978.

Russell, Peter. *Johannes Brahms and Klaus Groth: The Biography of a Friendship*. Aldershot, Hampshire, UK, and Burlington, VT: Ashgate, 2006.

s.v. "Volksfest." In *Pierer's Universal-Lexikon*, 4th ed. 19 vols. Altenburg: H. A. Pierer, 1859–65. Vol. 18 (1864): 658–59.

Sandberger, Wolfgang, ed. *Brahms Handbuch*. Stuttgart and Weimer: J. B. Metzler, 2009.

Sandberger, Wolfgang, ed. *Konfrontationen. Symposium: Musik im Spannungsfeld des deutsch-französischen Verhältnisses 1871–1918. Johannes Brahms und Frankreich*. Lübeck: Brahms-Institut an der Musikhochschule Lübeck; Munich: Edition Text + Kritik im Richard Boorberg Verlag, 2018.

Schäfer, Kirstin Anne. "Die Völkerschlacht." In *Deutsche Erinnerungsorte*. 3 vols. Edited by Etienne François and Hagen Schulze. Vol. 2: 187–201. Munich: C. H. Beck, 2001.

Schellack, Fritz. *Nationalfeiertage in Deutschland von 1871 bis 1945*. Frankfurt am Main: Peter Lang, 1990.

Scherer, Wilhelm. *Vorträge und Aufsätze zur Geschichte des geistigen Lebens in Deutschland und Österreich*. Berlin: Weidmannsche, 1874.

Scherr, Johannes. *1870–1871: Vier Bücher deutscher Geschichte*. 2 vols. Leipzig: Otto Wigand, 1879.

Schieder, Theodor. *Das deutsche Kaiserstaat von 1871 als Nationalstaat*. Wiesbaden: Springer Fachmedien, 1961.

Schilling, Heinz. *Martin Luther: Rebel in an Age of Upheaval*. Oxford: Oxford University Press, 2017.

Schmitz, Peter. *Johannes Brahms und der Leipziger Musikverlag Breitkopf & Härtel*. Göttingen: V & R unipress, 2009.

Schneider, Ute. "Einheit ohne Einigkeit: Der Sedantag im Kaiserreich." In *Inszenierungen des Nationalstaats: Politische Feiern in Italien und Deutschland seit 1860/71*, edited by Sabine Behrenbeck and Alexander Nützenadel, 27–44. Cologne: SH-Verlag, 2000.

Schneider, Ute. "Die Erfindung des Bösen: Der Welsche." In *"Gott mit uns": Nation, Religion und Gewalt im 19. und frühen 20. Jahrhundert*, edited by Gerd Krumeich and Hartmut Lehmann, 39–51. Göttingen: Vandenhoeck & Ruprecht, 2000.

Schneider, Ute. "Nationalfeste ohne politisches Zeremoniell? Der Sedantag (2. September) und die Erinnerung an die Befreiungskriege (18. Oktober) im Kaiserreich." In *Das politische Zeremoniell im Deutschen Kaiserreich 1871–1918*, edited by Andreas Biefang, Michael Epkenhans, and Klaus Tenfelde, 163–87. Düsseldorf: Droste, 2008.

Scholze-Stubenrecht, Werner, and Anja Steinhauer, eds. *Zitate und Aussprüche*. 3rd ed. Mannheim, Leipzig, Vienna, Zurich: Dudenverlag, 2008.

Schröder, E. *Ein Tagebuch Kaiser Wilhelms II., 1888–1902 nach Hof- und anderem Berichte*. Breslau: S. Schottlaender, 1902.

Schulz, Ekkehard. "Brahms' Karlsruher Freundes- und Bekanntenkreis." In *Johannes Brahms in Baden-Baden und Karlsruhe*, 35–57.

Schumann, Robert. "Neue Bahnen." *Neue Zeitschrift für Musik* 39 (October 28, 1853): 185–86.

Schüssler-Bach, Kerstin. "'Einigermaßen zeitgemäß': Brahms' Männerchöre im politischen Kontext der 1860-er Jahre." *Brahms-Studien*, vol. 16, edited by Beatrix Borchard and Kerstin Schüssler-Bach, 113–26. Tutzing: Hans Schneider, 2011.

Schüssler-Bach, Kerstin. "Vom Nutzen und Nachteil der Historie: Brahms' Triumphlied und die Signatur seiner Zeit." In *Musik-Kontexte: Festschrift für Hanns-Werner Heister*, edited by Wieland Reich and Thomas Phleps. 2 vols, 2: 861–79. Münster: Monsenstein und Vannerdat, 2011.

Sell, Sophie Charlotte von. *Fürst Bismarcks Frau: Lebensbild*. Berlin: Trowitzsch & Sohn, 1914.

Sell, Sophie Charlotte von. *Johannes Brahms: Ein deutscher Künstler*. Stuttgart: J. F. Steinkopf, 1931.

Senelick, Laurence. *Jacques Offenbach and the Making of Modern Culture*. Cambridge: Cambridge University Press, 2017.

Sheehan, James J. *German History 1770–1866*. Oxford: Clarendon Press, 1989.

Sieg, Ulrich. "'Radikaler Konservatismus' im Deutschen Reich." In Braune et al., *Einigkeit und Recht, doch Freiheit*, 249–65.

Silverman, Lisa, and Deborah Holmes. "Jewish Difference in the Austrian Context." *Austrian Studies* 24 (2016): 1–12.

Smith, Helmut Walser. *German Nationalism and Religious Conflict*. Princeton: Princeton University Press, 1995.

Smith, Helmut Walser. *Germany: A Nation in Its Time: Before, During, and After Nationalism, 1500–2000*. New York: Liveright, 2020.

Specht, Richard. *Johannes Brahms*. Translated by Eric Blom. London: Dent, 1930.

Speirs, Ronald. "German Literature and the Foundation of the Second Empire." In *Germany's Two Unifications: Anticipations, Experiences, Responses*, edited by Ronald Speirs and John Breuilly, 185–208. Houndsmill, Basingstoke, UK, and New York: Palgrave Macmillan, 2005.

Spitta, Philipp. "Johannes Brahms." In his *Zur Musik: Sechszehn Aufsätze*, 385–427. Berlin: Gebrüder Paetel, 1892.

Steinberg, Jonathan. *Bismarck: A Life*. Oxford: Oxford University Press, 2011.

Steinmeister, Anne. *Im Weltgarten zu Hamburg: Die internationalen Hamburger Gartenbauausstellungen des 19. Jahrhunderts*. Munich: Akademische Verlagsgemeinschaft, 2014.

Stekel, Hanns Christian. "Brahms und die Bibel—historisch-theologische Aspekte." *Brahms-Studien* 11 (1997): 49–54.

Stekel, Hanns Christian. *Sehnsucht und Distanz: Theologische Aspekte in den wortgebundenen religiösen Kompositionen von Johannes Brahms*. Frankfurt am Main: Peter Lang, 1997.

Stephenson, Kurt. *Johannes Brahms und die Familie von Beckerath.* Hamburg: Christians Verlag, 1979.

Sterkenburgh, Frederik Frank. "Staging a Monarchical-Federal Order: Wilhelm I as German Emperor." *German History* 39 (2021): 519–41.

Stern, Fritz Richard. *The Politics of Cultural Despair: A Study in the Rise of the Germanic Ideology.* Berkeley and Los Angeles: University of California Press, 1961.

Stockem, Michel. "Armand Parent, Brahms et la France." *Revue belge de Musicologie/Belgisch Tijdschrift voor Muziekwetenschap* 47 (1993): 177–88.

Stolberg-Wernigerode, Otto Graf zu. "Ein unbekanntes Bismarckgespräch aus dem Jahre 1865." *Historische Zeitschrift* 194/2 (April 1962): 357–62.

Sybel, Heinrich von. *Die Begründung des Deutschen Reiches durch Wilhelm I.* 7 vols. Munich and Leipzig: R. Oldenbourg, 1889–94.

Szabolcs, Czire. "The Beelzebul Controversy—A Mediterranean Cultural Reading." In *Hellenistischer und Judaistischer Hintergrund des Neuen Testaments,* edited by György Szabolcs, 69–81. Szeged: JATE Press, 2018.

Tadday, Ulrich. "Brahms' Bremer Triumphlied." In *Brahms am Werk: Konzepte-Texte-Prozesse,* edited by Siegfried Oechsle and Michael Struck with Katrin Eich, 150–69. Munich: Henle, 2016.

Taruskin, Richard. *The Oxford History of Western Music.* 6 vols. Oxford and New York, 2005.

Taruskin, Richard. *On Russian Music.* Berkeley and Los Angeles: University of California Press, 2009.

Taruskin, Richard. "Nationalism." Grove Music Online. Oxford Music Online. Oxford University Press, accessed March 6, 2017, http://www.oxfordmusiconline.com/subscriber/article/grove/music/50846.

Tebbe, Jason. "Revision and 'Rebirth': Commemoration of the Battle of Leipzig." *German Studies Review* 33 (2010): 618–40.

Thompson, Alistair. "'Prussians in a Good Sense': German Historians as Critics of Prussian Conservatism, 1890–1920." In *Writing National Histories: Western Europe since 1800,* edited by Stefan Berger, Mark Donovan, and Kevin Passmore, 97–110. London and New York: Routledge, 1999.

Tittel, Luiz. *Das Niederwalddenkmal.* Hildesheim: Gerstenberg, 1979.

Treitschke, Heinrich von. *Ein Wort über unser Judenthum.* Berlin: G. Reiner, 1880.

Treitschke, Heinrich von. *Zwei Kaiser. 15 Juni 1888. Abdruck aus dem 62. Bande der Preußischen Jahrbücher.* Berlin: Georg Reimer, 1888.

Turk, Eleanor. "The Press in Imperial Germany." *Central European History* 10 (1977): 329–37.

280 &❧ BIBLIOGRAPHY

Uhland, Ludwig. *Alte hoch- und niederdeutsche Volkslieder mit Abhandlung und Anmerkungen herausgegeben.* 2 vols. Stuttgart & Tübingen: J. G. Cotta'schen Buchhandlung, 1844–45.

Usinger, Rudolf. "Deutschland in der Französische Zeit." *Preussische Jahrbücher* 26 (1870): 297–43.

Vaughan, William. "Visual Arts." In Loges and Hamilton, *Brahms in Context*, 286–95.

Venturini, Carl. *Rußlands und Deutschlands Befreiungskriege von der Franzosen-Herrschaft unter Napoleon Buonaparte in den Jahren 1812–1815.* Leipzig and Altenburg: F. A. Brockhaus, 1816.

Verhandlungen zwischen Senat und Bürgerschaft im Jahre 1889. Hamburg: Lücke & Wulff, 1890.

Vick, Brian E. *Defining Germany: The 1848 Frankfurt Parliamentarians and National Identity.* Cambridge, MA, and London: Harvard University Press, 2002.

Vick, Brian E. *The Congress of Vienna: Power and Politics after Napoleon.* Cambridge, MA, and London: Harvard University Press, 2014.

Vignal, Marc. "Brahms und Frankreich." In *Internationaler Brahms-Kongress Gmunden 1997: Kongress Bericht*, edited by Ingrid Fuchs, 281–88. Tutzing: Hans Schneider, 2001.

Vondung, Klaus. *The Apocalypse in Germany.* Translated by Stephen D. Ricks. Columbia and Lincoln: University of Missouri Press, 2000.

Wagner, Kim A. "'Calculated to Strike Terror': The Amritsar Massacre and the Spectacle of Colonial Violence." *Past and Present* 233/1 (November 2016): 185–225.

Wagner, Richard. *Gesammelte Schriften und Dichtungen.* 10 vols. Leipzig: E. W. Fritsch, 1871–83.

Wawro, Geoffrey. *The Franco-Prussian War: The German Conquest of France in 1870–1871.* Cambridge: Cambridge University Press, 2003.

Webster, James. "Schubert's Sonata Form and Brahms's First Maturity (II)," *19th-Century Music* 3 (1979/80): 52–71.

Weinmann, Alexander. *J. P. Gotthard als später Originalverleger Franz Schuberts.* Vienna: Ludwig Krenn, 1979.

Wetzel, David. *A Duel of Giants: Bismarck, Napoleon III, and the Origins of the Franco-Prussian War.* Madison, WI: University of Wisconsin Press, 2001.

Wetzel, David. *A Duel of Nations: Germany, France, and the Diplomacy of the War of 1870–71.* Madison, WI: University of Wisconsin Press, 2012.

Whaley, Joachim. "Obedient Servants? Lutheran Attitudes to Authority and Society in the First Half of the Seventeenth Century: The Case of Johann Balthasar Schupp." *The Historical Journal* (1992): 27–42.

BIBLIOGRAPHY 281

Wheeldon, Marianne. "Anti-Debussyism and the Formation of French Neoclassicism." *Journal of the American Musicological Society* 70 (2017): 433–74.

Widmann, J. V. *Johannes Brahms in Erinnerungen*. Berlin: Gebrüder Paetel, 1898. Reprint ed., Zurich: Rotapfel-Verlag, 1980.

Widmann, J[oseph] V[iktor]. *Johannes Brahms in Erinnerungen*. Berlin: Gebrüder Paetel, 1898.

Widmann, Josef Viktor. *"Ein Journalist aus Temperament": Ausgewählte Feuilletons*. Edited by Elspeth Pulver and Rudolf Käser. Bern: Zytglogge, 1992.

Widmann, Max. *Josef Viktor Widmann: Ein Lebensbild. Zweite Lebenshälfte*. Leipzig: Frauenfeld, 1924.

Wierzbicka, Anna. *Understanding Culture through Their Key Words: English, Russian, Polish, German, and Japanese*. New York and Oxford: Oxford University Press, 1997.

Williamson, George S. "Protestants, Catholics, and Jews, 1760–1871: Enlightenment, Emancipation, New Forms of Piety." In *The Oxford Handbook of Modern German History*, edited by Helmut Walser Smith, 211–33. Oxford: Oxford University Press, 2011.

Winkler, H. A. *Germany: The Long Road West. Vol. 1: 1789–1933*. Translated by A. J. Sager. Oxford and New York: Oxford University Press, 2000.

Winterhager, Wolfgang. "Text und Musik im Triumphlied von Johannes Brahms." In *Musik, Transfer, Kultur: Festschrift für Horst Weber*, edited by Stefan Drees, Andreas Jacob, and Stefan Orgass, 135–48. Hildesheim and New York: G. Olms, 2009.

Wischmeyer, Johannes. "Buße, Andacht, patriotische Erhebung: Protestantische Inszenierungen der Reichsgründung 1871." In Fischer, Senkel, and Tanner, *Reichsgründung 1871: Ereignis–Beschreibung–Inszenierung*, 15–37.

With, Christopher B. "Adolph von Menzel and the German Revolution of 1848." *Zeitschrift für Kunstgeschichte* 42 (1979): 195–214.

Zimmer, Hasko. *Auf dem Altar des Vaterlands: Religion und Patriotismus in der deutschen Kriegslyrik des 19. Jahrhunderts*. Frankfurt am Main: Thesen Verlag, 1971.

Autograph Materials Cited

Brahms-Nachlass, Gesellschaft der Musikfreunde in Wien, Vienna

Autograph letters from Sophie Charlotte von Sell to Johannes Brahms
Certificate of Brahms's Honorary Presidency of the Vienna branch of the Association for the Unhitching of the Horses

Handschriftensammlung, Wienbibliothek im Rathaus, Vienna

Autograph letter from Sophie Charlotte von Sell to Johannes Brahms
Brahms's notebook of biblical citations

Historisches Archiv der Wiener Philharmoniker, Vienna

Autograph letter from Johannes Brahms to J. P. Gotthard

Pierpont Morgan Library, New York

Autograph letter from Johannes Brahms to Clara Schumann

Staatliches Institut für Musikforschung, Berlin

Joseph Joachim's membership card, Association for the Unhitching of the Horses

Staats- und Universitätsbibliothek Hamburg Carl von Ossietzky, Hamburg

Autograph letter from Laura von Beckerath to Johannes Brahms
Autograph manuscript: "Meine persönlichen Beziehungen zu Wiener Künstlern und insbesonders zum Meister Johannes Brahms während seines zeitweisen Wiener Aufenthaltes von 1861 bis 1872, Biographischer Beitrag von J. P. Gotthard, Vöslau 15./9/1901"

Contemporary Periodicals

Arbeiter Zeitung. Vienna
Berliner Tageblatt. Berlin
Blätter für Musik, Theater u[nd] Kunst. Vienna
Bund, Der. Bern
Cincinnati Daily Enquirer. Cincinnati
Deutsche Revue über das gesamte nationale Leben der Gegenwart. Berlin
Deutsche Zeitung. Vienna
Deutscher Reichs-Anzeiger und Königlich-Preußischer Staats-Anzeiger. Berlin
Floh, Der. Vienna
Grenzboten, Die. Leipzig
Figaro. Vienna
Frankfurter Zeitung. Frankfurt
Fremdenblatt. Vienna
Guide musical, Le. Brussels and Paris
Hamburger Abendblatt. Hamburg
Hamburger Nachrichten. Hamburg
Hamburgische Musikzeitung. Hamburg
Kemptner Zeitung. Kempten
Kladderadatsch. Berlin
Klagenfurter Zeitung. Klagenfurt
Liedgenossen. Vienna
Manchester Guardian. Manchester
Musical Times and Singing Class Circular. London
Musikalisches Wochenblatt. Leipzig
National-Zeitung. Berlin.
Neue Freie Presse. Vienna
Neue preussische Zeitung (Kreuzzeitung). Berlin
Neue Zeitschrift für Musik. Leipzig
Neues Wiener Tagblatt. Vienna
New York Times. New York
Norddeutsche Allgemeine Zeitung. Berlin
Norddeutsches Protestantenblatt. Bremen
Ost-Deutsche Post. Vienna
Outlook, The. New York
Presse, Die. Vienna
Preussische Jahrbücher. Berlin
Radio Times. London
Revue blanche, La. Paris
San Francisco Chronicle. San Francisco
Signale für die musikalische Welt. Leipzig

284 ❧ BIBLIOGRAPHY

Sonntags-Blatt. Vienna
Times, The. London
Tonhalle, Die: Organ für Musikfreunde. Leipzig
Vaterland, Das. Vienna
Vossische Zeitung. Berlin
Weser-Zeitung. Bremen
Wiener Zeitung. Vienna
Zwischen-Akt, Der. Vienna

Index

Aegidi, Ludwig, 19
Allgeyer, Julius, 63–65, 119, 136
Altonaer Singakademie, 27n7, 28n10, 50n11
Ambros, August Wilhelm, 78, 105
anti-Napoleonic Wars, 10–12, 11n11
antisemitism, 25, 188, 188n16, 190, 236, 236n38, 237–38
Applegate, Celia, 6–7, 118
Arndt, Ernst Moritz, 110–11, 152, 212, 219; "Was ist des Deutschen Vaterland?," 9
Arnim, Ludwig Archim von: "Siegeslied nach Aussprüchen des Paracelsus," 1833), 95
Auersperg, Carl, 117n9
Austria, 5, 13–14, 20, 31–42, 63–67, 74, 83, 99, 117
Austria-Hungary, 75, 160, 201–2
Austro-Prussian War, 82, 92
Avé-Lallement, Theodor, 17, 19

Bach, Johann Sebastian, 77, 79, 139; *Gottes Zeit ist die allerbeste Zeit,* BWV 106, 78
Battle of Dybbøl, 55, 60–61, 61n27
Battle of Leipzig, 11n11, 12, 94, 153, 173, 179, 212. *See also* Battle of Nations, 12, 53
Battle of Leuthen, 1, 3, 127
Battle of Nations, 12, 53
Battle of Sedan, 89, 96, 98, 152–53, 173, 179, 205, 217–18
Battle of Wörth, 153
Becker, Nikolaus: "Rheinlied," 52–53

Beckerath, Laura von, 158–59, 225–26, 228, 235
Beckerath, Rudolf von, 158
Beethoven, Ludwig van, 103, 124, 145; *Cantata on the Accession of Leopold II,* WoO 88, 190; *Cantata on the Death of Joseph II,* WoO 87, 190
Beller-McKenna, Daniel, 6, 30, 80–84, 149, 178–79, 183–84, 212, 217, 224
Beneke, Otto, 167, 171
Bergamenter, Gottfried, 33
Berry, Paul, 77–78
Beuerle, Hans Michael, 29
Bible, 12, 78, 81, 120–21, 124n36, 131n22, 170, 185, 191–96, 200, 218–19. *See also specific books*
Billroth, Theodor, 77n3, 93, 117n9, 118–20, 120n18, 134, 172, 182, 212, 228–30, 244
Binzer, August Daniel von, 13
Bismarck, Otto von, 43–45, 61, 63–66, 70, 74; admirers, 239–43; Austro-Prussian War and, 92; birthday of, 159–64; dismissal of, 231–35; expansionism and, 5; Franco-Prussian War and, 92; National Liberals and, 114; nationalism and, 139–40; rise of, 20, 31; Sybel and, 226; *Triumphlied* and, 20–21, 90, 120, 132; William II and, 230
Blackbourn, David, 14, 82, 114
Blücher, Gebhard Leberecht von, 50

286 ❧ INDEX

Blunthschli, Johann Caspar, 152n4
Bock, Katrin, 100n32
Bodelschwingh, Friedrich von, 153–54
Botstein, Leon, 149
Boulanger, Georges, 202, *203,* 204, 220
Brachmann, Jan, 194–95
Brahms, Johannes, admiration for Bismarck after 1866, 90, 119; death of, 243, 244, 246; early antipathy toward Bismarck, 43–44, 61, 63–64, 70–71, 119–21, 134, 160, 163–64, 225–43; early political formation, 8–21; family, 56; political disillusionment in later years, 239–46. *Works cited*: *Ave Maria,* op. 13, 77; Clarinet Quintet, op. 115, 236; Clarinet Sonatas, op. 120, nos. 1 and 2, 236; Clarinet Trio, op. 114, 236; *Drei Intermezzzi* for Piano, op. 118, 236; Duets for Alto and Baritone, op. 28, 35n31; *Deutsche Volkslieder,* WoO 33, 236; *Elf Choral-Vorspielen* for Organ, op. posth. 122, 236; *Es ist das Heil uns kommen her,* op. 29, no. 1, 77; *Geistliches Wiegenlied,* op. 91, no. 2, 77; *Klavierstücke,* op. 118, 236; *Klavierstücke,* op. 119, 236; *Marienlieder,* op. 22, 77; *Schicksalslied,* op. 54, 120; *Fantasien* for Piano, op. 116, 236; Symphony No. 3, op. 90, 5–6, *Vier ernste Gesänge,* op. 121, 196–99, *198,* 199n47; *See also Ein deutsches Requiem; Fest- und Gedenksprüche, Fünf Lieder für Männerchor,* and *Triumphlied*
Brinkman, James M., 40
Bruckner, Anton, 147
Brusniak, Friedhelm, 30

Büchner, Gottfried, 195; *Biblische Real-und Verbal-Hand-Concordanz,* 194
Bülow, Hans von, 167, 171–73, 177–78, 244
Bürgerministerium, 75, 75n59, 99
Burschenschaft movement, 11–13

Caprivi, Leo von, 234, 238
Carlsbad Decrees, 12–13
Catholicism (see also Roman Catholicism), 12, 80, 82–83, 99, 114–15, 123
Chickering, Robert, 140
Christian IX, King of Denmark, 55
Christian Socialism, 245
Christianity, 81, 89, 105–6, 199. *See also* Bible; Catholicism; Jesus Christ; Protestantism
Chrysander, Friedrich, 235
Cohen, Gary B., 31–32
Compromise of 1867, 99, 116
Congress of Vienna, 11, 111
Conway, J. S., 124
Corinthians, First Letter to, 196–97, *198*
Culture Protestantism, 81–82, 114, 123, 151

Denmark, 15, 20, 54–55, 61
Dennis, David B., 81
Ein deutsches Requiem nach Worten der heiligen Schrift, op. 45 (Brahms), 6, 76–85, 96,100, 119, 150
Dierick, Augustinius P., 229
Dietrich, Albert, 17, 94n16
Doppler, Franz, 39
Drinker, Sophie, 27n7
Dual Alliance, 227

Ecclesiastes, Book of, *192,* 193, 196, *198*

INDEX ❧ 287

Ecclesiasticus, Book of, *192*, 193, 196, *198*
Eichner, Barbara, 91
"Ein feste Burg ist unser Gott" (Luther), 13
Elben, Otto, 46
Enderes, Karl von, 39
Engelmann, Theodor, 230
Eulenberg, Philipp, 237
Exner, Adolf, 230
Exodus, Book of, 185

Faber, Arthur, 243
Favre, Jules, 205
Fest- und Gedenksprüche, op. 109 (Brahms), 5–6, 83, 172; Bible and, 170, 185; musical setting of, 209–24; nota bene in, 187–88; patriotism and, 178, 184; perfomance of, 175–77; title of, 171–72; *Vermischte Schriften* (Lichtenberg) and, 196; Wüllner and, 181–82; *Zwei Kaiser. 15. Juni 1888* (Treitschke) and, 187
Festival of All Germans, 152
Fichte, Johann Gottlieb, 9, 12
Fleming, Albert von, 63
France, 9, 11–12, 20, 31, 50, 53, 89, 144–45
Francis Joseph I, Emperor of Austria (later Emperor-King of Austria-Hungary), 31, 44–45, 75, 99, 115–16
Franco-Prussian War, 91–98, 92n10, 131
Frankfurt National Assembly, 14
fraternities, 11
Frederick I (Frederick Barbarossa), Holy Roman Emperor, 133
Frederick I, Grand Duke of Baden, 152
Frederick III, German Emperor, 183, 188–89, 191, 193–94

Frederick II (Frederick the Great), King of Prussia 2–4, 191
Frederick VII of Denmark, 54–55
Frederick William, Crown Prince of Prussia (later German Emperor Frederick III), 152, 183
Frederick William IV, King of Prussia, 14, 18, 54
Freiligrath, Ferdinand, 17; *Neuere politische und soziale Gedichte,* 16; "Die Todten an die Lebenden," 16
French Empire, 9
Freytag, Gustav, 64; *Bilder aus der deutschen Vergangenheit,* 71
Fuchs, Ingrid, 106n42
Fünf Lieder für Männerchor, op. 41 (Brahms), 5–6, 25, 27–31, 76; "Freiwillige her!," op. 41, no. 2, 28, 28n10, 29, 49–52, 56–61, 73; "Gebt Acht," op. 41, no. 5, 28–29, 49, 50n11, 59–62, 73; *Geistliches Wiegenlied,* op. 91, no. 2, 77; "Geleit," op. 41, no. 3, 28, 28n10, 38–42, 45–46, 56

Gabrieli, Giovanni, 174
Gade, Niels, 36
Gambetta, Léon, 207
Garibaldi, Giuseppe, 207
Gastein Convention, 63
Gehring, Franz, 25–26, 135, 137–39
Geibel, Emanuel, 27n6; "Am 3. September," 112; "Goldne Brücke seien alle Lieder mir," 27n6
Geiringer, Karl, 30, 147
Gerlach, Ernst Ludwig von, 65
German Confederation, 11–12, 15, 44–46, 50, 53–56, 63, 66, 70
German Question, 13, 63–66, 89, 157
German Reich, 13, 113, 115–17, 131, 155–56, 173, 186

288 ❧ INDEX

Germania (feminine personification of the German nation), 185–86
Gesellschaft der Musikfreunde (Musikverein), 118
Glassbrenner, Adolf, 15
Goeler, Herren von, 64
Goldmark, Carl, 33–34
Gotthard, J. P., 34–36, 35n31, 36–37, 36n33, 37–38, 45, 56
Gottlieb-Billroth, Otto, 225
Grädener, Carl Georg Peter, 17
Greece, 236
Green, Abigail, 55
Griffiths, Paul, 148
Grimes, Nicole, 197, 199–200
Grimm, Julius Otto, 17
Groth, Klaus, 187, 190, 208
Grove, George: *Dictionary of Music and Musicians*, 25–26
Gurlt, Ernst Julius, 118

Hallier, Emil, 19
Hallier, Johann Gottfried, 19
Hamburg, 14–15, 18, 44, 167–68, 171, 181
Hamburg Senate, 14
Hamburg Women's Chorus, 27
Hancock, Virginia, 182
Handel, George Frideric, 127, 149
Hanslick, Eduard, 48, 98–99, 190, 228, 230
Harden, Maximilian, 234
Häusser, Ludwig: *Deutsche Geschichte vom Tode Friedrichs des Großen bis zur Gründung des Deutschen Bundes*, 95
Hegel, Georg, 110
"Heil Dir im Siegerkranz" (Prussian national anthem), 103–4
Heine, Heinrich, 13
Hellborn, Heinrich Kreissle von, 33
Henschel, George, 142, 142n68

Herbeck, Johann, 36, 95
Hergenhahn, August Friedrich Carl von, 159
Hermann, Ulrich, 48
Herwegh, Georg: *Gedichte eines Lebendigen*, 16–17
Herzogenberg, Elisabeth von, 186, 186n12, 191, 199n47, 244
Heubner, Heinrich Leonhard, 194–95
Hill, Ralph, 146–47
Hoffmann von Fallersleben, August Heinrich, 17, 17n31; "Die Freiwilligen," 52–53; "Lied der Deutschen" (Song of the Germans), 17
Hohenwart, Karl Sigmund, 115, 117n9
Hölderlin, Friedrich: *Hyperion*, 120
Holst, Karl Heinz, 8
Holtzendorff, Franz, 151–52
Hornstein, Robert von: *Die Pagen von Versailles*, 48–49
Hungary, 99, 116
Hurd, Madeleine, 18

Imbert, Hugues, 144
Imperial Proclamation at Versailles (1871), 131–32, 154, 170
India, 95n19
International Agricultural Exhibition in Hamburg (1863), 43–44
Iron Ring, 164
Italian War of 1859, 50

Jahn, Friedrich Ludwig, 9
James, Book of, 185
Jesus Christ, 79, 84, 133, 218–19
Jireček, Josef, 115–16
Joachim, Joseph, 17, 19, 121, 239–40
Johann, Archduke of Austria, 16
Joseph II, Holy Roman Emperor, 190–91, 194

Kalbeck, Max, 1–3, 1n1, 5; on
  Brahms's first performance, 8;
  on *Fest- und Gedenksprüche,* 183;
  J. P. Gotthard and, 34–35; Julius
  Magg and, 73–74; on monarchism,
  194; Musikverein (Gesellschaft
  der Musikfreunde) and,
  96n22; Schubert and, 244–45;
  Triumphlied and, 106; *Vier ernste
  Gesänge* and, 197n44
Kalliwoda, Johann Wenzel, 34
Kings, First Book of, 191, *192,* 193,
  196, *198*
Klein, Bernhard, 25
Klinger, Max, 198
Kohn, Hans, 25
Körner, Theodor: "Männer und
  Buben," 52
Kotzebue, August von, 12
Kradolfer, Jacob, 89, 151–52
Kral, Edward, 33
Kretzschmar, Hermann, 103n34, 140
Kross, Siegfried, 29, 61, 172, 177
Krummacher, Friedhelm, 107, 148
Kufferath, Maurice, 141
Kugler, Franz, 3
Kulturkampf (cultural struggle), 114

Lamentations, Book of, 185
Landsmannschaften, 11
Langbehn, August Julius, 229n17;
  Rembrandt als Erzieher, 228–29,
  228n14
Laufer, Jack, 148
Lemcke, Carl, 49, 51–53; *Lieder und
  Gedichte,* 28–29, 49
Levi, Hermann, 63–64, 96n22, 119–
  20, 121n26, 122, 134, 136–37
Leyen, Rudolf von der, 242–43
Lichtenberg, Georg Christoph,
  195–96
Liedertafel, 25–26

Limberger, Paul, 180
Lokalposse, 43–44
London Protocol (1852), 54–55
Lübke, Wilhelm, 93
Lueger, Karl, 246
Luke, Gospel of, 212, 217, 219–20
Luther, Martin, 12–13, 120, 199
Lützow Free Corps, 12

MacDonald, Malcolm, 148, 175, 196
Magg, Julius, 73–74
Mair, Franz, 33
Mandyczewski, Eusebius, 107,
  220n26
March Revolution of 1848, 12
Matthew, Gospel of, 218
Maximilian I, Holy Roman Emperor, 70
Maxwell, Alexander, 25
Mayer, Sigmund, 117, 117n9
McCorkle, Margit, 28n10, 50–51
Meischein, Burkhard, 29–30
Mendelssohn, Felix, 36; "Es ist
  bestimmt in Gottes Rath," op. 47,
  no. 4, 42
Menzel, Adolph, 1–3, 5
Metternich, Klemens von, 11–13, 74
militarism, 143, 145, 149, 201
Minor, Ryan, 6, 178, 179n37, 212,
  217, 220
Mirsch, Paul, 212–13, 217
Moltke, Helmut von, 172
Moltke, Kuno von, 237
Morelly, Franz, 45
Mühlfeld, Richard, 236
Müller, Frank Lorenz, 188n16
Müller, Wilhelm: "Postillions
  Morgenlied," 27n6
Musikverein (Gesellschaft der
  Musikfreunde), 95–96, 96n22–23,
  118

Nägeli, Hans Georg, 26

INDEX

Napoleon Bonaparte, Emperor of the French, 8–11, *10,* 53, 85, 92
Napoleon III, Emperor of France, 50, 91–93, 98, 112, 219
Napoleonic Wars, 97
national chauvinism, 48, 91, 188, 188n16
National Liberals, 70, 114, 116, 151, 184, 226, 230
National Socialism, 80, 146–47
National-Denkmal auf dem Niederwald (Schilling), 155–58, *157,* 209
nationalism, 6, 9–10, 25, 30, 80, 110, 139–40, 150, 183, 236
nation-building, 122–34
neo-Absolutism, 14, 26, 31
Nietzsche, Friedrich: *Der Antichrist,* 199
Nipperdey, Thomas, 158
Nordau, Max, 245
North German Confederation, 66, 104, 112, 114, 226
Notley, Margaret, 229n17, 244
"Nun danket alle Gott," 127–28, 131–32, 155

Oncken, Wilhelm: *Unser Heldenkaiser,* 243
Otten, Georg Dietrich, 17
Ottoman Empire, 236

Paris Commune, 119
Paris, Siege of (1870–71), 100
patriotism, 9, 91, 99, 147, 174, 178, 183–84
Peace of Prague (1866), 66
Petersen, Carl, 167–69, 171–72
Pflanze, Otto, 233, 240n55, 244
Potocki, Alfred Józef, 99, 115
Protestantism, 6, 81–82, 123–24
Progressive Party (Prussia), 70

Prussia, 13–14, 20, 43–44n43, n46, 63, 65, 67, 83, 99, 179
Prussian expansionism, 103–4
Psalms, Book of, 185

Ravizza, Victor, 137n55, 149
Rechbauer, Karl, 117n9
Reformation, 12–13
Reichardt, Gustav, 34
Reinecke, Carl, 112, 112n55
Reinsurance Treaty, 202
Reinthaler, Carl, 79–80, 83, 100, 104, 118, 122n27
Reményi, Eduard, 27n6
Revelation, Book of, 84–85, 89, 103, 105, 110–12, 124, 124n36
Rhine Crisis of 1840, 53, 85
Rhineland, 9, 114, 114n3
Riemann, Hugo, 167, 175, 212–13
Rieter-Biedermann, J. Melchior, 35, 39, 71–73, 82
Rogge, Bernhard, 131, 177
Roman Catholicism (see also Catholicism), 114
Romans, Epistle to the, 120, 131n22
Rostand, Claude, 147
Rubinstein, Anton, 118, 136
Rückert, Friedrich, 185
Russia, 115, 201–2

Sand, Karl Ludwig, 12
Schiller, Friedrich, 110
Schilling, Johannes, 155–56, *157,* 209
Schleswig-Holstein Question, 53
Schneckenburger, Max: "Die Wacht am Rhein," 53
Schneider, Ute, 154
Schöbel, Louis, 47
Scholz, Bernhard, 107
Schubert, Ferdinand, 39
Schubert, Franz, 32, 36–37, 42, 244–45

INDEX ❧ 291

Schultze, Carl, 43
Schumann, Clara, 17, 19, 45n53, 76–78, 119, 122, 178–79, 197, 244
Schumann, Marie, 198
Schumann, Robert, 17, 76, 78, 138–39; "Neue Bahnen," 138–39
Schupp, Johan Balthazar: *Salomo, oder Regenten-Spiegel,* 193–94
Schüssler-Bach, Kerstin, 31, 49n7, 50, 148–49
Schütz, Heinrich, 174; *Psalmen Davids,* 175
Sell, Sophie Charlotte von, 239, 239n51, 240n56, 245
Senff, Bartholf, 100, 123
Seven Years' War (1756–1763), 49–50, 65
Seydlitz, Friedrich Wilhelm von, 49–50
Sheehan, James J., 54
Simrock, Clara, 1n1
Simrock, Fritz, 1n1, 3, 67–72, 83, 90, 95, 100, 133n45, 171, 181–82, 228, 245–46
Simrock, P. J., 66
Smith, Helmut Walser, 122
Social Democracy, 245
Social Question, 231
Speidel, Ludwig, 117n10; "Der Gott im deutschen Lager," 117–18
Spengel, Julius, 169, 171, 178, 181
Spina, C. A., 35–36, 39
Spitta, Philipp, 174–75
Sterkenburgh, Frederik Frank, 153, 179
Stockem, Michel, 145
Stoecker, Adolph, 205
Strauss, Johann, Jr., 45
Sybel, Heinrich von: *Die Begründung des Deutschen Reiches durch Wilhelm I,* 225–27, 230–32, 235

Taaffe, Eduard von, 164
Tadday, Ulrich, 100n32
Taruskin, Richard, 149–50
Third Punic War (149 BCE–146 BCE), 187–88
Third Silesian War (1756–1763), 3
Thirty Years' War (1618–1648), 65
Three Emperors' Agreement (1881), 201–2
Treaty of Frankfurt (1871), 154
Treitschke, Heinrich von, 119, 208, 225–26; *Zwei Kaiser. 15. Juni 1888,* 187–90, *189*
Triumphlied, op. 55 (Brahms), 5–6, 119; "Am 3. September" and, 112; Battle of Sedan and, 96; Bismarck and, 20–21, 132; Christ in, 133; expansion of, 118; first performance of, 134–40; Gehring on, 137–39; Imperial Proclamation and, 131; Levi and, 120; nationalism and, 110, 150; nation-building and, 124–34; overview of music of, 89–90; patriotism and, 99–100; performances of, 91, 134–40; popularity of, 115; reception of, 140–46; in repertoire, 148–49; Revelation and, 89, 105; revision of, 100n32; Rubinstein and, 136; sheet music, 108–9, 125–26, 128–30; Simrock and, 121–22; title page, 90, 95n19; William I and, 191; World War II and, 146–48
Turnverein movement, 9

Ulrich, Duke of Württemberg, 27
United Kingdom, 95n19, 145–48
Urburschenschaft, 11, 74

Veit, Philipp, 156
Verein "zur Ausspannung der Pferde," 239–42, *241,* 245

292   INDEX

Vienna, 31–42, 75–76, 118
Vienna Men's Choral Society, 32–33, 36–37, 72, 72n52, 238
Vienna Mercantile Choral Society, 36, 38, 45
Volgemann, Heinrich (and Heinrich Wilken): *Wilhelm Keenich und Fritze Fischmarkt aus Berlin auf der Reise zur Ausstellung in Hamburg*, 43–44
voluntary associations, 18, 31–32
Vondung, Klaus, 85
Vormärz, 12, 15, 17, 26, 194, 212

Wagner, Friedchen, 27n7
Wagner, Richard, 147; *Eine Kapitulation*, 145
Waldersee, Alfred von, 204
War of Austrian Succession, 49, 100
Wars of Liberation, 10–12, 53, 131, 156, 173, 209
Wartburg Castle, 12
Wehner, Arnold, 17
Wetzel, David, 92
Whaley, Joachim, 193
Wheeldon, Marianne, 7
Widmann, Joseph Viktor, 186, 206–9, 219–20, 220n26, 234, 236
Wilken, Heinrich (and Heinrich Volgemann): *Wilhelm Keenich und*

Fritze Fischmarkt aus Berlin auf der Reise zur Ausstellung in Hamburg, 43–44
Wilhelm der Große, 245n72
William, Prince of Prussia (later King Wilhelm I of Prussia, and German Emperor Wilhelm I), 18, 20
William I, German Emperor, 5, 43–47, 112, 127, 133, 155, 183, 191, 196. *See also* Wilhelm der Große
William I, King of Prussia (later German Emperor), 89–90, 94
William II, German Emperor, 143, 196, 204–5, 207–8, 224, 230, 245n72
Wilt, Marie, 64
Winkler, H. A., 64n36, 119n17, 123, 163, 204
"Wir hatten gebaut ein stattliches Haus" (Binzer), 13, 74
Wisdom of Solomon, 196–97
World War I, 131, 145
World War II, 146–48
Wüllner, Franz, 168, 180–82, 231

Zelter, Carl Friedrich, 25–26
Ziethen, Hans Joachim von, 49–50

Printed in the United States
by Baker & Taylor Publisher Services